# Methodist Records of Baltimore City Maryl~

## (East City Station)

## Henry C. Peden, Jr.

HERITAGE BOOKS
2020

# HERITAGE BOOKS

*AN IMPRINT OF HERITAGE BOOKS, INC.*


**Books, CDs, and more—Worldwide**

For our listing of thousands of titles see our website
at
www.HeritageBooks.com


Published 2020 by
HERITAGE BOOKS, INC.
Publishing Division
5810 Ruatan Street
Berwyn Heights, Md. 20740


Originally published 2004

International Standard Book Number
Paperbound: 978-1-68034-614-5

# PREFACE

This book is the third volume in a planned series and contains marriages, births, baptisms, and deaths gleaned from the records for the East City Station of Baltimore's Methodist Episcopal Church from 1840 through 1850 inclusive.

The previous two volumes covered the years from 1799 through 1839. Some corrections to information in those volumes are as follows:

Vol. 1, p. 64: Zachariah Rhodes, Harriet Cunningham, John Frederick, and Ruthy Collins are missing from the index;

Vol. 1, p. 192: "Harrison L. P. Dixon" should be "Harrison Dixon, L. P." (signifying "Local Preacher"); and,

Vol. 2, p. 158: "E. Popless" should be "E. Fopless"

The names of people within this third volume have been arranged alphabetically and then cross-referenced, thus negating the necessity for a separate index. It should be noted that there were times when the handwriting in the register was illegible or the names were strangely spelled or misspelled. Consequently I conducted research into marriage records and newspaper accounts which led to comments that I have placed in brackets and preceded them with [*Ed. Note:*] in the text.

For those interested in viewing the church records of the East City Station in Baltimore, the microfilm accession numbers at the Maryland State Archives are M408 through M412, and M1380. The Library of the Maryland Historical Society microfilm numbers are BAL 21-A (#698) through BAL 21-D (#701), and BAL CR#1. One may also wish to contact the Lovely Lane United Methodist Museum, 2200 St. Paul Street, Baltimore, MD 21219, with respect to their holdings.

Henry C. Peden, Jr.
Bel Air, Maryland
2004

# METHODIST EPISCOPAL RECORDS OF BALTIMORE, MD
## EAST CITY STATION, 1840-1850

----, Amelia Elizabeth Jennet, dau. of Alexander and Amelia ---- [blank], b. ---- [blank], bapt. 6 Jul 1844 by Rev. Wesley Stevenson

----, Elizabeth Harper, dau. of Alexander and Amelia ---- [blank], aged 3 months [b. 1844], bapt. 6 Jul 1844 by Rev. Wesley Stevenson

----, Helen M., dau. of Rev. J. Randolph and Helen M. ---- [blank], b. 28 Jun 1841, bapt. 2 Dec 1841 by Rev. Robert Emory

----, John J., son of John and Sarah ---- [blank], b. 20 Feb 1835, bapt. 12 Feb 1843 by Rev. Elisha D. Owen

----, Wesley (colored), son of Polly at Mr. Royston's, b. 3 Oct 1845, bapt. 25 Dec 1845 by Rev. Dr. George C. M. Roberts

Aaron, Ann and Samuel Boston m. 2 Aug 1847 by Rev. Dr. George C. M. Roberts

Abbert, Ann and Francis Olivet m. 1 Jun 1843 by Rev. Henry Slicer, lic. dated same day

Abbott, Mary Elizabeth, dau. of George and Elizabeth Abbott, b. 27 Apr 1836, Delaware, bapt. 7 Jan 1841, Baltimore City, by Rev. Isaac P. Cook [*Ed. Note:* Another entry, however, stated she was b. 26 Apr 1836 (place not given) and bapt. 30 Aug 1840.]

Abbott, William H. Harrison, son of William and Sophia Abbott, aged 8 months [b. 1480, Baltimore City], bapt. 30 May 1841 by Rev. Gerard Morgan

Abell, Jane, d. circa 1845 (death noted in Class List) [*Ed. Note:* Death notice in the *Baltimore Sun* stated that Jane Abell, dau. of Richard and Catherine Abell, d. 4 Apr 1846.]

Abell, Thomas and Elenour Armitage m. 12 Nov 1846 by Rev. Joseph Shane

Abrahams, Tabitha S. and Perry G. Buckingham m. 3 Jul 1845 by Rev. James Sewell, lic. dated same day

Aburn, James W. and Caroline Schley m. 29 Jul 1849 by Rev. John S. Martin, lic. dated 27 Jul 1849

Aburn, Johnson B. and Emily Jane Smith m. 16 May 1849 by Rev. John S. Martin, lic. dated 15 May 1849

Adams, Charles and Dorothy Ann Woods m. 14 May 1843 by Rev. Dr. George C. M. Roberts

Adams, Edward and Miss ---- [blank] Beckley, both of Baltimore County, m. 26 Jan 1841 by Rev. Bernard H. Nadal [*Ed. Note:* Their marriage notice in the *Baltimore Sun* indicated her first name was Margaret.]

Adams, Elizabeth and James R. Loane m. 27 Aug 1849 by Rev. Isaac P. Cook

Adams, Elizabeth and Robert McCaslind m. 28 Jan 1847 by Rev. Joseph Shane

Adams, Harriet and Stephen Peck m. 9 May 1849 by Rev. Joseph Shane

Adams, John F. and Sidney A. Powell m. 10 May 1848 by Rev. Dr. George C. M. Roberts

Adams, Joseph, see "Mary Ann Elizabeth Adams," q.v.

Adams, Joseph Jacob Grant, son of Joseph and Margaret Ann Adams, b. 1 Apr 1845, bapt. 15 Apr 1845 by Rev. Dr. George C. M. Roberts

Adams, Mary and John C. Bixby m. 26 Jul 1849 by Rev. John S. Martin, lic. dated 25 Jul 1849

Adams, Mary Ann and Daniel Simmering m. 5 Jan 1846 by Rev. Dr. George C. M. Roberts

Adams, Mary Ann and John A. Smith m. 29 Nov 1843 by Rev. Dr. George C. M. Roberts

Adams, Mary Ann Elizabeth, dau. of Joseph and Margaret Ann Adams, b. 11 May 1846, bapt. 19 May 1846 by Rev. Dr. George C. M. Roberts

Adams, Matthias, see "Thomas J. Adams" and "William H. Adams," q.v.

Adams, Nathan and Frances Whapping m. 3 Dec 1846 by Rev. Wesley Stevenson

Adams, Sarah E. and Richard E. Smith m. 5 Jun 1845 by Rev. James Sewell, lic. dated same day

Adams, Thomas Jefferson, son of Matthias and Mary Adams, b. 11 Oct 1838, Fells Point, Baltimore City, bapt. 25 Jun 1840 by Rev. Samuel Keppler

Adams, William Henry, son of Matthias and Mary Adams, b. 20 Jun 1840, Fells Point, Baltimore City, bapt. 25 Jun 1840 by Rev. Samuel Keppler

Adare, Elizabeth and Uriah Mitchel m. 1 Jun 1843 by Rev. Joseph Shane

Addison, Elizabeth and Samuel H. Travers m. 11 Jan 1848 by Rev. Littleton F. Morgan, lic. dated same day

Addison, Francess Roberts, dau. of George C. and Susanna Addison, b. 9 Apr 1840, bapt. 17 Apr 1840 by Rev. Dr. George C. M. Roberts

Addison, Isabella Cook, dau. of George C. and Susan Addison, b. 6 Feb 1842, bapt. 14 Feb 1842 by Rev. Dr. George C. M. Roberts

Addison, Robert Bohn, son of George C. and Susanna Addison, b. 6 Mar 1845, bapt. 15 Mar 1845 by Rev. Dr. George C. M. Roberts

Addison, Sarah Jane, dau. of George C. and Susan Addison, b. 14 Nov 1843, bapt. 22 Nov 1843 by Rev. Dr. George C. M. Roberts

Adler, Mary Louisa, dau. of George and Elizabeth Adler, b. 31 Jul 1839, bapt. 15 Jun 1840 by Rev. Joseph Shane

Ady, James and Catherine Brittingham m. 15 Oct 1850 by Rev. Henry Slicer, lic. dated same day

Aelman, Catherine and Alexander Haskell m. 26 May 1844 by Rev. James Sewell, lic. dated 25 May 1844

Agel, Jane and John R. Kirwan m. 13 Sep 1845 by Rev. Dr. George C. M. Roberts

Ahern, Eugene and Frances Augusta Kline m. 28 Sep 1844 by Rev. Isaac P. Cook

Ahl, Sarah Emily and Maximen Ardison m. 11 Oct 1849 by Rev. John S. Martin, lic. dated 8 Oct 1849 [Ed. Note: Their marriage notice in the Baltimore Sun gave their names as Chas. Ardisson and Sarah E. Ahl.]

Ailman, Sophia and Charles Leach m. 10 Aug 1847 by Rev. Stephen A. Roszel, lic. dated same day

Airey, William and Eliza Jane Young m. 30 Oct 1844 by Rev. Joseph Shane

Airs, James Henry, son of James H. and Elizabeth Airs, aged 6 months [b. 1840], bapt. 25 Apr 1841 by Rev. Gerard Morgan

Airy, Mary and William Cerrick m. 30 Nov 1842 by Rev. Wesley Stevenson

Albaugh, Grafton and Mary Elizabeth Harris m. 31 May 1842 by Rev. Samuel Brison

Albers, Elizabeth, d. circa 1847-1850 (exact date not given in Record of Members)

Albert, Joseph S. and Elizabeth Botfield m. 16 Jun 1842 by Rev. Dr. George C. M. Roberts

Alday, Neriah Wesley, son of John and Sarah Alday, b. 5 May 1841, Baltimore City, bapt. 6 Jun 1841 by Rev. William Prettyman

Alderson, James B. and Susan Varsans, both of Baltimore County, m. ---- [date not given] by Rev. George Hildt, lic. dated 13 Jan 1846 [*Ed. Note:* Their marriage notice in the *Baltimore Sun* gave her name as Susan Vansant and the marriage date as 14 Jan 1846.]

Aler, George Edward, son of George W. and Elizabeth Aler, b. 17 May 1836, bapt. 20 Nov 1840 by Rev. Charles B. Tippett

Aler, George W., see "George E. Aler" and "Reuben A. Aler," q.v.

Aler, Jesse Sanks, son of John and Elizabeth Aler, b. 22 Jul 1849, 22 Jul 1849, bapt. 1849 (exact date not given) by Rev. John S. Martin

Aler, John, see "Jesse S. Aler," q.v.

Aler, Mary and Allen G. Shaffer m. 29 May 1845 by Rev. Isaac P. Cook

Aler, Rachel and James McCurley m. 23 Jan 1848 by Rev. Joseph Shane

Aler, Reuben Albert, son of George W. and Elizabeth Aler, b. 15 Jul 1839, bapt. 20 Nov 1840 by Rev. Charles B. Tippett

Alexander, Amanda M. and William Porter m. 1 Feb 1848 by Rev. Dr. George C. M. Roberts

Alford, James E. and Mary Jane Edmondson m. 6 Oct 1847 by Rev. Littleton F. Morgan, lic. dated 15 [*sic*] Oct 1847 [*Ed. Note:* Their marriage notice in the *Baltimore Sun* stated that James E. Alford and Mary J. Edmundson m. 6 Oct 1847, so they obviously obtained their license on 5 Oct 1847, not 15 Oct 1847.]

Algie, Jane and William P. Lightner m. 8 Dec 1845 by Rev. Dr. George C. M. Roberts

Allen, Ann, d. 1845 (death noted in Class List) [*Ed. Note:* Death notice in the *Baltimore Sun* stated that Ann Allen d. 1 Aug 1845.]

Allen, Catherine E. and Joseph J. Daneker m. 20 Jan 1842 by Rev. Dr. George C. M. Roberts

Allen, Celestia Ann, dau. of Robert and Catherine Allen, b. 4 Nov 1839, bapt. 1 May 1840 by Rev. Dr. George C. M. Roberts

Allen, Charles and Hester A. E. Jones m. 25 Aug 1845 by Rev. Joseph Shane

Allen, James W. and Caroline J. Deaver m. 1 Nov 1843 by Rev. Joseph Shane

Allen, Maria and Daniel D. Vaughn m. 27 Oct 1841 by Rev. Gerard Morgan, lic. dated same day

Allen, Robert, see "Celestia A. Allen," q.v.

Allen, Solomon, see "William P. Allen," q.v.

Allen, William H. and Henrietta E. Scott m. 31 Jan 1844 by Rev. Joseph Shane

Allen, William Miller, son of William M. and Mary M. Allen, b. 14 Jul 1847, bapt. 24 Jan 1848 by Rev. Dr. George C. M. Roberts

Allen, William Patterson, son of Solomon and Elizabeth Allen, b. 3 Aug 1840, bapt. 9 Dec 1840 by Rev. Dr. George C. M. Roberts

Allison, Eliza and Baptist Higden m. 4 Apr 1850 by Rev. Joseph Shane

Alloway, Gabriel, d. circa 1840-1847 (exact date not given in Record of Members)

Allwell, Sarah (coloured adult), dau. of Wesley and Eliza Allwell, b. ---- [blank], bapt. 22 Nov 1840 by Rev. Dr. George C. M. Roberts

Allwell, William Wesley, son of Wesley and Eliza Allwell, b. 1840, bapt. 28 Nov 1840 by Rev. Dr. George C. M. Roberts

Alton, Lewis and Charlotte V. Herold m. ---- [blank] by Rev. John S. Martin, lic. dated 16 Jul 1850 [*Ed. Note:* Their marriage notice in the *Baltimore Sun* stated Lewis Alton m. Charlotte V. Harrold, dau. of John Harrold, on 16 Jul 1850.]

Alvey, Jane Biays and William C. Hammer m. 9 Oct 1845 by Rev. James Sewell, lic. dated 8 Oct 1845

Ames, Georgianna and Charles G. Williams m. 21 Jan 1845 by Rev. Dr. George C. M. Roberts

Amey, Catherine E. and Francis T. Clutcher m. 21 Apr 1845 by Rev. Joseph Shane

Amey, Elizabeth and Bladen Dulaney m. 2 Dec 1841 by Rev. Dr. George C. M. Roberts

Amick, Daniel, d. circa 1840-1847 (exact date not given in Record of Members)

Amos, Alfred P., son of Alfred P. and Jane Amos, b. 23 Feb 1841, bapt. 29 Jul 1841 by Rev. John A. Hening

Amos, Ann Rebecca and John B. Roberts m. 29 Jan 1848 by Rev. James H. Brown, lic. dated same day

Amos, James, d. circa 1845-1847 (exact date not given in Record of Members) [Ed. Note: Death notice in the Baltimore Sun stated that James Amoss d. 30 Oct 1845.]

Amoss, A. P., see "Sarah Harrison," q.v.

Amoss, Margaret H. and John J. Myers m. 14 Jan 1840 at John Haskitt's house in Baltimore by Rev. Beverly Waugh, lic. dated 13 Jan 1840

Amoss, Sarah A. and Richard Garrett m. 4 Sep 1842 by Rev. Henry Slicer, lic. dated 3 Sep 1842

Amoss, William W. and Margaret S. Harrison m. 8 Jan 1848 by Rev. Benjamin F. Brooke

Anderson, Agnes C. and Henry G. Mills m. 21 Apr 1847 by Rev. Benjamin F. Brooke

Anderson, Anna Jane, dau. of Joseph N. and E. Jane Anderson, b. 14 Jan 1848, bapt. 16 May 1848 by Rev. Dr. George C. M. Roberts

Anderson, Benjamin F. and Catherine D. Daley m. 14 May 1849 by Rev. Aquila A. Reese, lic. dated 12 May 1849

Anderson, Catharine Kenes, dau. of David and Jane Anderson, aged 2 years and 3 months [b. 1840], bapt. 3 Apr 1842 by Rev. John A. Hening

Anderson, Charles and Eliza J. Franklin m. 20 Feb 1846 by Rev. Dr. George C. M. Roberts

Anderson, David, see "Catharine K. Anderson" and "Margaret A. Anderson," q.v.

Anderson, Ellen Jane and James G. Makibben m. 25 Oct 1846 by Rev. Littleton F. Morgan, lic. dated 5 Oct 1846

Anderson, James Alexander and Adeline Seggrave Lechler m. 27 May 1840 by Rev. Samuel Keppler, lic. dated same day

Anderson, Jane, see "Catharine K. Anderson" and "Margaret A. Anderson," q.v.

Anderson, Jesse and Elizabeth Carmean m. 26 Dec 1843 by Rev. Dr. George C. M. Roberts

Anderson, John and Elizabeth Houseman m. 22 Jun 1843 by Rev. Dr. George C. M. Roberts

Anderson, Joseph N., see "Anna J. Anderson," q.v.

Anderson, Margaret Ann, dau. of David and Jane Anderson, aged 1 year, bapt. 3 Apr 1842 by Rev. John A. Hening

Andreon, Phoebe, dau. of Pearson and Harriet Adreon, b. 4 Mar 1846, Baltimore, bapt. 7 Jun 1847 by Rev. Stephen A. Roszel

Andrews, Anne and Henry W. S. Evans m. 14 Oct 1847 by Rev. Stephen A. Roszel, lic. dated same day

Andrews, Caroline M. and John Wilson m. 14 Oct 1849 by Rev. John S. Martin, lic. dated 13 Oct 1849

Andrews, Charles and Margaret Smith m. 3 Oct 1850 by Rev. Dr. George C. M. Roberts

Andrews, Jacob M. and Amanda M. Gorsuch m. 12 Jul 1840 by Rev. Samuel Keppler, lic. dated 9 Jul 1840

Andrews, James B. and Ann Wall, both of Baltimore County, m. 10 Mar 1845 by Rev. William Hamilton

Andrews, John Benjamin and Elizabeth Leary m. 28 Aug 1850 by Rev. John S. Martin, lic. dated 24 Aug 1850

Andrews, Mary E. and Rev. John Lannahan m. ---- [blank] by Rev. Littleton F. Morgan, lic. dated 13 May 1846

Andrews, Matilda and Thomas Lytle m. 19 Mar 1844 by Rev. Isaac P. Cook

Anschultz, Mary Catherine, dau. of Henry and Martha Anschultz, b. 15 Sep 1840, Baltimore City, bapt. 31 Jan 1841 by Rev. Samuel Keppler

Anthony, William and Mary Ann Patterson m. 28 Nov 1842 by Rev. Job Guest, lic. dated same day

Appleby, John Plumer, son of George and Mary Appleby, b. 16 Apr 1831, Baltimore City, bapt. 1841 (exact date not given) by Rev. Gerard Morgan

Appleby, Virginnia Hervey, dau. of George and Mary Appleby, b. 5 Jul 1838, Baltimore City, bapt. 1841 (exact date not given) by Rev. Gerard Morgan

Applegarth, Mary Jane and William Pugh m. 10 Jan 1850 by Rev. John S. Martin, lic. dated 8 Jan 1850

Appold, Ann Maria and Alexander Robinson, both of Baltimore County, m. 17 Nov 1840 by Rev. Bernard H. Nadal

Appold, Virginia and John R. Hall m. 1 Nov 1849 at the house of her father in Baltimore by Rev. Beverly Waugh, lic. dated same day

Ardison, Maximen and Sarah Emily Ahl m. 11 Oct 1849 by Rev. John S. Martin, lic. dated 8 Oct 1849 [Ed. Note: Their marriage notice in the Baltimore Sun gave their names as Chas. Ardisson and Sarah E. Ahl.]

Armager, Elizabeth, d. circa 1844-1847 (exact date not given in Record of Members)

Armitage, Elenour and Thomas Abell m. 12 Nov 1846 by Rev. Joseph Shane

Armour, Emeline and Joseph Harvey, Jr. m. 24 Mar 1840 by Rev. John Bear

Armstrong, Emilya Isabelle, dau. of Andrew and Eliza Armstrong, b. 3 Mar 1849, bapt. 1 Jul 1849 by Rev. Dr. George C. M. Roberts

Armstrong, Henry and Angeline Clarke, both of Baltimore City, m. 2 Oct 1845 by Rev. William Hamilton

Armstrong, James S. and Susan Chaney m. 13 Jul 1847 by Rev. Stephen A. Roszel, lic. dated 29 Jun 1847

Armstrong, John and Henrietta M. Ruff m. 22 Dec 1842 by Rev. Job Guest, lic. dated 6 Dec 1842

Armstrong, Thomas, d. "2 years ago" (note dated Feb 1850 was written on an 1849 Class List) [Ed. Note: Death notice in the Baltimore Sun stated that Thomas Armstrong d. 21 Nov 1848.]

Armstrong, William and Susanna Simonson m. 25 Aug 1847 by Rev. Dr. George C. M. Roberts

Armstrong, William and Mary Elizabeth Crouch m. 7 Dec 1847 by Rev. Stephen A. Roszel, lic. dated 6 Dec 1847

Arnold, Achsah and Daniel Newlin m. 6 Nov 1842 by Rev. Joseph Shane

Arnold, Benedict, see "Theodore F. Arnold," q.v

Arnold, Eliza and William Arnold m. 19 Aug 1841 by Rev. Joseph Shane

Arnold, Elizabeth and James Wirt m. 31 Dec 1850 by Rev. Joseph Shane

Arnold, Elizabeth and George H. Houck m. 7 Dec 1848 by Rev. Isaac P. Cook

Arnold, James and Mary Ann Young m. 2 Aug 1846 by Rev. Joseph Shane

Arnold, John Henry, son of John Henry and Susan Arnold, b. 28 Oct 1839, bapt. 18 Aug 1840 by Rev. Joseph Shane

Arnold, Roderick and Ann Rebecca Jenkins m. 26 Mar 1850 by Rev. Joseph Shane

Arnold, Susan Ann and Samuel Briden m. 2 Mar 1843 by Rev. Joseph Shane

Arnold, Theodore Franklin, son of Benedict and Mary Arnold, aged 19 months [b. 1838], bapt. 8 Jan 1840 by Rev. Gerard Morgan

Arnold, William and Eliza Arnold m. 19 Aug 1841 by Rev. Joseph Shane

Arrington (Anington?), Thomas D. and Mary E. Browning m. 16 Aug 1849 by Rev. Joseph Shane

Arthur, Henry and Elizabeth Maynard m. 12 Jan 1842 by Rev. Job Guest, lic. dated 10 Jan 1842

Arthur, Henry and Elizabeth Mainard m. ---- [date not given] by Rev. George D. Chenoweth, lic. dated 10 Jan 1842 [Ed. Note: Their marriage notice in the Baltimore Sun stated Henry Arthur and Elizabeth Maynard m. 12 Jan 1842.]

Ashcroft, Matilda, d. 1844 (death noted in Class List) [Ed. Note: Death notice in the Baltimore Sun stated that Matilda Ashcroft d. 12 Jul 1844.]

Ashcroft, Robert and Ann Emily Hall m. 6 Nov 1845 by Rev. Samuel Keppler (date of lic. not recorded)

Ashcroft, Thomas, d. 1845 (death noted in Class List)

Ashcum, George W., son of Alexander and Amelia Ashcum, b. 27 Nov 1841, bapt. 27 Sep 1842 by Rev. Elisha D. Owen

Ashley, Mary J. and William K. Shumler m. 9 Jun 1846 by Rev. Dr. George C. M. Roberts

Ashman, Rebecca, d. 19 May 184- (year not given; noted in Record of Members) [Ed. Note: Death notice in the Baltimore Sun stated that Rebecca Ashman, widow of William Ashman and mother-in-law of C. R. Coleman, d. 19 May 1847.]

Ashman, William, d. "years ago" (date not given; death noted in Record of Members) [Ed. Note: Death notice in the Baltimore Sun stated that William Ashman d. 28 Jan 1846.] See "Rebecca Ashman," q.v.

Askew, Charles L. and Laura S. Reynolds m. 30 Apr 1848 by Rev. Dr. George C. M. Roberts

Asparkin, Emily and William C. Stallings m. 9 Oct 1844 by Rev. Dr. George C. M. Roberts

Atkinson, Elizabeth Ann, d. 1841 (death noted in Class List) [Ed. Note: Death notice in the Baltimore Sun stated that Elizabeth A. Atkinson, wife of Angelo Atkinson, d. 28 Aug 1841.]

Atkinson, Margery Frances, son of David and Araminta Atkinson, b. 7 Nov 1839, bapt. 18 Mar 1842 by Rev. Dr. George C. M. Roberts

Atkinson, William George, son of David and Araminta Atkinson, b. 29 Feb 1842, bapt. 18 Mar 1842 by Rev. Dr. George C. M. Roberts

Atkinson, William T. and Elizabeth J. Aulderdike m. 24 May 1849 by Rev. John S. Martin, lic. dated 23 May 1849

Atwell, Rebecca A. and Thomas Booze m. 25 Jul 1841 by Rev. Gerard Morgan, lic. dated 21 Jul 1841

Audoun, Eliza Jane, d. 1849 (death noted in Class List)

Audoun, Joseph H. and Sarah A. Fuller m. 10 Apr 1845 by Rev. James Sewell, lic. dated 9 Apr 1845

Auld, Arianna A. and John L. Sears m. 6 Dec 1843 by Rev. Dr. George C. M. Roberts

Auld, David N. and Mary Ann Wright m. 5 Aug 1848 by Rev. James H. Brown, lic. dated 2 Aug 1848

Auld, Lavinia Sarah, dau. of Edward and Virginia Auld, b. 20 Nov 1841, bapt. 10 Dec 1841 by Rev. Dr. George C. M. Roberts

Aulderdike, Elizabeth J. and William T. Atkinson m. 24 May 1849 by Rev. John S. Martin, lic. dated 23 May 1849

Auskins, James and Henrietta Fitzgerald m. 12 Jun 1849 by Rev. John S. Martin, lic. dated 11 Jun 1849

Austin, William and Elisabeth Ford m. 21 Oct 1841 by Rev. Gerard Morgan, lic. dated 19 Oct 1841

Avis, Ann, dau. of Mr. & Mrs. Avis, aged 16 years, bapt. 31 Jan 1841 by Rev. Dr. George C. M. Roberts [Ed. Note: A later entry in the register stated she was b. 1824 and bapt. 5 Feb 1841.]

Ayres, George Wesley and Harriet Ann Jefferson m. 5 Mar 1848 by Rev. Stephen A. Roszel, lic. dated 4 Mar 1848

Ayres, Martha Ann, dau. of Charles and Elizabeth Ayres, b. 29 Jan 1840, bapt. 6 Jun 1840 by Rev. Dr. George C. M. Roberts

Ayres, Samuel and Ketura Cooper, of Baltimore City, m. 7 Dec 1846 by Rev. George Hildt

Backman, James E. and Susan Freeberger m. 6 Jan 1846 by Rev. Dr. George C. M. Roberts

Bacon, Phillip and Sarah Purner m. 26 Dec 1850 by Rev. Joseph Shane

Badger, Ezekiel and Louisa Plant, both of Baltimore, m. 25 Oct 1841 by Rev. Bernard H. Nadal

Bailey, Agnes A. and John M. E. Mennick m. 25 Jun 1846 by Rev. Littleton F. Morgan, lic. dated same day

Bailey, Anna L. and John A. Reese m. 12 Dec 1849 by Rev. Aquila A. Reese, lic. dated 11 Dec 1849

Bailey, George and Margaret S. Dormon m. 17 Apr 1844 by Rev. James Sewell, lic. dated same day

Bailey, Hellen, dau. of Henry and Mary Ann Bailey, b. -- Sep 1833, bapt. 31 [sic] Jun 1844 by Rev. James Sewell

Bailey, Henry, see "Hellen Bailey," q.v.

Bailey, John and Elvey Ann Pulley m. 11 Sep 1845 by Rev. Samuel Keppler (date of lic. not recorded)

Bailey, Sarah A. and Hiram Estlack m. 2 Jan 1848 by Rev. Dr. George C. M. Roberts

Bailey, Sarah, dau. of Thomas and Matilda Bailey, b. 14 Mar 1833, bapt. 13 Sep 1840 by Rev. Thomas Myers

Bailey, Thomas, see "Sarah Bailey," q.v.

Bailey, William W. F. and Ann McManus m. 7 Sep 1842 by Rev. Dr. George C. M. Roberts

Baily, Charles Bradenbaugh, son of William F. and Margaret Baily, b. 15 Oct 1840, bapt. 3 Jan 1842 by Rev. Dr. George C. M. Roberts

Baily, Eliza J. W. and William Downing, both of Baltimore County, m. 28 May 1844 by Rev. William Hamilton

Baily, Hamilton J., see "Martha A. Baily" and "Thomas R. Baily," q.v.

Baily, Isabella, d. 1845 (death noted in Class List) [*Ed. Note:* Death notice in the *Baltimore Sun* stated that Isabella Bailey, wife of Edwin Bailey and dau. of James Frazier, d. 25 Jun 1845.]

Baily, Martha Ann, dau. of Hamilton J. and Martha Ann Baily, b. 16 Aug 1847, bapt. 31 Oct 1854 by Rev. Dr. George C. M. Roberts

Baily, Sarah, d. 25 Aug 1842 (death noted in Record of Members)

Baily, Thomas Robb, son of Hamilton J. and Martha Ann Baily, b. 3 Jul 1843, bapt. 31 Oct 1854 by Rev. Dr. George C. M. Roberts

Baily, William Henry Clay, son of William F. and Margaret Baily, b. 20 Aug 1838, bapt. 3 Jan 1842 by Rev. Dr. George C. M. Roberts

Baker, Charles, son of Charles J. and Elizabeth Baker, b. 5 Feb 1845, bapt. 24 Oct 1845 by Rev. Dr. George C. M. Roberts

Baker, Charles and Mary A. Jackson m. 3 Oct 1842 by Rev. Henry Slicer, lic. dated same day

Baker, Cynthia Ann and Samuel D. Reed m. 28 Nov 1844 by Rev. Isaac P. Cook

Baker, Elizabeth, see "Charles Baker," q.v.

Baker, Elizabeth D. and George W. Cobb m. 19 Mar 1843 by Rev. Henry Slicer, lic. dated 16 Mar 1843

Baker, Frederick S., see "Matilda E. Baker," q.v.

Baker, Henry and Mary Mackelfresh, both of Baltimore County, m. ---- [date not given] by Rev. George Hildt, lic. dated 3 Jun 1845

Baker, James, see "Mary R. Baker" and "James M. Baker," q.v.

Baker, James Madison, son of James and Rebecca Baker, b. 18 Feb 1840, Fells Point, Baltimore City, bapt. 7 Jan 1841 by Rev. Isaac P. Cook [*Ed. Note:* Another entry in the church register stated he was bapt. 30 Aug 1840.]

Baker, John L. and Angeline Kelman m. 26 Dec 1849 by Rev. William Hirst, lic. dated same day

Baker, Joseph, d. 1849 (death noted in Class List)

Baker, Margaret G., see "Matilda E. Baker," q.v.

Baker, Martha A. and Lewis Rayns m. 13 Mar 1844 by Rev. Dr. George C. M. Roberts

Baker, Mary Rebecca, dau. of James and Rebecca Baker, b. 11 Jul 1841, bapt. 9 Dec 1841 by Rev. Dr. George C. M. Roberts

Baker, Matilda Elizabeth, dau. of Frederick S. and Margaret G. Baker, b. 12 Mar 1847, bapt. 22 Nov 1847 by Rev. Dr. George C. M. Roberts

Baker, Rebecca, see "James M. Baker" and "Mary R. Baker," q.v.

Baker, Sarah and David Biggart m. 7 May 1845 by Rev. James Sewell, lic. dated same day

Baker, Susanna H. and Edward H. Wilkinson m. 15 Dec 1840 by Rev. Samuel Keppler, lic. dated 5 Dec 1840

Baker, William and Margaret Lynch m. 21 Apr 1844 by Rev. Dr. George C. M. Roberts

Baldwin, Edmund, son of Robert and Mary Baldwin, b. 16 Apr 1843, bapt. 13 Jul 1843 by Rev. Dr. George C. M. Roberts

Ball, John and Lydia Jefferson m. 1 Jan 1850 by Rev. John S. Martin (date of lic. not recorded)

Ballard, Charles W. and Anna E. Harris m. 2 Feb 1850 at the house of her mother in Baltimore by Rev. Beverly Waugh, lic. dated same day

Ballard, James and Sarah Ann Woods m. 13 Jun 1843 by Rev. Wesley Stevenson

Ballow, Henrietta and Edward F. Irwin m. 24 Jun 1846 by Rev. Wesley Stevenson

Ballow(?), Sarah W. and William H. Robinson m. 22 Oct 1843 by Rev. Isaac P. Cook

Bamberger, Rebecca Ellen, dau. of Rebecca Bamberger, aged 11 years [b. 1846], bapt. 26 May 1857 by Rev. William A. Snively

Banbell, Charles Michael, son of Michael and Clarissa Banbell, aged 7 months [b. 1840, Baltimore City], bapt. 1841 (exact date not given) by Rev. Gerard Morgan

Bandel, Decatur Armisted, son of John and Ebelina [sic] Bandel, aged 2 months [b. 1840], bapt. 1 Dec 1841 by Rev. Gerard Morgan

Bandel, Thomas Fabus, son of John and Ebelina [sic] Bandel, aged 2 years [b. 1839], bapt. 1 Dec 1841 by Rev. Gerard Morgan

Bankard, Jacob Jackson, son of Jacob Jackson and Susan O. Bankard, b. 28 Aug 1847, bapt. 9 Sep 1847

Bankard, Pauline Emert, dau. of Jacob Jackson and Susanna O. Bankard, b. 27 Sep 1845, bapt. 28 Nov 1845 by Rev. Dr. George C. M. Roberts

Banker, Alfred, son of Mr. ---- [blank] and Susan Banker, aged 2 years [b. 1839], bapt. 16 Oct 1841 by Rev. Robert Emory

Banks, David and Sarah Justice m. 5 Sep 1841 by Rev. Gerard Morgan, lic. dated 3 Sep 1841

Banks, Wesley and Margaret Ann Stubbens, of Baltimore County, m. 29 Apr 1841 by Rev. John Rice, lic. dated 28 Apr 1841

Bannen, Betsey and George Turner m. 20 Nov 1843 by Rev. Dr. George C. M. Roberts

Bans, Samuel, son of James D. and Agness Bans, aged 5 months [b. 1841], bapt. 29 Aug 1841 by Rev. Gerard Morgan

Barbine, Joseph and Catherine Schults m. 22 Dec 1850 by Rev. Dr. George C. M. Roberts

Bargar, Susan and Samuel A. Smith m. 2 Jan 1850 by Rev. Aquila A. Reese, lic. dated same day

Barger, Sarah, d. circa 1840 (exact date not given in Record of Members) [Ed. Note: Death notice in the Baltimore Sun stated that Sarah Barger d. 28 Nov 1840.]

Barker, Alexander R. and Rebecca J. Woelper m. 8 Oct 1850 by Rev. John S. Martin, lic. dated 7 Oct 1850

Barker, Frances Ann, dau. of Francis and Harriet Ann Barker, b. 29 Mar 1834, bapt. 7 Dec 1840 by Rev. John Rice

Barker, George Yearly, son of Francis and Harriet Ann Barker, b. 8 Oct 1840, bapt. 7 Dec 1840 by Rev. John Rice

Barker, Harriet M. and Henry S. Lawson m. 13 Jan 1848 by Rev. Stephen A. Roszel, lic. dated same day

Barker, John Alexander, son of Francis and Harriet Ann Barker, b. 12 Aug 1835, bapt. 7 Dec 1840 by Rev. John Rice

Barker, Joseph Haines, son of Francis and Harriet Ann Barker, b. 3 Aug 1837, bapt. 7 Dec 1840 by Rev. John Rice

Barker, Louisa and James Franklin Towson, both of Baltimore, MD, m. 6 Apr 1842 by Rev. John A. Hening

Barker, William H. Sands, son of William Henry and Mary A. Barker, b. 6 Nov 1841, bapt. 1 Nov 1842 by Rev. Henry Slicer

Barkey, Emily Jane and Eli Dugent m. ---- [blank] by Rev. John S. Martin, lic. dated 22 Dec 1849 [*Ed. Note:* Their marriage notice in the *Baltimore Sun* stated Eli Dugent m. Emily J. Barker, dau. of William Barker, on 23 Dec 1849.]

Barkley, Joseph Henry, son of Hugh and Elizabeth Barkley, b. 1 Apr 1835, bapt. 27 Aug 1840 by Rev. Dr. George C. M. Roberts

Barling, Henry A. and Elizabeth Ann Hough m. 28 Dec 1843 by Rev. Isaac P. Cook

Barlow, Joseph and Ariann Norwood, both of Baltimore County, m. 2 Feb 1841 by Rev. Bernard H. Nadal

Barnard, Pauline and Joseph Hathaway Whittier m. 28 Nov 1849 by Rev. John S. Martin, lic. dated 27 Nov 1849

Barnes, Agnes Victoria, dau. of Mrs. Agnes Barnes, aged 12 years [b. 1845], bapt. 1 Jul 1857 by Rev. William A. Snively

Barnes, Emily Elizabeth, dau. of Robinson and Jemima Barnes, b. 22 Jan 1844, bapt. 21 Jul 1844 by Rev. Dr. George C. M. Roberts

Barnes, Eugene Ramsay, son of Mrs. Agnes Barnes, aged 13 years [b. 1844], bapt. 1 Jul 1857 by Rev. William A. Snively

Barnet, Charles, son of Charles J. and Ann M. Barnet, b. 20 Oct 1840, bapt. same day by Rev. Dr. George C. M. Roberts

Barnet, George Edward, son of Edward and Laura Amanda Barnet, b. 24 Dec 1846, bapt. 3 Jan 1848 by Rev. Dr. George C. M. Roberts

Barnett, Alexander Marion, son of James and Elizabeth Barnett, b. 18 Nov 1835, Easton, MD, bapt. 13 Apr 1840, Baltimore City, by Rev. Samuel Keppler

Barns, Margaret Ann, dau. of Christian and Sarah J. Barns, b. 25 Apr 1839, bapt. 17 Jan 1843 by Rev. Elisha D. Owen

Barns, Mary and Samuel C. Biscoe m. 4 Dec 1844 by Rev. James Sewell, lic. dated 2 Dec 1844

Barns, Mary A., d. circa 1841 (death noted in Class List)

Baron, John H. and Eleanor Owen m. 5 Jan 1843 by Rev. Dr. George C. M. Roberts

Barren, Rebecca Jane and William E. Patterson, both of Baltimore County, m. 4 Nov 1845 by Rev. William Hamilton

Barrett, Ann and Joseph Stating m. 13 Jul 1845 by Rev. Dr. George C. M. Roberts

Barrett, John and Elizabeth Cain m. 2 Nov 1845 by Rev. Samuel Keppler (date of lic. not recorded)

Barrick, Sarah J., see "Sarah J. Burrick," q.v.

Barros, Antonio and Isabelle Leme m. 4 May 1849 by Rev. John S. Martin, lic. dated same day

Barrow, Henry T. and Mary F. Stewart m. 14 Jul 1842 by Rev. Henry Slicer, lic. dated same day

Barrus, George W. and Mary Corsey m. 22 Apr 1848 by Rev. William Hirst

Barry, James Henry, son of John L. and Mary H. Barry, b. 20 Jan 1847, bapt. 27 Mar 1847 by Rev. Dr. George C. M. Roberts

Barston, Mary Eliza, dau. of George J. and Susan M. Barston, b. 16 Oct 1845, bapt. 24 May 1846 by Rev. Dr. George C. M. Roberts

Bartle, Susan and Joshua Clements m. 6 Jan 1848 by Rev. Joseph Shane

Bartlett, Hester Ann, dau. of James B. and Sophia Bartlett, b. -- Nov 1848, bapt. 1849 (exact date not given) by Rev. John S. Martin

Barton, Samuel L. and Mary Jane Johnson m. 13 Apr 1847 by Rev. Stephen A. Roszel, lic. dated same day

Bartzell, Jacob G. and Elizabeth Hartman m. 19 Aug 1841 by Rev. Dr. George C. M. Roberts

Basford, Isaac T. and Louisa B. Jenkins m. 18 Apr 1847 by Rev. Littleton F. Morgan, lic. dated 17 Apr 1847

Bassard, Henry and Elisa W. Berry m. 29 Jul 1845 by Rev. Dr. George C. M. Roberts

Bassett, Amelia and James R. Wiseman m. 27 May 1845 by Rev. James Sewell, lic. dated same day

Bassford, John T. and Adelia T. Dugent m. 6 Jun 1850 by Rev. John S. Martin, lic. dated 5 Jun 1850

Basten, Jane, dau. of Sarah Basten, aged 5 years [b. 1836], bapt. 5 Jan 1841 by Rev. Charles B. Tippett

Bateman, James O. and Mary Ann Brien m. 11 Feb 1847 by Rev. Dr. George C. M. Roberts

Bateman, Pamelia, d. circa 1840-1841 (death noted in Class List) [*Ed. Note:* Death notice in the *Baltimore Sun* stated that Pamelia Bateman d. 5 Jan 1841.]

Bateman, William and Ann Pontz m. 21 May 1846 by Rev. Samuel Keppler (date of lic. not recorded)

Bates, Elizabeth and Luke Brown m. 16 Jan 1843 by Rev. Wesley Stevenson

Batson, Mary Ann and James Parden, both of Baltimore, m. ---- [date not given] by Rev. John A. Hening, lic. dated 10 Sep 1841

Battee, Hannah, d. circa 1840 (exact date not given in Class Record)

Battow, Haman and Charlotte F. Leach m. 10 Mar 1845 by Rev. James Sewell, lic. dated 2 Mar 1845

Baughman, George, son of George and Mary Jane Baughman, b. 17 Apr 1837, bapt. 13 Sep 1841 by Rev. Dr. George C. M. Roberts

Baughman, Greer, son of George and Mary Jane Baughman, b. 17 Feb 1840, bapt. 13 Sep 1841 by Rev. Dr. George C. M. Roberts

Baunner, James G. W. and Catherine Robinson m. 7 Oct 1850 by Rev. Dr. George C. M. Roberts

Baxley, Mary G. and Elijah D. Williams m. 28 Sep 1847 by Rev. James H. Brown, lic. dated same day

Baxter, Ann Maria and William Chenwith m. 12 May 1846 by Rev. Samuel Keppler (date of lic. not recorded)

Baxter, Rebecca and John Tipton m. 30 Apr 1848 by Rev. Isaac P. Cook

Bayard, Aloesanna [*sic*] and John Boyd m. 22 Aug 1849 by Rev. Dr. George C. M. Roberts

Bayard, Thomas C. and Catherine L. Haden m. 20 May 1850 by Rev. Henry Slicer, lic. dated same day

Bayler, Mary A. and Asbury Hartlove m. 19 Sep 1841 by Rev. Dr. George C. M. Roberts

Bayliss, Jane, d. circa 1847-1848 (exact date not given in Record of Members) [*Ed. Note:* Death notice in the *Baltimore Sun* stated that Jane Bayless d. 26 Nov 1847.]

Bayzard, Samuel and Elizabeth Bustings m. 10 Mar 1844 by Rev. Joseph Shane

Beacham, John S. and Elizabeth Ann Murphy m. 5 May 1846 by Rev. Samuel Keppler (date of lic. not recorded)

Beacham, Mary Jane and John Wesley Stevens m. 6 Dec 1848 by Rev. Dr. George C. M. Roberts

Beacham, Mary Baldwin and John William Merchant m. 2 Dec 1845 by Rev. James Sewell, lic. dated same day

Beachamp, Jesse, see "Jesse Beecham," q.v.

Bean, Emily and Ezekiel Bell m. 5 Sep 1850 by Rev. Joseph Shane

Bean, Mary, d. -- Mar 1847 (death noted in Class List)

Bean, Mary E. and Alexander Sword m. 21 Apr 1840 by Rev. Samuel Keppler, lic. dated 20 Apr 1840

Bean, Thomas A. and Isabel Jones m. 9 Oct 1844 by Rev. James Sewell, lic. dated 8 Oct 1844

Bear, John Breckenridge, son of Dr. M. S. and Matilda Bear, b. 17 Mar 1843, bapt. 1 Jun 1843 by Rev. Dr. George C. M. Roberts

Beard, Lewis and Walamina M. Hunt m. 15 Jan 1845 by Rev. Dr. George C. M. Roberts

Beason, George Washington, son of John ad Julia Beason, b. 21 Jan 1842, bapt. 11 Mar 1842 by Rev. Robert Emory

Beaston, Sarah Augusta, dau. of George J. and Susan Beaston, b. 17 Feb 1847, bapt. 23 Apr 1847 by Rev. Dr. George C. M. Roberts

Beaty, Sarah, d. circa 1841-1842 (death noted in Class List) [*Ed. Note:* Death notice in the *Baltimore Sun* stated that Sarah Beatty, wife of George Beatty, d. 1 Feb 1842.]

Beauchamp, George Roberts, son of John and Mary E. Beauchamp, b. 14 Feb 1848, bapt. 15 Mar 1849 by Rev. Dr. George C. M. Roberts

Beauchamp, Mary, d. circa 1841 (death noted in Class List)

Beaum, Elizabeth, d. 1844 (exact date not given in Record of Members)

Beaumount, Isaac P. and Elizabeth Jeans, both of Baltimore County, m. ---- [date not given] by Rev. George Hildt, lic. dated 2 May 1846 [*Ed. Note:* Their marriage notice in the *Baltimore Sun* stated Isaac Beaumont and Elizabeth Jean m. 2 May 1846.]

Bechum, Ann M. and William Mason m. 17 Apr 1845 at the house of B. Waugh in Baltimore by Rev. Beverly Waugh, lic. dated 16 Apr 1845

Beck, George W. and Mary A. Dickenson m. 10 Dec 1841 by Rev. Joseph Shane

Becker, Hamilton and Hariot *[sic]* Frazer m. 11 Jul 1844 by Rev. James Sewell, lic. dated 2 Jul 1844

Beckley, Ann Maria and Perry G. Mitchell, both of Baltimore County, m. 19 May 1840 by Rev. Bernard H. Nadal

Beckley, Miss ---- [blank] and Edward Adams, both of Baltimore County, m. 26 Jan 1841 by Rev. Bernard H. Nadal [*Ed. Note:* Their marriage notice in the *Baltimore Sun* indicated her first name was Margaret.]

Beckwith, Mary A., d. 1849 (death noted in Class List) [*Ed. Note:* Death notice in the *Baltimore Sun* stated that Mary A. Beckwith d. 9 May 1849.]

Beebe, Samuel and Sarah Ann Chenowith m. 9 Jul 1850 by Rev. Dr. George C. M. Roberts

Beecham, Jesse, d. circa 1845-1847 (exact date not given in Record of Members) [*Ed. Note:* Death notice in the *Baltimore Sun* stated that Jesse Beachamp d. 13 Jan 1847.]

Beckly (Beekly?), Isaiah and Mary Jane Bishop m. 19 Feb 1846 by Rev. James Sewell, lic. dated same day

Bell, Catharine, d. 1849 (death noted in Class List) [*Ed. Note:* Death notice in the *Baltimore Sun* stated that Catharine Bell d. 20 Jun 1849.] See "Rachel Clark," q.v.

Bell, Catharine Fowler, dau. of ---- [blank], b. 24 May 1841, bapt. 28 Nov 1841 by Rev. William Prettyman

Bell, Davis, see "Henry E. Bell," q.v.

Bell, Edward J. and Sarah E. Dutton m. ---- [blank] by Rev. John S. Martin, lic. dated 21 Mar 1850 [*Ed. Note:* Their marriage notice in the *Baltimore Sun* stated Edward J. Bell m. Sarah E. Dutton, dau. of Robert Dutton, on 21 Mar 1850.]

Bell, Elizabeth and Alexander Kerr m. 8 Jan 1850 by Rev. Aquila A. Reese, lic. dated 7 Jan 1850

Bell, Ezekiel and Emily Bean m. 5 Sep 1850 by Rev. Joseph Shane

Bell, George W. and Mary E. Cope m. 7 Jun 1849 by Rev. Aquila A. Reese, lic. dated 6 Jun 1849

Bell, Georgietta Roberts, dau. of Nicholas R. and Henrietta Bell, b. 1 Jul 1848, bapt. 13 Jul 1848 by Rev. Dr. George C. M. Roberts

Bell, Henrietta, see "Georgietta R. Bell," q.v.

Bell, Henry Edwards, son of Davis and Susan A. McK. Bell, b. 23 May 1845, bapt. 16 Mar 1846 by Rev. Dr. George C. M. Roberts

Bell, James and Lydia A., see "Margaret A. Bell," q.v.

Bell, Margaret Ann, dau. of James E. and Lydia A. Bell, b. 5 Jul 1839, bapt. 20 Nov 1840 by Rev. Charles B. Tippett

Bell, Mary, d. circa 1847-1848 (death noted in Class List) [*Ed. Note:* Death notice in the *Baltimore Sun* stated that Mary F. Bell, wife of Edward J. Bell and dau. of David Fowler, d. 5 Dec 1848.]

Bell, Mary Ann and Samuel Craig m. 18 Jun 1846 by Rev. Dr. George C. M. Roberts

Bell, Nicholas R., see "Georgietta R. Bell," q.v.

Bell, Richard, d. circa 1849-1850 (death noted in Class List) [*Ed. Note:* Death notice in the *Baltimore Sun* stated that Richard Bell d. 9 Dec 1850.] See "Rachel Clark," q.v.

Bell, Sarah Isabella and Thomas S. Clarke m. 27 Apr 1843 by Rev. Henry Slicer, lic. dated same day

Bell, Susan A. McK., see "Henry E. Bell," q.v.

Bell, Theophilus and Mary Ann Elizabeth Burke m. 2 Apr 1840 by Rev. John Bear

Bell, William and Mary E. White m. 8 Mar 1842 by Rev. Gerard Morgan, lic. dated 7 Mar 1842

Bender, Charles S. and Eliza Grace m. ---- [blank] by Rev. John S. Martin, lic. dated 30 Oct 1849

Benjamin, Caroline and Charles Brosins (Brosius?) m. 12 Nov 1845 by Rev. Dr. George C. M. Roberts

Bennet, Mary Ann and Robert Mothland m. 14 Jan 1845 by Rev. James Sewell, lic. dated 13 Jan 1845

Bennet, Mary L. and John H. Davidson m. 29 Nov 1844 by Rev. James Sewell, lic. dated 28 Nov 1844

Bennett, B. F. and E. A. Ward m. 23 Aug 1848 by Rev. William Hirst [*Ed. Note:* Their marriage notice in the *Baltimore Sun* states Benjamin F. Bennett and E. A. Ward m. 24 Aug 1848.]

Bennett, Catherine and Martin Rash m. 2 Jul 1846 by Rev. Dr. George C. M. Roberts

Bennett, E. H. and John R. Lamben m. 4 May 1849 by Rev. William Hirst

Bennett, Francis W. and Margaret J. Patterson m. 10 Dec 1845 by Rev. Dr. George C. M. Roberts

Bennett, Jesse C. and Elizabeth Lyus m. 5 May 1841 by Rev. Joseph Shane

Bennett, John and Margaret Ross m. 21 Aug 1845 by Rev. Samuel Keppler (date of lic. not recorded)

Bennett, Littleton S. and Eliza S. Boon m. 18 Dec 1843 by Rev. Dr. George C. M. Roberts

Bennett, Mary Ann, dau. of William and Mary B. Bennett, b. 24 Sep 1846, bapt. 14 Nov 1846 by Rev. Dr. George C. M. Roberts

Bennett, Rufus and Louisa Walter m. 11 Oct 1849 by Rev. Aquila A. Reese, lic. dated 10 Oct 1849

Bennett, Sarah Ward, dau. of Benjamin F. and Eleanor Ann Bennett, b. 31 Jul 1849, bapt. 2 Sep 1849 by Rev. Dr. George C. M. Roberts

Bennett, William, see "Mary Ann Bennett," q.v.

Bennit, William Henry Harrison, son of Henry and Mary Ann Bennit, aged 5 months [b. 1840], bapt. 20 Jul 1840 by Rev. Gerard Morgan

Benoreti(?), Sarah B. and William F. Sicoden(?) m. 2 Apr 1843 by Rev. Job Guest, lic. dated 1 Apr 1843

Benson, John L. and Mary Rutter m. 13 May 1848 by Rev. William Hirst

Benson, Lloyd N. and Ann M. Carson m. 20 May 1847 by Rev. James H. Brown, lic. dated same day

Benson, Lucy, d. circa 1840-1847 (exact date not given in Record of Members)

Benthall, Thomas Watson, son of Robert and Isabella F. Benthall, b. 27 Oct 1837, bapt. 26 Jun 1842 by Rev. Joseph Merriken

Benthall, William McRea, son of Robert and Isabella F. Benthall, b. 17 Apr 1834, bapt. 26 Jun 1842 by Rev. Joseph Merriken

Bentley, Thomas, son of Thomas and Catherine Bentley, b. 11 Nov 1839, bapt. 18 Sep 1840 by Rev. Joseph Shane

Berry, ---- [blank], child of Jesse L. C. and Emily Berry, b. ---- [blank], bapt. 2 Apr 1849 by Rev. Dr. George C. M. Roberts

Berry, Ann C. and Lemuel Waggnier m. 26 Dec 1844 by Rev. James Sewell, lic. dated same day

Berry, Benjamin, see "Eleanor C. Morrow," q.v.

Berry, Benjamin Franklin, son of Benjamin D. and Sudney E. Berry, b. 23 Apr 1846, bapt. 29 Oct 1846 by Rev. Dr. George C. M. Roberts

Berry, Elisa W. and Henry Bassard m. 29 Jul 1845 by Rev. Dr. George C. M. Roberts

Berry, Elizabeth, see "Mary Elizabeth Bell," q.v.

Berry, James, d. circa 1843 (death noted in Probationers Book)

Berry, James W. and Lorinda Teal m. 25 Nov 1844 by Rev. Dr. George C. M. Roberts

Berry, Jesse L., see "Mary Elizabeth Bell," q.v.

Berry, Martha and Stephen Donaldson m. 6 Nov 1845 by Rev. James Sewell, lic. dated same day

Berry, Mary Eleanor, dau. of B. Dorsey and Sydney E. Berry, b. 22 Dec 1848, bapt. 11 Feb 1849 by Rev. Dr. George C. M. Roberts

Berry, Mary Elizabeth, dau. of Jesse L. and Elizabeth B. Berry, b. 21 Oct 1846, bapt. 29 Oct 1846 by Rev. Dr. George C. M. Roberts

Berry, Sydney E., see "Benjamin F. Bell," q.v.

Berry, William Lees, son of Mary Ann Berry, b. 18 Apr 1846, Baltimore, bapt. 27 Jun 1847 by Rev. Stephen A. Roszel

Betsworth, Emily, d. circa 1847-1850 (exact date not given in Record of Members)

Betts, William and Julian A. Peddicord m. 13 Jan 1842 by Rev. Joseph Shane

Beukler, Charles and Ellen Fife m. 20 Sep 1841 by Rev. Gerard Morgan, lic. dated same day

Bevan, Sarah J., d. circa 1840-1847 (exact date not given in Record of Members)

Beverage, Ann, d. circa 1844-1847 (exact date not given in Record of Members)

Bidderson, Ruth Ann, of Baltimore City, and James Morford, of Baltimore County, m. 13 Oct 1840 by Rev. John A. Hening

Biden, James and Jane Elizabeth Elkins m. 14 Mar 1850 by Rev. Joseph Shane

Bigby, Austen Johnson, son of Henry and Mary H. Bigby, aged 9 months [b. 1840], bapt. 27 Aug 1841 by Rev. Gerard Morgan

Biggart, David and Sarah Baker m. 7 May 1845 by Rev. James Sewell, lic. dated same day

Biggins, William H. and Catharine P. Lingril m. 22 Dec 1844 by Rev. Isaac P. Cook

Billingslea, Barzillai and Elizabeth A. Billingslea m. 16 Dec 1848 by Rev. Isaac P. Cook

Billington, Gover S. and Mary Marfield m. 7 Sep 1848 by Rev. Stephen A. Roszel, lic. dated same day

Bilson, E. G. and Samuel Hazelhurst, both of Baltimore County, m. 18 Feb 1840 by Rev. Bernard H. Nadal

Bilson, Emeline and James Hissey m. 12 Apr 1840 by Rev. Joseph Shane

Binley, Elizabeth and Thomas McMackin m. 21 Mar 1844 by Rev. Isaac P. Cook

Binnix, Rebecca and John F. Carey m. 11 Mar 1847 by Rev. Isaac P. Cook

Bird, Emma Adela, dau. of John Edward and Emeline Bird, b. 19 Jan 1842, bapt. 26 Mar 1844 by Rev. Dr. George C. M. Roberts

Bird, Emeline and John E., see "Emma A. Bird" and "Susan A. Bird," q.v.

Bird, Maria L. and Moses Kempton m. 29 aug 1848 by Rev. Dr. George C. M. Roberts

Bird, Mary E., d. circa 1847-1850 (exact date not given in Record of Members) [Ed. Note: The name "Gist" was initially written in, subsequently lined out, and the name "Bird" was written above it.]

Bird, Matilda and Jesse Brownly m. 1 Oct 1847 by Rev. Benjamin F. Brooke

Bird, Susan Amelia, dau. of John Edward and Emeline Bird, b. 3 Mar 1844, bapt. 26 Mar 1844 by Rev. Dr. George C. M. Roberts

Birth, Eleanor and Thomas M. Wilson m. 20 Oct 1842 by Rev. Samuel Brison

Biscoe, Samuel C. and Mary Barns m. 4 Dec 1844 by Rev. James Sewell, lic. dated 2 Dec 1844

Biscoe, William M. and Elizabeth Davis m. ---- [blank] by Rev. John S. Martin, lic. dated 2 Nov 1850

Bishop, Amelia Ringgold, dau. of Elijah and Harriet A. Bishop, b. 19 May 1846, bapt. 8 Aug 1847 by Rev. Dr. George C. M. Roberts

Bishop, Catharine A. and Patrick McLease m. 10 Jun 1847 by Rev. Stephen A. Roszel, lic. dated 8 Jun 1847

Bishop, Harriet and Elijah, see "Amelia R. Bishop," q.v.

Bishop, Henry and Harriet Poe m. 8 Mar 1849 by Rev. Joseph Shane

Bishop, J. T. and Elizabeth Ann Mungan m. 30 Dec 1841 by Rev. Wesley Stevenson [Ed. Note: However, another entry in the marriage register stated John T. Bishop and Eliza Ann Mangan were m. 4 Jan 1842 by Rev. Wesley Stevenson; perhaps the first date was the date of the license; no marriage notice was found in the Baltimore Sun newspaper.]

Bishop, Mary Jane and Isaiah Beckly (Beekly?) m. 19 Feb 1846 by Rev. James Sewell, lic. dated same day

Bixby, John C. and Mary Adams m. 26 Jul 1849 by Rev. John S. Martin, lic. dated 25 Jul 1849

Black, Ann Eliza, d. circa 1842-1847 (exact date not given in Record of Members)

Black, John R. and Eliza Ann Schrote, both of Baltimore County, m. 26 Nov 1840 by Rev. Thomas Myers, lic. dated 25 Nov 1840

Black, John R. and Sarah Jane Jacob m. 18 Feb 1847 by Rev. Isaac P. Cook

Black, Sarah Jane and James Taylor m. 2 Jun 1841 by Rev. Gerard Morgan, lic. dated 1 Jun 1841

Black, Susanna C. and Gerard Chesnut m. ---- [blank] by Rev. John S. Martin, lic. dated 9 May 1850 [Ed. Note: Their marriage notice in the Baltimore Sun stated Girard Chesnut m. Susanna C. Black on 15 May 1850.]

Blackburn, Franklin and Mildred C. Sutton m. 1 Sep 1843 by Rev. Samuel Brison

Blackman, Martha A. and Horace Fox m. 28 Aug 1842 by Rev. Dr. George C. M. Roberts

Blade, Ann Maria and James McLaughlin m. 15 Oct 1849 by Rev. Aquila A. Reese, lic. dated 14 Oct 1849

Blade, Rebecca and Thomas Reese m. 16 Oct 1844 by Rev. James Sewell, lic. dated same day

Blades, John L. and Frances E. Gale m. ---- [blank] by Rev. John S. Martin, lic. dated 21 Nov 1850 [Ed. Note: Their marriage notice in the Baltimore Sun initially stated John L. Blades m. Fanny E. Gill on 21 Nov 1850, but her name was later corrected to Frances Gayle.]

Blades, Sarah and Nathan Sherlock m. 28 Sep 1843 by Rev. Dr. George C. M. Roberts

Blake, Almira Augusta, dau. of Charles and Eliza C. Blake, b. 13 Sep 1849, bapt. 3 Mar 1850 by Rev. Dr. George C. M. Roberts

Blake, Charles William Woodcock, son of Charles and Eliza C. Blake, b. 31 Oct 1845, bapt. 18 May 1846 by Rev. Dr. George C. M. Roberts

Blake, John S., d. circa 1850 (exact date not given in Record of Members) [Ed. Note: Death notice in the Baltimore Sun stated that John S. Blake d. 13 Aug 1850.]

Blaney, Maria and Isaac Swan m. 6 Jan 1845 by Rev. Isaac P. Cook

Bloomer, Frederick and Harriet C. Wood m. 19 Jan 1840 by Rev. Samuel Keppler, lic. dated 27 Jan 1840

Bobard, Charles, son of Charles and Charlotte Bobard, b. 3 May 1842, bapt. 17 May 1842 by Rev. Elisha D. Owen

Bobeth, Helen L. and Jacob Rimby m. 10 Dec 1846 by Rev. Isaac P. Cook

Bockman, Virginia and Warren P. Kemp m. 7 May 1846 by Rev. Dr. George C. M. Roberts

Bocree, Rosina and John Seeman m. 7 Jun 1849 by Rev. Dr. George C. M. Roberts

Boden, Elizabeth and David L. Hammersley m. 8 Sep 1842 by Rev. Henry Slicer, lic. dated 13 Aug 1842

Bodensick, Catharine and Charles Roberts m. 30 Nov 1843 by Rev. Isaac P. Cook

Bodensick, Mary M. and Jacob T. Neighoof m. 23 Nov 1848 by Rev. Isaac P. Cook

Bodfield, Ann and George R. Carmine m. 28 Sep 1845 by Rev. Dr. George C. M. Roberts

Boeston, George, son of George J. and Susan Boeston, b. 10 Sep 1839, bapt. 23 Jun 1844 by Rev. Dr. George C. M. Roberts

Boeston, James Mitchell, son of George J. and Susan Boeston, b. 26 Oct 1843, bapt. 23 Jun 1844 by Rev. Dr. George C. M. Roberts

Boeston, Laura Susanna, dau. of George J. and Susan Boeston, b. 6 Nov 1841, bapt. 23 Jun 1844 by Rev. Dr. George C. M. Roberts

Bohen, Jenet and Leven Jones, both of Baltimore, MD, m. 24 Dec 1840

Bolby, Ann Louisa, dau. of J. D. and Elizabeth Ann Bolby, aged 21 months [b. 1840], bapt. 2 Apr 1842 by Rev. Gerard Morgan

Bolding, Lewis, son of John and Sophia Bolding, b. 28 Oct 1842, bapt. 30 Dec 1842 by Rev. Henry Slicer

Bolgiano, Francis W., son of John H. and Hannah Bolgiano, b. 6 Apr 1839, bapt. 15 Dec 1847 by Rev. Dr. George C. M. Roberts

Bolgiano, James Slater, son of John H. and Hannah Bolgiano, b. 19 Jun 1847, bapt. 15 Dec 1847 by Rev. Dr. George C. M. Roberts

Bolgiano, Sarah Elizabeth, dau. of John H. and Hannah Bolgiano, b. 7 Jul 1843, bapt. 15 Dec 1847 by Rev. Dr. George C. M. Roberts

Bolour, Albert R. and Adaline King, of Baltimore, m. 11 Oct 1840 by Rev. John A. Hening

Bolster, Thomas, d. circa 1840-1847 (exact date not given in Record of Members)

Bond, Elizabeth and Read S. Owen m. 28 Dec 1845 by Rev. Dr. George C. M. Roberts

Bond, James Jr. and Elizabeth A. Smith m. 15 Nov 1842 by Rev. Henry Slicer, lic. dated 14 Nov 1842

Bond, Rachel and Thomas Laird m. 17 Sep 1843 by Rev. Phillip B. Reese (date of lic. not recorded)

Bond, Sarah and James Hadaway m. 15 Dec 1845 by Rev. Dr. George C. M. Roberts

Bond, Thomas and Elizabeth Crosby m. 7 Oct 1843 by Rev. Henry Slicer, lic. dated same day

Bonssell, Sarah R. and William H. Stonnan(?) m. 11 Nov 1841 by Rev. Job Guest, lic. dated 8 Nov 1841

Bookhultz, Mary Elizabeth, dau. of George and Sarah J. Bookhultz, b. 15 Jun 1840, bapt. 28 Nov 1840 by Rev. Dr. George C. M. Roberts

Boon, Benjamin F. and Margaret C. Carback m. 18 Aug 1844 by Rev. Dr. George C. M. Roberts

Boon, Eliza S. and Littleton S. Bennett m. 18 Dec 1843 by Rev. Dr. George C. M. Roberts

Boone, Benjamin Francis, son of Burly and Rebecca Boone, aged 3 years [b. 1837, Baltimore City], bapt. 1840 (exact date not given) by Rev. Gerard Morgan

Booth, Josephine, dau. of John R. and Ariadus Booth, b. 18 Feb 1843, bapt. 26 Jul 1843 by Rev. Dr. George C. M. Roberts

Booth, M. A. and ---- [blank] Lawrence m. 1 May 1849 by Rev. William Hirst [Ed. Note: Their marriage notice in the Baltimore Sun gave their names as Matthew A. Booth and Anna L. Lawrence.]

Booz, Thomas H. and Elisabeth Carbeck m. 15 Aug 1841 by Rev. Gerard Morgan, lic. dated 10 Aug 1841

Booze, Mary Loiza, dau. of Benjamin and Ann Maria Booze, aged 15 months [b. 1840], bapt. 20 Feb 1842 by Rev. Gerard Morgan

Booze, Thomas and Rebecca A. Atwell m. 25 Jul 1841 by Rev. Gerard Morgan, lic. dated 21 Jul 1841

Borgelt, John, d. circa 1842-1843 (exact date not given in Record of Members) [Ed. Note: Death notice in the Baltimore Sun stated that John Borgelt d. 17 Sep 1843.]

Boring, Sarah Ann and William Hopkins m. 2 Dec 1847 at the house of Mrs. Daniel Fosbenner in Baltimore by Rev. Beverly Waugh, lic. dated 29 Nov 1847

Bose, Henry H. and Ann Maria Foreman m. 30 Nov 1844 by Rev. Joseph Shane

Bosley, George, d. circa 1847-1848 (death noted in Probationers Book) [Ed. Note: Death notice in the Baltimore Sun stated that George M. Bosley d. 1 Jan 1848.]

Bosley, Kezia Ann and Archibald McNeal m. 28 Sep 1843 by Rev. Samuel Brison

Bosley, Rachel, d. circa 1849-1850 (death noted in Class List) [Ed. Note: Death notice in the Baltimore Sun stated that Rachel Bosley d. 11 Apr 1850.]

Bosley, Sarah and George C. Redman m. 31 May 1846 by Rev. Joseph Shane

Bosley, Talbot and Rebecca Patterson m. 5 Mar 1843 by Rev. Dr. George C. M. Roberts

Boss, John, d. 1840 (death noted in Class List) [Ed. Note: Death notice in the Baltimore Sun stated that John Boss d. 29 Oct 1840.]

Boston, Daniel (colored) and Elizabeth Thomas (colored) m. 17 Sep 1846 by Rev. Samuel Keppler

Boston, Joseph S. and Caroline Stevens m. 19 Jan 1845 by Rev. Dr. George C. M. Roberts

Boston, Samuel and Ann Aaron m. 2 Aug 1847 by Rev. Dr. George C. M. Roberts

Boswick, Elmira and Nelson Gray m. 3 Oct 1841 by Rev. Isaac P. Cook

Bosworth, Mary Frances and John J. Whiteford, both of Baltimore County, m. 29 Jan 1843 by Rev. Nelson Head

Boteler, Sarah Jane, dau. of George McKendree and Ellen Boteler, b. 10 Aug 1847, bapt. 12 Sep 1847 by Rev. Dr. George C. M. Roberts

Botfield, Elizabeth and Joseph S. Albert m. 16 Jun 1842 by Rev. Dr. George C. M. Roberts

Botler, Charles W. Jr. and Catharine Pentz, both of Baltimore County, m. 8 Mar 1840 by Rev. Bernard H. Nadal

Bougheraft, Sarah, dau. of George and Eliza Bougheraft, b. 8 Aug 1840, bapt. 5 Aug 1842 by Rev. Elisha D. Owen

Boures, Mary and Samuel Mardy m. 21 Sep 1848 by Rev. William Hirst

Bourgelt, George, d. circa 1840 (exact date not given in Class Record)

Bourgelt, Jacob, d. circa 1840 (exact date not given in Class Record)

Bowden, Rosana and Joseph R. Davis m. 11 Apr 1844 by Rev. Joseph Shane

Bowdle, Jane and William T. Shaw m. 11 Dec 1842 by Rev. Dr. George C. M. Roberts

Bowe, Nathaniel F. and Elizabeth Ann Crenshaw m. 5 Aug 1842 at Brawne's(?) Hotel in Baltimore by Rev. Beverly Waugh, lic. dated same day

Bowen, Ann E. and Thomas B. Watkins m. 7 Apr 1846 by Rev. Dr. George C. M. Roberts

Bowen, Ann, d. circa 1845-1846 (death noted in Class List) [Ed. Note: Death notice in the Baltimore Sun stated that Ann Bowen d. 2 Sep 1846.]

Bowen, Edward L. and Mary Ann Willett m. 21 Feb 1850 by Rev. Aquila A. Reese, lic. dated 20 Feb 1850

Bowen, Eliza Ann, dau. of Nathaniel and Emeline Bowen, b. 2 Jun 1837(?), bapt. 15 Jun 1840 by Rev. Dr. George C. M. Roberts

Bowen, Imogene, dau. of ---- [blank] and Elizabeth Bowen, b. ---- [blank], bapt. 25 Jun 1840 by Rev. Dr. George C. M. Roberts

Bowen, Mary, d. circa 1845-1847 (death noted in Class List) [Ed. Note: Death notice in the Baltimore Sun stated that Mary Bowen, widow of John Bowen, d. 14 Jan 1847.]

Bowen, Nathaniel, see "Eliza Ann Bowen," q.v.

Bowers, Anna and William J. Hartley m. ---- [blank] by Rev. John S. Martin, lic. dated 13 Sep 1850

Bowers, Elmira A. and Robert Stewart m. 28 May 1845 by Rev. Dr. George C. M. Roberts

Bowling, James P. Jr. and Mary H. M. Dashiel m. ---- [blank] by Rev. John S. Martin, lic. dated 13 Jul 1850 [Ed. Note: Their marriage notice in the Baltimore Sun stated James P. Bowling, Jr. m. Henrietta Dashiel, dau. of Levin F. Dashiel, on 30 Jul 1850.]

Bowling, William J. and Caroline M. Hamal m. 15 Jul 1850 by Rev. John S. Martin, lic. dated 13 Jul 1850

Bowser, Sophia (colored) and Thomas Patterson (colored) m. 4 Nov 1841 by Rev. Gerard Morgan, lic. dated 28 Oct 1841

Boyd, Agness C. and James T. Randolph m. 8 Oct 1840 by Rev. Samuel Keppler, lic. dated 6 Oct 1840

Boyd, Elizabeth J. M., d. 21 Feb 1848 (death noted in Record of Members)

Boyd, Ellinor and Wesley McMachen m. 3 Jan 1850 by Rev. Aquila A. Reese, lic. dated 2 Jan 1850

Boyd, Francis S. A. B. and Sarah Ann Hopkins m. 29 Aug 1841 by Rev. Gerard Morgan, lic. dated 25 Aug 1841

Boyd, Henry and Catherine Cross m. 14 Feb 1850 by Rev. Aquila A. Reese, lic. dated 13 Feb 1850

Boyd, John and Aloesanna [sic] Bayard m. 22 Aug 1849 by Rev. Dr. George C. M. Roberts

Boyd, John and Mary E. Chard m. 25 Jul 1850 by Rev. John S. Martin, lic. dated 24 Jul 1850

Boyd, Joseph H. and Mary Jane Reese, both of Baltimore County, m. 2 Sep 1845 by Rev. J. Hoffman Waugh, lic. dated same day

Boyd, Mary, d. circa 1844-1847 (exact date not given in Record of Members)

Boyd, Weston, see "William R. Boyd," q.v.

Boyd, William Robert, son of Weston and Hannah Boyd, b. 25 Aug 1841, bapt. 12 Oct 1842 by Rev. Elisha D. Owen

Boyer, John, son of John and Ann Boyer, b. 25 Aug 1841, bapt. 21 Oct 1841 by Rev. Gerard Morgan

Boyer, John, d. circa 1845-1847 (exact date not given in Record of Members)

Boyer, Teverly Evan, son of John and Nancy Boyer, b. 11 Dec 1842, bapt. 12 Jan 1843 by Rev. Elisha D. Owen

Boyer, William, son of John and Elizabeth Boyer, b. 24 Sep 1840, bapt. 5 Oct 1840 by Rev. Dr. George C. M. Roberts

Bradford, John and Susan Reese, both of Baltimore County, m. ---- [date not given] by Rev. George Hildt, lic. dated 20 Dec 1845 [*Ed. Note:* Their marriage notice in the *Baltimore Sun* stated they married on 21 Dec 1845.]

Bradford, Margaret, d. circa 1849 (death noted in Class List)

Bradford, Samuel Drew, son of Charles H. and Frances P. Bradford, b. 8 May 1847, bapt. 21 Oct 1847 by Rev. Dr. George C. M. Roberts

Bradshaw, Mary Ann and Thomas Flood m. 19 Sep 1843 by Rev. Samuel Brison

Bradshaw, Samuel and Mary Ann Dawson m. 13 Jun 1844 by Rev. Joseph Shane

Brady, Elisabeth (colored) and George Scott (colored) m. 5 Aug 1841 by Rev. Gerard Morgan, lic. dated 4 Aug 1841

Brady, William and Mary Ann Vickers m. 29 Nov 1840 by Rev. Samuel Keppler, lic. dated 23 Nov 1840

Bragg, William F. and Henrietta E. Briscoe m. 29 May 1849 by Rev. Aquila A. Reese, lic. dated 28 May 1849

Bramble, Laura Jane, dau. of ---- [blank] and Maria Bramble, b. ---- "not given" [*sic*], bapt. 27 Oct 1844 by Rev. Isaac P. Cook

Bramble, Martha L. and William H. Reno m. 25 Oct 1848 by Rev. Dr. George C. M. Roberts

Brannaman, Margaret S. and Alexander M. Olen, both of Baltimore County, m. 18 May 1842 by Rev. Nelson Head

Brannan, Alexander, see "Ann E. Brannan" and "Ellen R. Brannan" and "William A. Brannan," q.v.

Brannan (Branan), Ann Maria and William M. Haney m. 27 Jul 1848 by Rev. Stephen A. Roszel, lic. dated same day

Brannan, Ann Elizabeth, dau. of Alexander and Eliza Brannan, b. 26 Feb 1840, bapt. 22 Dec 1844 by Rev. Isaac P. Cook

Brannan (Branan), Christianna, d. circa 1846 (death noted in Probationers Book)

Brannan, Eliza J., dau. of James M. Brannan, b. 31 Jul 1840(?), bapt. 14 Sep 1840 by Rev. John A. Hening

Brannan, Ellen Rebecca, dau. of Alexander and Eliza Brannan, b. 9 Mar 1841, bapt. 22 Dec 1844 by Rev. Isaac P. Cook

Brannan, Emily and Jesse Brown m. 5 Nov 1845 by Rev. Samuel Keppler (date of lic. not recorded)

Brannan, James M., see "Eliza J. Brannan," q.v.

Brannan, William Alexander, son of Alexander and Eliza Brannan, b. 20 Nov 1843, bapt. 22 Dec 1844 by Rev. Isaac P. Cook

Brant, Creighton W. and Martha Ann Riley m. ---- [no date given] by Rev. John Miller, lic. dated 31 Dec 1850

Brass, Joseph and Hannah Johnson m. 6 Oct 1847 by Rev. Benjamin F. Brooke

Bratt, Noah and Martha Ann Harris m. 7 Sep 1841 by Rev. Dr. George C. M. Roberts

Brazier, Robert and Sarah Horn m. 24 Mar 1846 by Rev. Isaac P. Cook

Brazier, Robert and Mary Ann Henderson m. 19 Sep 1844 by Rev. Dr. George C. M. Roberts

Brazier, William W. and Margaret Ann Dulen m. 28 Feb 1843 by Rev. Samuel Brison [*Ed. Note:* Their marriage notice in the *Baltimore Sun* gave their names as William H. Brazier and Margaret A. Dewling.]

Brett, George Roberts, son of Cyrus K. Sr. and Sarah Brett, b. 30 Mar 1845, bapt. 2 Apr 1845 by Rev. Dr. George C. M. Roberts

Brett, Sarah Emma, dau. of Cyrus K. and Sarah A. Brett, b. 5 Oct 1846, bapt. 10 Oct 1846 by Rev. Dr. George C. M. Roberts

Brewer, Daniel, d. circa 1840-1841 (exact date not given in Record of Members) [*Ed. Note:* Death notice in the *Baltimore Sun* stated that Daniel Brewer d. 14 Jan 1841.]

Brian, Eliza and James P. Smith, both of Baltimore County, m. ---- [date not given] by Rev. George D. Chenoweth, lic. dated 21 Mar 1842

Brian, John and Emily Sterrett, both of Baltimore County, m. ---- [date not given] by Rev. George Hildt, lic. dated 1 Nov 1845 [*Ed. Note:* Their marriage notice in the *Baltimore Sun* stated they married on 2 Nov 1845.]

Briant, Isabella C., see "Isabella Bryan," q.v.

Briden, Samuel and Susan Ann Arnold m. 2 Mar 1843 by Rev. Joseph Shane

Bridener, Philip and Clementine Stansbury m. 20 Oct 1847 by Rev. James H. Brown, lic. dated same day

Brien, Catharine E., see "Catherine E. Bryan," q.v.

Brien, Mary Ann and James O. Bateman m. 11 Feb 1847 by Rev. Dr. George C. M. Roberts

Briggs, John W., d. 1849 (death noted in Class List) [*Ed. Note:* Death notice in the *Baltimore Sun* stated that John W. Briggs d. 27 Oct 1849.]

Briggs, Mary and Benjamin Earlaugher m. 15 Aug 1840 by Rev. Joseph Shane

Briggs, Temperance, d. 1847 (death noted in Class List) [*Ed. Note:* Death notice in the *Baltimore Sun* stated that Temperance Briggs, mother-in-law of Joseph Perrigo, d. 13 Sep 1847.]

Brinkley, Elizabeth, d. circa 1844-1847 (exact date not given in Record of Members)

Briscoe, Cordelia Ann and Dr. John T. Grey m. 17 Aug 1841 by Rev. Dr. George C. M. Roberts

Briscoe, Henrietta E. and William F. Bragg m. 29 May 1849 by Rev. Aquila A. Reese, lic. dated 28 May 1849

Briscoe, Lavinia and William Hubbard m. 29 Mar 1847 by Rev. Dr. George C. M. Roberts

Brison(?), Avarilla and Joshua Whitaker m. 21 Apr 1842 by Rev. Job Guest, lic. dated same day

Brittingham, Catherine and James Ady m. 15 Oct 1850 by Rev. Henry Slicer, lic. dated same day

Britton, Thomas Jefferson and Sarah Sophia Nevil m. 2 Jul 1845 by Rev. James Sewell, lic. dated same day

Brome, William H. and Susan E. Faulkner m. 16 May 1843 by Rev. Henry Slicer, lic. dated 15 May 1843

Bromly, Jesse and Josephine Lory m. 19 Nov 1843 by Rev. Dr. George C. M. Roberts

Brooke, Elizabeth and John B. Davis m. 10 Apr 1844 by Rev. Isaac P. Cook

Brooks, Eliza Lavinia, dau. of William and Martha T. Brooks, b. 18 Sep 18-- [blank], bapt. 24 Jan 1846 by Rev. Dr. George C. M. Roberts

Brooks, Emily and George A. Nagel m. 5 Jan 1844 by Rev. Dr. George C. M. Roberts

Brooks, George Walter, son of William and Martha T. Brooks, b. 22 Dec 1845, bapt. 24 Jan 1846 by Rev. Dr. George C. M. Roberts

Brooks, James (Thomas) [sic], son of Robert and Mary Brooks, b. 14 Dec 1840, bapt. -- Oct 1841 by Rev. Robert Emory

Brooks, Jinnette, dau. of William and Martha T. Brooks, b. 27 Nov 1841, bapt. 24 Jan 1846 by Rev. Dr. George C. M. Roberts

Brooks, John Thomas and Mary Jane Buck m. 5 Aug 1841 by Rev. Gerard Morgan, lic. dated 4 Aug 1841

Brooks, Margaret and Joseph Lyles m. 2 Jan 1850 by Rev. Aquila A. Reese, lic. dated same day

Brooks, William Harrison, son of William and Martha T. Brooks, b. 16 Sep 1843, bapt. 24 Jan 1846 by Rev. Dr. George C. M. Roberts

Broom, William and Mary E. Irvin m. 4 Jun 1845 by Rev. James Sewell, lic. dated same day

Brosins (Brosius?), Charles and Caroline Benjamin m. 12 Nov 1845 by Rev. Dr. George C. M. Roberts

Brown, Alice, see "Ophelia A. Brown," q.v.

Brown, Ann M., see "Joshua J. Brown," q.v.

Brown, Ann Maria and James Taylor m. 30 Apr 1848 by Rev. Dr. George C. M. Roberts

Brown, Carlton T. and Elizabeth A. Risteau m. 10 Apr 1843 by Rev. Henry Slicer, lic. dated same day

Brown, Catherine Eleanor, dau. of James R. and Hester Ann Brown, b. 1 Nov 1848, bapt. 13 Nov 1848 by Rev. Dr. George C. M. Roberts

Brown, Charles and Eliza Wilson m. 8 Jun 1842 by Rev. Dr. George C. M. Roberts

Brown, Charles N. and Mary A. Reece m. 24 May 1848 by Rev. Joseph Shane

Brown, Dixon and Catharine Rhodes, both of Baltimore County, m. 8 Nov 1840 by Rev. Bernard H. Nadal

Brown, Edward William and Amelia Klockgelter m. 9 Aug 1841 by Rev. Job Guest, lic. dated same day

Brown, Elenor and James E. White m. 4 Apr 1841 by Rev. Gerard Morgan, lic. dated 3 Apr 1841

Brown, Elizabeth C. and Marshal D. Maxwell m. 4 Feb 1843 by Rev. Job Guest, lic. dated 3 Feb 1843

Brown, Emma, d. 23 Apr 1847 (death noted in Record of Members) [Ed. Note: Death notice in the Baltimore Sun stated that Emma Brown, widow of Jacob S. Brown, d. 17 Apr 1847.]

Brown, George W., see "Gerahty W. Brown" and "James M. Brown," q.v.

Brown, Gerahty W., son of George Washington and Mary M. Brown, aged 16 months [b. 1839], bapt. -- Sep 1841 by Rev. John A. Hening

Brown, Harriett C., d. circa 1845-1847 (exact date not given in Record of Members) [*Ed. Note:* Death notice in the *Baltimore Sun* stated that Harriet C. Brown d. 21 Aug 1846.]

Brown, Hester A., see "Catherine E. Brown," q.v.

Brown, Isaiah and Mary Ann Wilcox m. 2 Jul 1850 by Rev. Isaac P. Cook

Brown, Jacob S., see "Emma Brown," q.v.

Brown, James, see "John C. Brown" and "Joshua K. Brown," q.v.

Brown, James M., son of George Washington and Mary M. Brown, aged 4 years [b. 1836], bapt. -- Sep 1841 by Rev. John A. Hening

Brown, James R., see "Catherine E. Brown," q.v.

Brown, James V. and Ann Caroline Ch---l(?) [page smudged] m. 15 Sep 1840 by Rev. Samuel Keppler, lic. dated 14 Sep 1840

Brown, Jesse and Emily Brannan m. 5 Nov 1845 by Rev. Samuel Keppler (date of lic. not recorded)

Brown, John C., son of James and Ann C. Brown, b. 2 Aug 1841, bapt. 17 Jan 1843 by Rev. Elisha D. Owen

Brown, Joshua J. and Eleanor Gregory m. 3 Jan 1844 by Rev. Henry Slicer, lic. dated 2 Jan 1844

Brown, Joshua Jackson, son of James M. and Ann M. Brown, b. 7 Nov 1840, bapt. 11 Apr 1841 by Rev. Isaac P. Cook

Brown, Josiah Washington, son of James and Ann Brown, b. ---- [blank], bapt. 8 Mar 1840 by Rev. Thomas Myers

Brown, Luke and Elizabeth Bates m. 16 Jan 1843 by Rev. Wesley Stevenson

Brown, Margaret and John Cooper m. 3 Oct 1841 by Rev. Gerard Morgan, lic. dated 2 Oct 1841

Brown, Margaret and William Hooper m. 1 Mar 1843 by Rev. Henry Slicer, lic. dated same day

Brown, Margaret E. and William Griffin m. 26 Dec 1848 by Rev. Stephen A. Roszel, lic. dated same day

Brown, Mary, d. 8 May 1844 (death noted in Class List)

Brown, Mary Ann and Joseph M. Shaw m. 10 Feb 1841 by Rev. Samuel Keppler, lic. dated 9 Feb 1841

Brown, Mary Ann and Patrick Dillon m. 6 Jan 1841 by Rev. Samuel Keppler, lic. dated 4 Jan 1841

Brown, Mary M., see "Gerahty W. Brown" and "James M. Brown," q.v.

Brown, Ophelia Alice, dau. of Jacob and Alice Brown, aged 7 years [b. 1850], bapt. 22 Apr 1857 by Rev. William A. Snively

Brown, Sarah Ann and Abel Brunner m. 10 Jun 1849 by Rev. Dr. George C. M. Roberts

Brown, Sophia and Richard Perine, both of Baltimore County, m. 18 Nov 1842 by Rev. Nelson Head

Brown, William C. and Emily C. Smythe m. 2 May 1850 by Rev. Joseph Shane

Browne, Ann, d. 3 Jan 184- (year not given; death noted in Record of Members) [*Ed. Note:* Death notice in the *Baltimore Sun* stated that Ann Browne, wife of John B. Browne, d. 8 Jan 1845.]

Browning, Louis H. and Ellen Lowrey m. 1 Mar 1841 by Rev. Wesley Stevenson

Browning, Mary E. and Thomas D. Arrington (Anington?) m. 16 Aug 1849 by Rev. Joseph Shane

Brownley, Thomas and Sarah A. Darby m. 16 Apr 1850 by Rev. Dr. George C. M. Roberts

Brownly, Jesse and Matilda Bird m. 1 Oct 1847 by Rev. Benjamin F. Brooke

Bruff, Charles L. and Anna M. Read m. 3 Sep 1846 by Rev. Dr. George C. M. Roberts

Bruff, Joseph D. and Martha Ann Guest m. 16 Nov 1841 by Rev. Job Guest, lic. dated 15 Nov 1841

Bruiman (Bwiman?), Jauelda(?) Catharine and George W. Pryor m. 24 Oct 1848 by Rev. Stephen A. Roszel, lic. dated same day

Brundage, William and Sarah Wylie m. 4 Dec 1849 by Rev. Aquila A. Reese, lic. dated 3 Dec 1849 [Ed. Note: Their marriage notice in the Baltimore Sun gave their names as William Brundige and Sarah Wiley.]

Brundidge, Thomas V. and Margaret Smith, both of Baltimore County, m. 21 Jul 1842 by Rev. Nelson Head

Brundige, Thomas Worthington, son of Thomas V. and Margaret T. Brundige, b. 30 Mar 1847, bapt. 16 Aug 1847 by Rev. Dr. George C. M. Roberts

Brune, Ellen, d. circa 1847-1850 (exact date not given in Record of Members)

Brunker, Luke and Susan Hadaway m. 29 Oct 1847 by Rev. Stephen A. Roszel, lic. dated same day

Brunner, Abel and Sarah Ann Brown m. 10 Jun 1849 by Rev. Dr. George C. M. Roberts

Brunner, Andrew, see "Elizabeth Gossage," q.v.

Brunner, Harriet and John Morrow m. 9 Apr 1850 by Rev. Dr. George C. M. Roberts

Brunner, Phebe, see "Elizabeth Gossage," q.v.

Bruscup, Elizabeth and John O. Cornthwait m. 19 Oct 1843 by Rev. Henry Slicer, lic. dated same day

Brusster, Martha M. and William C. Stockton m. 12 May 1842 by Rev. Henry Slicer, lic. dated same day

Bryan, Catherine E. and John Fefil m. 30 Apr 1846 by Rev. Dr. George C. M. Roberts [Ed. Note: Their marriage notice in the Baltimore Sun stated that John Fefill and Catharine E. Brien m. 29 Apr 1846.]

Bryan, Christopher, see "Sarah R. Bryan," q.v.

Bryan, Emma Street, dau. of John A. W. and Mary A. Bryan, b. 30 Jan 1850, bapt. 30 Mar 1850 by Rev. Dr. George C. M. Roberts

Bryan, Isabella, d. circa 1847-1850 (exact date not given in Record of Members) [Ed. Note: Death notice in the Baltimore Sun stated that Isabella C. Briant d. 25 Jan 1850.]

Bryan, John A. W. and Mary A. Mowbray m. 27 Mar 1849 at Light Street Church in Baltimore by Rev. Beverly Waugh, lic. dated 26 Mar 1849. See "Emma S. Bryan," q.v.

Bryan, Sarah R., dau. of Christopher and Ellen Bryan, b. 22 Aug 1840, bapt. 5 Sep 1840 by Rev. John A. Hening

Bryan, William and Margaret Reith m. 7 Apr 1846 by Rev. Dr. George C. M. Roberts

Bryden (Buyden?), John and Ann O. Wade m. 16 Dec 1841 by Rev. Joseph Shane

Buchanan, Ann and William P. Mills m. 6 Dec 1842 by Rev. Benjamin H. Crever, lic. dated same day

Buck, Elizabeth A. and John J. Keys m. 12 May 1842 by Rev. Joseph Shane

Buck, George W. and Virginia Irving m. 24 Aug 1848 by Rev. James H. Brown, lic. dated 24 May 1848

Buck, James B. and Mary C. McCormick m. 17 May 1849 by Rev. Isaac P. Cook

Buck, Mary Jane and John Thomas Brooks m. 5 Aug 1841 by Rev. Gerard Morgan, lic. dated 4 Aug 1841

Buck, Susan Green and Edward Thomas Owens m. 15 Dec 1840 by Rev. Samuel Keppler, lic. dated same day

Buckey, David D. and Sarah Ann Greenfield m. 8 Jun 1847 by Rev. Littleton F. Morgan, lic. dated 7 Jun 1847

Buckingham, Charles E. and Mary Hagner m. 31 Jan 1847 by Rev. Dr. George C. M. Roberts

Buckingham, Perry G. and Tabitha S. Abrahams m. 3 Jul 1845 by Rev. James Sewell, lic. dated same day

Buckless, Henry Slicer, son of Henry and Barbary Buckless, b. 19 Jan 1841, bapt. 1 Jul 1842 by Rev. Henry Slicer

Buckley, David and Mary Stevenson m. 28 Aug 1842 by Rev. Dr. George C. M. Roberts

Buckley, Elizabeth and Robert Donaldson m. 20 Oct 1850 by Rev. Dr. George C. M. Roberts

Buckmaster, Henry and Frances E. Vetry m. ---- [blank] by Rev. John S. Martin, lic. dated 21 Mar 1850

Bull, Christopher W. and Lavinia M. Corbitt m. 30 Dec 1849 by Rev. Aquila A. Reese, lic. dated 28 Dec 1849

Bull, Edmund and Rachel Isaacs m. 16 Jun 1846 by Rev. Littleton F. Morgan, lic. dated same day

Bull, Mary, d. 1844 (exact date not given in Record of Members) [Ed. Note: Death notice in the Baltimore Sun stated that Mary Bull, wife of Edmund Bull, d. 1 Jun 1844.]

Bunting, George and Amelia Thompson, both of Baltimore County, m. 1 Apr 1841 by Rev. John Rice

Burch, Thomas B. and Maria Evritt m. 6 Nov 1845 by Rev. Samuel Keppler (date of lic. not recorded)

Burcheral, Frances Virginia, dau. of Jeremiah and Mary Burcheral, b. 10 May 1842, bapt. 4 Aug 1844 by Rev. Isaac P. Cook

Burcheral, Joseph Thomas, son of Jeremiah and Mary Burcheral, b. 19 May 1840, bapt. 4 Aug 1844 by Rev. Isaac P. Cook

Burcheral, Luther James, son of Jeremiah and Mary Burcheral, b. 10 Nov 1843, bapt. 4 Aug 1844 by Rev. Isaac P. Cook

Burdich, Oscar Edwin, son of Joseph A. and Emmeline H. Burdich, b. 6 Aug 1847, bapt. 19 Aug 1847 by Rev. Dr. George C. M. Roberts

Burgess, Caleb, see "Samuel O. Burgess," q.v.

Burgess, George Roberts, son of Stephen and Mary Burgess, b. 11 Sep 1842, bapt. 6 Jan 1843 by Rev. William Prettyman

Burgess, Mary, d. circa 1841 (death noted in Class List)

Burgess, Samuel O., son of Caleb and Elizabeth Burgess, b. 18 Nov 1841, bapt. 10 Oct 1842 by Rev. William Prettyman

Burgess, Sarah A., d. circa 1840 (exact date not given in Record of Members) [Ed. Note: Death notice in the Baltimore Sun stated that Sarah A. Burgess d. 6 Feb 1840.]

Burgess, Stephen, see "George R. Burgess," q.v.

Burgess, William and Ruth Jones m. 15 Sep 1844 by Rev. Joseph Shane

Burke, Elizabeth, d. circa 1846-1847 (exact date not given in Record of Members) [*Ed. Note:* Death notice in the *Baltimore Sun* stated that Elizabeth Burke, wife of David Burke, d. 15 Jul 1846.]

Burke, Ester Louisa, dau. of Richard and Mary Burke, b. 8 Oct 1839, bapt. 20 Jul 1840 by Rev. Thomas Myers

Burke, Mary Ann Elizabeth and Theophilus Bell m. 2 Apr 1840 by Rev. John Bear

Burke, Richard, d. circa 1842-1847 (exact date not given in Record of Members) [*Ed. Note:* Death notice in the *Baltimore Sun* stated that Richard Burke d. 12 Aug 1842.]

Burke, Sarah and George T. Pool m. 1 Sep 1846 by Rev. Littleton F. Morgan, lic. dated same day

Burke, Sarah A. and Stephen Woolford m. 22 Mar 1842 by Rev. Dr. George C. M. Roberts

Burkhead, Christopher and Eliza Ann Ford, both of Baltimore County, m. 28 Apr 1840 by Rev. Thomas Myers, lic. dated same day

Burkholder, Mary A. and Andrew F. Wilson m. 2 Dec 1843 by Rev. Isaac P. Cook

Burnel, Samuel Rowe, son of Samuel and Sarah Ann Burnel, b. 2 Sep 1844, bapt. 22 Sep 1844 by Rev. Dr. George C. M. Roberts

Burneston, Isaac, see "Ann Burniston," q.v.

Burnet, Ellen Virginia Spedden, dau. of Samuel and Sarah Ann Burnet, b. 23 Nov 1847, bapt. 11 Dec 1847 by Rev. Dr. George C. M. Roberts

Burnet, George Roberts, son of Samuel and Sarah Ann Burnet, b. 1 Mar 1842, bapt. same day by Rev. Dr. George C. M. Roberts

Burnet, James Edgar, son of Samuel and Sarah Ann Burnet, b. 26 Jun 1846, bapt. 14 Jan 1847 by Rev. Dr. George C. M. Roberts

Burnet, Susanna Reese, dau. of Samuel and Sarah Ann Burnet, b. 2 Jan 1840, bapt. 25 Jul 1841 by Rev. Dr. George C. M. Roberts

Burnham, Charles F. and Mahala Watson m. 9 Sep 1840 by Rev. Samuel Keppler, lic. dated same day

Burnham, Mahala and Lucius A. R. Tisdale m. 28 May 1843 by Rev. Henry Slicer, lic. dated 27 May 1843

Burniston, Ann, d. 1842 (exact date not given in Record of Members) [*Ed. Note:* Death notice in the *Baltimore Sun* stated that Anna Burneston, widow of Isaac Burneston, d. 7 Apr 1842.]

Burns, Ann and David C. Zimmerman m. 4 Oct 1849 by Rev. Aquila A. Reese, lic. dated 3 Oct 1849

Burns, Ann Catharine and Randolph Richards m. 1 Sep 1847 by Rev. Isaac P. Cook

Burns, Elizabeth Grace, dau. of Samuel and Catherine Wilkes Burns, b. 19 Jun 1842, bapt. 5 Apr 1855 by Rev. Dr. George C. M. Roberts

Burns, Mary Kimmall, dau. of Samuel and Catherine Wilkes Burns, b. 7 Sep 1847, bapt. 5 Apr 1855 by Rev. Dr. George C. M. Roberts

Burress, George Washington, son of John and Jane Burress, aged 5, bapt. 17 Oct 1841 by Rev. Gerard Morgan

Burress, Jane Elisabeth, dau. of John and Jane Burress, aged 5 weeks, bapt. 17 Oct 1841 by Rev. Gerard Morgan

Burress, John Alexander, son of John and Jane Burress, aged 17, bapt. 17 Oct 1841 by Rev. Gerard Morgan

Burress, Joseph Loan, son of John and Jane Burress, aged 3, bapt. 17 Oct 1841 by Rev. Gerard Morgan

Burress, Mary, dau. of John and Jane Burress, aged 13, bapt. 17 Oct 1841 by Rev. Gerard Morgan

Burress, Susan Virginia, dau. of John and Jane Burress, aged 7, bapt. 17 Oct 1841 by Rev. Gerard Morgan

Burrick, Sarah J. and James Shelder m. 22 Aug 1850 by Rev. Dr. George C. M. Roberts [Ed. Note: Their marriage notice in the Baltimore Sun gave their names as James Sheldon and Sarah J. Barrick.]

Burroughs, William and Ellen Scott m. 23 Sep 1844 by Rev. James Sewell, lic. dated same day

Busch, George Washington, son of George and Ann Eliza Busch, b. 1 Jan 1841, bapt. 2 Sep 1841 by Rev. Dr. George C. M. Roberts

Busch, Mary A. and James Forrest m. 7 May 1843 by Rev. Dr. George C. M. Roberts

Busch, William and Caroline Forrest m. 26 Jan 1843 by Rev. Dr. George C. M. Roberts

Busey, Arneda and Thomas Mortimer m. 14 Dec 1841 by Rev. Joseph Shane

Busey, Richard G. and Mary E. Fitzgerald m. 22 Jan 1844 by Rev. Joseph Shane

Bush, Amelia, bapt. in her 17th year on 3 Oct 1841 by Rev. John A. Hening

Bush, Cain, see "Isabella Bush," q.v.

Bush, Cassandra A. and William F. Gambill m. 23 Dec 1849 by Rev. Aquila A. Reese, lic. dated 22 Dec 1849 [Ed. Note: Their marriage notice in the Baltimore Sun gave their names as William F. Gambrill and Casandra Bush, dau. of David Bush.]

Bush, Charlotte, dau. of George W. and Susanna Bush, b. 2 Mar 1839(?), bapt. 11 Aug 1840 by Rev. Charles B. Tippett

Bush, David, see "Cassandra A. Bush," q.v.

Bush, Isabella, dau. of Cain and Elizabeth Bush, aged 3 years and 11 months [b. 1839], bapt. 25 Dec 1842 by Rev. Henry Slicer

Bushman, Samuel and Ann Elizabeth Salisbury m. 2 Aug 1847 by Rev. Dr. George C. M. Roberts

Busk, Thomas B. and Talitha A. Keirle m. 5 Apr 1843 at the house f her father Joshua Dryden in Baltimore by Rev. Beverly Waugh, lic. dated 2 Apr 1843

Bustings, Elizabeth and Samuel Bayzard m. 10 Mar 1844 by Rev. Joseph Shane

Butcher, Charles and Hannah Winchester m. 26 Nov 1848 by Rev. Dr. George C. M. Roberts. See "Mary W. Butcher," q.v.

Butcher, Margaret and James Pew m. 11 May 1841 by Rev. Isaac P. Cook

Butcher, Mary Winchester, dau. of Charles M. and Hannah E. Butcher, b. 10 Mar 1849, bapt. 18 Mar 1849 by Rev. Dr. George C. M. Roberts

Butcher, William H. and Emeline Cromwell m. 9 Oct 1849 by Rev. Aquila A. Reese, lic. dated 8 Oct 1849

Butler, Amelia H., dau. of ---- [blank], b. 25 Jul 1841, bapt. 2 Aug 1841 by Rev. Gerard Morgan

Butler, Amelia Henryta, dau. of ---- [blank], b. 18 Jul 1841, East Baltimore, bapt. 25 Jul 1841 by Rev. Gerard Morgan

Butler, Charlotte, see "Valeria Jane Butler," q.v.

Butler, Emily J. and William Halsey m. 12 Mar 1846 by Rev. Joseph Shane

Butler, James and Mary Young m. 8 Aug 1846 by Rev. Isaac P. Cook

Butler, John, see "William Butler," q.v.

Butler, Mary A., d. 1845 (exact date not given in Record of Members) [*Ed. Note:* Death notice in the *Baltimore Sun* stated that Mary A. Butler d. 22 Jan 1845.]

Butler, Samuel, see "Valeria Jane Butler," q.v.

Butler, Valeria Jane, dau. of Samuel and Charlotte Butler, b. 1 Jan 1845, bapt. 13 Jan 1845 by Rev. Dr. George C. M. Roberts

Butler, William, son of John and ---- [blank] Butler, b. 24 Oct 1839, bapt. 24 Aug 1840 by Rev. Isaac P. Cook

Button, Joseph, d. circa 1841 (death noted in Class List)

Button, Sarah, d. circa 1841-1842 (death noted in Class List) [*Ed. Note:* Death notice in the *Baltimore Sun* stated that Sarah Button, widow of Elias Button, d. 3 Jun 1842.]

Buxton, Charlotte Jane, dau. of Benjamin and Eunice Buxton, b. 27 Nov 1846, Baltimore, bapt. 25 Jul 1847 by Rev. William M. D. Ryan

Buxton, Julia Ellen, dau. of Benjamin and Eunice Buxton, b. 10 Oct 1841, bapt. 9 Oct 1842 by Rev. Henry Slicer

Buxton, Mary Eliza, dau. of Benjamin and Eunice Buxton, b. 7 Feb 1839, bapt. 9 Oct 1842 by Rev. Henry Slicer

Byas, Rebecca, d. 21 Jul 1847 (death noted in Record of Members)

Byers, Frederick and Susan Wells m. 27 Jun 1844 by Rev. Isaac P. Cook

Byrne, Adeline Gertrude, dau. of William W. and Elizabeth M. Byrne, b. 17 Jun 1845, bapt. 20 Jun 1846 by Rev. Dr. George C. M. Roberts

Byrne, Ann Elizabeth Jenkins, dau. of William W. and Elizabeth M. Byrne, b. 10 Apr 1843, bapt. 24 Oct 1843 by Rev. Dr. George C. M. Roberts

Byrne, Charles Thomas Jenkins, son of William W. and Elizabeth Byrne, b. -- Jul 1844, bapt. 21 Jul 1844 by Rev. Dr. George C. M. Roberts

Byrne, Eugene Martin, son of William W. and Elizabeth M. Byrne, b. 19 Feb 1850, bapt. 28 Jul 1850 by Rev. Dr. George C. M. Roberts

Byrne, Henry F. and Ann M. D. Lee m. 18 Nov 1847 by Rev. Dr. George C. M. Roberts

Byrne, Margaret Hester, dau. of William W. and Elizabeth M. Byrne, b. 10 May 1841, bapt. 22 May 1840 *[sic]* by Rev. Dr. George C. M. Roberts

Byron, Charles Henry and Sarah Jane Houston m. 10 Jun 1847 by Rev. Dr. George C. M. Roberts

Byus, Anna M., d. circa 1847-1850 (exact date not given in Record of Members)

Cacey, Mary and Parker C. Thomas m. 15 Nov 1849 by Rev. Dr. George C. M. Roberts

Cain, Elizabeth and John Barrett m. 2 Nov 1845 by Rev. Samuel Keppler (date of lic. not recorded)

Cain, Ellen Frances and Rufus King Cain m. 30 Oct 1845 by Rev. James Sewell, lic. dated same day

Cain, Jesse and Elizabeth Milburn m. 15 Oct 1846 by Rev. Littleton F. Morgan, lic. dated 14 Oct 1846

Cain, Rufus King and Ellen Frances Cain m. 30 Oct 1845 by Rev. James Sewell, lic. dated same day

Caine, Frances M., d. 28 Nov 1840 (death noted in Record of Members)

Callender, Mary Ann and John C. Sullivan m. 29 Nov 1840 by Rev. Samuel Keppler, lic. dated 28 Nov 1840

Camerline, Catharine, d. circa 1847-1850 (exact date not given in Record of Members)

Cameron, Samuel and Sarah Ann Phillips m. 30 Jan 1849 by Rev. Dr. George C. M. Roberts

Cameron, Sarah J. and Joseph Skinner m. 2 Jul 1846 by Rev. Dr. George C. M. Roberts

Camm, Simerimis and Thomas A. Owens m. 18 Feb 1845 by Rev. James Sewell, lic. dated same day

Campbell, George R. and Sarah A. Cross m. 18 Aug 1842 by Rev. Isaac P. Cook

Campbell, Jane and James McCann m. 29 Nov 1840 by Rev. Joseph Shane

Campbell, John and Catherine Lemmon m. 19 Jan 1842 by Rev. Joseph Shane

Campbell, John and Angelina Orchard m. 23 Jan 1849 by Rev. Dr. George C. M. Roberts

Campbell, John W. and Margaret Clarke m. 27 May 1847 by Rev. Dr. George C. M. Roberts

Campbell, Martha and Arthur McKee m. 19 Aug 1844 by Rev. Joseph Shane

Campbell, Sarah, d. -- Jun 1847 (death noted in Record of Members) [Ed. Note: Death notice in the Baltimore Sun stated that Sarah Campbell, widow of George Campbell, d. 2 Jun 1847.]

Camper, Mary E., d. 1844 (exact date not given in Record of Members) [Ed. Note: Death notice in the Baltimore Sun stated that Mary E. Camper d. 30 Dec 1844.]

Cann, Mary and William Sapp m. 29 Aug 1845 by Rev. James Sewell, lic. dated same day

Cannon, Harriet, d. 1841 (death noted in Class List) [Ed. Note: Death notice in the Baltimore Sun stated that Harriet Canon, wife of Thomas Canon, d. 22 Mar 1841.]

Canon, Thomas, see "Harriet Cannon," q.v.

Caples, Frederick and Rachel Wells m. 28 Jan 1841 by Rev. Joseph Shane

Caragan, Elizabeth and William Deaver m. 3 Sep 1840 by Rev. Joseph Shane

Carback, Margaret C. and Benjamin F. Boon m. 18 Aug 1844 by Rev. Dr. George C. M. Roberts

Carback, Mary, d. circa 1846-1847 (exact date not given in Record of Members) [Ed. Note: Death notice in the Baltimore Sun stated that Mary Carback d. 27 Jan 1847.]

Carbeck, Elisabeth and Thomas H. Booz m. 15 Aug 1841 by Rev. Gerard Morgan, lic. dated 10 Aug 1841

Carcaud, Gilbert and Elizabeth Smith m. 1 Oct 1850 by Rev. Henry Slicer, lic. dated same day

Care, Sarah and Charles Maidlow m. 21 Apr 1846 by Rev. Littleton F. Morgan, lic. dated 17 Apr 1846

Carey, John F. and Rebecca Binnix m. 11 Mar 1847 by Rev. Isaac P. Cook

Carey, Rebecca, d. circa 1845-1847 (exact date not given in Record of Members)

Carman, William and Catherine Wilson m. 8 Oct 1843 by Rev. Joseph Shane

Carmean, Elizabeth and Jesse Anderson m. 26 Dec 1843 by Rev. Dr. George C. M. Roberts

Carmichael, Samuel, d. before 1847 (exact date not given in Record of Members) [Ed. Note: Death notice in the Baltimore Sun stated that Achsah Carmichael, widow of Samuel Carmichael, d. 29 Jul 1849.]

Carmine, George R. and Ann Bodfield m. 28 Sep 1845 by Rev. Dr. George C. M. Roberts

Carmon, Edward, son of William and Susan Carmon, b. 15 Oct 1841, bapt. 30 Mar 1842 by Rev. Isaac P. Cook

Carmon, Thomas Jefferson, son of William and Susan Carmon, b. 1 Feb 1839, bapt. 30 Mar 1842 by Rev. Isaac P. Cook

Carnalier (Cavnalier?), George W. L. and Amelia Catherine Mette m. 8 Sep 1846 by Rev. Job Guest, being then in Alexandria D. C., lic. dated 7 Sep 1846

Carpenter, William H. and Ann A. West m. 20 Nov 1848 by Rev. William Hirst

Carr, Benjamin D. and Mary R. Croxall m. 24 Feb 1842 by Rev. Job Guest, lic. dated same day

Carr, James and Amanda M. Wright m. 15 Nov 1849 by Rev. Aquila A. Reese, lic. dated 14 Nov 1859

Carr, Mary E. and William Curley m. 15 Dec 1845 by Rev. Wesley Stevenson

Carroll, Bernard and Marcella A. Philips m. 20 Jul 1850 by Rev. Dr. George C. M. Roberts, lic. dated 17 Jul 1850

Carroll, Margarett and John Lewis m. 7 Jun 1840 by Rev. Joseph Shane

Carson, Ann M. and Lloyd N. Benson m. 20 May 1847 by Rev. James H. Brown, lic. dated same day

Carson, Ann Rebecca, dau. of Elijah and Hannah Carson, b. 31 Dec 1848, bapt. 29 Jul 1855 by Rev. Dr. George C. M. Roberts

Carson, George and Catherine Cross m. 14 Aug 1842 by Rev. Joseph Shane

Carson, John and Ellen F. Hogg, both of Baltimore County, m. 7 Apr 1840 by Rev. Bernard H. Nadal

Carson, Joseph and Mary C. Sanders m. 2 Sep 1843 by Rev. Henry Slicer, lic. dated 27 Aug 1843

Carter, Ann and James Sapp m. 13 Sep 1846 by Rev. Dr. George C. M. Roberts

Carter, Asbury, see "George R. Carter," q.v.

Carter, Catharine, d. circa 1849-1850 (exact date not given in Record of Members) [*Ed. Note:* Death notice in the *Baltimore Sun* stated that Catharine Carter, widow of Solomon Carter, d. 30 Jul 1849.]

Carter, Cloud and Mary G. Plummer, both of Baltimore County, m. 27 Apr 1840 by Rev. Thomas Myers, lic. dated same day

Carter, Elizabeth, dau. of Isaac and Mary Ann Carter, b. 1 May 1846, bapt. 27 Sep 1846 by Rev. Samuel Keppler

Carter, Francis and Caroline F. Lemmon m. 16 Sep 1849 by Rev. Aquila A. Reese, lic. dated 15 Sep 1849

Carter, George Roberts, son of William and Sarah Carter, b. 4 Jan 1840, bapt. 25 Jan 1841 by Rev. Dr. George C. M. Roberts

Carter, George Roberts, son of Asbury and Mary C. Carter, b. 25 Mar ---- [blank], bapt. 25 May 1846 by Rev. Dr. George C. M. Roberts

Carter, Isaac, see "Elizabeth Carter," q.v.

Carter, John W., see "Laura A. Carter," q.v.

Carter, Laura Alverta, dau. of John W. and Elizabeth Carter, b. 6 Sep 1840, bapt. 29 Nov 1840 by Rev. John Bear

Carter, Solomon, see "Catharine Carter," q.v.

Carter, William, see "George R. Carter," q.v.

Carter, William and Sarah Pruitt m. 31 Mar 1845 by Rev. Dr. George C. M. Roberts

Carty, Ann and William A. Swift, Jr. m. 20 Jul 1847 by Rev. Stephen A. Roszel, lic. dated same day

Case, John H. and Martha E. Jones m. 13 Dec 1849 by Rev. Dr. George C. M. Roberts

Case, Susan R. and Caleb Hipsley m. 21 May 1850 by Rev. Joseph Shane

Casey, Catherine and George Smith m. 30 May 1841 by Rev. Joseph Shane

Casey, Catherine, d. after 1841 (exact date not given in Class Record)

Casey, Jane, d. circa 1844-1847 (exact date not given in Record of Members)

Casey, Maria Sewell, dau. of William and Mary Jane Casey, b. 16 Jan 1844, bapt. 11 Jun 1844 by Rev. James Sewell

Casey, Mary A., d. 1844 (death noted in Class List) [Ed. Note: Death notice in the Baltimore Sun stated that Mary Casy d. 11 Sep 1844.]

Casey, William and Mary Jane Ward m. 6 Nov 1842 by Rev. Job Guest, lic. dated 5 Nov 1842. See "Maria S. Casey," q.v.

Caskey, John Campbell Black(?), son of Joseph and Julia Ann Caskey, b. 5 Jan 1840, bapt. -- Oct 1840 by Rev. Charles B. Tippett

Caskey, Samuel and Mary R. Hyson m. 28 Jul 1841 by Rev. Dr. George C. M. Roberts

Cassell, Edward A. and Mary Elizabeth Ing m. 11 Oct 1848 by Rev. Dr. George C. M. Roberts

Cassey, Sarah and William Price m. 19 Jan 1841 by Rev. Samuel Keppler, lic. dated same day

Cassnill, Augustus W. and Margaret A. Woods m. 5 May 1849 by Rev. John S. Martin, lic. dated same day

Cathcart, Mary Jane and Joseph S. Cleveland m. 17 Dec 1840 by Rev. Samuel Keppler, lic. dated same day

Cathcart, Robert Edward, son of Robert and Martha A. Cathcart, b. 21 Nov 1841, bapt. 12 Oct 1842 by Rev. Elisha D. Owen

Cather, Robert William, son of ---- [blank], b. 1 Nov 1838, bapt. 20 Jun 1841 by Rev. Job Guest

Cather, Susanna Elizabeth, dau. of ---- [blank], b. 15 Aug 1840, bapt. 20 Jun 1841 by Rev. Job Guest

Cathwood, Sarah and James Johnson m. 1 Apr 1844 by Rev. Dr. George C. M. Roberts

Causell, Mary Jane and John H. Deer m. 29 Jul 1849 by Rev. Aquila A. Reese, lic. dated 28 Jul 1849 [Ed. Note: Their marriage notice in the Baltimore Sun gave their names as John H. Derr and Mary J. Cassell.]

Cavnalier, George, see "George Carnalier," q.v.

Cerrick, William and Mary Airy m. 30 Nov 1842 by Rev. Wesley Stevenson

Ch---l(?) [page smudged], Caroline and James V. Brown m. 15 Sep 1840 by Rev. Samuel Keppler, lic. dated 14 Sep 1840

Chalk, Ann and George Flindell(?) m. 20 Feb 1846 by Rev. Wesley Stevenson

Chalk, Hannah and Henry Horn m. 26 May 1846 by Rev. Wesley Stevenson [Ed. Note: His name was given as "Henry Hohn" in their Baltimore Sun marriage notice.]

Chalk, Leah and William L. Jackson m. 6 Nov 1843 by Rev. Wesley Stevenson

Chalmers, Henrietta, d. circa 1849-1850 (exact date not given in Record of Members) [Ed. Note: Death notice in the Baltimore Sun stated that Henrietta Chalmers, widow of James Chalmers, d. 10 Jun 1849.]

Chalmers, Isabella E. and Henry Clay Smith m. 25 Jul 1850 by Rev. Isaac P. Cook

Chalmers, Lydia Marrion, dau. of James and Ann Maria Chalmers, aged 10 months [b. 1839], bapt. -- Jul 1840 by Rev. Charles B. Tippett

Chamberlain, Alexander B., d. 1844 (death noted in Class List)

Chamberlain, Alexena, dau. of Alexander B. and Rebecca Chamberlain, b. 14 Jun 1842, bapt. 25 Dec 1842 by Rev. Henry Slicer

Chamberlain, Frederick, see "Frederick Chamberland," q.v.

Chamberlain, John, son of John and Rebbecca [sic] A. Chamberlain, b. 11 Jul 1840, bapt. 22 Jul 1840 by Rev. Dr. George C. M. Roberts

Chamberlain, Sarah Louisa, dau. of Alexander B. and Rebecca Chamberlain, b. 9 Mar 1840, bapt. 25 Dec 1842 by Rev. Henry Slicer

Chamberland, Ferdinand and Lare Ann Dawson m. 23 Sep 1843 by Rev. Phillip B. Reese (date of lic. not recorded) [Ed. Note: Their marriage notice in the Baltimore Sun indicated Ferdinand Chamberlain and Lear A. Dawson m. 24 Sep 1843.]

Chambers, Catharine, d. circa 1850 (death noted in Class List) [Ed. Note: Death notice in the Baltimore Sun stated that Catharine Chambers, widow of Alexander Chambers, d. 10 Apr 1850.]

Chambers, John Thomas, son of John and Elizabeth Chambers, b. ---- "not given" [sic], bapt. 27 Oct 1844 by Rev. Isaac P. Cook

Chambers, Margaret, d. 1845 (exact date not given in Record of Members)

Chance, Ann Maria and James H. Hadaway m. 23 Dec 1845 by Rev. Dr. George C. M. Roberts

Chandler, John R., d. circa 1845-1847 (death noted in Class List) [Ed. Note: Death notice in the Baltimore Sun stated that John R. Chandler d. 16 Jan 1847.]

Chandler, Mary C., d. circa 1847-1848 (death noted in Class List) [Ed. Note: Death notice in the Baltimore Sun stated that Mary C. Chandler d. 22 Feb 1848.]

Chandley, James S. and Ann Taylor m. 21 Dec 1840 by Rev. Joseph Shane

Chaney, Angeline and William Phelps m. 14 Dec 1843 by Rev. Joseph Shane

Chaney, John and Eliza Ann Coleman m. 6 Jan 1846 by Rev. Joseph Shane

Chaney, Louisa and George W. Tharle m. 28 Sep 1847 by Rev. Joseph Shane

Chaney, Susan and James S. Armstrong m. 13 Jul 1847 by Rev. Stephen A. Roszel, lic. dated 29 Jun 1847

Chapline, James L. and Sarah E. Warfield m. 9 May 1844 by Rev. Joseph Shane

Chapman, Charlotte and John Munotten m. 15 Jun 1841 by Rev. Gerard Morgan, lic. dated 31 May 1841

Chappell, Amanda J. and Dr. Pembrook M. Womble m. 20 Dec 1849 by Rev. William Hirst, lic. dated 18 Dec 1849

Chappell, Marshall Fanerdon, son of John G. and Priscilla E. Chappell, b. 4 Dec 1845, bapt. 14 May 1846 by Rev. Dr. George C. M. Roberts

Chard, Mary E. and John Boyd m. 25 Jul 1850 by Rev. John S. Martin, lic. dated 24 Jul 1850

Chase, Eugenia and James Orem, both of Baltimore County, m. ---- [date not given] by Rev. George D. Chenoweth, lic. dated 14 Jan 1842

Chase, George W. and Ellen Murray m. 9 Jun 1847 by Rev. James H. Brown, lic. dated 8 Jun 1847

Chase, Hanibal, see "Hannah Ann Chase," q.v.

Chase, Hannah Ann, dau. of Hanibal and Susan Chase, b. 20 Feb 1840, bapt. 1 Jun 1840 by Rev. Joseph Shane

Chase, John, see "William H. H. Chase," q.v.

Chase, William and Elizabeth Norris m. 8 May 1849 by Rev. Aquila A. Reese, lic. dated 7 May 1849

Chase, William H. H., son of John and Mary A. Chase, b. 4 Feb 1841, bapt. 4 Aug 1842 by Rev. Elisha D. Owen

Chaytor, Daniel, see "Sarah Chaytor," q.v.

Chaytor, Mary and Frederick W. Marston m. 13 Feb 1844 at the house of Mrs. Chaytor in Baltimore by Rev. Beverly Waugh, lic. dated same day

Chaytor, Mrs., see "Thomas L. Hall" and "Frederick W. Marston," q.v.

Chaytor, Rebecca P., see "Rebecca Poits," q.v.

Chaytor, Sarah, d. "2 years ago" (death noted in Record of Members in 1847 which spelled her name "Chator") [Ed. Note: Death notice in the Baltimore Sun stated that Sarah Chaytor, widow of Daniel Chaytor, d. 4 Jul 1845.]

Chenowith, Sarah Ann and Samuel Beebe m. 9 Jul 1850 by Rev. Dr. George C. M. Roberts

Chenwith, William and Ann Maria Baxter m. 12 May 1846 by Rev. Samuel Keppler (date of lic. not recorded)

Chesney, William H. and Frances Hawkins m. 7 Dec 1847 by Rev. Littleton F. Morgan, lic. dated 6 Dec 1847

Chesnut, Gerard and Susanna C. Black m. ---- [blank] by Rev. John S. Martin, lic. dated 9 May 1850 [Ed. Note: Their marriage notice in the Baltimore Sun stated Girard Chesnut m. Susanna C. Black on 15 May 1850.]

Chester, Ann Matilda (coloured), dau. of William and Eliza Chester, b. 15 Oct 1841, bapt. 20 Feb 1842 by Rev. Isaac P. Cook

Chickering, Alvin A. and Mary H. Kervil m. 27 Jul 1847 by Rev. Dr. George C. M. Roberts

Chickering, E. Clinton and Mary E. Richardson m. 16 Mar 1848 by Rev. Dr. George C. M. Roberts

Child, Margaret Ann and William Henry Hiss m. 11 Jan 1848 at the house of her father in Baltimore by Rev. Beverly Waugh, lic. dated 10 Jan 1848

Child, Mary Catharine and James Cortlan, Jr. m. 9 Jan 1844 at the house of her father in Baltimore by Rev. Beverly Waugh, lic. dated 8 Jan 1844

Childs, William and Eleanor Marshall m. 14 Jul 1840 by Rev. Samuel Keppler, lic. dated 13 Jul 1840

Chisall, Mary Ann and William Sheldon m. 24 Jul 1843 by Rev. Dr. George C. M. Roberts

Chival, Brittania and George Robinson m. 12 Dec 1843 by Rev. Isaac P. Cook

Chiveral, Ellen E., dau. of Alexander and Susan Chiveral, b. 14 Oct 1842, bapt. 11 Jan 1842 by Rev. Elisha D. Owen

Chiverell, Virginia C. and Lyttleton N. B. Long m. ---- [blank] by Rev. John S. Martin, lic. dated 8 Jul 1850 [Ed. Note: Their marriage notice in the Baltimore Sun stated Littleton N. B. Long and Virginia C. Chiverfill [sic] m. 9 Jul 1850, even though his last name looked more like "Laig" or "Lang" in the church register.]

Christie, Eliza, d. circa 1847-1850 (exact date not given in Record of Members)

Christopher, Josiah and Anna Mellor m. 21 Apr 1844 by Rev. Joseph Merriken

Church, Susanna A. and Columbus Huzza m. 14 Jan 1845 by Rev. Dr. George C. M. Roberts

Cissel, Margaret Ann and George C. Pierce, both of Montgomery County, MD, m. 15 Sep 1840 by Rev. Thomas Myers, lic. dated 13 Sep 1840

Clampitt, Elias and Margaret Miller, both of Baltimore County, m. ---- [date not given] by Rev. George Hildt, lic. dated 21 Aug 1845 [*Ed. Note:* Their marriage notice in the *Baltimore Sun* stated they married on 21 Aug 1845.]

Clanahan, Catherine A. and James H. Glanding m. 8 Oct 1849 by Rev. Aquila A. Reese, lic. dated 7 Oct 1849

Clare, Ann Elizabeth, dau. of Thomas I. and Eliza Clare, b. 16 Apr 1841, bapt. 2 Sep 1841 by Rev. Dr. George C. M. Roberts

Clare, Eliza Jane, dau. of Thomas I. and Eliza J. Clare, b. 14 Jan 1848, bapt. 14 May 1848 by Rev. Dr. George C. M. Roberts

Clare, Gustavus Brown, son of Thomas I. and Eliza J. Clare, b. 14 Aug 1849, bapt. 18 Apr 1850 by Rev. Dr. George C. M. Roberts

Clare, Helen Augusta, dau. of Thomas I. and Eliza Clare, b. 16 Aug 1838, bapt. 2 Sep 1841 by Rev. Dr. George C. M. Roberts

Clare, John James, son of Thomas Isaac and Eliza J. Clare, b. 9 Jan 1846, bapt. 3 Aug 1847 by Rev. Dr. George C. M. Roberts

Clark, Alexander, d. circa 1841-1843 (death noted in Class List) [*Ed. Note:* Death notice in the *Baltimore Sun* stated that Alexander Clark d. 2 Feb 1843.]

Clark, Benjamin Edward, son of Benjamin and Hester A. Clark, b. 14 Oct 1842, bapt. 21 Feb 1843 by Rev. Henry Slicer

Clark, Elizabeth E. and John Marley m. 7 Dec 1843 by Rev. Isaac P. Cook

Clark, George, see "Robert H. Clark," q.v.

Clark, George P. and Eliza J. Gardner m. 3 Aug 1845 by Rev. Joseph Shane

Clark, Hester Ann and Francis Downs m. ---- [blank] by Rev. John S. Martin, lic. dated 15 Aug 1850 [*Ed. Note:* Their marriage notice in the *Baltimore Sun* stated they married on 18 Aug 1850.]

Clark, Jane Ann Adeline and John L. S. McClamar m. 14 Dec 1840 by Rev. Samuel Keppler, lic. dated same day

Clark, John and Sarah Gillespie m. 29 Aug 1842 by Rev. Dr. George C. M. Roberts

Clark, John and Amanda E. Ellender m. 2 Jul 1850 by Rev. Isaac P. Cook

Clark, John W. and Elizabeth Waters m. 28 Aug 1845 by Rev. Dr. George C. M. Roberts

Clark, Joseph F. and Mary C. Jacob m. 30 Jun 1842 by Rev. Isaac P. Cook

Clark, Martha and Joseph Latham m. 24 Sep 1846 by Rev. Dr. George C. M. Roberts

Clark, Mary Ann and Rev. Andrew Jameson m. 28 Mar 1850 by Rev. Isaac P. Cook

Clark, Rachel, d. circa 1841-1842 (death noted in Class List) [*Ed. Note:* Death notice in the *Baltimore Sun* stated that Rachel Clark, wife of Thomas S. Clark and dau. of Richard and Catherine Bell, d. 20 Jan 1842.]

Clark, Robert Henry, son of George and Sophia Clark, b. 21 Oct 1840, bapt. 28 Feb 1841 by Bishop Waugh

Clark, Sarah and John T. Norvell m. 22 Aug 1841 by Rev. Dr. George C. M. Roberts

Clarke, Angeline and Henry Armstrong, both of Baltimore City, m. 2 Oct 1845 by Rev. William Hamilton

Clarke, Ann and Stephen H. Fitch m. 21 Jun 1842 by Rev. Job Guest, lic. dated same day

Clarke, Bartus and Ann L. Fellow m. 19 Sep 1844 by Rev. James Sewell, lic. dated same day

Clarke, James, d. circa 1845 (death noted in Class List) [*Ed. Note:* Death notices in the *Baltimore Sun* stated that one James Clark d. 26 Jan 1844 and another James Clark d. 28 Jul 1846.]

Clarke, Margaret and John W. Campbell m. 27 May 1847 by Rev. Dr. George C. M. Roberts

Clarke, Thomas S. and Sarah Isabella Bell m. 27 Apr 1843 by Rev. Henry Slicer, lic. dated same day

Clash, Jonathan and Maria Green m. 12 May 1842 by Rev. Samuel Brison

Clash, Susan Ann and Josiah K. Smith m. 19 Aug 1844 by Rev. Dr. George C. M. Roberts

Clavell, Edward and Caroline Thompson m. 1 Feb 1848 by Rev. Stephen A. Roszel, lic. dated 30 Jan 1848 [*Ed. Note:* His last name looked like "Claivell" in the church register, but their marriage notice in the *Baltimore Sun* gave their names as Edward Clavell and Caroline D. Thompson.]

Clayton, Samuel S. and Catharine Ann Essex m. 15 Sep 1846 by Rev. Littleton F. Morgan, lic. dated same day

Cleaveland, Elizabeth Eleanor, dau. of Joseph S. and Mary J. Cleaveland, b. 24 Oct 1841, bapt. 26 Jun 1842 by Rev. Joseph Merriken. See "Joseph S. Cleveland," q.v.

Clement, Elizabeth Ann and William A. Pennington m. 25 Feb 1844 by Rev. Isaac P. Cook

Clement, Mary and Reuben Dare m. 2 May 1840 by Rev. Joseph Shane

Clements, Joshua and Susan Bartle m. 6 Jan 1848 by Rev. Joseph Shane

Clemmons, Catharine and Joseph Earpe m. 16 Dec 1841 by Rev. Isaac P. Cook

Clemmons, Charlotte and David Crouch m. 17 Oct 1848 by Rev. Joseph Shane

Clemmons, William, see "Ann Coleman," q.v.

Clendinen, Jane and John Suick m. 9 Sep 1850 by Rev. Isaac P. Cook

Cleveland, Joseph S. and Mary Jane Cathcart m. 17 Dec 1840 by Rev. Samuel Keppler, lic. dated same day. See "Eleanor E. Cleveland," q.v.

Clifford, Austen and Mary Ann Williams m. 9 Feb 1843 by Rev. Dr. George C. M. Roberts

Cline, Albensinda(?) and Thomas Tyson m. 13 Jan 1845 by Rev. James Sewell, lic. dated same day

Cline, Emeline and George Edward Hartley m. 27 Dec 1847 by Rev. Stephen A. Roszel, lic. dated same day

Cline, Georgeanna, dau. of Anthony and Eliza Cline, b. 22 Oct 1842, bapt. 12 Feb 1843 by Rev. Elisha D. Owen

Cline, Rebecca, dau. of Henry and Maria Cline, b. 18 Feb 1842, bapt. 12 Feb 1843 by Rev. Elisha D. Owen

Cline, Sarah Elizabeth, dau. of Jacob C. and Sarah Cline, b. 8 Dec 1849, bapt. 15 Dec 1849 by Rev. Dr. George C. M. Roberts

Cline, Sarah, b. 26 Jun 1811, bapt. 15 Dec 1849 by Rev. Dr. George C. M. Roberts

Clineline, Abigail, dau. of John and Ann Maria Clineline, b. 12 Aug 1845, bapt. 1849 (exact date not given) by Rev. John S. Martin

Close, Ambrose Bearden, son of Alexander and Mary Ann Close, b. 28 Mar 1840, bapt. 22 Nov 1840 by Rev. Joseph Shane

Clutcher, Francis T. and Catherine E. Amey m. 21 Apr 1845 by Rev. Joseph Shane

Coale, James J. and Mary A. Eareckson, both of Baltimore County, m. 5 Oct 1846 by Rev. George Hildt, lic. dated same day

Coates, Sarah A. L. and Joshua G. McIntire m. 18 Oct 1846 by Rev. Dr. George C. M. Roberts

Coath, Sarah Harriet, dau. of William S. and Sarah Harriet Coath, b. 26 Jul 1835, bapt. 21 Oct 1840 by Rev. Charles B. Tippett

Cobb, George W. and Elizabeth D. Baker m. 19 Mar 1843 by Rev. Henry Slicer, lic. dated 16 Mar 1843

Cobb, Nathaniel G. and Eliza Hunt m. 9 Apr 1840 by Rev. Samuel Keppler, lic. dated same day

Cochran, Catherine Amelia Roberts, dau. of Charles and Hester A. Cochran, b. 6 Jan 1850, bapt. 2 Jul 1850 by Rev. Dr. George C. M. Roberts

Cochran, Emily A. and William B. Dail m. 10 Nov 1846 by Rev. Dr. George C. M. Roberts

Cochran, Hiram, see "Maria Walters," q.v.

Cochran, Sarah Elizabeth Byrne, dau. of Charles and Hester A. Cochran, b. 31 Jan 1848, bapt. 6 Apr 1848 by Rev. Dr. George C. M. Roberts

Cockran, Ann Robinson, dau. of William and Rachel J. Cockran, b. 31 Jan 1844, bapt. 5 May 1844 by Rev. Dr. George C. M. Roberts

Codd, Pilkington C. and Ann Matilda Sears m. 21 Nov 1841 by Rev. Dr. George C. M. Roberts

Coffin, Obed M. and Caroline T. Marshall m. 14 Mar 1844 by Rev. Joseph Shane

Coker, Daniel Abner (coloured), son of Philip and Louisa Coker, b. 9 Mar 1839, Fells Point, Baltimore City, bapt. 4 Feb 1841 by Rev. Samuel Keppler

Coker, Rebecca Malvina (coloured), dau. of Philip and Louisa Coker, b. 28 Sep 1840, Fells Point, Baltimore City, bapt. 4 Feb 1841 by Rev. Samuel Keppler

Colbart, William J. and Mary Ann Fennell m. 9 Oct 1844 by Rev. Dr. George C. M. Roberts

Cole, Charity Gertrude, dau. of Jane Cole, b. 8 Jul 1844, bapt. same day by Rev. James Sewell

Cole, Charles Boston, son of George H. and Elizabeth Cole, b. 18 Jul 1839, Baltimore City, bapt. 25 Feb. 1841 by Rev. Samuel Keppler

Cole, George H., see "Charles B. Cole," q.v.

Cole, Jane, see "Charity G. Cole," q.v.

Cole, Margaret and Michael Dulack m. 21 May 1845 by Rev. Joseph Shane

Cole, Michael and Margaret S. H. Vickers m. ---- [blank] by Rev. John S. Martin, lic. dated 13 Mar 1850 [*Ed. Note:* Their marriage notice in the *Baltimore Sun* stated they married on 31 Mar 1850.]

Cole, Richard and Lucretia Wadman m. 16 Jan 1843 by Rev. Joseph Shane

Coleman, Alexander and Margaret Ann Hartlove m. 7 Jan 1849 by Rev. Joseph Shane

Coleman, Ann, d. 1847 (exact date not given in Record of Members) [*Ed. Note:* Death notice in the *Baltimore Sun* stated that Ann Coleman, aunt of William Clemmons, d. 23 Oct 1847.]

Coleman, C. R., see "Rebecca Ashman," q.v.

Coleman, Catherine, d. 1849 (death noted in Class List) [*Ed. Note:* Death notice in the *Baltimore Sun* stated that Catharine Coleman, wife of Samuel Coleman, d. 16 Mar 1849.]

Coleman, Charles R., see "Sarah E. Coleman," q.v.

Coleman, Eliza Ann and John Chaney m. 6 Jan 1846 by Rev. Joseph Shane

Coleman, Emily, dau. of Thomas and Martha Coleman, b. 26 Oct 1841, bapt. --
May 1842 by Rev. William Prettyman

Coleman, Samuel, see "Catherine Coleman," q.v.

Coleman, Samuel G. and Ruth Ann Wallace m. 23 Mar 1847 by Rev. Isaac P. Cook

Coleman, Sarah A. and David McCleester m. 2 Jun 1844 by Rev. James Sewell, lic.
dated 31 May 1844

Coleman, Sarah Ellen, dau. of Charles R. and Rebecca B. Coleman, b. 10 Nov
1840, bapt. 6 Dec 1840 by Rev. Dr. George C. M. Roberts

Coleman, Sarah Ann and William K. Frazier m. 20 May 1847 by Rev. Dr. George
C. M. Roberts

Coleman, Thomas, see "Emily Coleman," q.v.

Coleman, Uriah and Georgiana R. Steever m. 17 Jul 1848 by Rev. Stephen A.
Roszel, lic. dated 26 Jun 1848

Coleman, William and Catherine Reese m. 13 May 1850 by Rev. Joseph Shane

Collen, Mary, d. 1847 (death noted in Class List)

Collier, Henry and Sarah Jane Ervine m. 12 Feb 1845 by Rev. James Sewell, lic.
dated same day

Collier, Henry and Martha Ann Peale m. 2 Dec 1849 by Rev. John S. Martin, lic.
dated 1 Dec 1849

Collier, John H. and Eliza A. Dewees m. 9 Nov 1842 by Rev. Henry Slicer, lic.
dated same day

Collins, Catharine and George T. Macgill m. 24 Dec 1844 by Rev. Isaac P. Cook

Collins, Cordelia Hollins, dau. of Rev. John A. and Camilla Collins, b. 10 Feb
1847, bapt. 4 Jan 1848 by Rev. Dr. George C. M. Roberts

Collins, Elizabeth and John Smith m. 28 Mar 1847 by Rev. Joseph Shane

Collins, Elizabeth and George Smith m. 10 Sep 1840 by Rev. John Bear

Collins, Emma Jane, dau. of James L. and Emma C. Collins, b. 1 Dec 1845, bapt.
26 May 1846 by Rev. Dr. George C. M. Roberts

Collins, Isaac, of Frederick County, MD, and Hannah Leakin, of Baltimore County,
m. 4 Jul 1843 by Rev. S. S. Roszel, lic. dated same day

Collins, James L., see "Emma J. Collins," q.v.

Collins, James S. and Mary C. Smith m. 11 Jan 1844 by Rev. Henry Slicer, lic.
dated 10 Jan 1844

Collins, John A., see "Cordelia H. Collins," q.v.

Collins, John W. and Susannah Thompson m. 29 Jan 1845 by Rev. James Sewell,
lic. dated 22 Jan 1845

Collins, John and Elizabeth Smarden m. 5 Dec 1843 by Rev. Samuel Brison

Collins, Louisa, d. circa 1844-1847 (exact date not given in Record of Members)

Collins, Samuel and Elizabeth Sherry, both of Baltimore County, m. 5 Dec 1844 by
Rev. William Hamilton

Collins, Samuel, d. circa 1846-1847 (exact date not given in Record of Members)
[Ed. Note: Death notice in the Baltimore Sun stated that Samuel Collins d. 17
Jan 1846.]

Collins, Ursilla, d. circa 1844 (exact date not given in Record of Members) [Ed.
Note: Death notice in the Baltimore Sun stated that Ursula Collins, wife of
Samuel Collins, d. 6 Sep 1844.]

Collins, William R. and Maria Higgins m. 4 Jun 1850 by Rev. John S. Martin, lic.
dated 3 Jun 1850

Collison, Eleanor, of Baltimore, and Levin Richardson, of Dorchester County, MD, m. 28 Oct 1841 by Rev. John A. Hening, lic. dated 25 Oct 1841

Collison, Henry Clay, son of William and Elizabeth R. Collison, b. 17 May 1847, bapt. 13 Jul 1847 by Rev. Dr. George C. M. Roberts

Collison, Kate, dau. of William and Elizabeth Collison, b. 13 Jun 1850, bapt. 25 Jul 1853 by Rev. Dr. George C. M. Roberts

Collison, Laura Bell, dau. of William and Elizabeth Collison, b. 21 Jun 1848, bapt. 25 Jul 1853 by Rev. Dr. George C. M. Roberts

Collison, Susan, d. circa 1840 (exact date not given in Class Record)

Collison, Susanna Hopkins, dau. of William and Elizabeth Collison, b. 22 Dec 1840, bapt. 19 Jul 1841 by Rev. Dr. George C. M. Roberts

Collitt, Ann and Thomas Dennison m. 16 Apr 1848 by Rev. Stephen A. Roszel, lic. dated 15 Apr 1848

Colton, George and Lydia J. Hamilton m. 27 Sep 1842 by Rev. Henry Slicer, lic. dated same day

Combes, John and Ann Catherine Wilson m. 5 Jan 1846 by Rev. Joseph Shane

Combus, Ann and Thomas Murray m. 28 Jan 1850 by Rev. William Hirst, lic. dated 26 Jan 1850

Comeges, Mary Ann and William Yehrman m. 10 Jul 1844 by Rev. Joseph Shane

Comegys, Cornelius and Clarissa Gosnell m. 25 Nov 1847 by Rev. Isaac P. Cook

Comine, Amanda and Sebastian Granite m. 2 Apr 1849 by Rev. Dr. George C. M. Roberts

Commine, Caroline and Josiah T. Powers m. 14 Jun 1847 by Rev. Stephen A. Roszel, lic. dated same day

Comnbs, Sarah Parmelia (adult), dau. of ---- "not given" [sic], b. ---- [blank], bapt. 24 May 1844 by Rev. Isaac P. Cook

Conaway, Thomas A. and Dolly Stocksdale m. 25 Jul 1850 by Rev. Henry Slicer, lic. dated same day

Conce, Margaret Ann and Henry Dunlop m. 8 Jul 1846 by Rev. Benjamin F. Brooke

Connels, Elizabeth and Joseph Dalrymple m. 2 Jun 1844 by Rev. James Sewell, lic. dated 31 May 1844

Conner, John Henry, son of Rogers and Mary Conner, b. aged 10 years [b. 1847], bapt. 3 May 1857 by Rev. William A. Snively

Conner, Rogers, son of Rogers and Mary Conner, b. aged 8 years [b. 1849], bapt. 3 May 1857 by Rev. William A. Snively

Connors, Michael and Mary Richards m. 10 Nov 1840 by Rev. Samuel Keppler, lic. dated same day

Connoway, James Henry and Eliza Livingston m. 10 Apr 1849 by Rev. Dr. George C. M. Roberts

Conolly, Anna Jane, dau. of James H. and Mary E. Conolly, b. 19 Jul 1847, bapt. 20 Oct 1847 by Rev. Dr. George C. M. Roberts

Conoway, John and Ellen S. Hazard m. 20 Dec 1849 by Rev. Joseph Shane

Constable, Caroline, d. circa 1840 (exact date not given in Class Record)

Constantine, John W. and Ann Barbara Prince m. 24 Jan 1850 by Rev. Wesley Stevenson

Constantine, Rachel and James Yeager m. 31 Jan 1843 by Rev. Wesley Stevenson

Cooch, Joseph Wilkins, son of Levi G. and Sarah C. Cooch, b. ---- [blank], bapt. 30 Jun 1841 by Rev. Job Guest

Cook, Ann Elisabeth and Zacharia Turner m. 15 Nov 1841 by Rev. Gerard Morgan, lic. dated 13 Nov 1841

Cook, Anthony L., see "Mary Cook," q.v.

Cook, Archibald Parker, son of Rev. J. P. and Laura M. Cook, b. 7 Apr 1848, bapt. 2 Nov 1848 by Rev. Dr. George C. M. Roberts

Cook, Christopher, son of William and Mary Ann Cook, b. 30 Mar 1843, bapt. 2 Jun 1844 by Rev. Dr. George C. M. Roberts

Cook, Eliza Jane and Charles Henry Martin m. 21 Nov 1841 by Rev. Isaac P. Cook

Cook, Hannah, d. circa 1840 (exact date not given in Record of Members) [*Ed. Note:* Death notice in the *Baltimore Sun* stated that Hannah Cook, wife of Jacob Cook, d. 23 Jul 1840.]

Cook, Isaac C., see "William P. Cook," q.v.

Cook, J. P., see "Archibald P. Cook," q.v.

Cook, Jacob, see "Hannah Cook," q.v.

Cook, James, see "Martha Jane Cook," q.v.

Cook, James Edward, son of Thomas and Mary Cook (residents of Baltimore County), b. 26 Dec 1841, bapt. 29 May 1842 by Rev. Isaac P. Cook

Cook, John H. and Sarah Ann Noble m. 4 Aug 1844 by Rev. Isaac P. Cook

Cook, Lewis C. and Sarah Foxwell m. 26 May 1850 by Rev. Isaac P. Cook. See "Mary Cook," q.v.

Cook, Martha Jane (coloured), dau. of James and Mary Cook, b. 7 Jan 1842, bapt. 20 Feb 1842 by Rev. Isaac P. Cook

Cook, Mary, d. circa 1840-1847 (exact date not given in Record of Members) [*Ed. Note:* Death notices in the *Baltimore Sun* stated that one Mary Cook, wife of Anthony L. Cook, d. 6 Feb 1844 and another Mary A. Cook, wife of Lewis C. Cook and dau. of Anthony Noblet, d. 11 Dec 1847.]

Cook, Thomas, see "James Edward Cook," q.v.

Cook, William, see "Christopher Cook," q.v.

Cook, William Chalmers, son of Isaac P. and Laura Ann Cook, b. 10 May 1846, bapt. 8 Jul 1846 by Rev. Dr. George C. M. Roberts

Cooper, Calvin, see "Frances Cooper," q.v.

Cooper, Dinah, d. 1849 (death noted in Class List) [*Ed. Note:* Death notice in the *Baltimore Sun* stated that Dinah Cooper, wife of Elisha Cooper, d. 19 Mar 1849.]

Cooper, Edward Wilson, son of Samuel and Mary Jane Cooper, b. 25 Jun 1841, bapt. 28 Nov 1841 by Rev. Job Guest

Cooper, Elisha, see "Dinah Cooper," q.v.

Cooper, Frances, d. circa 1845-1846 (death noted in Class List) [*Ed. Note:* Death notice in the *Baltimore Sun* stated that Frances Cooper, widow of Calvin Cooper, d. 7 Jan 1846.]

Cooper, John and Margaret Brown m. 3 Oct 1841 by Rev. Gerard Morgan, lic. dated 2 Oct 1841

Cooper, John, d. circa 1846-1847 (death noted in Class List) [*Ed. Note:* Death notice in the *Baltimore Sun* stated that John Cooper, Sr. d. 3 Feb 1847.]

Cooper, Ketura and Samuel Ayres, of Baltimore City, m. 7 Dec 1846 by Rev. George Hildt

Cooper, Lord Nelson, son of Lord Nelson and Elizabeth Cooper, b. 27 Feb 1840, bapt. 22 Apr 1840 by Rev. Joseph Shane

Cooper, Margaret (colored) and James Hanson (colored) m. 5 Sep 1842 by Rev. Henry Slicer, lic. dated same day

Cooper, Rachel and Stephen Linsey m. 7 Aug 1842 by Rev. Henry Slicer, lic. dated 6 Aug 1842

Cooper, Robert, d. 1841 (death noted in Class List)

Cope, Mary E. and George W. Bell m. 7 Jun 1849 by Rev. Aquila A. Reese, lic. dated 6 Jun 1849

Copes, Giles, d. circa 1840-1841 (exact date not given in Record of Members) [Ed. Note: Death notice in the Baltimore Sun stated that Giles L. Copes d. 21 Jul 1841.]

Copper, George P. and Elizabeth Downey m. 22 Jan 1849 by Rev. William Hirst

Copper, Robert James Norris, son of Robert and Emily Copper, b. -- Feb 1840, bapt. 28 Jan 1841 by Rev. Thomas Myers

Corbitt, Emanuel and Esther Watchman m. 9 Oct 1849 by Rev. Dr. George C. M. Roberts

Corbitt, Lavinia M. and Christopher W. Bull m. 30 Dec 1849 by Rev. Aquila A. Reese, lic. dated 28 Dec 1849

Cord, Cassandra, d. circa 1847-1850 (exact date not given in Record of Members)

Cord, Susan and Robert W. B. Foster m. 17 Oct 1844 by Rev. Isaac P. Cook

Cordray, Henry, see "Elizabeth Cordrey," q.v.

Cordrey, Elizabeth, d. circa 1845-1847 (exact date not given in Record of Members) [Ed. Note: Death notice in the Baltimore Sun stated that Elizabeth Cordray, widow of Henry Cordray, dau. of William Furlong, and mother-in-law of George W. Yeates, d. 11 Sep 1846.]

Cordry, James and Julia Ann Murray m. 17 Oct 1844 by Rev. James Sewell, lic. dated same day

Corkran, William Benjamin Withgott, son of William and Rachel J. Corkran, b. 9 Nov 1847, bapt. 7 May 1848 by Rev. Dr. George C. M. Roberts

Corkran, William Samuel, son of William and Rachel Corkran, b. 8 Apr 1846, bapt. 8 Nov 1846 by Rev. Dr. George C. M. Roberts

Corner, Agness V., dau. of Mr. and Mrs. Corner, b. 30 Jun 1843, bapt. 18 Sep 1843 by Rev. Philip B. Reese

Corner, Baptist Mezick and Sarah Ann Welch m. 14 Jan 1841 by Rev. Samuel Keppler, lic. dated 12 Jan 1841. See "Sarah Ann Corner," q.v.

Corner, James Coleman, d. circa 1841 (death noted in Class List)

Corner, John B., see "Sarah A. Corner," q.v.

Corner, Margaret, d. circa 1844 (death noted in Class List)

Corner, Sarah A., d. circa 1845 (death noted in Class List) [Ed. Note: Death notice in the Baltimore Sun stated that Sarah A. Corner, wife of John B. Corner, d. 10 Jul 1845.]

Corner, Sarah Ann, d. circa 1842 (death noted in Class List) [Ed. Note: Death notice in the Baltimore Sun stated that Sarah Ann Corner, wife of B. Mezick Corner and dau. of John Welch, d. 1 Sep 1842.]

Corner, Theodore and Rachel Littig Shaffer m. 26 Oct 1848 by Rev. Stephen A. Roszel, lic. dated 25 Oct 1848

Corns, William and Ann Elizabeth Whiteford m. 12 Apr 1849 by Rev. Isaac P. Cook

Cornthwait, Henrietta Clementine, dau. of Robert and Martha Ann Cornthwait, b. 19 Aug 1840, Baltimore City, bapt. 21 Jan 1841 by Rev. Samuel Keppler

Cornthwait, John O. and Elizabeth Bruscup m. 19 Oct 1843 by Rev. Henry Slicer, lic. dated same day

Cornthwait, Lewis Austen, son of Robert and Martha Ann Cornthwait, b. 14 May 1839, Baltimore City, bapt. 21 Jan 1841 by Rev. Samuel Keppler

Cornthwait, William, d. circa 1842 (death noted in Class List) [*Ed. Note:* Death notice in the *Baltimore Sun* stated that William Cornthwaite, Sr. d. 18 Aug 1842.]

Corph(?), Ephraim Taylor, son of Samuel and Mary Jane Corph(?), b. 19 Aug 1839, bapt. 26 Feb 1840 by Rev. Dr. George C. M. Roberts

Corprell, Thomas and Lowraine Morgan m. 11 Oct 1849 by Rev. John S. Martin, lic. dated 10 Oct 1849 [*Ed. Note:* Their marriage notice in the *Baltimore Sun* gave their names as Thomas Corprew and Lowraine Morgan.]

Corrie, Teresa J. and George Wilson m. 28 Jun 1844 by Rev. Dr. George C. M. Roberts

Corsey, Elizabeth and Frederick Henry Wasmus m. 2 Jun 1845 by Rev. Dr. George C. M. Roberts

Corsey, Mary and George W. Barrus m. 22 Apr 1848 by Rev. William Hirst

Cortlan, James Jr. and Mary Catharine Child m. 9 Jan 1844 at the house of her father in Baltimore by Rev. Beverly Waugh, lic. dated 8 Jan 1844

Cost, George W. and Rebecca Parks m. 12 Sep 1850 by Rev. John S. Martin, lic. dated 11 Sep 1850

Cost, Mary, d. 1849 (death noted in Class List) [*Ed. Note:* Death notice in the *Baltimore Sun* stated that Mary E. A. Cost, wife of George W. Cost, d. 25 Mar 1849.]

Cotman, Eliza (adult), b. ---- [blank], bapt. 15 Apr 1840 by Rev. Dr. George C. M. Roberts

Cottrell, John Clark, son of Clark and Mary Adeline Cottrell, b. 1 Aug 1846, bapt. 8 Sep 1846 by Rev. Dr. George C. M. Roberts

Cottrell, Lucy Ellen Winter, dau. of Capt. Clark and Mary Adeline Cottrell, b. 17 Apr 1847, bapt. 9 Jun 1848 by Rev. Dr. George C. M. Roberts

Coulson, Eleanor and Douglass E. Gosnell m. 16 May 1850 by Rev. Henry Slicer, lic. dated 29 Jan 1850

Coulter, John and Mary Hillary m. 11 Jul 1848 by Rev. Joseph Shane

Coulter, Sarah J. and William Wood m. 11 Feb 1841 by Rev. Joseph Shane

Councilman, Sarah Amelia, dau. of Charles and Catherine Councilman, b. 25 May 1845, bapt. 28 Sep 1845 by Rev. Dr. George C. M. Roberts

Courtney, Sarah E. and Benjamin F. Cronin m. -- Mar 1846 [page torn] by Rev. James Sewell, lic. dated 4 Mar 1846 [*Ed. Note:* Benjamin F. Cronin and Sarah Elizabeth Courtney obtained a marriage lic. in Harford County on 4 Mar 1846.] [*Ed. Note:* Their marriage notice in the *Baltimore Sun* stated they married on 31 Mar 1850.]

Couzens, John Edward, son of Michael and Elizabeth Couzens, b. 10 Jun 1840, Fells Point, Baltimore City, bapt. 28 Oct 1840 by Rev. Samuel Keppler

Covell, John Thomas Jefferson, son of Joel and Mary Covell, b. 21 Sep 1838, bapt. 29 May 1840 by Rev. Joseph Shane

Covington, Zachariah, d. circa 1847-1850 (exact date not given in Record of Members)

Cowan, Thomas and Caroline Sophia Norwood m. 10 Sep 1846 by Rev. Littleton F. Morgan, lic. dated same day

Cowman, Philip Auld, son of Joseph and Lucretia Cowman, b. 23 Nov 1846, bapt. 19 Jun 1847 by Rev. Dr. George C. M. Roberts

Cowman, Thomas Edward, son of Joseph and Lucretia Cowman, b. 11 Jul 1848, bapt. 6 Aug 1848 by Rev. Dr. George C. M. Roberts

Cox, Agnes and John Williams m. 14 Jan 1847 by Rev. Joseph Shane

Cox, Ann M., see "Thomas J. Cox," q.v.

Cox, Elizabeth and William Murry m. 29 May 1847 by Rev. Littleton F. Morgan, lic. dated same day

Cox, Hester and Charles Webb, Jr., both of Baltimore County, m. 7 Oct 1844 by Rev. William Hamilton

Cox, Nathaniel, see "Thomas J. Cox," q.v.

Cox, Samuel and Hannah Eliza Duncan m. 21 Apr 1845 at the house of her father Mr. Palmer in Baltimore by Rev. Beverly Waugh, lic. dated 19 Apr 1845

Cox, Thomas Jefferson, son of Nathaniel and Ann M. Cox, b. 31 Aug 1840, bapt. 7 Sep 1840 by Rev. John Bear

Coxwell, James H. (colored) and Ann Hill (colored) m. 6 Jul 1842 by Rev. Henry Slicer (date of lic. not recorded)

Craber, Eliza, d. circa 1840-1847 (exact date not given in Record of Members)

Craif, John and Mary Peterson m. 9 Jul 1845 by Rev. Dr. George C. M. Roberts

Craig, A. Juliet and John R. Scott m. 25 Dec 1842 by Rev. Henry Slicer, lic. dated 22 Dec 1842

Craig, Samuel and Mary Ann Bell m. 18 Jun 1846 by Rev. Dr. George C. M. Roberts

Cramer, Eliza Jane, dau. of John and Elizabeth Cramer, aged 10 years [b. 1830], bapt. 14 Jun 1840 by Rev. Thomas Myers

Cramer, Mary Elizabeth and James Howard m. 3 Dec 1840 by Rev. Joseph Shane

Crane, Mary, d. circa 1840 (exact date not given in Class Record)

Crane, Susan E., dau. of Thomas and Ann Crane, b. 3 Jun 1842, bapt. 17 Jan 1843 by Rev. Elisha D. Owen

Crangle, Henrietta and William Dorbacker, both of Baltimore City, m. 20 Sep 1845 by Rev. William Hamilton

Crapster, Mary J. and George H. Little m. 25 Jul 1850 by Rev. Henry Slicer, lic. dated same day

Crawford, Eliza and Thomas Hooper m. 3 May 1848 by Rev. William Hirst

Crawford, Francis and Eliza Salvador m. 4 Oct 1846 by Rev. Dr. George C. M. Roberts

Creighton, Louisa E. and Barclay Spear m. 18 Dec 1849 by Rev. William Hirst, lic. dated 10 Dec 1849

Creighton, Sarah Ann and Daniel P. Riggs m. 17 May 1849 by Rev. William Hirst, lic. dated 14 May 1849

Crenshaw, Elizabeth Ann and Nathaniel F. Bowe m. 5 Aug 1842 at Brawne's(?) Hotel in Baltimore by Rev. Beverly Waugh, lic. dated same day

Cridler, Jacob and Diana Sanders m. 14 Jan 1846 by Rev. Dr. George C. M. Roberts

Crisall, George W. and Ellen Knight m. 9 Jul 1846 by Rev. Dr. George C. M. Roberts

Crisp, Charles F. and Sarah J. Kirby m. 31 Jul 1842 by Rev. Henry Slicer, lic. dated 29 Jul 1842

Crockett, Nehemiah and Elizabeth F. Cross, both of Baltimore County, m. 16 Jun 1840 by Rev. Bernard H. Nadal

Crogan, Thomas and Margaret A. Manning m. 12 Sep 1843 by Rev. Samuel Brison

Cromwell, Emeline and William H. Butcher m. 9 Oct 1849 by Rev. Aquila A. Reese, lic. dated 8 Oct 1849

Cromwell, Sarah A., d. circa 1840 (exact date not given in Class Record)

Cromwell, Thomas and Sarah E. Noyes m. 27 Apr 1843 at the house of Dr. Noyes in Baltimore by Rev. Beverly Waugh, lic. dated 26 Apr 1843

Croney, Charles William Kirk, son of John W. and Catherine Croney, b. 11 Apr 1846, bapt. 27 Aug 1846 by Rev. Samuel Keppler

Cronin, Benjamin F. and Sarah E. Courtney m. -- Mar 1846 [page torn] by Rev. James Sewell, lic. dated 4 Mar 1846 [*Ed. Note:* Benjamin F. Cronin and Sarah Elizabeth Courtney obtained a marriage lic. in Harford County on 4 Mar 1846.]

Cronise, William H. V. and Mary O. George m. 21 Jan 1845 at the house of her mother in Baltimore by Rev. Beverly Waugh, lic. dated 20 Jan 1845

Cronmiller, Elizabeth, d. circa 1850 (exact date not given in Record of Members) [*Ed. Note:* Death notice in the *Baltimore Sun* stated that Elizabeth Cronmiller d. 31 Jul 1850.]

Crook, Walter, see "Mary Crooke," q.v.

Crooke, Mary, d. circa 1849-1850 (exact date not given in Record of Members) [*Ed. Note:* Death notice in the *Baltimore Sun* stated that Mary Crook, widow of Walter Crook, d. 12 May 1849.]

Crookshanks, John and Roda [*sic*] S. Robinson m. 28 Oct 1846 by Rev. Benjamin F. Brooke

Crookshanks, Mary Virginia, dau. of John and Mary Ann Crookshanks, b. 6 Nov 1838, bapt. 3 Jan 1841 by Rev. Dr. George C. M. Roberts

Crookshanks, Phebe Augusta, dau. of Johnathan and Mary Ann Crookshanks, b. 26 Mar 1843, bapt. 19 Nov 1845 by Rev. Dr. George C. M. Roberts

Crosby, Elizabeth and Thomas Bond m. 7 Oct 1843 by Rev. Henry Slicer, lic. dated same day

Cross, Anthony and Amelia Knight m. 26 Feb 1843 by Rev. Job Guest, lic. dated 25 Feb 1843

Cross, Catherine and George Carson m. 14 Aug 1842 by Rev. Joseph Shane

Cross, Catherine and Henry Boyd m. 14 Feb 1850 by Rev. Aquila A. Reese, lic. dated 13 Feb 1850

Cross, Christianna and John Grubb m. 13 Jun 1843 by Rev. Dr. George C. M. Roberts

Cross, Elizabeth F. and Nehemiah Crockett, both of Baltimore County, m. 16 Jun 1840 by Rev. Bernard H. Nadal

Cross, Henrietta G. and Henry Jones, both of Baltimore County, m. 26 Sep 1840 by Rev. Bernard H. Nadal

Cross, Sarah A. and George R. Campbell m. 18 Aug 1842 by Rev. Isaac P. Cook

Crouch, David and Charlotte Clemmons m. 17 Oct 1848 by Rev. Joseph Shane

Crouch, Mary Elizabeth and William Armstrong m. 7 Dec 1847 by Rev. Stephen A. Roszel, lic. dated 6 Dec 1847

Croxall, Mary R. and Benjamin D. Carr m. 24 Feb 1842 by Rev. Job Guest, lic. dated same day

Crugin, Charles H. and Mary McKenney, both of Georgetown, District of Columbia, m. 2 Oct 1845 by Rev. William Hamilton, lic. dated 1 Oct 1845

Cruikshanks, Mary, d. circa 1845-1847 (exact date not given in Record of Members)

Cruise, Henry Harrison, son of George and Matilda Cruise, b. 3 May 1840, Fells Point, Baltimore City, bapt. 7 Jan 1841 by Rev. Samuel Keppler

Cudlipp, Mary Jane and Charles Warren m. 14 Oct 1848 by Rev. Isaac P. Cook

Culbertson, James Henry, son of James and Louisa Culbertson, b. 17 Feb 1840, bapt. 7 May 1841 by Rev. Robert Emory

Cullen, Ann Rebecca, dau. of Thomas and Emily M. Cullen, b. 18 Mar 1849, bapt. 1860 (exact date not given) by Rev. William R. Mills

Culley, Elizabeth Jane and James Nash m. 2 Oct 1846 by Rev. Joseph Shane

Cullison, George W. and Amanda L. Page m. 28 Apr 1847 by Rev. Stephen A. Roszel, lic. dated same day

Cummins, Jonathan P. and Mary J. Dell, both of Baltimore County, m. ---- [date not given] by Rev. George Hildt, lic. dated 25 Jun 1845 [*Ed. Note:* Their marriage notice in the *Baltimore Sun* stated they married on 26 Jun 1845. His first name was spelled "Johnathan" in the church register.]

Cunningham, Eveline and George Kell m. 29 Dec 1847 by Rev. Stephen A. Roszel, lic. dated 23 Dec 1847

Cunningham, John, d. after 1845 (death noted in Class List) [*Ed. Note:* Death notice in the *Baltimore Sun* stated that John Cunningham d. 10 Mar 1848.]

Cunoal, Louisa and John Visher m. 27 Mar 1845 by Rev. Isaac P. Cook

Curlett, Edward W. and Caroline Moss m. 23 May 1849 by Rev. John S. Martin, lic. dated same day

Curley, Emily J. and William D. Dalyrmple m. 16 Dec 1847 by Rev. James H. Brown, lic. dated 15 Oct 1847

Curley, William and Mary E. Carr m. 15 Dec 1845 by Rev. Wesley Stevenson

Curmine, Ann Rebecca and Joseph Liddle m. 19 Mar 1840 by Rev. Joseph Shane

Curran, Francis, son of Richard and Matilda Curran, b. 8 May 1836, bapt. 24 Jan 1841 by Rev. Dr. George C. M. Roberts

Curran, Margaret, dau. of Richard and Matilda Curran, b. 1 Oct 1840, bapt. 24 Jan 1841 by Rev. Dr. George C. M. Roberts

Curren (Curven?), Caroline and John H. Humes m. 20 Mar 1845 by Rev. Dr. George C. M. Roberts

Curtain, Thomas, see "Jane Curtean," q.v.

Curtean, Jane, d. 1847 (death noted in Class List) [*Ed. Note:* Death notice in the *Baltimore Sun* stated that Jane Curtain, widow of Thomas Curtain, d. 23 Jul 1847.]

Curvall, Alvina, dau. of John and Mary Curvall, aged 7 years [b. 1836], bapt. 1843 (exact date not given) by Rev. Wesley Stevenson

Curvall, Charles, son of John and Mary Curvall, aged 11 years [b. 1832], bapt. 1843 (exact date not given) by Rev. Wesley Stevenson

Curvall, Gertrude, dau. of John and Mary Curvall, aged 4 years [b. 1839], bapt. 1843 (exact date not given) by Rev. Wesley Stevenson

Cutler, Charles S. and Mary R. Little m. 19 Dec 1850 by Rev. Dr. George C. M. Roberts

Daddz, Susanna and Robert M. Plummer m. 5 Nov 1850 by Rev. Dr. George C. M. Roberts [*Ed. Note:* Their marriage notice in the *Baltimore Sun* gave their names as Robert Plumer and Susanna Dadds.]

Dagner, Ann, d. circa 1840 (exact date not given in Class Record)

Dail, William B. and Emily A. Cochran m. 10 Nov 1846 by Rev. Dr. George C. M. Roberts

Dairy (Dany?), Charles H. and Mary E. Pool m. 11 May 1843 by Rev. Dr. George C. M. Roberts

Dales, Samuel and Mary Potter m. 15 Feb 1842 by Rev. Joseph Shane

Daley, Catherine D. and Benjamin F. Anderson m. 14 May 1849 by Rev. Aquila A. Reese, lic. dated 12 May 1849

Dallam, Margaret, d. circa 1844-1847 (exact date not given in Record of Members)

Dalyrmple, Joseph and Elizabeth Connels m. 2 Jun 1844 by Rev. James Sewell, lic. dated 31 May 1844

Dalyrmple, William D. and Emily J. Curley m. 16 Dec 1847 by Rev. James H. Brown, lic. dated 15 Oct 1847

Daneker, Joseph J. and Catherine E. Allen m. 20 Jan 1842 by Rev. Dr. George C. M. Roberts

Daneker, Nancy, d. circa 1840-1847 (exact date not given in Record of Members)

Daniel, Edward, son of Edward and Adeline Daniel, b. ---- [blank], bapt. 24 Aug 1841 by Rev. Dr. George C. M. Roberts

Daniel, Elizabeth and Richard H. Hayden m. 29 Nov 1850 by Rev. Isaac P. Cook

Danneker, George C. M. Roberts, son of John J. and Catherine E. Danneker, b. 16 Feb 1848, bapt. 5 Jun 1848 by Rev. Dr. George C. M. Roberts

Danneker, Mary Eliza, dau. of Henry B. and Sarah A. Danneker, b. 17 Jan 1840, bapt. 11 Apr 1840 by Rev. Dr. George C. M. Roberts

Danneker, Samuel Hinds, son of John J. and Ann Danneker, b. 9 Dec 1839, bapt. 11 Apr 1840 by Rev. Dr. George C. M. Roberts

Dany (Dairy?), Charles H. and Mary E. Pool m. 11 May 1843 by Rev. Dr. George C. M. Roberts

Darby, Elizabeth and Henry Williams m. 8 Apr 1850 by Rev. Dr. George C. M. Roberts

Darby, Sarah A. and Thomas Brownley m. 16 Apr 1850 by Rev. Dr. George C. M. Roberts

Dare, Cassandra S. and Sutton J. Weems m. 10 Dec 1845 by Rev. Dr. George C. M. Roberts

Dare, Reuben and Mary Clement m. 2 May 1840 by Rev. Joseph Shane

Darringon, Caroline and Robert Hutson m. 29 Apr 1840 by Rev. Samuel Keppler, lic. dated 28 Apr 1840

Darrington, James J. and Rebecca Ann Leary m. 12 Nov 1844 by Rev. James Sewell, lic. dated 9 Nov 1844

Darrington, William H. and Mary E. Lowrey m. 9 Apr 1848 by Rev. Stephen A. Roszel, lic. dated 7 Apr 1848

Dashiel, Mary H. M. and James P. Bowling, Jr. m. ---- [blank] by Rev. John S. Martin, lic. dated 13 Jul 1850 [Ed. Note: Their marriage notice in the Baltimore Sun stated James P. Bowling, Jr. m. Henrietta Dashiel, dau. of Levin F. Dashiel, on 30 Jul 1850.]

Dashields, Margaret, dau. of James and Ann Dashields, aged 14 months [b. 1840, Baltimore City], bapt. 1841 (exact date not given) by Rev. Gerard Morgan

Dashiell, Emily, d. circa 1847-1850 (exact date not given in Record of Members)

Daughaday, Jemima and Isaac C. Forney m. 18 Apr 1850 by Rev. Isaac P. Cook

Davey, William, d. circa 1849-1850 (death noted in Class List) [Ed. Note: Death notice in the Baltimore Sun stated that William Davy d. 16 Jul 1850.]

David, Mary E. and Samuel H. Grafton m. 4 Sep 1847 by Rev. Benjamin F. Brooke

Davidson, Elizabeth, d. circa 1850 (exact date not given in Record of Members) [*Ed. Note:* Death notice in the *Baltimore Sun* stated that Elizabeth Davidson d. 4 Jul 1850.]

Davidson, John H. and Mary L. Bennet m. 29 Nov 1844 by Rev. James Sewell, lic. dated 28 Nov 1844

Davidson, Permelia, of Anne Arundel County, and Rev. Samuel Keppler, of the Baltimore Annual Conference, m. ---- [date not given], lic. dated 15 Apr 1846

Davis, Abigail, d. circa 1840 (exact date not given in Class Record)

Davis, Albin P. and Eliza Ann Wesley m. 8 Jan 1850 by Rev. Aquila A. Reese, lic. dated 7 Jan 1850

Davis, Ann E., see "Charles McN. Davis," q.v.

Davis, Ann O., see "Mary Jane Davis," q.v.

Davis, Benjamin and Emily Stembler m. 18 Mar 1849 by Rev. Aquila A. Reese, lic. dated 17 Mar 1849

Davis, Charles McNight, son of Edward W. and Ann E. Davis, b. 15 Sep 1839, bapt. 27 Aug 1840 by Rev. Dr. George C. M. Roberts

Davis, Charlotte and William H. Harrison m. 1 Dec 1845 by Rev. Wesley Stevenson

Davis, Dorcas, d. circa 1841 (death noted in Class List) [*Ed. Note:* Death notice in the *Baltimore Sun* stated that Dorcas Davis, widow of Robert Davis, d. 23 Feb 1842.]

Davis, Dr., see "Rev. Matthew G. Hamilton," q.v.

Davis, Edward W., see "Charles McN. Davis," q.v.

Davis, Elizabeth and David S. Sumwalt m. 10 Mar 1847 by Rev. Wesley Stevenson

Davis, Elizabeth and William M. Biscoe m. ---- [blank] by Rev. John S. Martin, lic. dated 2 Nov 1850

Davis, Elizabeth E., see "George C. M. R. Davis," q.v.

Davis, Frances, d. circa 1847-1850 (exact date not given in Record of Members)

Davis, George C. M. Roberts, son of James C. and Elizabeth E. Davis, b. 22 Oct 1848, bapt. 24 Oct 1848 by Rev. Dr. George C. M. Roberts

Davis, H. H., see "John A. C. Davis" and "Mary W. Davis," q.v.

Davis, Jacob C. and Martha A. Diffey m. 4 Nov 1849 by Rev. Isaac P. Cook

Davis, James, see "Mary Virginia Davis," q.v.

Davis, James C., see "George C. M. R. Davis" and "James R. Davis" and "Elizabeth Rooke," q.v.

Davis, James Robert, son of James C. and Elizabeth E. Davis, b. 22 Oct 1848, bapt. 24 Oct 1848 by Rev. Dr. George C. M. Roberts

Davis, John and Anna Ivans m. 20 Nov 1848 by Rev. Dr. George C. M. Roberts

Davis, John A. Collins, son of H. H. and Elizabeth Davis, aged 7 years and 8 months [b. 1837], bapt. 24 Mar 1845 by Rev. Wesley Stevenson

Davis, John W. and Mary F. Warns m. 21 Dec 1848 by Rev. Wesley Stevenson

Davis, John B. and Elizabeth Brooke m. 10 Apr 1844 by Rev. Isaac P. Cook

Davis, Joseph R. and Rosana Bowden m. 11 Apr 1844 by Rev. Joseph Shane. See "Mary Ann Davis," q.v.

Davis, Josephine E. and Thomas Willis m. 18 Dec 1849 by Rev. Aquila A. Reese, lic. dated 17 Dec 1849

Davis, Mary Virginia, dau. of James and Sarah Ann Davis, b. 4 Jun 1840, Fells Point, Baltimore City, bapt. 23 Jun 1840 by Rev. Samuel Keppler

Davis, Mary Ellen and Henry N. Night m. 14 Jan 1849 by Rev. Dr. George C. M. Roberts

Davis, Mary Watts, dau. of H. H. and Elizabeth Davis, aged 2 weeks, bapt. 4 Apr 1845 by Rev. Wesley Stevenson

Davis, Mary Ann, dau. of Joseph R. and Rosanna Davis, b. 26 Dec 1844, bapt. 18 May 1845 by Rev. Dr. George C. M. Roberts

Davis, Mary Jane, dau. of Robert and Ann O. Davis, b. 15 Aug 1840, bapt. 29 Nov 1840 by Rev. Isaac P. Cook

Davis, Phoebe and Adams Gray m. 19 Nov 1840 by Rev. Samuel Keppler, lic. dated same day

Davis, Rebecca H. and Henry R. Lyons m. 21 Feb 1844 by Rev. Samuel Brison

Davis, Richard E. and Martha A. Mangles m. 29 Aug 1845 by Rev. James Sewell, lic. dated 27 Aug 1845

Davis, Robert, see "Mary Jane Davis" and "Dorcas Davis," q.v.

Davis, Robert and Eleanor McNelly m. 3 Sep 1850 by Rev. Henry Slicer, lic. dated 2 Sep 1850

Davis, Rosanna, see "Mary Ann Davis," q.v.

Davis, Rose P. and Isaac Dryden m. 20 Dec 1842 by Rev. Job Guest, lic. dated same day

Davis, Sally A. and Henry Poole m. 15 Nov 1849 by Rev. Aquila A. Reese, lic. dated 14 Nov 1849

Davis, Samuel and E. V. Tydings m. 6 Apr 1848 by Rev. William Hirst

Davis, Sarah Ann, see "Mary Virginia Davis," q.v.

Davis, Susan A. and William J. Hitchcock m. 23 Jul 1849 by Rev. Isaac P. Cook

Davis, Thomas and Margaretta Reese m. 26 Feb 1848 by Rev. Dr. George C. M. Roberts

Davis, William G. and Mary Jones m. 26 May 1848 by Rev. Joseph Shane

Davis, William H. H. and Elizabeth Hays, both of Baltimore County, m. 3 Oct 1842 by Rev. Nelson Head

Dawson, Ann Eliza R. and Thomas H. Wrightson m. 28 Jun 1849 by Rev. John S. Martin, lic. dated 21 Jun 1849

Dawson, Debora and William R. Whitten m. 22 Oct 1844 by Rev. James Sewell, lic. dated same day

Dawson, Jane L., d. circa 1847 (death noted in Class List)

Dawson, Lare Ann and Ferdinand Chamberland m. 23 Sep 1843 by Rev. Phillip B. Reese (date of lic. not recorded) [Ed. Note: Their marriage notice in the Baltimore Sun indicated Ferdinand Chamberlain and Lear A. Dawson m. 24 Sep 1843.]

Dawson, Maria S. and Isaiah G. Sanbourn m. 20 May 1840 at her father's house in Baltimore by Rev. Beverly Waugh, lic. dated same day

Dawson, Mary Ann and Samuel Bradshaw m. 13 Jun 1844 by Rev. Joseph Shane

Dawson, Philip O. and Mary Wilson, both of Baltimore County, m. 31 Oct 1844 by Rev. William Hamilton

Dawson, Sarah, d. 1845 (death noted in Class List) [Ed. Note: Death notice in the Baltimore Sun stated that Sarah Dawson d. 7 Apr 1845.]

Dawson, Sarah A., d. circa 1844-1847 (exact date not given in Record of Members) [Ed. Note: Death notice in the Baltimore Sun stated that Sarah Dawson, wife of William Dawson and dau. of Peter A. Jay, d. 9 Jan 1846.]

Dawson, William, see "Sarah A. Dawson," q.v.

Day, Joseph H. and Margaret B. Ireland m. 15 Apr 1845 by Rev. Dr. George C. M. Roberts

Day, Mary E. and James W. Orem m. 21 Aug 1847 by Rev. Isaac P. Cook

Dean, John William, son of Stephen and Christiana Dean, b. 6 Feb 1840, bapt. 23 Aug 1840 by Rev. Charles B. Tippett

Dean, V. Mary and Robert W. Trott, both of Baltimore County, m. 4 Oct 1843 by Rev. S. S. Roszel, lic. dated same day

Dean, William, d. circa 1840 (exact date not given in Class Record) [Ed. Note: Death notice in the Baltimore Sun stated that William Dean d. 21 Jul 1839.]

Deaver, Caroline J. and James W. Allen m. 1 Nov 1843 by Rev. Joseph Shane

Deaver, William and Elizabeth Caragan m. 3 Sep 1840 by Rev. Joseph Shane

Deaver, William and Angelina Hopkins m. 5 Apr 1847 by Rev. Isaac P. Cook

Debaugh, Charles and Mary Jane McCulloh m. 25 Jan 1844 by Rev. Isaac P. Cook

Debow, John Jr. and Almira Knight m. 10 Jan 1847 by Rev. Dr. George C. M. Roberts

Debrow, Martha and William Thompson m. 4 May 1845 by Rev. Isaac P. Cook

Debuler, Mary Ann, dau. of Bennett and Mary Ann Debuler, b. ---- [blank], bapt. 6 Jun 1840 by Rev. Dr. George C. M. Roberts

Decoursey, Henry and Sarah Jane Keller m. 2 Nov 1848 by Rev. Stephen A. Roszel, lic. dated same day

Deems, Adam W. and Catherine Semon m. 23 Jun 1846 by Rev. Joseph Shane

Deer, John H. and Mary Jane Causell m. 29 Jul 1849 by Rev. Aquila A. Reese, lic. dated 28 Jul 1849 [Ed. Note: Their marriage notice in the Baltimore Sun gave their names as John H. Derr and Mary J. Cassell.]

Deer, Susan and John Montgarret m. 3 Jul 1846 by Rev. Joseph Shane

DeGraff, Gerritt and Wilhelmina Harback m. 7 Sep 1850 by Rev. Isaac P. Cook

Delacour, William Louis and Martha Ann Myers, both of Baltimore County, m. 8 Oct 1842 by Rev. Nelson Head

Delay, James and Ellen Hagan m. 1 Aug 1842 by Rev. Job Guest, lic. dated same day

Delcher, John W. and Sarah J. Lafferty m. 9 Oct 1842 by Rev. Henry Slicer, lic. dated 8 Oct 1842

Delcher, William G. and Margaret Thompson m. 28 May 1843 by Rev. Dr. George C. M. Roberts

Dell, Margaret Ann and John H. Hagan, both of Baltimore County, m. 1 Jan 1843 by Rev. Nelson Head

Dell, Mary J. and Jonathan P. Cummins, both of Baltimore County, m. ---- [date not given] by Rev. George Hildt, lic. dated 25 Jun 1845 [Ed. Note: Their marriage notice in the Baltimore Sun stated they married on 26 Jun 1845. His first name was spelled "Johnathan" in the church register.]

Dell, William A. and Hester J. Pressley m. 3 Oct 1850 by Rev. Henry Slicer, lic. dated same day

Dellow, William and Susan Dellow, both of Baltimore County, m. ---- [date not given] by Rev. George Hildt, lic. dated 7 Apr 1846 [Ed. Note: Their marriage notice in the Baltimore Sun stated William Dillow and Susan Dillow married on 9 Mar 1846.]

Dempster, Mary, d. before 1847 (exact date not given in Record of Members) [Ed. Note: Death notice in the Baltimore Sun stated that Mary A. Dempster, wife of James Dempster, d. 27 Oct 1843.]

Denney, Hariot *[sic]* and Richard J. Robinson m. 26 Jul 1844 by Rev. James Sewell, lic. dated 25 Jul 1844

Denney, William H. and Elizabeth Ellen Hubbard m. 9 Sep 1845 by Rev. James Sewell, lic. dated 8 Sep 1845 [*Ed. Note:* Their marriage notice in the *Baltimore Sun* stated that William H. Denny and Elizabeth E. Hubbard m. 8 Sep 1845.]

Dennis, C. A. and E. A. Edmondson m. 16 Dec 1848 by Rev. William Hirst [*Ed. Note:* Their marriage notice in the *Baltimore Sun* gave their names as Charles A. Dennis and Ann E. Edmondson, dau. of Robert Edmondson.]

Dennison, Thomas and Ann Collitt m. 16 Apr 1848 by Rev. Stephen A. Roszel, lic. dated 15 Apr 1848

Denny, Charles Henry, son of Thomas O. and Elizabeth T. Denny, b. 25 Sep 1825, bapt. 13 Oct 1842 by Rev. Henry Slicer

Denny, Elizabeth and Charles W. Elton m. 26 Sep 1844 by Rev. Dr. George C. M. Roberts

Denny, Louisa, d. circa 1847-1850 (exact date not given in Record of Members)

Denny, William H., see "William H. Denney," q.v.

Depo, John and Sarah Smith m. 21 Aug 1842 by Rev. Henry Slicer, lic. dated same day

Derr, John H., see "John H. Deer," q.v.

Despeaux, Margaret Ann and John Van Trump m. 20 Oct 1850 by Rev. John S. Martin, lic. dated 17 Oct 1850

Devalin, Rose and Stephen Moore m. 4 Jan 1848 by Rev. Stephen A. Roszel, lic. dated same day

Dever, Ruth Ann, dau. of John D. and Caroline J. Dever, b. 14 Nov 1839, bapt. 19 Feb 1840 by Rev. Dr. George C. M. Roberts

Devilbiss, Ruth A. and John M. Fetterling m. 24 Feb 1849 by Rev. James H. Brown, lic. dated 21 Feb 1849

Devitch, Julius and Johanna Shoemacker m. 20 Dec 1841 by Rev. Dr. George C. M. Roberts

Devlin, Nancy and James Diggs m. 5 Apr 1847 by Rev. Stephen A. Roszel, lic. dated 1 Apr 1847

Devline, Eugene and Sarah A. E. Stiver m. 7 Aug 1849 by Rev. Joseph Shane [*Ed. Note:* Their marriage notice in the *Baltimore Sun* gave their names as Eugene Devlin and Sarah A. E. Stivers.]

Dew, Ann M. V. and Jacob Gravenstine m. 9 May 1844 by Rev. Joseph Shane [*Ed. Note:* Their marriage notice in the *Baltimore Sun* gave her name as Anna M. V. Dew, dau. of William Dew.]

Dew, George, d. circa 1850 (exact date not given in Record of Members) [*Ed. Note:* Death notice in the *Baltimore Sun* stated that George Dew d. 9 Oct 1850.]

Dew, Mary Jane and Alexander McAllister m. 14 Dec 1841 by Rev. Dr. George C. M. Roberts

Dew, William, see "Ann N. V. Dew," q.v.

Dewees, Eliza A. and John H. Collier m. 9 Nov 1842 by Rev. Henry Slicer, lic. dated same day

Dickenson, Mary A. and George W. Beck m. 10 Dec 1841 by Rev. Joseph Shane

Dickerson, George W. and Rebecca Elizabeth Dickerson m. 23 Sep 1840 by Rev. Samuel Keppler, lic. dated 22 Sep 1840

Dickson, Mary Louisa and Harvey J. McCready m. 18 Nov 1847 by Rev. Littleton
F. Morgan, lic. dated same day

Dickson, Sophia J. and Asa Howard m. ---- [no date given] by Rev. John Miller, lic.
dated 17 Dec 1850 [Ed. Note: Their marriage notice in the Baltimore Sun
stated they married on 19 Dec 1850.]

Dicus, James and Mary Ellen Gosnell m. 8 Jun 1845 by Rev. Isaac P. Cook

Diffey, Martha A. and Jacob C. Davis m. 4 Nov 1849 by Rev. Isaac P. Cook

Diggs, Beverly, son of Henry and Rebecca Ann Diggs, b. 24 Dec 1836, Fells Point,
Baltimore City, bapt. 15 May 1840 by Rev. Samuel Keppler

Diggs, Elizabeth and Joseph Jenkins m. 10 Aug 1845 by Rev. Joseph Shane

Diggs, Henry Slicer, son of Henry and Rebecca Ann Diggs, b. 27 Sep 1841, bapt.
30 Oct 1842 by Rev. Henry Slicer. See "Virginia Van Buren Diggs," q.v.

Diggs, James and Nancy Devlin m. 5 Apr 1847 by Rev. Stephen A. Roszel, lic.
dated 1 Apr 1847

Diggs, Virginia Van Buren, dau. of Henry and Rebecca Ann Diggs, b. 14 Sep 1839,
Fells Point, Baltimore City, bapt. 15 May 1840 by Rev. Samuel Keppler

Dill, Thomas T. and Bethia C. Etchberger m. 24 Jan 1841 by Rev. Samuel Keppler,
lic. dated 23 Jan 1841

Dillen, Sarah (colored) and Edward M. Wilson (colored) m. 3 Jul 1844 by Rev.
James Sewell

Dillon, Mary and Cornelius McFaddon m. 12 Mar 1840 by Rev. Joseph Shane

Dillon, Patrick and Mary Ann Brown m. 6 Jan 1841 by Rev. Samuel Keppler, lic.
dated 4 Jan 1841

Dillow, Ann, d. circa 1847-1850 (exact date not given in Record of Members)

Dillow, William, see "William Dellow," q.v.

Disney, Ann, d. circa 1840 (exact date not given in Class Record) [Ed. Note: Death
notice in the Baltimore Sun stated that Ann Disney, mother of William Disney,
Jr., d. 3 Aug 1838.]

Disney, Ann, d. circa 1849-1850 (exact date not given in Record of Members) [Ed.
Note: Death notice in the Baltimore Sun stated that Ann Disney, aunt of
William Sullivan, d. 16 Dec 1849.]

Disney, Caroline, see "Eli L. Disney" and "James E. Disney," q.v.

Disney, Eli Lilly, son of William A. and Caroline Disney, b. 5 Feb 1846, bapt. 25
Feb 1846 by Rev. Dr. George C. M. Roberts

Disney, George W. and Elizabeth Todd m. 16 Apr 1844 by Rev. Joseph Shane

Disney, James Eli, son of William A. and Caroline Disney, b. 25 Jan 1842, bapt. 26
Jan 1842 by Rev. Dr. George C. M. Roberts

Disney, James R., d. after 1840 (exact date not given in Class Record)

Disney, Joshua P. and Rebecca S. Hutchins m. 20 Dec 1849 by Rev. Isaac P. Cook

Disney, Louisa Polk and Conrad Schumacher m. 25 Jul 1850 by Rev. Dr. George
C. M. Roberts

Disney, Margaret A. and John W. Wright m. 8 Jun 1848 at the house of her father
in Baltimore by Rev. Beverly Waugh, lic. dated 7 Jun 1848

Disney, Mary E. and Edward C. Varina m. 15 May 1842 by Rev. Dr. George C. M.
Roberts

Disney, Mary Jane and John William Quick m. 30 May 1848 by Rev. Isaac P. Cook

Disney, Rachel Ann and Richard Talbott m. -- Sep 1843 by Rev. Joseph Shane

Disney, William A., see "Eli L. Disney" and "James E. Disney," q.v.

Disney, William Jr., see "Ann Disney," q.v.

Ditterich, Frederick H. and Susan A. Larkin m. 19 Dec 1847 by Rev. Dr. George C. M. Roberts

Dobbins, Francis M. and Susanna S. Franklin m. 23 May 1847 by Rev. Dr. George C. M. Roberts

Dodd, George, d. 1841 (death noted in Class List) [Ed. Note: Death notice in the Baltimore Sun stated that George Dodd d. 21 Dec 1841.]

Dodson, George Washington, son of Susan Dodson (widow), aged 2 years and 8 months [b. 1839], bapt. 16 Jan 1842 by Rev. Gerard Morgan

Dodson, James B. and Henrietta Waugh m. 28 Sep 1840 at her father's house in Washington, D.C. by Rev. Beverly Waugh, lic. dated same day

Dolan, Lawrence and Mary A. Hiskey m. 29 Mar 1847 by Rev. Dr. George C. M. Roberts

Donahue, John Holton, son of James and Elizabeth Donahue, b. 24 May 1844, bapt. 8 Jul 1844 by Rev. James Sewell

Donaldson, Moses and Rachel A. Elder m. 4 May 1841 by Rev. Joseph Shane [Ed. Note: Her name was misspelled "Eleder" in the church register.]

Donaldson, Plummer and Rachel E. Shipley m. 16 Jul 1848 by Rev. William Hirst

Donaldson, Robert and Elizabeth Buckley m. 20 Oct 1850 by Rev. Dr. George C. M. Roberts

Donaldson, Sarah and William Price m. 29 Oct 1843 by Rev. Isaac P. Cook

Donaldson, Stephen and Martha Berry m. 6 Nov 1845 by Rev. James Sewell, lic. dated same day

Donallen, Andrew and Mary A. Dubleman m. 8 Jun 1845 by Rev. Dr. George C. M. Roberts

Donohu, Margaret, d. after 1841 (death noted in Class List) [Ed. Note: Death notice in the Baltimore Sun stated that Margaret Donohoo d. 17 Jun 1846]

Donohue, James and Elizabeth Holton m. 11 Sep 1842 by Rev. Henry Slicer, lic. dated 10 Sep 1842

Donohue, Rebecca, dau. of James and Margaret Donohue, b. 9 Dec 1841, bapt. 9 May 1842 by Rev. Henry Slicer

Dorbacker, William and Henrietta Crangle, both of Baltimore City, m. 20 Sep 1845 by Rev. William Hamilton

Dormon, Margaret S. and George Bailey m. 17 Apr 1844 by Rev. James Sewell, lic. dated same day

Dorsey, Ann and Stephen Woolford m. 24 Jan 1850 by Rev. Joseph Shane

Dorsey, Catharine E. and Louis H. Lentz m. 21 Nov 1841 by Rev. Gerard Morgan, lic. dated 20 Nov 1841

Dorsey, Elizabeth, d. circa 1840-1844 (exact date not given in Probationers Book circa 1840 or in Record of Members in 1844) [Ed. Note: Death notice in the Baltimore Sun stated that Elizabeth Dorsey d. 18 Jun 1844.]

Dorsey, James B., see "William T. Dorsey," q.v.

Dorsey, John Thomas, son of Dr. Edwin and Matilda Dorsey, b. 2 Oct 1844, bapt. 6 May 1845 by Rev. Dr. George C. M. Roberts

Dorsey, Paul E. and Virginia E. Thomas, both of Baltimore County, m. 21 Apr 1841 by Rev. Thomas Myers, lic. dated same day

Dorsey, Rozina, see "William T. Dorsey," q.v.

Dorsey, Stephen B. and Sally E. Owens, both of Baltimore County, m. 24 Nov 1842 by Rev. Nelson Head

Dorsey, William Thomas, son of James B. and Rozina Dorsey, b. 20 Mar 1833, bapt. 4 Apr 1840 by Rev. Dr. George C. M. Roberts

Doughlas, Elizabeth and Richard Wood m. 30 Mar 1844 by Rev. Joseph Shane

Douglas, William H. and Ann Eliza Wheeler m. 11 Aug 1845 by Rev. Samuel Keppler (date of lic. not recorded)

Douglass, Elizabeth, d. after 1847 (exact date not given in Record of Members) [*Ed. Note:* Death notice in the *Baltimore Sun* stated that Elizabeth Douglass, wife of A. B. Douglass, d. 4 Sep 1848.]

Douglass, John, of Washington City, and Miss Syney [*sic*] V. Smith, of Baltimore County, m. 21 Jun 1845 by Rev. William Hamilton

Dove, Elijah and Sarah Howes m. 21 Nov 1849 by Rev. Isaac P. Cook

Dover, Mary Ann, dau. of John and Sarah Dover, b. 26 Dec 1844, bapt. 31 May 1845 by Rev. Dr. George C. M. Roberts

Dover, Rebecca Conner, dau. of John and Sarah Dover, b. 26 May 1849, bapt. 7 Apr 1850 by Rev. Dr. George C. M. Roberts

Dowell, John Summerfield, son of John and Catherine Dowell, b. 20 Aug 1842, bapt. 10 Oct 1842 by Rev. William Prettyman

Downes, Eliza Ann and John W. Simpson m. 24 Sep 1844 by Rev. Dr. George C. M. Roberts

Downey, Elizabeth and George P. Copper m. 22 Jan 1849 by Rev. William Hirst

Downey, Julia Ann and Jesse Jarrett m. 3 Oct 1850 by Rev. Henry Slicer, lic. dated same day

Downing, William and Eliza J. W. Baily, both of Baltimore County, m. 28 May 1844 by Rev. William Hamilton

Downs, Anna and Francis Pearce m. 31 May 1841 by Rev. Dr. George C. M. Roberts

Downs, Francis and Hester Ann Clark m. ---- [blank] by Rev. John S. Martin, lic. dated 15 Aug 1850 [*Ed. Note:* Their marriage notice in the *Baltimore Sun* stated they married on 18 Aug 1850.]

Downs, William H. and Amanda Mason m. 22 Jan 1850 by Rev. Aquila A. Reese, lic. dated 21 Jan 1850

Doxson, Mary Ann and Lewis Jones m. 3 Aug 1842 by Rev. Dr. George C. M. Roberts

Doyle, Angeline and William D. Moon m. 18 Jun 1844 by Rev. Joseph Shane

Doyle, William T. and Sarah E. Shueman m. 4 Dec 1845 by Rev. Dr. George C. M. Roberts

Draden, Hellen, dau. of James and Catharine Draden, aged 7 months [b. 1842], bapt. 9 Feb 1843 by Rev. Wesley Stevenson

Drakeley, George, son of Henry W. and Mary E. Drakeley, b. 8 Aug 1844, bapt. 28 Sep 1845 by Rev. Dr. George C. M. Roberts

Drakeley, Thomas, son of Henry W. and Mary E. Drakeley, b. 10 Jun 1846, bapt. 20 Sep 1846 by Rev. Dr. George C. M. Roberts

Draper, Rachel B. and William Price m. 16 Jan 1840 by Rev. John Bear

Driver, Ann and Henry Kauffman m. 10 Dec 1848 by Rev. Joseph Shane

Driver, Silas and Olivia Wilson m. 23 Apr 1846 by Rev. Joseph Shane

Drury, Mary Frances, dau. of Charles H. and Mary E. Drury, b. 12 Jul 1845, bapt. 25 Nov 1848 by Rev. Dr. George C. M. Roberts

Dryden, Isaac and Rose P. Davis m. 20 Dec 1842 by Rev. Job Guest, lic. dated same day

Dryden, Joshua, see "Thomas B. Busk," q.v.

Dryden, Laura L. and James Salisbury m. 31 Oct 1848 by Rev. James H. Brown, lic. dated 30 Oct 1848

Dryden, Sarah Jane and Theodore Thomas Hall m. 6 Jul 1847 by Rev. Littleton F. Morgan, lic. dated same day

Dubard, William and Susan A. Wisner m. 4 May 1845 by Rev. Joseph Shane

Dubleman, Mary A. and Andrew Donallen m. 8 Jun 1845 by Rev. Dr. George C. M. Roberts

Duckworth, Maria and John Lewis m. 7 Oct 1849 by Rev. Aquila A. Reese, lic. dated 6 Oct 1849

Duddle, Ann, d. after 1840 (exact date not given in Record of Members) [Ed. Note: Death notice in the Baltimore Sun stated that Ann Duddell, wife of J. Duddell, d. 18 Mar 1841.]

Duff, John Watchman, son of William and Elizabeth Ann Duff, b. 3 Jun 1839, Fells Point, Baltimore City, bapt. 4 Jun 1840 by Rev. Samuel Keppler

Dugent, Adelia T. and John T. Bassford m. 6 Jun 1850 by Rev. John S. Martin, lic. dated 5 Jun 1850

Dugent, Eli and Emily Jane Barkey m. ---- [blank] by Rev. John S. Martin, lic. dated 22 Dec 1849 [Ed. Note: Their marriage notice in the Baltimore Sun stated Eli Dugent m. Emily J. Barker, dau. of William Barker, on 23 Dec 1849.]

Duges, Benjamin (colored) and Charlotte Sanders (colored) m. 11 Aug 1847 by Rev. Dr. George C. M. Roberts

Duhaey, Margaret and Joseph S. Walker m. 6 Jul 1845 by Rev. Isaac P. Cook

Duhurst, Mary Ann Catherine, dau. of Granbury and Ann Duhurst, b. ---- [blank], bapt. 12 Apr 1840 by Rev. Joseph Shane

Duke, Adam and Julia Freeman m. 17 Jul 1845 by Rev. Dr. George C. M. Roberts

Dukehart, Samuel M. and Martha Ereckson m. 2 Nov 1847 by Rev. Littleton F. Morgan, lic. dated 1 Nov 1847

Dulack, Michael and Margaret Cole m. 21 May 1845 by Rev. Joseph Shane

Dulaney, Ann Eliza Josephine, dau. of Bladen T. and Elizabeth Ann Dulaney, b. 26 Oct 1844, bapt. 1 Mar 1845 by Rev. Dr. George C. M. Roberts

Dulaney, Bladen and Elizabeth Amey m. 2 Dec 1841 by Rev. Dr. George C. M. Roberts

Dulaney, Theodore Thomas Jefferson, son of Bladen and Elizabeth Dulaney, b. 10 Oct 1842, bapt. 19 May 1844 by Rev. Dr. George C. M. Roberts

Dulany, Peter M. and Elizabeth Stirling m. 2 Sep 1846 by Rev. Samuel Keppler (date of lic. not recorded)

Dulen, Margaret Ann and William W. Brazier m. 28 Feb 1843 by Rev. Samuel Brison [Ed. Note: Their marriage notice in the Baltimore Sun gave their names as William H. Brazier and Margaret A. Dewling.]

Duling, James and Mary Mullin m. 26 Nov 1844 by Rev. James Sewell, lic. dated 25 Nov 1844

Dull, Permelia S. and Alexander Yeo m. ---- [blank] by Rev. John S. Martin, lic. dated 7 Feb 1850 [Ed. Note: Their marriage notice in the Baltimore Sun stated Alexander Yeo m. Permelia J. Dull, dau. of James and Jane R. Dull, on 7 Feb 1850.]

Dunbar, J. A. and Ann E. Langley, both of Baltimore County, m. 10 Sep 1840 by Rev. Bernard H. Nadal [*Ed. Note:* Her first name was misspelled "Aan" in the marriage register.]

Duncan, Alexander and Sophia Lehman m. 3 Sep 1850 by Rev. Dr. George C. M. Roberts

Duncan, Elizabeth and Robert Pulley m. 24 Jul 1843 by Rev. Henry Slicer, lic. dated same day

Duncan, Hannah Eliza and Samuel Cox m. 21 Apr 1845 at the house of her father Mr. Palmer in Baltimore by Rev. Beverly Waugh, lic. dated 19 Apr 1845

Dungan, Susannah and Henry H. Watson m. 15 Jun 1847 by Rev. Dr. George C. M. Roberts

Dunkin, Ann, d. 1841 (death noted in Class List)

Dunlop, Henry and Margaret Ann Conce m. 8 Jul 1846 by Rev. Benjamin F. Brooke

Dunn, Charlotte and George W. Mills m. 4 Jan 1848 by Rev. Stephen A. Roszel, lic. dated 31 Dec 1847

Dunn, Jemima C. and Joel Hinman m. 8 Nov 1849 by Rev. Dr. George C. M. Roberts

Dunn, Julia A. C. and George W. Wright m. 27 Jun 1843 by Rev. Henry Slicer, lic. dated same day

Dunn, Mary Ann, dau. of Curtis and Sarah Dunn, b. 17 Apr 1833, Fells Point, Baltimore City, bapt. 14 Jul 1840 by Rev. Samuel Keppler

Dunn, Matilda Jane, dau. of William and Mary D. Dunn, b. 22 Sep 1843, bapt. 27 Jun 1847 by Rev. Dr. George C. M. Roberts

Dunning, Ann and John James m. 1 Oct 1842 by Rev. Wesley Stevenson

Dunnington, Thomas R. and Josephine Rorback m. 29 Jan 1843 by Rev. Job Guest, lic. dated 28 Jan 1843

Dunnington, William M. and Sarah B. Keenor, both of Baltimore County, m. 7 Jan 1846 by Rev. William Hamilton

Dunsford, Julia and John Murry m. 27 Oct 1842 by Rev. Henry Slicer, lic. dated same day

Durand, Amelia Hulse, dau. of John H. and Jane Durand, b. 3 Feb 1848, bapt. 16 Jan 1848 by Rev. Dr. George C. M. Roberts

Durand, Eliza Roberts, dau. of John H. and Jane Durand, b. 15 Sep 1843, bapt. 1 Oct 1843 by Rev. Dr. George C. M. Roberts

Durand, John Alexander, son of John H. and Mary Jane Durand, b. 25 Jul 1850, bapt. 13 Oct 1850 by Rev. Dr. George C. M. Roberts

Durand, Mary Lawrence, dau. of John Henry and Jane Durand, b. 2 Oct 1845, bapt. 6 Nov 1845 by Rev. Dr. George C. M. Roberts

Durham, John M. and Alice Simmonds m. 8 Dec 1850 by Rev. Isaac P. Cook

Durham, Lemuel and Catharine Hovell (Hevell?) m. 13 May 1843 by Rev. Wesley Stevenson

Durham, Sarah Ann and Orman Knight m. 28 Sep 1848 by Rev. Joseph Shane

Durkee, John A. and Elizabeth C. Wheeler m. 4 Feb 1841 by Rev. Samuel Keppler, lic. dated 1 Feb 1841

Durkee, Mary and Patrick Kelly m. 14 Jan 1849 by Rev. Dr. George C. M. Roberts

Dushon, Mary, d. circa 1840-1847 (exact date not given in Record of Members)

Dutton, Emma, dau. of Robert and Mary Ann Button, b. 22 Sep 1846, Baltimore, bapt. 25 Jul 1847 by Rev. William M. D. Ryan

Dutton, Robert, see "Sarah Murray," q.v.

Dutton, Sarah E. and Edward J. Bell m. ---- [blank] by Rev. John S. Martin, lic. dated 21 Mar 1850 [*Ed. Note:* Their marriage notice in the *Baltimore Sun* stated Edward J. Bell m. Sarah E. Dutton, dau. of Robert Dutton, on 21 Mar 1850.]

Duvall, Adeline, dau. of Edward and Adeline Duvall, b. 26 May 1846, bapt. 12 Feb 1845 by Rev. Dr. George C. M. Roberts. See "John H. Duvall" and "Mary R. Duvall" and "Mary W. Duvall," q.v.

Duvall, Alexander, see "Lewis E. Duvall," q.v.

Duvall, Augusta Walton, dau. of Richard C. and Sarah Duvall, b. 21 May 1839, bapt. 22 Jul 184- [page torn] by Rev. ---- (name not indicated) [*Ed. Note:* Information was written on a piece of paper and inserted in the church register.]

Duvall, Carver Mercer, son of Claudius and Julia A. Duvall, b. 8 Jun 1843, bapt. 13 Jul 1843 by Rev. Dr. George C. M. Roberts

Duvall (Duval), Charlotte and William Jessop, both of Baltimore County, m. 22 Jan 1841 by Rev. John Rice, lic. dated 21 Jan 1841

Duvall, Claudius, see "Carver M. Duvall," q.v.

Duvall, Edward, see "Adeline Duvall" and "John H. Duvall" and "Mary R. Duvall" and "Mary W. Duvall," q.v.

Duvall, George W. and Maria Louisa Wood m. 19 Nov 1845 at the house of her father in Baltimore by Rev. Beverly Waugh, lic. dated 18 Nov 1845

Duvall, John Henry, son of Edward and Adeline Duvall, b. 11 Aug 1846, bapt. 18 Aug 1846 by Rev. Dr. George C. M. Roberts

Duvall, Lewis Eugene, son of Alexander and Elizabeth Anna Duvall, b. 7 Jun 1843, bapt. 14 Oct 1843 by Rev. Dr. George C. M. Roberts

Duvall, Martha A. and William L. Fendall, both of Baltimore County, m. 19 Jul 1842 by Rev. Nelson Head

Duvall, Mary Rebecca, dau. of Edward and Adeline Duvall, b. 5 Sep 1848, bapt. 4 Feb 1849 by Rev. Dr. George C. M. Roberts

Duvall, Mary Winchester, dau. of Edward and Adeline Duvall, b. 3 Sep 1842, bapt. 13 Jul 1843 by Rev. Dr. George C. M. Roberts

Duvall, Richard C., see "Augusta W. Duvall," q.v.

Duvall, Sarah J. and William H. Foley, both of Baltimore, m. 5 May 1841 by Rev. John A. Hening

Dyer, Charles Walter, son of Benjamin and Caroline Dyer, b. 6(?) Jun 1839, bapt. 9 Aug 1840 by Rev. Charles B. Tippett

Dykes, Mary Ann, d. circa 1840-1847 (exact date not given in Record of Members)

Eagen, Rachel and John Simonson m. 3 Apr 1845 by Rev. Dr. George C. M. Roberts

Eagleston, Joshua and Mary Ann Myres m. 27 Oct 1842 by Rev. Dr. George C. M. Roberts

Eaisbouns(?), Eliza Ann and John Wallis m. 19 Mar 1846 by Rev. Joseph Shane

Eames, Ann Amelia, dau. of William A. and Hannah Eames, b. 23 Dec 1843, bapt. 22 May 1844 by Rev. Dr. George C. M. Roberts

Eareckson, Mary A. and James J. Coale, both of Baltimore County, m. 5 Oct 1846 by Rev. George Hildt, lic. dated same day

Earheart, George W. and Elizabeth A. Leatch, both of Baltimore County, m. 8 Feb 1843 by Rev. Nelson Head

Earlaugher, Benjamin and Mary Briggs m. 15 Aug 1840 by Rev. Joseph Shane

Earpe, James and Catharine Weaver m. 10 Apr 1849 by Rev. Isaac P. Cook

Earpe, Jemima and Dennis Mewshaw m. 7 Oct 1841 by Rev. Isaac P. Cook

Earpe, Joseph and Catharine Clemmons m. 16 Dec 1841 by Rev. Isaac P. Cook

Earpe, William P. and Mary M. Smith m. 13 Aug 1846 by Rev. Isaac P. Cook

Eastman, Samuel, d. circa 1840 (exact date not given in Record of Members) [*Ed. Note:* Death notice in the *Baltimore Sun* stated that Samuel Eastman d. 5 Jun 1840.]

Ebaugh, Rebecca and Levi Taylor m. 7 Jun 1849 by Rev. Dr. George C. M. Roberts

Eddleman, Gotlieb Henry and Mary Jane Franklin m. 18 Jul 1849 by Rev. Isaac P. Cook

Edmondson, E. A. and C. A. Dennis m. 16 Dec 1848 by Rev. William Hirst [*Ed. Note:* Their marriage notice in the *Baltimore Sun* gave their names as Charles A. Dennis and Ann E. Edmondson, dau. of Robert Edmondson.]

Edmondson, Mary Jane and James E. Alford m. 6 Oct 1847 by Rev. Littleton F. Morgan, lic. dated 15 [*sic*] Oct 1847 [*Ed. Note:* Their marriage notice in the *Baltimore Sun* stated that James E. Alford and Mary J. Edmundson m. 6 Oct 1847, so they obviously obtained their license on 5 Oct 1847, not 15 Oct 1847.]

Edmondson, Moses L. and Matilda A. Stiner m. 1 Jan 1850 by Rev. William Hirst, lic. dated 31 Dec 1849 [*Ed. Note:* Their marriage notice in the *Baltimore Sun* gave their names as Moses Edmonson and Matilda A. Steiner.]

Edmondson, Robert, see "E. A. Edmondson," q.v.

Edmonson, John P. and Sarah C.(?) Mitchell m. 30 Nov 1847 by Rev. Benjamin F. Brooke

Edwards, Anna E. and Richard E. Jenkins m. 21 Mar 1848 by Rev. Benjamin F. Brooke

Edwards, Ellen E. and William H. Neilson m. 27 Jan 1848 by Rev. Stephen A. Roszel, lic. dated same day

Edwards, Jane, d. circa 1845-1847 (exact date not given in Record of Members) [*Ed. Note:* Death notice in the *Baltimore Sun* stated that Jane Edwards, wife of Joseph Edwards, d. 14 Jul 1845.]

Edwards, Thomas James and Mary Elizabeth Jones m. 2 Jan 1843 by Rev. Job Guest, lic. dated same day

Egarrer, Eliza Jane and Joseph Roberts, Jr. m. 13 May 1849 by Rev. Dr. George C. M. Roberts [*Ed. Note:* Her last name was given as "Legar" in their *Baltimore Sun* marriage notice.]

Elam, William A. and Sarah Emanly m. 27 May 1845 by Rev. James Sewell, lic. dated same day

Elder, Rachel A. and Moses Donaldson m. 4 May 1841 by Rev. Joseph Shane [*Ed. Note:* Her name was misspelled "Eleder" in the church register.]

Elder, Rebecca, d. circa 1840 (exact date not given in Class Record)

Elder, Sarah, d. circa 1840 (exact date not given in Class Record)

Elder, Sarah J. and William J. Webb m. 3 Oct 1850 by Rev. Joseph Shane

Eldred, Eliza Jane and Owen T. Humphreys m. 2 Aug 1841 by Rev. Dr. George C. M. Roberts

Eliason, Joseph, son of Ereck and Julia A. Eliason, b. 1 May 1840, bapt. 23 Sep 1840 by Rev. Charles B. Tippett

Elkington, Harriett A. and John H. Rutter m. 14 Feb 1841 by Rev. John Bear

Elkins, Jane Elizabeth and James Biden m. 14 Mar 1850 by Rev. Joseph Shane
Ellender, Amanda E. and John Clark m. 2 Jul 1850 by Rev. Isaac P. Cook
Elliott, Amelia M. and John S. Schwitzer m. 21 Jun 1849 by Rev. Aquila A. Reese,
    lic. dated 20 Jun 1849
Elliott, Catherine A. and William H. Kirkwood m. 30 Jun 1846 by Rev. Dr. George
    C. M. Roberts
Elliott (Elliot), Elizabeth, d. circa 1847-1850 (exact date not given in Record of
    Members) [Ed. Note: Death notice in the Baltimore Sun stated that Elizabeth
    Elliott, wife of William Elliott, d. 28 Oct 1848.]
Elliott (Elliot), Emily Jane, dau. of Hooper and Lurania Elliot, b. 30 May 1842,
    bapt. 21 Feb 1843 by Rev. Henry Slicer
Elliott, Hooper, son of Burket and Retty [sic] Elliott, aged 26, bapt. 21 Feb 1843
    by Rev. Henry Slicer
Elliott (Elliot), John and Mary Lusby m. 5 Aug 1841 by Rev. Dr. George C. M.
    Roberts
Elliott (Elliot), Nathan Jackson, son of Nathan and Eliza Elliot, aged 7 weeks, bapt.
    4 Jan 1842 by Rev. Gerard Morgan. See "William S. Elliott," q.v.
Elliott, Robert and Ann Elizabeth Mobery m. 16 Jan 1848 by Rev. Stephen A.
    Roszel, lic. dated 15 Jan 1848
Elliott, William, see "Elizabeth Elliott," q.v.
Elliott, William Smallwood, son of Nathaniel J. and Eliza Elliott, b. 5 Feb 1840,
    Baltimore City, bapt. 28 Jul 1840 by Rev. Samuel Keppler. See "Nathan J.
    Elliott," q.v.
Ellis, Abraham and Ann Johnson m. 22 Sep 1841 by Rev. Gerard Morgan, lic.
    dated 20 Sep 1841
Ellis, Mary E. and James T. Walmsley m. 30 May 1850 by Rev. Henry Slicer, lic.
    dated same day [Ed. Note: His last name was spelled "Wamsley" in the church
    register.]
Ellis, Susan and George Monk m. 21 Mar 1844 by Rev. Isaac P. Cook
Ellis, William and Mary Ann Evans m. 24 Oct 1848 by Rev. Dr. George C. M.
    Roberts
Elsby, Rachel, d. circa 1847-1850 (exact date not given in Record of Members)
Elsby, Thomas, see "Thomas Helsby," q.v.
Elssrode, Elizabeth A. and Richard M. Green m. 1 May 1846 by Rev. Wesley
    Stevenson [Ed. Note: Her name was given as "A. Elsrode" in their Baltimore
    Sun marriage notice.]
Elton, Charles W. and Elizabeth Denny m. 26 Sep 1844 by Rev. Dr. George C. M.
    Roberts
Eltonhead, Jane B. and Hugh Pursell m. 13 Jun 1844 by Rev. Isaac P. Cook
Emanly, Sarah and William A. Elam m. 27 May 1845 by Rev. James Sewell, lic.
    dated same day
Embret, Susanna C. and John R. Jeffres m. 26 Oct 1847 by Rev. Dr. George C. M.
    Roberts
Emerson, William C. and Margaret Zeigler m. 7 Apr 1850 by Rev. Dr. George C.
    M. Roberts
Emich, Charles A. and Elizabeth M. Severson m. 27 Jul 1847 by Rev. Dr. George
    C. M. Roberts
Emory, Catharine and William Little, both of Baltimore County, m. 24 Dec 1840
    by Rev. Bernard H. Nadal

Emory, Mary Eliza, dau. of William H. and Eliza Emory, b. 7 Dec 1847, bapt. 23 Apr 1848 by Rev. Dr. George C. M. Roberts

Emory, William Hopper, son of William H. and Eliza Emory, b. 28 Jun 1849, bapt. 30 Dec 1849 by Rev. Dr. George C. M. Roberts

Ereckson, George Wesley, son of Federal and Henrietta Ereckson, b. 28 Jul 1841, bapt. 28 Jan 1842 by Rev. William Prettyman [Ed. Note: A later entry stated George Wesley Erickson was bapt. -- Mar 1842.]

Ereckson, Martha and Samuel M. Dukehart m. 2 Nov 1847 by Rev. Littleton F. Morgan, lic. dated 1 Nov 1847

Erick, Sarah Ann and Benjamin F. Gawthorp m. ---- [blank] by Rev. James H. Brown, lic. dated 7 Nov 1848

Erpenbeck, Henry and Fredericka Peterson m. 8 Jul 1845 by Rev. Dr. George C. M. Roberts [Ed. Note: Their marriage notice in the Baltimore Sun gave her name as Fredericker Petersen.]

Erven, Mary Jane, dau. of Joseph and Ann E. Erven, b. 3 Jun 1842, bapt. 20 Jun 1842 by Rev. Elisha D. Owen

Ervin, E. Gifford and John W. Hack m. 6 Sep 1846 by Rev. Littleton F. Morgan, lic. dated 5 Sep 1846

Ervine, Sarah Jane and Henry Collier m. 12 Feb 1845 by Rev. James Sewell, lic. dated same day

Espey, Mary Jane and William Henry Smith m. 2 Mar 1848 by Rev. Stephen A. Roszel, lic. dated 1 Mar 1848

Espey, William S. and Sarah Ann Tier m. 28 Nov 1843 by Rev. Henry Slicer, lic. dated same day

Essender, Lewis W. and Mary E. Towson m. 26 Nov 1850 by Rev. Henry Slicer, lic. dated 20 Nov 1850

Essex, Catharine Ann and Samuel S. Clayton m. 15 Sep 1846 by Rev. Littleton F. Morgan, lic. dated same day

Essex, Rebecca and Samuel H. Smith m. 16 Jan 1844 by Rev. Joseph Shane

Estes, Garland, son of Elisha B. and Matilda Estes, b. 11 Aug 1840, bapt. 25 Oct 1840 by Rev. Dr. George C. M. Roberts

Estlack, Hiram and Sarah A. Bailey m. 2 Jan 1848 by Rev. Dr. George C. M. Roberts

Etchberger, Bethia C. and Thomas T. Dill m. 24 Jan 1841 by Rev. Samuel Keppler, lic. dated 23 Jan 1841

Etchberger, Charles Edwin, son of James and Frances Ann Etchberger, b. 24 Jul 1844, Baltimore, bapt. 28 Dec 1846 by Rev. Samuel Keppler

Etchberger, Charlotte, d. after 1841 (death noted in Class List) [Ed. Note: Death notice in the Baltimore Sun stated that Charlotte Etchberger d. 28 Jan 1844.]

Etchberger, Elsey, d. circa 1840 (death noted in Class List)

Etchberger, Frances Ann, dau. of James and Frances Ann Etchberger, b. 13 Jan 1841, Baltimore, bapt. 28 Dec 1846 by Rev. Samuel Keppler

Etchberger, James, see "Charles E. Etchberger" and "Frances A. Etchberger" and "William C. Etchberger," q.v.

Etchberger, Ralph P. and Mary E. Williams m. 10 May 1840 by Rev. Samuel Keppler, lic. dated 8 May 1840

Etchberger, William Clifford, son of James and Frances Ann Etchberger, b. 12 Apr 1846, Baltimore, bapt. 28 Dec 1846 by Rev. Samuel Keppler

Eubanks, Augusta and Benjamin Howard m. 18 Nov 1845 by Rev. Dr. George C. M. Roberts

Evans, Daniel Thomas and Frances Ann Harrington m. 16 Jul 1848 by Rev. Stephen A. Roszel, lic. dated 14 Jul 1848

Evans, Elizabeth, d. circa 1840 (exact date not given in Class Record)

Evans, Fanny M. and William Murdock m. 17 Oct 1849 by Rev. John S. Martin, lic. dated 16 Oct 1849

Evans, Harriet Jane and John West m. 3 Sep 1844 by Rev. Dr. George C. M. Roberts

Evans, Henry W. S. and Anne Andrews m. 14 Oct 1847 by Rev. Stephen A. Roszel, lic. dated same day

Evans, Mary Ann and William Ellis m. 24 Oct 1848 by Rev. Dr. George C. M. Roberts

Evans, Susanna and Robert W. Register, both of Baltimore, MD, m. 10 Nov 1840 by Rev. John A. Hening

Evans, Thomas W. and Margaret S. Leatherbury m. 27 Jan 1848 by Rev. Dr. George C. M. Roberts

Everet, Rachel and John Fenney m. 16 Aug 1846 by Rev. Samuel Keppler (date of lic. not recorded)

Everett, Hezekiah M. and Mary M. Riggins m. 25 Nov 1845 by Rev. Dr. George C. M. Roberts

Everrett, Alexander B., son of George and Christiana Everrett, b. 3 Nov 1837, bapt. 27 Sep 1842 by Rev. Elisha D. Owen

Everrett, Mary M., son of George and Christiana Everrett, b. 5 Feb 1842, bapt. 27 Sep 1842 by Rev. Elisha D. Owen

Everton, Elizabeth, d. 1847 (death noted in Class List)

Evritt, Maria and Thomas B. Burch m. 6 Nov 1845 by Rev. Samuel Keppler (date of lic. not recorded)

Ewell, Tabitha and Benjamin Venables, both of Baltimore County, m. 29 Oct 1844 by Rev. William Hamilton

Ewin, James and Eliza Hindel m. 30 Apr 1846 by Rev. Littleton F. Morgan, lic. dated same day

Ewing, Scott and Ann Johnson m. 18 Dec 1842 by Rev. Henry Slicer, lic. dated 17 Dec 1842

Faithful, Henry and Catherine Ross m. 14 Sep 1842 by Rev. Joseph Shane

Fance, George and Sarah Gaber m. 18 Aug 1844 by Rev. Joseph Shane

Fardwell, Elizabeth and Richard J. Tutsel m. 25 Jul 1842 by Rev. Samuel Brison

Fardwell, Elizabeth and Thomas Helsby m. 27 Nov 1847 by Rev. Benjamin F. Brooke [Ed. Note: Their marriage notice in the Baltimore Sun states Thomas Elsby and Elizabeth Fardwell, dau. of Isaac Fardwell, m. 28 Nov 1847.]

Fardwell, Isaac, see "Elizabeth Fardwell" and "Thomas Helsby," q.v.

Fardwell, William A. and Sarah F. Mister m. 10 Sep 1850 by Rev. Henry Slicer, lic. dated 28 May 1850

Farlan, Margaret and Oliver Thompson m. 9 Mar 1847 by Rev. Joseph Shane

Farling, Margaret E. and Jphar(?) A. Thompson m. 12 Nov 1847 by Rev. Stephen A. Roszel, lic. dated same day [Ed. Note: His first name is unusual as written in the church register and it is difficult to read. Their marriage notice in the Baltimore Sun gave his name only as J. A. Thompson.]

Farlow, Sarah Ann and David Nichol m. 24 Dec 1840 by Rev. Samuel Keppler, lic. dated same day

Farnandis, Walter Jr. and Mary E. Griffith m. 17 Oct 1850 by Rev. Dr. George C. M. Roberts

Farringer, Martha A. and Allen Kirby m. 26 Apr 1845 by Rev. James Sewell, lic. dated 8 May [sic] 1845

Farrow, Mary Elizabeth, dau. of Joseph and Maria Farrow, b. 7 Mar 1843, bapt. 12 Jun 1843 by Rev. Isaac P. Cook

Faulkner, John R. and Elizabeth Ann Woods m. 15 Sep 1846 by Rev. Dr. George C. M. Roberts

Faulkner, Susan E. and William H. Brome m. 16 May 1843 by Rev. Henry Slicer, lic. dated 15 May 1843

Fefel, Frederick and Jane Nelson m. 25 May 1843 by Rev. Dr. George C. M. Roberts

Fefil, John and Catherine E. Bryan m. 30 Apr 1846 by Rev. Dr. George C. M. Roberts [Ed. Note: Their marriage notice in the Baltimore Sun stated that John Fefill and Catharine E. Brien m. 29 Apr 1846.]

Fell, Elizabeth, d. circa 1847-1850 (exact date not given in Record of Members)

Fellow, Ann L. and Bartus Clarke m. 19 Sep 1844 by Rev. James Sewell, lic. dated same day

Fendall, William L. and Martha A. Duvall, both of Baltimore County, m. 19 Jul 1842 by Rev. Nelson Head

Fenix, James H. and Mary Ann Godwin m. 11 Sep 1849 by Rev. John S. Martin, lic. dated same day

Fennaghan, John Oliver, son of Thomas H. and Elizabeth Ann Fenneghan, b. 11 Feb 1849, bapt. 21 Jun 1849 by Rev. Dr. George C. M. Roberts

Fennell, Mary Ann and William J. Colbart m. 9 Oct 1844 by Rev. Dr. George C. M. Roberts

Fenney, John and Rachel Everet m. 16 Aug 1846 by Rev. Samuel Keppler (date of lic. not recorded)

Ferguson, Elizabeth Ann, dau. of Andrew and Sarah Ferguson, b. 15 Aug 1848, bapt. 7 Apr 1855 by Rev. Dr. George C. M. Roberts

Ferguson, Marshall H. and Mary Thomas m. 8 Aug 1847 by Rev. Isaac P. Cook

Ferrel, Catharine R. and Jabez Wilkes m. 16 May 1849 by Rev. John S. Martin, lic. dated same day

Fetterling, John M. and Ruth A. Devilbiss m. 2 4 Feb 1849 by Rev. James H. Brown, lic. dated 21 Feb 1849

Feury, Caroline, an orphan in the Female Asylum in Mulberry Street, b. 6 Mar 1836, bapt. 4 Oct 1840 by Rev. Thomas Myers

Fife, Ellen and Charles Beukler m. 20 Sep 1841 by Rev. Gerard Morgan, lic. dated same day

Fifer, Christopher and Sarah Sumwalt m. 7 Dec 1846 by Rev. Wesley Stevenson

Fish, Robert and Sarah Gregory m. 31 Mar 1844 by Rev. Joseph Merriken

Fish(?), Orell and John M. Flowers m. 10 Feb 1848 by Rev. Benjamin F. Brooke

Fisher, Abraham, see "Mary A. Fitzgerald," q.v.

Fisher, Elizabeth and John O'Brien m. 28 Jun 1845 by Rev. Wesley Stevenson

Fisher, Elizabeth, d. circa 1846-1847 (exact date not given in Record of Members) [Ed. Note: Death notice in the Baltimore Sun stated that Elizabeth A. Fisher d. 15 Jan 1847.]

Fisher, George Washington, son of William and Elizabeth Fisher, b. 31 Oct 1850, bapt. 8 Mar 1852 by Rev. Dr. George C. M. Roberts

Fisher, Hannah, dau. of George and Mary Fisher, b. 15 Mar 1846, bapt. 13 Jun 1846 by Rev. Dr. George C. M. Roberts

Fisher, John, d. 7 Jan 1840 (death noted in Class Record) [*Ed. Note:* Death notice in the *Baltimore Sun* stated that John Fisher d. 9 Jan 1840.]

Fisher, Mary and Louis Hamberd m. 8 Nov 1850 by Rev. Isaac P. Cook

Fisher, Mary, d. circa 1847 (exact date not given in Record of Members) [*Ed. Note:* Death notice in the *Baltimore Sun* stated that Mary M. Fisher d. 5 Mar 1846.]

Fitch, Stephen H. and Ann Clarke m. 21 Jun 1842 by Rev. Job Guest, lic. dated same day

Fitzgerald, Ellen, d. circa 1840 (exact date not given in Class Record)

Fitzgerald, George W. and Ann Maria Poteet m. 16 Jan 1844 by Rev. Joseph Shane

Fitzgerald, Henry, see "Mary A. Fitzgerald," q.v.

Fitzgerald, Henrietta and James Auskins m. 12 Jun 1849 by Rev. John S. Martin, lic. dated 11 Jun 1849

Fitzgerald, Mary A., d. circa 1840 (exact date not given in Record of Members) [*Ed. Note:* Death notice in the *Baltimore Sun* stated that Mary A. Fitzgerald, wife of Henry Fitzgerald and dau. of Abraham Fisher, d. 7 Nov 1840.]

Fitzgerald, Mary E. and Richard G. Busey m. 22 Jan 1844 by Rev. Joseph Shane

Fitzgerald, Thomas H. and Eliza Jane Hardy m. 7 Oct 1847 by Rev. Benjamin F. Brooke

Fitzgerald, Victoria and William Williams m. 25 Jan 1848 by Rev. Dr. George C. M. Roberts

Fitzpatrick, Elizabeth, dau. of Thomas and Mary Fitzpatrick, b. 2 Feb(?) 1848, bapt. 4 Mar 1849 by Rev. Dr. George C. M. Roberts

Fitzpatrick, Mary E. and Charles L. Woods m. 9 Dec 1841 by Rev. Dr. George C. M. Roberts

Fitzpatrick, Thomas and Mary McCall m. 18 May 1846 by Rev. Dr. George C. M. Roberts

Flack, Mary Grace, dau. of George W. and Rebecca Flack, b. 20 Oct 1850, bapt. 30 Jun 1851 by Rev. Dr. George C. M. Roberts

Flannegon, Eleanor, d. by 1840 (exact date not given in Class Record) [*Ed. Note:* Death notice in the *Baltimore Sun* stated that Eleanor Flanagan d. 6 Jun 1838.]

Flannigan, William and Susan Kirby m. 12 Apr 1848 by Rev. Dr. George C. M. Roberts

Flayhart, Edward and Margaret Yost m. 22 Jan 1843 by Rev. Isaac P. Cook

Flayhart, Sarah and Thomas Whittle m. 20 Oct 1842 by Rev. Isaac P. Cook

Fleming, William H. and Elizabeth W. Pruitt m. 26 Mar 1843 by Rev. Dr. George C. M. Roberts [*Ed. Note:* Their marriage notice in the *Baltimore Sun* stated that William H. Flemming m. Elizabeth W. Prueitt, dau. of Severn Prueitt.]

Fletcher, William G. and Hester Ann Griffin m. 14 Dec 1843 by Rev. Dr. George C. M. Roberts

Flindell(?), George and Ann Chalk m. 20 Feb 1846 by Rev. Wesley Stevenson

Flint, Thomas, see "Anna Israel," q.v.

Flood, Thomas and Mary Ann Bradshaw m. 19 Sep 1843 by Rev. Samuel Brison

Flowers, Chatham C. and Catherine P. Pollard, both of Baltimore County, m. 15 May 1846 by Rev. George Hildt, lic. dated same day

Flowers, John M. and Orell Fish(?) m. 10 Feb 1848 by Rev. Benjamin F. Brooke

Floyd, Elizabeth, d. after 1845 (death noted in Class List) [*Ed. Note:* Death notice in the *Baltimore Sun* stated that Elizabeth Floyd d. 6 Mar 1846.]

Floyd, Thomas and Margaret W. Wilkerson m. 21 Oct 1841 by Rev. Gerard Morgan, lic. dated 19 Oct 1841

Flyn, Mary Ann and Francis Johnson m. 23 Apr 1840 by Rev. John Bear

Foard, Mary A. and Benjamin Taylor m. 26 Sep 1843 by Rev. Henry Slicer, lic. dated same day

Foley, William H. and Sarah J. Duvall, both of Baltimore, m. 5 May 1841 by Rev. Bernard H. Nadal

Folgar, Maria and Henry Jones m. 8 Oct 1840 by Rev. Samuel Keppler, lic. dated 6 Oct 1840

Folsum, Charles and Mary Martin m. 16 Jan 1844 by Rev. Samuel Brison

Fonce, Amos and Margaret Ann Franklin m. 3 Jun 1849 by Rev. Aquila A. Reese, lic. dated 2 Jun 1849

Forbes, Nector A. and Eliza Jane Hines m. 4 Aug 1841 by Rev. Dr. George C. M. Roberts

Forbush, Barthy A. and Cyrus Sutton m. 11 Apr 1845 by Rev. Dr. George C. M. Roberts

Ford, Clement Roberts, son of Rufus K. and Mary Ann Ford, b. 10 Jul 1845, bapt. 14 Jul 1845 by Rev. Dr. George C. M. Roberts

Ford, Elisabeth and William Austin m. 21 Oct 1841 by Rev. Gerard Morgan, lic. dated 19 Oct 1841

Ford, Eliza Ann and Christopher Burkhead, both of Baltimore County, m. 28 Apr 1840 by Rev. Thomas Myers, lic. dated same day

Ford, Frederick Augustus, son of George E. and Laura E. Ford, b. 15 Aug 1849, bapt. 17 Jun 1850 by Rev. Dr. George C. M. Roberts

Ford, George A. and Laura E. Mitchell m. 9 Nov 1848 by Rev. Dr. George C. M. Roberts

Ford, John S. and Aschah Ann Paul m. 2 Jan 1845 by Rev. Dr. George C. M. Roberts

Ford, John S. and Alverda Shoemaker m. ---- [no date given] by Rev. John Miller, lic. dated 22 Oct 1850 [*Ed. Note:* Their marriage notice in the *Baltimore Sun* stated that John S. Ford and Alverda Shoemaker, dau. of George Shoemaker, m. 22 Oct 1850.]

Ford, Margaret Ann and John T. Glenn m. 11 Nov 1841 by Rev. Dr. George C. M. Roberts

Ford, Mary Elizabeth, dau. of Rufus K. and Mary Ann Ford, b. 17 Dec 1850, bapt. 27 Dec 1850 by Rev. Dr. George C. M. Roberts

Ford, Rufus King, son of Rufus K. and Mary Ann Ford, b. 16 Jun 1848, bapt. 24 Oct 1848 by Rev. Dr. George C. M. Roberts

Ford, Sarah Catharine, dau. of Michael and Mary Ford, b. 21 Nov 1838, bapt. 21 Jun 1840 by Rev. John Bear

Ford, Thomas and Susan Tidings m. 14 May 1843 by Rev. Henry Slicer, lic. dated 13 May 1843

Fordes, William C. and Emeline Matrona Hartzell, both of Baltimore County, m. 14 Mar 1841 by Rev. John Rice

Foreman, Ann Maria and Henry H. Bose m. 30 Nov 1844 by Rev. Joseph Shane

Foreman, John and Mary Jane Posey, both of Baltimore County, m. 31 Dec 1840 by Rev. Bernard H. Nadal

Foreman, Leonard, d. 1840 (death noted in Class List) [*Ed. Note:* Death notice in the *Baltimore Sun* stated that Leonard Forman d. 23 Aug 1840.]

Forice, Elizabeth and John Wilds m. 24 Aug 1849 by Rev. Joseph Shane

Forman, Margaret (colored) and John Steward (colored) m. 13 Dec 1842 by Rev. Henry Slicer (date of lic. not recorded)

Forney, Isaac C. and Jemima Daughaday m. 18 Apr 1850 by Rev. Isaac P. Cook

Forrest, Caroline and William Busch m. 26 Jan 1843 by Rev. Dr. George C. M. Roberts

Forrest, James and Mary A. Busch m. 7 May 1843 by Rev. Dr. George C. M. Roberts

Forrest, Mary Virginia, dau. of William A. and Eliza Jane Forrest, b. 27 Mar 1846, bapt. 31 Dec 1847 by Rev. Dr. George C. M. Roberts

Forrester, John and Henrietta Kennell m. 5 Dec 1844 by Rev. Joseph Shane

Forsyth, Jane Anna, dau. of Emanuel T. and Eliza Forsyth, b. 27 Aug 1843, bapt. 11 Apr 1844 by Rev. Dr. George C. M. Roberts

Forsyth, Manuel Thomas, son of Manuel T. and Eliza Forsyth, b. 27 May 1840, bapt. 29 Nov 1840 by Rev. Isaac P. Cook

Fort, Deborah and William Wells m. 11 Feb 1844 by Rev. Joseph Shane

Fort, Rebecca and William R. McKenley m. 5 Mar 1850 by Rev. Isaac P. Cook

Fosbenner, Mrs. Daniel, see "William Hopkins," q.v.

Foster, Ann and Washington Holt m. 26 Aug 1841 by Rev. Gerard Morgan, lic. dated same day

Foster, Charlotte M. and Thomas W. Killmon m. 20 May 1849 by Rev. John S. Martin, lic. dated 15 May 1849 by Rev. John S. Martin, lic. dated [*Ed. Note:* Their marriage notice in the *Baltimore Sun* gave his name as Thomas W. Killmon even though it looked more like Thomas St. Killmon in the church register.]

Foster, David B. and Elizabeth P. Free m. 6 Nov 1849 by Rev. William Hirst, lic. dated same day

Foster, Hamilton and Charlotte Oscuby, both of Baltimore County, m. 24 Dec 1844 by Rev. William Hamilton [*Ed. Note:* Their marriage notice in the *Baltimore Sun* gave her name as Charlotte Osgodby.]

Foster, Jane and Reuben Jubbs m. 25 Oct 1840 by Rev. Samuel Keppler, lic. dated 24 Oct 1840

Foster, Maria and James Sammon m. 10 Feb 1840 by Rev. Joseph Shane

Foster, Robert W. B. and Susan Cord m. 17 Oct 1844 by Rev. Isaac P. Cook

Foulk, Elizabeth Ann, dau. of Louis and Eliza Foulk, b. ---- [blank], bapt. 12 Apr 1846 by Rev. Dr. George C. M. Roberts

Fouse, Henry L. and Teresa Jones m. 24 Oct 1847 by Rev. Stephen A. Roszel, lic. dated 23 Oct 1847

Fowble, William H., d. circa 1843 (death noted in Probationers Book) [*Ed. Note:* Death notice in the *Baltimore Sun* stated that William H. Fowble d. 14 Mar 1844.]

Fowler, Annette and Owen Morris m. 22 Jun 1843 by Rev. Isaac P. Cook

Fowler, David, see "Mary Bell," q.v.

Fowler, Mary and John S. Sanders, both of Baltimore County, m. ---- [date not given] by Rev. George Hildt, lic. dated 18 Dec 1845

Fowler, Rebecca Jane and Francis Robbson, of Baltimore County, m. 4 Apr 1841 by Rev. John Rice, lic. dated 3 Apr 1841

Fowler, William and Jane Spillman m. 6 May 1849 by Rev. Joseph Shane

Fowler, Wilsey and Martha Sullivan, both of Virginia, m. 14 Apr 1845 by Rev. William Hamilton

Fox, Horace and Martha A. Blackman m. 28 Aug 1842 by Rev. Dr. George C. M. Roberts

Foxwell, Sarah and Lewis C. Cook m. 26 May 1850 by Rev. Isaac P. Cook

Foy, William H. Harrison, son of William and Louisa Foy, b. 9 Feb 1841, bapt. 11 Jun 184- [page torn] by Rev. ---- (name not indicated) [*Ed. Note:* Information was written on a piece of paper and inserted in the church register.]

Franklin, Eliza J. and Charles Anderson m. 20 Feb 1846 by Rev. Dr. George C. M. Roberts

Franklin, Elizabeth Ann and Edward Simmonds m. 25 Jul 1847 by Rev. Stephen A. Roszel, lic. dated 21 Jul 1847

Franklin, Margaret Ann and Amos Fonce m. 3 Jun 1849 by Rev. Aquila A. Reese, lic. dated 2 Jun 1849

Franklin, Maria, d. by 1840 (exact date not given in Class Record) [*Ed. Note:* Death notice in the *Baltimore Sun* stated that Maria Franklin, wife of William Franklin, d. 31 Aug 1838.]

Franklin, Mary Jane and Gotlieb Henry Eddleman m. 18 Jul 1849 by Rev. Isaac P. Cook

Franklin, Susanna S. and Francis M. Dobbins m. 23 May 1847 by Rev. Dr. George C. M. Roberts

Franklin, William, see "Maria Franklin," q.v.

Frantom, Hester, d. 1845 (death noted in Class List)

Franton, George and Louisa C. Martin m. 16 Jul 1844 by Rev. Dr. George C. M. Roberts

Franton, Harriet Ann, dau. of George W. and Louisa C. Franton, b. 17 Apr 1845, bapt. 24 Nov 1845 by Rev. Dr. George C. M. Roberts

Fray, George and Emeline Letsinger m. 24 Dec 1843 by Rev. Henry Slicer, lic. dated 22 Dec 1843

Frazer, Hariot *[sic]* and Hamilton Becker m. 11 Jul 1844 by Rev. James Sewell, lic. dated 2 Jul 1844

Frazier, Barbara A. and John A. Frazier m. 9 Jul 1848 by Rev. Joseph Shane

Frazier, Catherine R. and Thomas Thomas m. 18 May 1845 by Rev. Dr. George C. M. Roberts

Frazier, Edwin Creswell and Narcissa Young m. 13 Jan 1848 at the house of her father in Shrewsbury, PA by Rev. Beverly Waugh, no lic. required

Frazier, Edwin, d. 1849 (death noted in Class List)

Frazier, Eleanor and Francis A. Gunby m. 25 Apr 1841 by Rev. Isaac P. Cook

Frazier, Emeline and George W. Wotten m. 25 Apr 1845 by Rev. Dr. George C. M. Roberts

Frazier, Harriet Ann Rebecca, dau. of John and Adeline Frazier, b. 21 Feb 1842, bapt. 30 Jun 1849 by Rev. Dr. George C. M. Roberts

Frazier, James, see "Thomas S. Frazier" and "Isabella Bailey," q.v.

Frazier, Jeremiah, d. 1849 (death noted in Class List) [*Ed. Note:* Death notice in the *Baltimore Sun* stated that Jeremiah Frazier, father-in-law of Jacob S. Morris, d. 1 Feb 1849.]

Frazier, John A. and Barbara A. Frazier m. 9 Jul 1848 by Rev. Joseph Shane

Frazier, Mary E., dau. of John and Jane Frazier, aged 5 months [b. 1840 or 1841], b. Baltimore City, bapt. 1841 (exact date not given) by Rev. Gerard Morgan

Frazier, Sidney A. and John H. Heald m. 2 Nov 1843 at the house of her father in Baltimore by Rev. Beverly Waugh, lic. dated 1 Nov 1843

Frazier, Thomas S., d. circa 1845 (death noted in Class List) [*Ed. Note:* Death notice in the *Baltimore Sun* stated that Thomas S. Frazier, son of James Frazier, d. 12 Jun 1846.]

Frazier, William and Mary Lee m. 12 Jul 1846 by Rev. Joseph Shane

Frazier, William Edward, son of William and Mary Ann Frazier, b. 12 Jun 1840, bapt. 29 Jul 1840 by Rev. Joseph Shane

Frazier, William K. and Sarah Ann Coleman m. 20 May 1847 by Rev. Dr. George C. M. Roberts

Frederick, John Henry, son of John Henry and Mary Frederick, b. 27 Sep 1846, bapt. 7 Oct 1846 by Rev. Dr. George C. M. Roberts

Frederick, Thomas and Mary Ann Freeberger m. 19 May 1844 by Rev. Dr. George C. M. Roberts

Frederick, William Thomas, son of Thomas and Mary Ellen Frederick, b. 6 Oct 1845, bapt. -- Jan 1846 by Rev. Dr. George C. M. Roberts

Free, Elizabeth P. and David B. Foster m. 6 Nov 1849 by Rev. William Hirst, lic. dated same day

Free, Milton Alexander Gabriel, son of Milton and Mary Free, b. 13 Sep 1839, bapt. 15 Jun 1840 by Rev. Joseph Shane

Freeberger, Columbus Marion, son of James M. and Emeline Freeberger, b. 8 Oct 1843, bapt. 19 May 1844 by Rev. Dr. George C. M. Roberts

Freeberger, George Washington, son of Henry and Sarah Freeberger, b. 17 Feb 1840, bapt. 19 May 1844 by Rev. Dr. George C. M. Roberts

Freeberger, Mary Ann and Thomas Frederick m. 19 May 1844 by Rev. Dr. George C. M. Roberts

Freeberger, Peter Van Buren, son of James M. and Emeline Freeberger, b. 5 May 1834, bapt. 19 May 1844 by Rev. Dr. George C. M. Roberts

Freeberger, Susan and James E. Backman m. 6 Jan 1846 by Rev. Dr. George C. M. Roberts

Freeman, George Henry, son of Thomas and Lavinia Freeman, b. 26 Sep 1840, Fells Point, Baltimore City, bapt. 28 Oct 1840 by Rev. Samuel Keppler

Freeman, Julia and Adam Duke m. 17 Jul 1845 by Rev. Dr. George C. M. Roberts

Freeman, William A. Francis, son of Charles and Caroline Freeman, b. 7 Oct 1841, Baltimore City, bapt. 10 Oct 1841 by Rev. Gerard Morgan

French, Charles and Margaretta Lambert m. 9 Jul 1850 by Rev. Dr. George C. M. Roberts

French, Martha Eddy and Henry H. McCabe m. 15 Dec 1840 by Rev. Joseph Shane

French, Susan and William C. Redman m. 8 Jul 1841 by Rev. Joseph Shane

Fretwell, Caroline, b. 11 Oct 1825, Yorkshire, England, bapt. 27 Sep 1846, Baltimore City, by Rev. Samuel Keppler

Frisby, Mary A. and Charles A. Mettee m. 23 Jun 1844 by Rev. Joseph Shane

Frizbe, Sarah, d. circa 1847-1850 (exact date not given in Record of Members)

Fryers, Frederick and Anna M. Gesang m. 18 Jul 1848 by Rev. Stephen A. Roszel, lic. dated 17 Jul 1848

Fulenger, Elizabeth and Gideon Herbert, Jr. m. 9 Aug 1840 by Rev. Joseph Shane

Fuller, Sarah A. and Joseph H. Audoun m. 10 Apr 1845 by Rev. James Sewell, lic. dated 9 Apr 1845

Fulton, James H. and Monemia Love m. 21 Jun 1849 by Rev. Dr. George C. M. Roberts

Fulton, Mary A. and David E. Small m. 13 Jun 1849 by Rev. Wesley Stevenson

Fultz, Lavinia and James Nicholson m. 12 Nov 1846 by Rev. Isaac P. Cook

Furlong, William, see "Elizabeth Cordrey," q.v.

Gaber, Sarah and George Fance m. 18 Aug 1844 by Rev. Joseph Shane

Gaither, Sarah L. and John Penn m. 4 Jun 1850 by Rev. Henry Slicer, lic. dated 27 May 1850

Galaspie, Hamilton and Elizabeth Amelia Loury m. 14 Oct 1846 by Rev. Joseph Shane

Gale, Frances E. and John L. Blades m. ---- [blank] by Rev. John S. Martin, lic. dated 21 Nov 1850 [Ed. Note: Their marriage notice in the Baltimore Sun initially stated John L. Blades m. Fanny E. Gill on 21 Nov 1850, but her name was later corrected to Frances Gayle.]

Gallan, Bridget and William H. Hayward m. 1 May 1842 by Rev. Isaac P. Cook

Gallagher, James, see "Frances Galliger," q.v.

Gallaway, Clarissa and Henry Holdbrook m. 13 Jan 1841 by Rev. Samuel Keppler, lic. dated same day

Gallaway, Joseph John, son of Thomas and Mary Gallaway, b. 8 Mar 1836, Fells Point, Baltimore City, bapt. 26 Jan 1840 by Rev. Samuel Keppler

Gallaway, Pamela Jane, dau. of Thomas and Mary Gallaway, b. 17 Mar 1833, Fells Point, Baltimore City, bapt. 26 Jan 1840 by Rev. Samuel Keppler

Galliger, Frances, d. circa 1850 (exact date not given in Record of Members) [Ed. Note: Death notice in the Baltimore Sun stated that Frances Gallagher, widow of James Gallagher, d. 25 Jul 1850.]

Galloway, Aquila, d. "years ago" (death noted in Record of Members in 1847) [Ed. Note: Death notice in the Baltimore Sun stated that Aquilla Galloway, Sr. d. 28 Jan 1843 and Aquilla Galloway, Jr. d. 21 Mar 1844.]

Galloway, Marion DeKalb and Martha Metz m. 29 Feb 1848 by Rev. Stephen A. Roszel, lic. dated 28 Feb 1848

Galloway, Mary Eliza, dau. of Aquilla and Margaret Galloway, aged 2 months [ b. 1839], bapt. 22 Feb 1840 by Rev. Thomas Myers

Gambill, William F. and Cassandra A. Bush m. 23 Dec 1849 by Rev. Aquila A. Reese, lic. dated 22 Dec 1849 [Ed. Note: Their marriage notice in the Baltimore Sun gave their names as William F. Gambrill and Casandra Bush, dau. of David Bush.]

Gamble, James (Rev.) and Julia Ann Rowe m. 21 Feb 1843 at the house of Mr. Mettee in Baltimore by Rev. Beverly Waugh, lic. dated 20 Feb 1843

Gamble, Mary and Henry Kone m. 1 Sep 1843 by Rev. Joseph Shane

Gamble, Ruth, d. circa 1840-1847 (exact date not given in Record of Members)

Gambrel, William and Eliza H. Heacock m. 2 Sep 1840 by Rev. Joseph Shane

Gambrill, William, see "William F. Gambill," q.v.

Gardner, Ann Maria, dau. of William and Ellen Gardner, b. 26 Jun 1840, bapt. 9 Aug 1840 by Rev. Isaac P. Cook

Gardner, Anna Jane, dau. of ---- [blank], b. 26 Feb 1844, bapt. 20 Sep 1863 by Rev. Alexander E. Gibson

Gardner, Anna Maria, dau. of Francis Robert and Lucretia Gardner, b. 9 Aug 1841, bapt. 12 Apr 1846 by Rev. Dr. George C. M. Roberts

Gardner, Catharine and John Jones m. 15 Apr 1847 by Rev. Stephen A. Roszel, lic. dated 13 Apr 1847

Gardner, Charles Henning, son of Francis Robert and Lucretia Gardner, b. 1 Dec 1839, bapt. 12 Apr 1846 by Rev. Dr. George C. M. Roberts

Gardner, Christopher and Elizabeth Peacock m. 23 Jun 1841 by Rev. Dr. George C. M. Roberts

Gardner, David A. and Ursula Reeve m. 30 Apr 1845 by Rev. James Sewell, lic. dated same day

Gardner, Eliza J. and George P. Clark m. 3 Aug 1845 by Rev. Joseph Shane

Gardner, Emeline Worth, dau. of Francis R. and Lucretia Gardner, b. 10 Aug 1847, bapt. 22 Aug 1847 by Rev. Dr. George C. M. Roberts

Gardner, George C. M. Roberts, son of Francis Robert and Lucretia Gardner, b. 27 Apr 1845, bapt. 12 Apr 1846 by Rev. Dr. George C. M. Roberts

Gardner, George and Maria Turner m. 20 Oct 1842 by Rev. Dr. George C. M. Roberts

Gardner, James and Ann Jane Torrence m. ---- [blank] by Rev. John S. Martin, lic. dated 15 Jan 1850 [Ed. Note: Their marriage notice in the Baltimore Sun stated James Gardiner m. Ann J. Torrance, dau. of William Torrance, on 23 Jan 1850.]

Gardner, Lucretia Glenn, dau. of Francis Robert and Lucretia Gardner, b. 11 Apr 1843, bapt. 12 Apr 1846 by Rev. Dr. George C. M. Roberts

Gardner, Virginia Thomas, dau. of Francis Robert and Lucretia Gardner, b. 27 Apr 1845, bapt. 12 Apr 1846 by Rev. Dr. George C. M. Roberts

Gardner, William K. and Marinda Sayward m. 18 Feb 1844 by Rev. Henry Slicer, lic. dated 17 Feb 1844

Garish, Ann E. and William Hosinow m. 19 Sep 1847 by Rev. Stephen A. Roszel, lic. dated 13 Sep 1847

Garrett, Anna M. and Truman Hinman m. 2 Sep 1847 by Rev. Dr. George C. M. Roberts

Garrett, Richard and Sarah A. Amoss m. 4 Sep 1842 by Rev. Henry Slicer, lic. dated 3 Sep 1842

Garrett, Robert, son of John W. and Rachel A. Garrett, b. 9 Apr 1847, bapt. 20 Jan 1861 by Rev. Dr. George C. M. Roberts

Garrett, Thomas Harrison, son of John W. and Rachel A. Garrett, b. 11 Feb 1849, bapt. 20 Jan 1861 by Rev. Dr. George C. M. Roberts

Garthwait, Isaac and Elizabeth Gray m. 4 Dec 1842 by Rev. Henry Slicer, lic. dated 3 Dec 1842

Gatch, Jane White, dau. of Conduce and Jane W. Gatch, b. 21 Dec 1839, bapt. 23 Aug 1840 by Rev. Charles B. Tippett

Gates, Ezra and Sarah Amelia Glasgow, both of Baltimore County, m. 11 Jan 1846 by Rev. J. Hoffman Waugh, lic. dated 10 Jan 1846

Gaunt, Mary and John Tweedall, John and Mary Gaunt m. 19 Aug 1849 by Rev. William Hirst, lic. dated 18 Aug 1849

Gawthorp, Benjamin F. and Sarah Ann Erick m. ---- [blank] by Rev. James H. Brown, lic. dated 7 Nov 1848

Gees, Alfred Smith and Martha Ann Shawn m. 4 Oct 1846 by Rev. Littleton F. Morgan, lic. dated 1 Oct 1846 [*Ed. Note:* Their marriage notice in the *Baltimore Sun* gave their names as Alfred S. Geer and Martha A. Shoon.]

Geese, Mary A., d. circa 1841-1842 (exact date not given in Record of Members) [*Ed. Note:* Death notice in the *Baltimore Sun* stated that Mary A. Gees, wife of George Gees, d. 1 Jan 1842.]

George, Mary O. and William H. V. Cronise m. 21 Jan 1845 at the house of her mother in Baltimore by Rev. Beverly Waugh, lic. dated 20 Jan 1845

George, Stephen and Margaret L. Shamburg m. 4 Mar 1845 by Rev. Dr. George C. M. Roberts

Gephart, John, son of John and Ann L. Gephart, b. 21 Nov 1848, bapt. 22 Nov 1848 by Rev. Dr. George C. M. Roberts

Germain, Mary Elizabeth and William L. Wrightson m. 4 Oct 1849 by Rev. John S. Martin, lic. dated 3 Oct 1849

German, Caroline and George Holmes m. 17 Sep 1844 by Rev. Isaac P. Cook

German, Sarah and Isaac Wood m. 16 Feb 1843 by Rev. Henry Slicer, lic. dated 15 Feb 1843

Gesang, Anna M. and Frederick Fryers m. 18 Jul 1848 by Rev. Stephen A. Roszel, lic. dated 17 Jul 1848

Gettier, Henry and Ellen Henricks m. 8 Dec 1844 by Rev. James Sewell, lic. dated 7 Dec 1844

Gibbons, Joseph and Ann E. Langwell m. 16 Aug 1846 by Rev. Samuel Keppler (date of lic. not recorded)

Gibbons, Mary, d. 1845 (exact date not given in Record of Members) [*Ed. Note:* Death notice in the *Baltimore Sun* stated that Mary Gibbons, widow of John Gibbons, d. 22 Jul 1845.]

Gibbs, Mary, d. circa 1840 (exact date not given in Class Record) [*Ed. Note:* Death notice in the *Baltimore Sun* stated that Mary Gibbs d. 28 Feb 1840.]

Gibson, Mary A. and Samuel K. Sheckells m. 1 Jun 1847 by Rev. Dr. George C. M. Roberts

Gibson, Mary Ann and Francis Owens, both of Baltimore County, m. ---- [date not given] by Rev. George D. Chenoweth, lic. dated 3 Feb 1842

Gibson, Sarah, d. 1844 (death noted in Class List) [*Ed. Note:* Death notice in the *Baltimore Sun* stated that Sarah Gibson d. 19 Feb 1844.]

Gibson, Susan Eliza, dau. of James and Elizabeth Gibson, b. 14 Oct 1841, bapt. 23 Oct 1842 by Rev. Henry Slicer

Gildea, Charlotte and Leroy C. Ross m. 3 Mar 1842 by Rev. Isaac P. Cook

Gildea, Mary Ann and George Nunemaker m. 23 Mar 1840 by Rev. Joseph Shane

Gill, Ann M. E., d. circa 1842 (death noted in Probationers Book) [*Ed. Note:* The name "McCanty" was initially written in the book, subsequently lined out, and the name "Gill" was written above it.]

Gill, Eliza Ann and William Paul m. 27 Jan 1840 in Baltimore by Rev. Beverly Waugh, lic. dated 13 Jan 1840

Gill, Washington and Elizabeth Thompson m. 30 Apr 1843 by Rev. Dr. George C. M. Roberts

Gillespie, Sarah and John Clark m. 29 Aug 1842 by Rev. Dr. George C. M. Roberts

Gillet, George Lemuel, son of James and Mary Ann Gillet, b. 29 Aug 1838, bapt. 24 Apr 1842 by Rev. Job Guest

Gillet, James Francis, son of James and Mary Ann Gillet, b. 21 Aug 1841, bapt. 24 Apr 1842 by Rev. Job Guest

Gillman, Judson and Mary Ann Willis m. 7 Jun 1845 by Rev. Dr. George C. M. Roberts

Gilman, George Roberts, son of Dr. Judson and Mary Ann Gilman, b. 1 Jan 1846, bapt. 4 Jan 1846 by Rev. Dr. George C. M. Roberts

Gilman, Mary Catharine and David W. Long m. 19 Jan 1847

Gilpin, Elizabeth R., d. circa 1850 (exact date not given in Record of Members) [Ed. Note: Death notice in the Baltimore Sun stated that Elizabeth P. Gilpin, wife of Henry L. Gilpin, d. 14 Jun 1850.]

Ginnevan, Anna P. and Columbus Tuttle m. 7 Jan 1845 by Rev. Dr. George C. M. Roberts

Girlett, Mary and Elijah R. Sinners m. 15 Aug 1847 by Rev. Isaac P. Cook

Gist, Margaret Louisa, dau. of William D. and Elizabeth F. Gist, b. 26 Feb 1820, bapt. 5 Sep 1848 by Rev. Dr. George C. M. Roberts

Gist, William, d. circa 1844 (exact date not given in Record of Members) [Ed. Note: Death notice in the Baltimore Sun stated that William Gist d. 4 Dec 1843.]

Gittings, Benjamin E. and Rachel M. Thompson m. 2 Jul 1850 by Rev. Henry Slicer, lic. dated same day

Gittings, Mary, d. 16 May 184- (year not given; death noted in Record of Members) [Ed. Note: Death notice in the Baltimore Sun stated that Mary Gittings, wife of Thomas Gittings, d. 16 May 1841.]

Given, William, son of George and Mary Given, b. 8 Apr 1840, bapt. 29 Apr 1840 by Rev. Thomas Myers

Gladding, Diana and John Walton m. 17 Nov 1847 by Rev. Dr. George C. M. Roberts

Glanding, James H. and Catherine A. Clanahan m. 8 Oct 1849 by Rev. Aquila A. Reese, lic. dated 7 Oct 1849

Glanville, Mary Catharine, dau. of James and Hannah Glanville, b. ---- [blank], bapt. 8 Mar 1840 by Rev. Thomas Myers

Glanville, Mary R. and David Ridgley m. 4 Aug 1846 by Rev. Isaac P. Cook

Glasgow, Elizabeth, d. circa 1845-1847 (exact date not given in Record of Members) [Ed. Note: Death notice in the Baltimore Sun stated that Elizabeth Glassgow, widow of William R. Glassgow, d. 26 Jan 1846.]

Glasgow, Sarah Amelia and Ezra Gates, both of Baltimore County, m. 11 Jan 1846 by Rev. J. Hoffman Waugh, lic. dated 10 Jan 1846

Glassgow, William H. and Ann B. Hooper, both of Baltimore County, m. 4 Jul 1840 by Rev. Thomas Myers, lic. dated 3 Jul 1840

Glassgow, William R., see "Elizabeth Glasgow," q.v.

Glenn, Elizabeth Starling, dau. of Michael and Martha Glenn, b. 24 Jan 1840, bapt. 19 Feb 1840 by Rev. Dr. George C. M. Roberts

Glenn, John T. and Margaret Ann Ford m. 11 Nov 1841 by Rev. Dr. George C. M. Roberts

Glinnin, Andrew and Mary Ann Miller, both of Baltimore County, m. ---- [date not given] by Rev. George D. Chenoweth, lic. dated 3 Feb 1842

Godwin, Ann Jane, dau. of Littleton and Ann Godwin, b. 10 Mar 1836 (1838?), bapt. 2 Feb 1840 by Rev. Isaac P. Cook

Godwin, David Mitchell, son of Littleton and Ann Godwin, b. 9 Oct 1839, bapt. 2 Feb 1840 by Rev. Isaac P. Cook

Godwin, Mary Ann and James H. Fenix m. 11 Sep 1849 by Rev. John S. Martin, lic. dated same day

Godwin, Walter Elijah, son of Littleton and Ann Godwin, b. 29 Dec 1833, bapt. 2 Feb 1840 by Rev. Isaac P. Cook

Goldman, Ann Maria and George W. Holdin m. 21 Nov 1847 by Rev. Dr. George C. M. Roberts

Goll, William and Elizabeth Hook m. 7 Nov 1844 by Rev. Dr. George C. M. Roberts

Gollibert, James Shutter, son of Simon R. and Mary Gollibert, b. 28 Dec 1849, bapt. 4 Jul 1851 by Rev. Dr. George C. M. Roberts

Goodfellow, Joseph and Agnes A. Robinson m. 10 Jul 1849 by Rev. John S. Martin, lic. dated 9 Jul 1849

Goodhand, Angelina, d. circa 1845-1847 (exact date not given in Record of Members) [Ed. Note: Death notice in the Baltimore Sun stated that Angeline P. Goodhand, wife of John Goodhand, d. 2 Jun 1846.]

Goodhand, James B. and Elizabeth Ann Horner, both of Baltimore County, m. 19 Jun 1845 by Rev. William Hamilton, lic. dated 18 Jun 1845

Goodhand, John, see "Angelina Goodhand," q.v.

Goodwin, Mary, dau. of William and Mary E. Goodwin, b. 8 Jun 1846,, bapt. 5 Oct 1846 by Rev. Dr. George C. M. Roberts

Gordon, Abraham M. E., son of George W. and Jane Gordon, b. 10 Sep 1841, bapt. 10 Oct 1842 by Rev. William Prettyman

Gordon, Ruthey Jane, dau. of John and Catherine Gordon, b. 28 Feb 1843, bapt. 20 Apr 1844 by Rev. James Sewell

Gorell, Robert Hayes, son of Edward and Mary Gorell, b. 19 Dec 1840, bapt. 28 Jan 1842 by Rev. William Prettyman

Gorman, James T. and Mary Ann Spencer m. 14 Dec 1847 by Rev. Stephen A. Roszel, lic. dated 9 Dec 1847

Gorsuch, Amanda M. and Jacob M. Andrews m. 12 Jul 1840 by Rev. Samuel Keppler, lic. dated 9 Jul 1840

Gorsuch, Charles D., see "Elizabeth Gossage," q.v.

Gorsuch, Elizabeth, see "Elizabeth Gossage," q.v.

Gorsuch, Susan, d. after 1840 (exact date not given in Record of Members) [Ed. Note: Death notice in the Baltimore Sun stated that Susannah Gorsuch d. 29 Dec 1841.]

Gorsuch, Thomas and Sarah Ann Hill m. 10 Sep 1845 by Rev. Samuel Keppler (date of lic. not recorded)

Goshell, Elezina and George Ravenset m. 17 Apr 1845 by Rev. James Sewell, lic. dated same day [Ed. Note: Their marriage notice in the Baltimore Sun gave their names as George Ravenot and Elezine Goshell.]

Gosloe, Bridget and David Inloes m. 26 Jul 1841 by Rev. Isaac P. Cook

Gosnell, Clarissa and Cornelius Comegys m. 25 Nov 1847 by Rev. Isaac P. Cook

Gosnell, Douglass E. and Eleanora Coulson m. 16 May 1850 by Rev. Henry Slicer, lic. dated 29 Jan 1850

Gosnell, Mary Ellen and James Dicus m. 8 Jun 1845 by Rev. Isaac P. Cook

Gosnell, Mary Ann, d. circa 1840-1847 (exact date not given in Record of Members)

Gosnell, Rachel and George W. Mellon m. 21 May 1845 by Rev. Joseph Shane

Gosnell, Susanna and Philip Sherwood m. 24 Sep 1840 by Rev. Samuel Keppler, lic. dated same day

Gossage, E lizabeth, d. "18 m onths a go" ( exact d ate n ot g iven; d eath n oted i n Record of Members compiled circa 1847-1849) [Ed. Note: She was possibly the Elizabeth Gorsuch in the Baltimore Sun (widow of Charles D. Gorsuch and dau. of Andrew and Phebe Brunner) who d. 10 Jan 1847.]

Got, Virginia Ford, dau. of Thomas J. Got, aged 6 weeks, b. Baltimore City, bapt. 1840 (exact date not given) by Rev. Gerard Morgan

Gott, Elizabeth A. and Edward Norwood Trimble m. 19 Mar 1850 by Rev. Joseph Shane

Gould, Moses Alexander, son of Alexander and Elizabeth H. Gould, b. 14 Oct 1847, bapt. 26 Nov 1847 by Rev. Dr. George C. M. Roberts

Goulden, Caroline and Basil W. Leary m. 5 Oct 1845 by Rev. Samuel Keppler (date of lic. not recorded)

Grace, Eliza and Charles S. Bender m. ---- [blank] by Rev. John S. Martin, lic. dated 30 Oct 1849

Graff, Araminta and Joseph S. Weathers m. 4 Oct 1842 by Rev. Job Guest, lic. dated -- Oct 1842

Grafflin, Christopher L. and Elizabeth A. Stansbury m. 25 Apr 1850 by Rev. Henry Slicer, lic. dated same day

Grafton, Samuel H. and Mary E. David m. 4 Sep 1847 by Rev. Benjamin F. Brooke

Graham, Julia Ann, d. 1849 (death noted in Class List)

Graham, Victorine and Jesse Walker m. 5 Aug 1845 by Rev. Isaac P. Cook

Graham, William and Ann Reese m. 10 Jul 1843 by Rev. Isaac P. Cook

Granite, Sebastian and Amanda Comine m. 2 Apr 1849 by Rev. Dr. George C. M. Roberts

Grant, Jane E. and Thomas Strider m. 17 Jan 1843 by Rev. Isaac P. Cook

Grapevine, Elizabeth, d. circa 1847-1850 (exact date not given in Record of Members) [Ed. Note: Death notice in the Baltimore Sun stated that Elizabeth Grapevine, widow of Frederick Grapevine, d. 9 Feb 1850.]

Grapevine, Frederick, d. circa 1840 (exact date not given in Class Record)

Gravenstine, Jacob and Ann M. V. Dew m. 9 May 1844 by Rev. Joseph Shane [Ed. Note: Their marriage notice in the Baltimore Sun gave her name as Anna M. V. Dew, dau. of William Dew.]

Graves, Harriet and John W. Zimmerman m. 27 Jan 1841 by Rev. Samuel Keppler, lic. dated same day

Graves, Robert, d. 1847 (death noted in Class List) [Ed. Note: Death notice in the Baltimore Sun stated that Robert Graves d. 20 Mar 1847.]

Gray, Adams and Phoebe Davis m. 19 Nov 1840 by Rev. Samuel Keppler, lic. dated same day

Gray, Amanda J. and John Gray m. 27 Oct 1842 by Rev. Henry Slicer, lic. dated 24 Oct 1842

Gray, Ann and James Thornes m. 17 Sep 1843 by Rev. Samuel Brison

Gray, Charles Edward and Mary Elizabeth Reese m. 3 Feb 1848 by Rev. Isaac P. Cook

Gray, Elizabeth and Isaac Garthwait m. 4 Dec 1842 by Rev. Henry Slicer, lic. dated 3 Dec 1842

Gray, Elizabeth Ann, dau. of George and Elizabeth Gray, b. 2 Oct 1840, bapt. 7 Oct 1840 by Rev. John Bear

Gray, George Washington, son of George and Elizabeth Gray, b. 23 Jul 1838, bapt. 6 Sep 1840 by Rev. John Bear

Gray, John and Amanda J. Gray m. 27 Oct 1842 by Rev. Henry Slicer, lic. dated 24 Oct 1842

Gray, Leonard Wood, son of George and Elizabeth Gray, b. 6 Dec 1835, bapt. 7 Oct 1840 by Rev. John Bear

Gray, Louisa and James J. Humphreys m. 29 Sep 1848 by Rev. Joseph Shane

Gray, Nelson and Elmira Boswick m. 3 Oct 1841 by Rev. Isaac P. Cook

Green, Amon and Mary Heaney m. 23 Aug 1842 by Rev. Isaac P. Cook

Green, Ann Rebecca and Thomas Henry Harrison m. 14 Nov 1850 by Rev. Joseph Shane

Green, Benjamin F. and Elizabeth Riley m. 20 Sep 1841 by Rev. Isaac P. Cook

Green, Frederick Clark, son of Frederick S. and Margaret Louisa Green, b. 3 Jul 1850, bapt. 30 Jul 1851 by Rev. Dr. George C. M. Roberts

Green, George G. and Diantha E. Jewett m. 4 Sep 1848 by Rev. Dr. George C. M. Roberts

Green, Maria and Jonathan Clash m. 12 May 1842 by Rev. Samuel Brison

Green, Martha and Joseph G. Summers, both of Baltimore County, m. 19 Jun 1845 by Rev. William Hamilton, lic. dated 18 Jun 1845

Green, Mary, d. circa 1850 (exact date not given in Record of Members) [Ed. Note: She was possibly the Mary A. Green reported in the Baltimore Sun who d. 17 Dec 1850.]

Green, Mary, d. 5 Feb 1848 (death noted in Record of Members) [Ed. Note: Death notice in the Baltimore Sun stated that Mary Green, wife of William Green, d. 25 Feb 1848.]

Green, Richard M. and Elizabeth A. Elssrode m. 1 May 1846 by Rev. Wesley Stevenson [Ed. Note: Her name was given as "A. Elsrode" in their Baltimore Sun marriage notice.]

Green, Sarah and John Walworthy m. 6 Jan 1846 by Rev. Dr. George C. M. Roberts

Green, William, see "Mary Green," q.v.

Greenfield, A. (male), d. circa 1850 (exact date not given in Record of Members) [Ed. Note: Death notice in the Baltimore Sun stated that Aquila H. Greenfield d. 14 Sep 1850.]

Greenfield, Joel and Josephine Tilghman m. 5 Sep 1844 by Rev. Isaac P. Cook

Greenfield, Sarah Ann and David D. Buckey m. 8 Jun 1847 by Rev. Littleton F. Morgan, lic. dated 7 Jun 1847

Greenly, Eliza and George H. Joyce m. 8 Oct 1843 by Rev. Dr. George C. M. Roberts

Greer, Robert A. and Laura E. Tyson m. 21 Jul 1847 by Rev. Dr. George C. M. Roberts

Greerson, Robert G. and Sophia A. Simmons m. 12 (13?) [ink smudged] Dec 1848 by Rev. William Hirst

Gregg, John and Ruth Ann Woodward m. 22 May 1845 by Rev. Dr. George C. M. Roberts

Gregory, Eleanor and Joshua J. Brown m. 3 Jan 1844 by Rev. Henry Slicer, lic. dated 2 Jan 1844

Gregory, Eliza and Augustus F. Montague m. 2 Jul 1844 by Rev. Dr. George C. M. Roberts

Gregory, Emilie A. and Charles B. Vickory m. 5 Dec 1847 by Rev. Stephen A. Roszel, lic. dated 4 Dec 1847

Gregory, Lavenia and David Noble m. 28 Dec 1848 by Rev. Joseph Shane

Gregory, Mary and Joseph Roberts m. 7 Aug 1842 by Rev. Henry Slicer, lic. dated 6 Aug 1842

Gregory, Sarah and Robert Fish m. 31 Mar 1844 by Rev. Joseph Merriken

Grey, John T. (M.D.), and Cordelia Ann Briscoe m. 17 Aug 1841 by Rev. Dr. George C. M. Roberts

Gridley, Catharine, d. circa 1840-1847 (exact date not given in Record of Members)

Gridley, Ruth, d. circa 1850 (exact date not given in Record of Members) [Ed. Note: Death notice in the Baltimore Sun stated that Ruth G. Gridley, widow of Samuel Gridley, d. before 10 Jul 1850.]

Grieves, Elizabeth A. and James N. Muir m. 28 Jun 1842 by Rev. Henry Slicer, lic. dated same day

Griffin, Elizabeth, dau. of Robert Burns and Elizabeth Griffin, b. 10 May 1848, bapt. 14 Aug 1848 by Rev. Dr. George C. M. Roberts

Griffin, Hester Ann and William G. Fletcher m. 14 Dec 1843 by Rev. Dr. George C. M. Roberts

Griffin, Hester Ann (coloured), son of Mary Griffin, b. ---- "not given" [sic], bapt. 15 Jan 1843 by Rev. Isaac P. Cook

Griffin, Julia A. and John F. Herbert, both of Baltimore County, m. 15 Sep 1842 by Rev. Nelson Head

Griffin, William and Margaret E. Brown m. 26 Dec 1848 by Rev. Stephen A. Roszel, lic. dated same day

Griffith, Georgiana and Rev. John Maclay m. 19 Apr 1849 by Rev. Dr. George C. M. Roberts

Griffith, Grace, d. 1849 (death noted in Class List)

Griffith, Henry Magruder, son of Richard H. and Susan M. Griffith, b. 25 Apr 1848, bapt. 19 Jun 1848 by Rev. Dr. George C. M. Roberts

Griffith, James T. and Maria Logan m. 13 Jun 1850 by Rev. Henry Slicer, lic. dated 29 May 1850

Griffith, John, see "Sarah Griffith," q.v.

Griffith, John Anna, child of John H. and Susan Emeline Griffith, b. 17 Jun 1849, bapt. 9 Jan 1853 by Rev. Dr. George C. M. Roberts

Griffith, Margaret, d. 1845 (death noted in Class List)

Griffith, Maria Elizabeth and George Sipe m. 14 Jan 1849 by Rev. Joseph Shane

Griffith, Mary E. and Walter Farnandis, Jr. m. 17 Oct 1850 by Rev. Dr. George C. M. Roberts

Griffith, Sarah, d. 1 Oct 1842 (death noted in Record of Members) [Ed. Note: Death notice in the Baltimore Sun stated that Sarah Griffith, widow of John Griffith, d. 1 Oct 1842.]

Griffith, Sophia and John S. Jones m. 21 Mar 1849 by Rev. William Hirst

Griffith, Susan Emily, dau. of Capt. John and Susan Griffith, b. 8 Apr 1841, bapt. 10 Aug 1843 by Rev. Dr. George C. M. Roberts

Griffith, Vermidella, dau. of John H. and Susan Emeline Griffith, b. 29 Nov 1843, bapt. 9 Jan 1853 by Rev. Dr. George C. M. Roberts

Grillett, James, d. circa 1845-1847 (exact date not given in Record of Members)

Grim, Hester Ann and John F. Wall m. 2 Jul 1850 by Rev. Henry Slicer, lic. dated same day

Grimes, Anna Maria and Joshua Owings m. 4 Dec 1849 by Rev. Joseph Shane

Grimes, Jesse W. and Sarah A. Thompson m. 12 Nov 1849 by Rev. Aquila A. Reese, lic. dated 11 Nov 1849

Grinnage, Elizabeth (colored) and George Johnson (colored) m. 2 Jul 1846 by Rev. Samuel Keppler

Griswold, Charles and Ann Johnson m. 29 Aug 1844 by Rev. Isaac P. Cook

Grivell, John, son of John and Sophia Grivell, b. 21 Jun 1840, bapt. 27 Jul 1841 by Rev. Isaac P. Cook

Grivell, Mary H., dau. of John and Sophia Grivell, b. 29 Mar 1838, bapt. 27 Jul 1841 by Rev. Isaac P. Cook

Grooms, Thomas and Isabella E. S. Sherington m. 20 Sep 1846 by Rev. Samuel Keppler (date of lic. not recorded)

Gross, Margaret and Frederick Shepherd m. 24 Jun 1849 by Rev. Joseph Shane

Grove, Daniel L. and Margaret C. Schaffer m. 19 Jan 1843 by Rev. Dr. George C. M. Roberts

Groverman, Anthony, son of Anthony and Helen Eliza Groverman, b. 17 Mar 1850, bapt. 20 Feb 1852 by Rev. Dr. George C. M. Roberts

Groves, John J. and Eliza P. Sank m. 25 Oct 1847 by Rev. Dr. George C. M. Roberts [*Ed. Note:* Their marriage notice in the *Baltimore Sun* gave their names as Eliza Sank and John T. Groves.]

Groves, Sarah H., d. circa 1840 (exact date not given in Class Record)

Grubb, John and Christianna Cross m. 13 Jun 1843 by Rev. Dr. George C. M. Roberts

Guest, Martha Ann and Joseph D. Bruff m. 16 Nov 1841 by Rev. Job Guest, lic. dated 15 Nov 1841

Guest, Richard W., d. circa 1840-1847 (exact date not given in Record of Members)

Gunby, Francis A. and Eleanora Frazier m. 25 Apr 1841 by Rev. Isaac P. Cook

Guyton, Ella, dau. of Beale S. and Mary L. Guyton, b. 13 Sep 1850, bapt. 1 Jan 1851 by Rev. Dr. George C. M. Roberts

Guyton, Orville, son of Beale S. and Mary L. Guyton, b. 22 Feb 1847, bapt. 1 Jan 1851 by Rev. Dr. George C. M. Roberts

Habner, Matilda A. and David O'Laughlin m. 9 Nov 1842 by Rev. Isaac P. Cook

Hack, John W. and E. Gifford Ervin m. 6 Sep 1846 by Rev. Littleton F. Morgan, lic. dated 5 Sep 1846

Hacket, Eliza Ann and Jacob H. Webb m. 23 Mar 1844 by Rev. Isaac P. Cook

Hackett, Edward and Mary Ann Riley m. 15 Jun 1848 by Rev. Isaac P. Cook

Hackett, James Franklin Green, son of Edward and Mary Ann Hackett, b. 26 Jun 1848, bapt. 24 Jul 1848 by Rev. Dr. George C. M. Roberts

Hackett, John B. and Lucinda Shipley m. 31 Jan 1850 by Rev. Isaac P. Cook

Hackett, Margaret A. and Allen L. Wilson m. 18 Mar 1849 by Rev. Aquila A. Reese, lic. dated 17 Mar 1849

Hackett, William and Mary Pennington m. 11 Apr 1844 by Rev. James Sewell, lic. dated same day

Hadaway, Harriet and Edward Hudson m. 5 Apr 1847 by Rev. Dr. George C. M. Roberts

Hadaway, James H. and Ann Maria Chance m. 23 Dec 1845 by Rev. Dr. George C. M. Roberts

Hadaway, James and Sarah Bond m. 15 Dec 1845 by Rev. Dr. George C. M. Roberts

Hadaway, Sarah A. and Absolem C. C. Thompson m. 30 May 1844 by Rev. James Sewell, lic. dated same day

Hadaway, Susan and Luke Brunker m. 29 Oct 1847 by Rev. Stephen A. Roszel, lic. dated same day

Haden, Catherine L. and Thomas C. Bayard m. 20 May 1850 by Rev. Henry Slicer, lic. dated same day

Hagan, Ellen and James Delay m. 1 Aug 1842 by Rev. Job Guest, lic. dated same day

Hagan, John H. and Margaret Ann Dell, both of Baltimore County, m. 1 Jan 1843 by Rev. Nelson Head

Hager, Sarah Jane, dau. of Charles and Sarah Hager, b. 21 Sep 1830, bapt. 24 Sep 1841 by Rev. Dr. George C. M. Roberts

Hagerty, Sarah, d. by 1840 (exact date not given in Class Record) [Ed. Note: Death notice in the Baltimore Sun stated that Sarah Haggerty, widow of John Haggerty, d. 30 Dec 1838.]

Haggerty, Georgeanna and George V. Keen m. 1 Jan 1845 by Rev. Dr. George C. M. Roberts

Hagner, Mary and Charles E. Buckingham m. 31 Jan 1847 by Rev. Dr. George C. M. Roberts

Hahn, James H. and Ann E. McCrone m. 19 Apr 1849 by Rev. Isaac P. Cook

Hainesworth, Henry S. and Sarah A. White m. 20 Sep 1847 by Rev. Dr. George C. M. Roberts

Hains, Sophia and Robert H. Shipley m. 28 May 1846 by Rev. Littleton F. Morgan, lic. dated same day

Hale, Ann Maria and John A. Scheerer m. 2 Sep 1845 by Rev. Dr. George C. M. Roberts

Hall, Adaline E., dau. of Alexander Hall, b. 24 Apr 1840, bapt. -- Jul 1840 by Rev. John A. Hening

Hall, Amelia, an orphan in the Female Asylum in Mulberry Street, b. 9 Dec 1837, bapt. 4 Oct 1840 by Rev. Thomas Myers

Hall, Ann Emily and Robert Ashcroft m. 6 Nov 1845 by Rev. Samuel Keppler (date of lic. not recorded)

Hall, Edward, d. after 1841 (death noted in Class List) [Ed. Note: Death notice in the Baltimore Sun stated that Edward Hall d. 1 Apr 1843.]

Hall, Eliza Ann, dau. of John and Eliza Hall, b. 6 Oct 1839, bapt. 6 Jun 1840 by Rev. Dr. George C. M. Roberts

Hall, Elizabeth Ann and Elbridge G. Kilbourn m. 6 Nov 1849 at the house of her mother in Baltimore by Rev. Beverly Waugh, lic. dated same day

Hall, Ellenor Forman, dau. of ---- and ---esa A. Hall [page torn], b. 6 Jan 1841, bapt. ---- 184- [page torn] by Rev. ---- (name not indicated) [Ed. Note: Information was written on a piece of paper and inserted in the church register.]

Hall, George, d. 1845 (death noted in Class List) [Ed. Note: Death notice in the Baltimore Sun stated that George N. O. Hall d. 2 Apr 1845.]

Hall, George and Esther Jane Taylor m. 13 Sep 1849 by Rev. John S. Martin, lic. dated same day

Hall, John R. and Virginia Appold m. 1 Nov 1849 at the house of her father in Baltimore by Rev. Beverly Waugh, lic. dated same day

Hall, John Thomas, son of ---- [blank], b. 19 Nov 1839, bapt. -- Jul 1840 by Rev. John A. Hening

Hall, John Wesley, son of John and Almira Hall, b. 25 Sep 1842, bapt. 6 Jan 1843 by Rev. William Prettyman

Hall, Joseph, son of ---- and ---esa A. Hall [page torn], b. 3 Jul 1839, bapt. ---- 184- [page torn] by Rev. ---- (name not indicated) [Ed. Note: Information was written on a piece of paper and inserted in the church register.]

Hall, Juliet S. and Francis A. Williams m. ---- [no date given] by Rev. John Miller, lic. dated 16 May 1850

Hall, Mary, d. circa 1841 (death noted in Class List) [Ed. Note: Death notice in the Baltimore Sun stated that Mary Hall, wife of S. H. Hall, d. 15 Mar 1840.]

Hall, Mary Ann and Samuel Hopkins m. 11 Nov 1847 by Rev. Littleton F. Morgan, lic. dated 10 Nov 1847

Hall, Robert J. and Rebecca A. Prill (Price?), both of Baltimore County, m. 26 Feb 1846 by Rev. William Hamilton

Hall, S. H., see "Mary Hall," q.v.

Hall, Theodore Thomas and Sarah Jane Dryden m. 6 Jul 1847 by Rev. Littleton F. Morgan, lic. dated same day

Hall, Thomas and Elizabeth Ratcliff m. 22 Jul 1843 by Rev. Joseph Shane

Hall, Thomas L. and Rebecca Poits m. 26 Oct 1843 at the house of her mother Mrs. Chaytor in Baltimore by Rev. Beverly Waugh, lic. dated 26 Oct 1843 [Ed. Note: Their marriage notice in the Baltimore Sun gave her name as Rebecca P. Chaytor.]

Hall, William, son of John and Almira Hall, b. 12 May 1840, bapt. 6 Jan 1843 by Rev. William Prettyman

Halsey, William and Emily J. Butler m. 12 Mar 1846 by Rev. Joseph Shane

Hamal, Caroline M. and William J. Bowling m. 15 Jul 1850 by Rev. John S. Martin, lic. dated 13 Jul 1850

Hamberd, Louis and Mary Fisher m. 8 Nov 1850 by Rev. Isaac P. Cook

Hamilton, Ann and John Perrian m. 24 Nov 1840 by Rev. Samuel Keppler, lic. dated same day

Hamilton, Caroline and Benjamin Jeffrey m. 3 Dec 1846 by Rev. Isaac P. Cook

Hamilton, Edward and Mary Vanderford m. 19 Feb 1846 by Rev. Dr. George C. M. Roberts

Hamilton, Louisa McClean, dau. of Philip and Rebecca Hamilton (residents of New York), b. 1 Jul 1844, bapt. 14 Oct 1844 by Rev. Dr. George C. M. Roberts

Hamilton, Lydia J. and George Colton m. 27 Sep 1842 by Rev. Henry Slicer, lic. dated same day

Hamilton, Matthew G. (Rev.) and Eliza P. Uhler m. 9 Jan 1843 at the house of Dr. Davis in Baltimore by Rev. Beverly Waugh, lic. dated 7 Jan 1843

Hamilton, Maxwell and Charlotte Redman m. 5 Sep 1841 by Rev. Joseph Shane

Hamilton, Philip and Rebecca, see "Louisa McClean Hamilton," q.v.

Hamilton, Washington and Catherine Parker m. 8 Apr 1849 by Rev. Aquila A. Reese, lic. dated 7 Apr 1849

Hamilton, Wesley and Henrietta Wilson m. 1 Oct 1843 by Rev. Joseph Shane

Hammer, William C. and Jane Biays Alvey m. 9 Oct 1845 by Rev. James Sewell, lic. dated 8 Oct 1845

Hammersley, David L. and Elizabeth Boden m. 8 Sep 1842 by Rev. Henry Slicer, lic. dated 13 Aug 1842

Hammett, Diana Narcissa, dau. of Samuel and Narcissa Hammett, b. 29 Mar 1818, bapt. 25 Sep 1742 by Rev. Henry Slicer

Hammock, George M. and Margaret Ann Murray m. 3 Jun 1847 by Rev. Stephen A. Roszel, lic. dated 2 Jun 1847

Hammond, Caroline, d. circa 1845-1847 (exact date not given in Record of Members)

Hammond, Clorinda and Nicholas Wyant m. 19 Nov 1843 by Rev. Dr. George C. M. Roberts

Hammond, Elvira and Leonard Hawk m. 4 May 1847 by Rev. Joseph Shane

Hammond, George Washington and Elvira Love m. 11 Apr 1843 by Rev. Samuel Brison

Hampton, Robert B. and Ann R. Weedon m. 12 Dec 1845 by Rev. Dr. George C. M. Roberts

Hance, Sarah J. and Samuel B. Wilson m. 5 Dec 1847 by Rev. Littleton F. Morgan, lic. dated 4 Dec 1847

Hancock, Ann, d. circa 1847-1850 (exact date not given in Record of Members)

Hancock, Nancy and William H. Kelly m. 18 Jan 1846 by Rev. Dr. George C. M. Roberts

Handy, George W. and Eliza J. Newton, both of Baltimore County, m. 19 Mar 1846 by Rev. J. Hoffman Waugh, lic. dated same day

Haney, Sarah and John Simone m. 21 Aug 1842 by Rev. Joseph Shane

Haney, William M. and Ann Maria Brannan m. 27 Jul 1848 by Rev. Stephen A. Roszel, lic. dated same day

Hanna, Charles Henry, son of John and Elizabeth Hanna, b. 1826, bapt. 26 Mar 1841, aged 15 by Rev. Gerard Morgan

Hanna, George Washington, son of John and Elizabeth Hanna, b. ---- [blank], bapt. 26 Mar 1841, aged 21 by Rev. Gerard Morgan

Hanson, James (colored) and Margaret Cooper (colored) m. 5 Sep 1842 by Rev. Henry Slicer, lic. dated same day

Harback, Wilhelmina and Gerritt DeGraff m. 7 Sep 1850 by Rev. Isaac P. Cook

Harden, Sophia Ann, dau. of Stephen and Mary Ann Harden, aged 14 years [b. 1829 or 1830], bapt. 7 Jan 1844 by Rev. Isaac P. Cook

Hardester, Benjamin, b. 22 Dec 1760, bapt. -- May 1842 by Rev. William Prettyman

Hardestie, Priscilla and John R. Paddy m. 14 Oct 1845 by Rev. James Sewell, lic. dated 23 Aug 1845

Hardesty, Benjamin, d. 1841 (death noted in Class List)

Hardesty, Daniel and Eliza J. Norfolk m. 5 Aug 1845 by Rev. Dr. George C. M. Roberts

Hardesty, Louisa A. and Nehemiah Miller m. 16 Dec 1845 by Rev. Dr. George C. M. Roberts

Hardesty, Priscilla and Joseph Parson m. 23 Dec 1849 by Rev. William Hirst, lic. dated 22 Dec 1849

Hardie, Emily Alice, dau. of Robert and Emily Hardie, b. -- Sep 1840, bapt. 30 Dec 1840 by Rev. Thomas Myers

Hardy, Ann and Louis J. Watkins m. 20 Apr 1843 by Rev. Dr. George C. M. Roberts

Hardy, Eliza Jane and Thomas H. Fitzgerald m. 7 Oct 1847 by Rev. Benjamin F. Brooke

Hardy, Lavinia A. and Alexander R. Medairy m. 15 Jul 1847 by Rev. Stephen A. Roszel, lic. dated 13 Jul 1847

Hare, Ephraim and Anna Owens m. 18 Nov 1848 by Rev. Joseph Shane

Harford, Elizabeth A. and Jesse House m. 11 Jan 1844 by Rev. Isaac P. Cook

Harford, Martha M., see "Martha M. Hartford," q.v.

Harlow, Caroline and Thomas W. Lucas m. 2 Jan 1844 by Rev. Henry Slicer, lic. dated same day

Harman, Margaret Ann and James Lawrence McPhail, both of Baltimore County, m. 5 Nov 1840 by Rev. Thomas Myers, lic. dated same day

Harman, Mary Ann Louisa and John Smith m. 24 Sep 1849 by Rev. Aquila A. Reese, lic. dated 23 Sep 1849

Harmon, Margaret C., d. -- Mar 1845 (death noted in Record of Members) [*Ed. Note:* Death notice in the *Baltimore Sun* stated that Margaret E. Harmon, wife of Joseph Harmon, d. 26 Mar 1845.]

Harney, Jacob and Ann Maria Smith m. 27 Jul 1843 by Rev. Joseph Shane

Harp, John and Cecelia Shaw m. 13 Sep 1842 by Rev. Henry Slicer, lic. dated 12 Sep 1842

Harp, Sarah A. and John A. Riddell m. 11 Aug 1847 by Rev. Stephen A. Roszel, lic. dated same day

Harriman, Mary Rebecca, dau. of William D. and Julia A. Harriman, b. 5 Nov 1839, bapt. 2 Mar 1843 by Rev. William Prettyman

Harriman, Sarah Elizabeth, dau. of William D. and Julia A. Harriman, b. 15 Aug 1842, bapt. 2 Mar 1843 by Rev. William Prettyman

Harrington, Deborah Zigler, dau. of Thomas and Louisa Harrington, b. 17 Sep 1842, bapt. 7 Apr 1850 by Rev. Dr. George C. M. Roberts

Harrington, Frances Ann and Daniel Thomas Evans m. 16 Jul 1848 by Rev. Stephen A. Roszel, lic. dated 14 Jul 1848

Harrington, James and Maria Hooper m. 2 Oct 1845 by Rev. Dr. George C. M. Roberts

Harrington, Maria and Samuel T. Newell m. 23 Jul 1844 by Rev. Dr. George C. M. Roberts

Harrington, Robert and Mary A. Logue m. 14 Dec 1848 by Rev. Stephen A. Roszel, lic. dated 13 Dec 1848

Harrington, Sophia Wilson, dau. of Thomas and Louisa Harrington, b. 9 Sep 1845, bapt. 7 Apr 1850 by Rev. Dr. George C. M. Roberts

Harrington, Thomas and Louisa Zigler m. 26 Aug 1841 by Rev. Dr. George C. M. Roberts

Harris, Anna E. and Charles W. Ballard m. 2 Feb 1850 at the house of her mother in Baltimore by Rev. Beverly Waugh, lic. dated same day

Harris, Benjamin F. and Mary J. Krager, both of Baltimore County, m. ---- [date not given] by Rev. George Hildt, lic. dated 25 Mar 1846

Harris, Caroline, d. 1841 (death noted in Class List)

Harris, Clarissa, d. circa 1840-1847 (exact date not given in Record of Members)

Harris, Elizabeth L. and William Harris, both of Baltimore County, m. 9 Oct 1844 by Rev. William Hamilton

Harris, James Henry and Mary Amanda Wellen m. 6 Sep 1846 by Rev. Dr. George C. M. Roberts

Harris, Margaret Ann and John Thomas Lloyd m. 11 Jul 1842 by Rev. Samuel Brison

Harris, Martha Ann and Noah Bratt m. 7 Sep 1841 by Rev. Dr. George C. M. Roberts

Harris, Mary, d. 1849 (death noted in Class List) [*Ed. Note:* Death notice in the *Baltimore Sun* stated that Mary Harris, wife of William Harris, d. 29 Aug 1849.]

Harris, Mary C., dau. of William and Mary Harris, b. 1 Sep 1842, bapt. 16 Dec 1842 by Rev. Elisha D. Owen

Harris, Mary Elizabeth and Grafton Albaugh m. 31 May 1842 by Rev. Samuel Brison

Harris, Rebecca H. and James B. Ringgold, both of Baltimore County, m. 8 Dec 1845 by Rev. J. Hoffman Waugh, lic. dated 6 Dec 1845

Harris, Rufus Cain, son of Joseph and Ann Harris, b. 5 Oct 1839, bapt. 16 Oct 1840 by Rev. Dr. George C. M. Roberts

Harris, Samuel and Margaret Ann Kinnman m. 16 Apr 1844 by Rev. Joseph Merriken

Harris, Thomas C., d. circa 1844 (exact date not given in Record of Members) [*Ed. Note:* Death notice in the *Baltimore Sun* stated that Thomas G. Harris d. 14 Oct 1844.]

Harris, William, see "Mary Harris," q.v.

Harris, William and Elizabeth L. Harris, both of Baltimore County, m. 9 Oct 1844 by Rev. William Hamilton

Harris, William D., see "Ann Lamb," q.v.

Harris, William T. and Margaret M. Vickers m. 8 Nov 1848 by Rev. Dr. George C. M. Roberts

Harrison, Ann, d. circa 1844 (exact date not given in Record of Members) [*Ed. Note:* Death notice in the *Baltimore Sun* stated that Ann Harrison d. 10 Oct 1844.]

Harrison, Ann, d. circa 1847 (exact date not given in Record of Members) [*Ed. Note:* Death notice in the *Baltimore Sun* stated that Ann Harrison, widow of Jonathan Harrison, d. 7 Mar 1847.]

Harrison, Ann Elizabeth and Levin Jones m. 7 Jan 1849 by Rev. Stephen A. Roszel, lic. dated 6 Jan 1849

Harrison, Champion W. and Ann E. Hope m. 25 Aug 1842 by Rev. Dr. George C. M. Roberts

Harrison, Emily and William H. Harrison m. 21 Nov 1844 by Rev. Dr. George C. M. Roberts

Harrison, Frances A., d. circa 1844 (exact date not given in Record of Members) [*Ed. Note:* Death notice in the *Baltimore Sun* stated that Frances A. Harrison, widow of John Harrison, d. 11 Mar 1844.]

Harrison, John, see "Frances A. Harrison," q.v.

Harrison, Jonathan, see "Ann Harrison," q.v.

Harrison, Margaret S. and William W. Amoss m. 8 Jan 1848 by Rev. Benjamin F. Brooke

Harrison, Sarah, d. -- Sep 1847 (death noted in Record of Members) [*Ed. Note:* Death notice in the *Baltimore Sun* stated that Sarah Harrison, mother-in-law of A. P. Amoss, d. 30 Sep 1847.]

Harrison, Thomas Henry and Ann Rebecca Green m. 14 Nov 1850 by Rev. Joseph Shane

Harrison, Thomas S., d. circa 1840 (death noted in Class List)

Harrison, William H. and Charlotte Davis m. 1 Dec 1845 by Rev. Wesley Stevenson

Harrison, William H. and Emily Harrison m. 21 Nov 1844 by Rev. Dr. George C. M. Roberts

Harryman, Sarah Elizabeth, dau. of Walter and Sarah Harryman, b. 7 Jun 1846, bapt. 26 Nov 1846 by Rev. Dr. George C. M. Roberts

Hart, Francis and Sarah Walts m. 16 May 1847 by Rev. Joseph Shane

Hart, Francis B. and Mary J. Mulligan m. 7 Feb 1850 by Rev. Aquila A. Reese, lic. dated same day

Hartford, Martha, d. 1849 (death noted in Class List) [*Ed. Note:* Death notice in the *Baltimore Sun* stated that Martha M. Harford d. 25 Dec 1849.]

Hartley, George Edward and Emeline Cline m. 27 Dec 1847 by Rev. Stephen A. Roszel, lic. dated same day

Hartley, William J. and Anna Bowers m. ---- [blank] by Rev. John S. Martin, lic. dated 13 Sep 1850

Hartlove, Asbury and Mary A. Bayler m. 19 Sep 1841 by Rev. Dr. George C. M. Roberts

Hartlove, Charles H. and Eliza J. Simpson m. 12 Sep 1844 by Rev. Dr. George C. M. Roberts

Hartlove, Margaret Ann and Alexander Coleman m. 7 Jan 1849 by Rev. Joseph Shane

Hartman, Daniel and Mary Jane Taylor, both of Baltimore County, m. 27 Mar 1841 by Rev. John Rice

Hartman, Elizabeth and Jacob G. Bartzell m. 19 Aug 1841 by Rev. Dr. George C. M. Roberts

Hartzell, Emeline Matrona and William C. Fordes, both of Baltimore County, m. 14 Mar 1841 by Rev. John Rice

Harvey, Ann S. and Joseph T. Johnson m. 23 Dec 1841 by Rev. Dr. George C. M. Roberts

Harvey, Frances and Henry W. Moore m. 7 Jan 1849 by Rev. Dr. George C. M. Roberts

Harvey, Joseph Jr. and Emeline Armour m. 24 Mar 1840 by Rev. John Bear

Harwood, Laura Ann Eugenia, dau. of Richard A. and Elizabeth G. Harwood, b. 9 Feb 1849, bapt. 24 May 1849 by Rev. Dr. George C. M. Roberts

Harwood, Richard A. and Elizabeth G. Mayo m. 16 Mar 1848 by Rev. Dr. George C. M. Roberts

Haskell, Alexander and Catherine Aelman m. 26 May 1844 by Rev. James Sewell, lic. dated 25 May 1844

Haskitt, John, see "John J. Myers," q.v.

Hastings, Flowrence Edward Dunbar, son of William Henry and Hester Hastings, b. 11 Oct 1846, bapt. 10 Jan 1850 by Rev. John S. Martin

Hastings, John Edgar Wilcox, son of William Henry and Hester Hastings, b. 5 Oct 1848, bapt. 10 Jan 1850 by Rev. John S. Martin

Hatch, Catharine T., d. circa 1850 (exact date not given in Record of Members) [*Ed. Note:* Death notice in the *Baltimore Sun* stated that Catharine T. Hatch d. 24 Jul 1850.]

Hatch, Lydia, "died s houting" *[sic]* c irca 1 840 ( exact d ate n ot g iven i n C lass Record) [*Ed. Note:* Death notice in the *Baltimore Sun* stated that Lydia Hatch d. 15 Feb 1839.]

Hatch, Sarah, d. 1840 (death noted in Class List) [*Ed. Note:* Death notice in the *Baltimore Sun* stated that Sarah Hatch d. 26 Dec 1840.]

Hatchison, Catharine E. and Benjamin F. Shakespeare m. 22 Jul 1847 by Rev. Stephen A. Roszel, lic. dated 20 Jul 1847

Havenner, Elizabeth H. and William N. Rowe m. 28 Apr 1842 in Washington City by Rev. Henry Slicer, lic. dated same day

Hawk, Leonard and Elvira Hammond m. 4 May 1847 by Rev. Joseph Shane

Hawkins, Frances and William H. Chesney m. 7 Dec 1847 by Rev. Littleton F. Morgan, lic. dated 6 Dec 1847

Hawkins, Isaac (colored) and Mary J. Preston (colored) m. 27 Dec 1842 by Rev. Henry Slicer (date of lic. not recorded)

Hawkins, Samuel, d. circa 1849-1850 (exact date not given in Record of Members) [*Ed. Note:* Death notice in the *Baltimore Sun* stated that Samuel M. Hawkins d. 12 Jan 1850.]

Hayden, Richard H. and Elizabeth Daniel m. 29 Nov 1850 by Rev. Isaac P. Cook

Hayes, Susannah and Robert M. Ling m. 14 Jun 1844 by Rev. James Sewell, lic. dated 13 Jun 1844

Haynes, Robert and Catherine Lucas m. 24 Apr 1845 by Rev. James Sewell, lic. dated same day

Hayns, William D., d. 1841 (death noted in Class List)

Hays, Elizabeth and William H. H. Davis, both of Baltimore County, m. 3 Oct 1842 by Rev. Nelson Head

Hays, Robert and Mary Ann Holtz, both of Baltimore County, m. 25 Feb 1840 by Rev. Bernard H. Nadal

Hayward, William H. and Bridget Gallan m. 1 May 1842 by Rev. Isaac P. Cook

Haywood, Sarah, d. circa 1847-1850 (exact date not given in Record of Members)

Hazard, Ellen S. and John Conoway m. 20 Dec 1849 by Rev. Joseph Shane

Hazelhurst, Elizabeth B., dau. of Samuel and Elizabeth Hazelhurst, b. 30 May 1842, bapt. 28 Feb 1843 by Rev. Isaac P. Cook

Hazelhurst, Hugh Jenkins, son of Samuel and Elizabeth G. Hazelhurst, b. 1 Sep 1843, bapt. 4 Jan 1844 by Rev. Isaac P. Cook [*Ed. Note:* Name was spelled "Hazlehurst" in the register.]

Hazelhurst, Samuel and E. G. Bilson, both of Baltimore County, m. 18 Feb 1840 by Rev. Bernard H. Nadal

Hazen, Eugene Everett, son of John H. and Margaret Ann Hazen, b. 24 Jul 1848, bapt. 24 Sep 1848 by Rev. Dr. George C. M. Roberts

Heacock, Eliza H. and William Gambrel m. 2 Sep 1840 by Rev. Joseph Shane

Heald, John H. and Sidney A. Frazier m. 2 Nov 1843 at the house of her father in Baltimore by Rev. Beverly Waugh, lic. dated 1 Nov 1843

Heaney, Mary and Amon Green m. 23 Aug 1842 by Rev. Isaac P. Cook

Hebb, Joseph and Mary E. Smith m. 15 Dec 1847 by Rev. Stephen A. Roszel, lic. dated same day

Hebum(?), Rebecca J. and John Timmerman m. 18 Mar 1844 by Rev. Isaac P. Cook

Heffner, George C. M. Roberts, son of Edward and Elizabeth Ann Heffner, b. 23 Aug 1847, bapt. 31 Dec 1847 by Rev. Dr. George C. M. Roberts

Helme, Celina Roszel, dau. of ---- [blank], b. 23 Jun 1848, bapt. -- Jul 1849 by Rev. John S. Martin

Helsby, Thomas and Elizabeth Fardwell m. 27 Nov 1847 by Rev. Benjamin F. Brooke [Ed. Note: Their marriage notice in the Baltimore Sun states Thomas Elsby and Elizabeth Fardwell, dau. of Isaac, m. 28 Nov 1847.]

Hemmack, William and Emily L. Wright m. 21 Feb 1850 by Rev. Aquila A. Reese, lic. dated 20 Feb 1850

Henderson, David D., son of William and Mary Jane Henderson, b. 13 Aug 1843, bapt. 1 May 1844 by Rev. James Sewell

Henderson, Mary Ann and Robert Brazier m. 19 Sep 1844 by Rev. Dr. George C. M. Roberts

Hening, Frances Virginia, dau. of John and Mary Ann Hening, b. -- Jun 1840, bapt. 2 Aug 1840 by Rev. Beverly Waugh

Hening, George Anna, dau. of Rev. J. A. and Mary Hening, b. ---- [blank], bapt. 1 Mar 1842 by Rev. Dr. George C. M. Roberts

Hennace, Virginia and Peter Wilson m. 28 Jul 1845 by Rev. Samuel Keppler (date of lic. not recorded)

Hennaman, William and Ann Shaw m. 5 May 1842 by Rev. Henry Slicer, lic. dated 4 May 1842

Hennick, John C. and Eliza Hunt m. 27 Feb 1845 by Rev. Dr. George C. M. Roberts

Henricks, Ellen and Henry Gettier m. 8 Dec 1844 by Rev. James Sewell, lic. dated 7 Dec 1844

Henrix, Robert, son of Thomas and Mary Henrix, b. 6 Apr 1842, bapt. 20 Jun 1842 by Rev. Isaac P. Cook

Henry, Jemima J. and Samuel Murdoch m. 15 Nov 1846 by Rev. Littleton F. Morgan, lic. dated 9 Nov 1846

Herald, George, son of George and Nancy Herald, b. 12 May 1845, bapt. 14 Nov 1846 by Rev. Dr. George C. M. Roberts

Herbert, Gideon Jr. and Elizabeth Fulenger m. 9 Aug 1840 by Rev. Joseph Shane

Herbert, John F. and Julia A. Griffin, both of Baltimore County, m. 15 Sep 1842 by Rev. Nelson Head

Herbert, Thomas Jefferson, son of John and Emeline Herbert, b. 13 Jun 1846, bapt. 8 Sep 1846 by Rev. Samuel Keppler

Hergesheimer, Mary Josephine, dau. of Charles and Sarah Hergesheimer, aged 11 years [b. 1846], bapt. -- Nov 1857 by Rev. William A. Snively

Herling, George and Martha A. Nicholson m. 12 Dec 1844 by Rev. Dr. George C. M. Roberts [Ed. Note: His last name was initially written as "Hawling" but it was lined out and "Herling" was written above it.]

Herold, Charlotte V. and Lewis Alton m. ---- [blank] by Rev. John S. Martin, lic. dated 16 Jul 1850 [Ed. Note: Their marriage notice in the Baltimore Sun stated Lewis Alton m. Charlotte V. Harrold, dau. of John Harrold, on 16 Jul 1850.]

Hervey, James R. and Susan Silva m. 16 Dec 1841 by Rev. Gerard Morgan, lic. dated same day

Hestings, Edward T. and Letitia Jane Hestings m. 22 Nov 1849 by Rev. Aquila A. Reese, lic. dated 21 Nov 1849

Hestings, Letitia Jane and Edward T. Hestings m. 22 Nov 1849 by Rev. Aquila A. Reese, lic. dated 21 Nov 1849

Hevell, Catharine and Lemuel Durham m. 13 May 1843 by Rev. Wesley Stevenson

Hewens, Elizabeth and James Stevenson m. 26 Jun 1843 by Rev. Henry Slicer, lic. dated 23 Jun 1843

Hickner, Jacob O. and Adaline Stone m. 18 Jun 1846 by Rev. Littleton F. Morgan, lic. dated 15 Jun 1846

Higden, Baptist and Eliza Allison m. 4 Apr 1850 by Rev. Joseph Shane

Higgins, Maria and William R. Collins m. 4 Jun 1850 by Rev. John S. Martin, lic. dated 3 Jun 1850

High, Elizabeth A., d. circa 1849-1850 (exact date not given in Record of Members) [*Ed. Note:* Death notice in the *Baltimore Sun* stated that an Eliza High d. 26 Feb 1849.]

High, Margaret Ann, dau. of William and Susan High, b. 20 Jan 1840, bapt. 1 Jun 1840 by Rev. Joseph Shane

High, William, d. circa 1840 (exact date not given in Class Record) [*Ed. Note:* Death notice in the *Baltimore Sun* stated that William High, Sr. d. 2 Dec 1839.]

Hilditch, Mary Ann and William Sutherland m. 3 May 1847 by Rev. Stephen A. Roszel, lic. dated same day

Hilgar, Abraham P. and Sarah Elizabeth Reed m. 30 May 1848 by Rev. Isaac P. Cook

Hill, Ann (colored) and James H. Coxwell (colored) m. 6 Jul 1842 by Rev. Henry Slicer (date of lic. not recorded)

Hill, Margaret and Thomas Tiser m. 5 Sep 1847 by Rev. Stephen A. Roszel, lic. dated 26 Aug 1847

Hill, Sarah Ann and Thomas Gorsuch m. 10 Sep 1845 by Rev. Samuel Keppler (date of lic. not recorded)

Hillary, Mary and John Coulter m. 11 Jul 1848 by Rev. Joseph Shane

Hillen, Dane(?), child of Mr. and Mrs. Hillen, b. 22 Sep 1842, bapt. 18 Sep 1843 by Rev. Philip B. Reese

Hilliard, Mary E., d. circa 1840 (exact date not given in Record of Members) [*Ed. Note:* Death notice in the *Baltimore Sun* stated that Mary E. Hillard d. 21 Aug 1840.]

Hindel, Eliza and James Ewin m. 30 Apr 1846 by Rev. Littleton F. Morgan, lic. dated same day

Hindes, Evelina Elizabeth, dau. of Samuel and H. E. Hindes, b. 29 Oct 1843, bapt. 23 Nov 1843 by Rev. Isaac P. Cook

Hinds, Ann Rebecca, dau. of John and Mary Ann Hinds, b. 27 Jul 1841, bapt. 13 Aug 1841 by Rev. Dr. George C. M. Roberts

Hines, Eliza Jane and Nector A. Forbes m. 4 Aug 1841 by Rev. Dr. George C. M. Roberts

Hinman, Joel and Jemima C. Dunn m. 8 Nov 1849 by Rev. Dr. George C. M. Roberts

Hinman, Truman and Anna M. Garrett m. 2 Sep 1847 by Rev. Dr. George C. M. Roberts

Hinson, Ann, d. circa 1845-1847 (exact date not given in Record of Members)

Hinton, Elizabeth A. and Judson W. Hunt m. 10 Jan 1850 by Rev. Aquila A. Reese, lic. dated 9 Jan 1850

Hinton, Susan J., d. 1849 (death noted in Class List) [*Ed. Note:* Death notice in the *Baltimore Sun* stated that Susan J. Hinton, wife of William Hinton, d. 28 Jun 1849.]

Hipsley, Caleb and Susan R. Case m. 21 May 1850 by Rev. Joseph Shane

Hiskey, Mary A. and Lawrence Dolan m. 29 Mar 1847 by Rev. Dr. George C. M. Roberts

Hiss, Elizabeth Rodgers and Thomas Beale Israel m. 11 May 1848 by Rev. James H. Brown, lic. dated 10 May 1848

Hiss, George R. A. and Mary Janes Israel m. 15 Jan 1850 at the house of her mother in Baltimore by Rev. Beverly Waugh, lic. dated 14 Jan 1850

Hiss, Joseph and Caroline M. Mason m. 28 Sep 1845 by Rev. Dr. George C. M. Roberts

Hiss, William Henry and Margaret Ann Child m. 11 Jan 1848 at the house of her father in Baltimore by Rev. Beverly Waugh, lic. dated 10 Jan 1848

Hissey, Ellenora and Samuel Wideman m. 15 Jun 1842 by Rev. Joseph Shane

Hissey, James and Emeline Bilson m. 12 Apr 1840 by Rev. Joseph Shane

Hissey, John Archibald, son of William and Eliza Hissey, b. 12 Feb 1840, bapt. 25 Oct 1840 by Rev. John Bear

Hitch, Catharine and Peter Williams m. 18 Oct 1847 by Rev. Stephen A. Roszel, lic. dated same day

Hitch, Marcellus R. and Mary J. Lankford m. 21 May 1845 by Rev. James Sewell, lic. dated 20 May 1845

Hitchcock, Catharine and John Miller m. 14 Jan 1841 by Rev. John Bear

Hitchcock, William J. and Susan A. Davis m. 23 Jul 1849 by Rev. Isaac P. Cook

Hitchkiss, William A. and Sophia Winchester m. 19 Oct 1848 by Rev. William Hirst

Hitzelberger, Elizabeth, d. circa 1844-1847 (exact date not given in Record of Members) [*Ed. Note:* Death notices in the *Baltimore Sun* stated that one Elizabeth Hitselberger, wife of Joseph Hitselberger and dau. of Andrew Shorb, d. 20 Nov 1845 and another Elizabeth Hitzelberger, widow of Joseph Hitzelberger, d. 18 Jul 1846.]

Hobbs, Daniel D. and Rebecca Parker m. 13 Aug 1850 by Rev. Isaac P. Cook

Hobbs, Littleton, see "Sarah Hobbs," q.v.

Hobbs, Lucretia and David Whittle m. 2 Apr 1843 by Rev. Isaac P. Cook

Hobbs, Sarah, d. 1845 (death noted in Class List) [*Ed. Note:* Death notice in the *Baltimore Sun* stated that Sarah Hobbs, wife of Littleton Hobbs, d. 2 Mar 1845.]

Hobbs, Thomas and Rhoda Rimby, both of Baltimore, MD, m. 11 Oct 1840 by Rev. John A. Hening [*Ed. Note:* Her name was misspelled "Rimbe" in the church register.]

Hodges, Robert Emory, son of John and ---- [blank] Hodges, b. ---- [blank], bapt. 21 Apr 1841 by Rev. Robert Emory

Hodges, Solomon and Jemima Parsons, both of Baltimore County, m. 9 Jan 1843 by Rev. Nelson Head

Hoffman, Angeline A. and Lawrence M. Strong m. 21 Dec 1846 by Rev. Dr. George C. M. Roberts

Hoffman, George W., d. before 1840 (exact date not given in Class Record) [*Ed. Note:* Death notice in the *Baltimore Sun* stated that George W. Hoffman d. 29 Sep 1838.]

Hoffman, Margaret and Abner Humphries m. 3 Sep 1843 by Rev. Henry Slicer, lic. dated 2 Sep 1843

Hoffman, Mary Elizabeth, dau. of John L. and Emeline Hoffman, b. 23 Dec 1843, bapt. 21 Oct 1844 by Rev. Dr. George C. M. Roberts

Hoffman, Sarah Virginia, dau. of John and Emelia Hoffman, b. 8 Dec 1840, bapt. 11 May 1840 *[sic]* by Rev. Dr. George C. M. Roberts

Hogans, Margaret and John Riley m. 28 May 1845 by Rev. Joseph Shane

Hogg, Ellen G. and John Carson, both of Baltimore County, m. 7 Apr 1840 by Rev. Bernard H. Nadal

Hogg, Robert E. and Mary Ann Lloyd m. 24 Aug 1847 by Rev. Dr. George C. M. Roberts

Hogg, Thomas Sargent, son of John W. and Martha A. Hogg, b. 4 Dec 1846, bapt. same day by Rev. Dr. George C. M. Roberts

Hohn, Henry, see "Henry Horn," q.v.

Holdbrook, Henry and Clarissa Gallaway m. 13 Jan 1841 by Rev. Samuel Keppler, lic. dated same day

Holdin, George W. and Ann Maria Goldman m. 21 Nov 1847 by Rev. Dr. George C. M. Roberts

Holebrook, Charlotte J. and Charles H. Trumbo, both of Baltimore County, m. ---- [date not given] by Rev. George Hildt, lic. dated 20 May 1845 [*Ed. Note:* Their marriage notice in the *Baltimore Sun* initially stated Charles H. Trumbo m. Charlotta I. Holbrook on 21 May 1845, but her name was later corrected to Charlotte J. Holbrook.]

Holland, Elizabeth A. and Oliver W. Wheeler m. 20 Dec 1849 by Rev. Aquila A. Reese, lic. dated 19 Dec 1849

Holland, Isaiah and Mary Ann Wempsat m. 15 Apr 1844 by Rev. Joseph Merriken

Holland, Samuel and Mary Jane McAllister m. 7 Oct 1847 by Rev. Stephen A. Roszel, lic. dated 4 Oct 1847

Holland, William Thomas, son of William and Margaret Holland, aged 3 months and 7 days, bapt. 21 Jun 1841 by Rev. John A. Hening

Hollingshead, Caroline Rebecca, dau. of Capt. F. and Amelia Hollingshead, b. 18 Aug 1842, bapt. 10 May 1845 by Rev. Dr. George C. M. Roberts

Hollingshead, Francis Isaak, son of Francis and Amelia Hollingshead, b. 11 Jun 1839, bapt. 17 Jan 1841 by Rev. Dr. George C. M. Roberts

Hollingshead, George Roberts, son of Francis and Amelia Hollingshead, b. 1 Jun 1836, bapt. 17 Jan 1841 by Rev. Dr. George C. M. Roberts

Hollingshead, James, son of Francis and Amelia Hollingshead, b. 2 Jun 1833, bapt. 17 Jan 1841 by Rev. Dr. George C. M. Roberts

Hollingshead, Mary Clare, dau. of Capt. Francis and Amelia R. Hollingshead, b. 1 Jan 1848, bapt. 13 Jan 1852 by Rev. Dr. George C. M. Roberts

Hollingshead, Samuel and Sarah Leaville m. 11 Jun 1846 by Rev. Dr. George C. M. Roberts

Hollingshead, Samuel Owens, son of Capt. F. and Amelia Hollingshead, b. 24 Apr 1845, bapt. 10 May 1845 by Rev. Dr. George C. M. Roberts

Hollingsworth, Colin F. and Ann Elizabeth Kepbron m. 15 Sep 1846 by Rev. Dr. George C. M. Roberts

Hollis, George C. M. Roberts, son of Charles and Jane Hollis, b. 8 Oct 1843, bapt. 11 Apr 1844 by Rev. Dr. George C. M. Roberts

Hollis, James, d. circa 1849-1850 (exact date not given in Record of Members) [*Ed. Note:* Death notices in the *Baltimore Sun* stated that one James Hollis d. 2 Jan 1849 and another James Hollis d. 19 Dec 1850.]

Holmes, Caroline L. and William A. Kemp m. 27 Oct 1846 by Rev. Benjamin F. Brooke

Holmes, George and Caroline German m. 17 Sep 1844 by Rev. Isaac P. Cook

Holmes, Joseph Milton, son of Joseph M. and Mary Elizabeth Holmes, b. 27 May 1849, bapt. 29 Jul 1850 by Rev. Dr. George C. M. Roberts

Holt, Joseph and Sarah C. Holton m. 21 Jul 1842 by Rev. Henry Slicer, lic. dated same day

Holt, Margaret and Charles Stewart m. 24 Dec 1840 by Rev. Joseph Shane

Holt, Mary and Isaac Moss m. 14 Apr 1844 by Rev. Joseph Shane

Holt, Washington and Ann Foster m. 26 Aug 1841 by Rev. Gerard Morgan, lic. dated same day

Holton, Elizabeth and James Donohue m. 11 Sep 1842 by Rev. Henry Slicer, lic. dated 10 Sep 1842

Holton, George J. and Catherine Myrtz m. 7 Jun 1842 by Rev. Henry Slicer, lic. dated 6 Jun 1842

Holton, Sarah C. and Joseph Holt m. 21 Jul 1842 by Rev. Henry Slicer, lic. dated same day

Holtstein, Elizabeth Ann and Richard Warner, both of Baltimore County, m. 21 Sep 1842 by Rev. Nelson Head

Holtz, Frederick and Mary A. Mountgarett m. 6 Apr 1845 by Rev. Dr. George C. M. Roberts

Holtz, Mary Ann and Robert Hays, both of Baltimore County, m. 25 Feb 1840 by Rev. Bernard H. Nadal

Holtzman, Henry Clay, son of George and Margaret H. Holtzman, b. 7 Jul 1839, bapt. 14 Jun 1840 by Rev. Thomas Myers

Honey, Susannah, d. circa 1847 (exact date not given in Record of Members) [*Ed. Note:* Death notice in the *Baltimore Sun* stated that Susannah Honey, widow of Amos Honey, d. 5 Jul 1847.]

Hood, John and Ann Lowman m. 11 Feb 1841 by Rev. Joseph Shane

Hoofnogle, John S. and Sarah Ann Lane m. 22 Dec 1842 by Rev. Dr. George C. M. Roberts

Hook, Elizabeth and William Goll m. 7 Nov 1844 by Rev. Dr. George C. M. Roberts

Hook, Ellen, dau. of Nelson and Rachel Hook, b. 1 Sep 1839, bapt. 18 Aug 1840 by Rev. Dr. George C. M. Roberts

Hook, Sophia and William Mushaw m. 17 Jan 1850 by Rev. John S. Martin, lic. dated 16 Jan 1850

Hooker, Elizabeth and John Willis m. 18 Jun 1840 by Rev. Samuel Keppler, lic. dated 2 Jun 1840

Hooper, Ann B. and William H. Glassgow, both of Baltimore County, m. 4 Jul 1840 by Rev. Thomas Myers, lic. dated 3 Jul 1840

Hooper, Anna Marietta, dau. of Capt. William and Amanda M. Hooper, b. 27 Oct 1848, bapt. 30 Jun 1849 by Rev. Dr. George C. M. Roberts

Hooper, Maria and James Harrington m. 2 Oct 1845 by Rev. Dr. George C. M. Roberts

Hooper, Thomas and Eliza Crawford m. 3 May 1848 by Rev. William Hirst

Hooper, William and Margaret Brown m. 1 Mar 1843 by Rev. Henry Slicer, lic. dated same day

Hoover, Peter and Sarah Zimmerman m. 19 Jul 1846 by Rev. Littleton F. Morgan, lic. dated 16 Jul 1846

Hope, Adeline Susan, dau. of William and Henrietta Hope, b. 26 Jul 1839, bapt. 21 Aug 1843 by Rev. Dr. George C. M. Roberts

Hope, Ann E. and Champion W. Harrison m. 25 Aug 1842 by Rev. Dr. George C. M. Roberts

Hope, Daniel, son of William and Henrietta Hope, b. 2 Jun 1842, bapt. 21 Aug 1843 by Rev. Dr. George C. M. Roberts

Hope, Oregon, child of William and Henrietta Hope, b. 10 Apr 1848, bapt. 21 Jan 1848 by Rev. Dr. George C. M. Roberts

Hopkins, Alice Ann, dau. of Franklin and Eliza Hopkins, b. 12 Oct 1846, Baltimore, bapt. 27 Jun 1847 by Rev. Stephen A. Roszel

Hopkins, Amanda Melvina and Edward Latham m. 31 Dec 1840 by Rev. Samuel Keppler, lic. dated 30 Dec 1840

Hopkins, Angelina and William Deaver m. 5 Apr 1847 by Rev. Isaac P. Cook

Hopkins, Edward Franklin, son of Franklin and Ann M. Hopkins, b. 19 Sep 1841, bapt. 7 Aug 1842 by Rev. Henry Slicer

Hopkins, Emma Virginia, dau. of Franklin and Eliza Hopkins, b. 6 Apr 1845, Baltimore, bapt. 27 Jun 1847 by Rev. Stephen A. Roszel

Hopkins, George C. M. Roberts, son of William L. and Rebecca S. Hopkins, b. 7 Oct 1843, bapt. 23 Jun 1844 by Rev. Dr. George C. M. Roberts

Hopkins, Howard H. and Mary McConkey, both of Baltimore County, m. 25 Nov 1844 by Rev. William Hamilton

Hopkins, Mary Eliza, dau. of Franklin and Ann M. Hopkins, b. 29 Jan 1840, bapt. 7 Aug 1842 by Rev. Henry Slicer

Hopkins, Rachel and Moses Malone m. -- Mar 1846 [page torn] by Rev. James Sewell, lic. dated 18 Mar 1846

Hopkins, Samuel and Mary Ann Hall m. 11 Nov 1847 by Rev. Littleton F. Morgan, lic. dated 10 Nov 1847

Hopkins, Samuel G. and Rebecca C. Skilman m. 3 Feb 1843 by Rev. Joseph Shane

Hopkins, Sarah, d. circa 1840-1847 (exact date not given in Record of Members) [Ed. Note: Death notice in the Baltimore Sun stated that Sarah Hopkins d. 4 Apr 1845.]

Hopkins, Sarah Alice, dau. of Jane Hopkins (colored), b. -- Dec 1842, bapt. 31 Jul 1848 by Rev. Dr. George C. M. Roberts

Hopkins, Sarah Ann and Francis S. A. B. Boyd m. 29 Aug 1841 by Rev. Gerard Morgan, lic. dated 25 Aug 1841

Hopkins, Sarah Ann and James J. Stover (Storer?) m. 17 Jun 1849 by Rev. John S. Martin, lic. dated 16 Jun 1849

Hopkins, Susan E., dau. of Franklin and Eliza Hopkins, b. 15 Apr 1843, Baltimore, bapt. 27 Jun 1847 by Rev. Stephen A. Roszel

Hopkins, William and Sarah Ann Boring m. 2 Dec 1847 at the house of Mrs. Daniel Fosbenner in Baltimore by Rev. Beverly Waugh, lic. dated 29 Nov 1847

Hopkins, William E. and Hannah P. Stevenson m. 16 Jun 1847 by Rev. Isaac P. Cook

Hopkins, William Ellis and Amelia Rebecca Sewell m. 4 Feb 1847 at Light Street Church in Baltimore by Rev. Beverly Waugh, lic. dated 2 Feb 1847

Hopkins, William Ryan, son of Joseph and Mary Hopkins, b. 26 Jan 1850, bapt. 24 Aug 1851 by Rev. Dr. George C. M. Roberts

Hopper, William J. and Sarah E. Stephens, both of Baltimore County, m. 27 May 1844 by Rev. William Hamilton

Horn, Henry and Hannah Chalk m. 26 May 1846 by Rev. Wesley Stevenson [Ed. Note: His name was given as "Henry Hohn" in their Baltimore Sun marriage notice.]

Horn, Sarah and Robert Brazier m. 24 Mar 1846 by Rev. Isaac P. Cook

Horner, Elizabeth Ann and James B. Goodhand, both of Baltimore County, m. 19 Jun 1845 by Rev. William Hamilton, lic. dated 18 Jun 1845

Horner, Mary A., d. circa 1847-1850 (exact date not given in Record of Members)

Horney, Ann and Edward Martin m. 21 Apr 1843 by Rev. Joseph Shane

Horney, Ann E. and Josiah Waggner m. 9 Nov 1845 by Rev. James Sewell, lic. dated 7 Nov 1845

Horney, Elizabeth E., dau. of Thomas and Mary A. Horney, b. 8 Aug 1840, bapt. 23 Sep 1849 by Rev. John S. Martin

Horney, Mary Charlotte, dau. of Mary Horney, b. 17 Jan 1847, Baltimore, bapt. 27 Jun 1847 by Rev. Stephen A. Roszel

Horney, Sarah F., dau. of Thomas and Mary A. Horney, b. 8 Feb 1843, bapt. 23 Sep 1849 by Rev. John S. Martin

Horney, Thomas F., dau. of Thomas and Mary A. Horney, b. 15 Aug 1848, bapt. 23 Sep 1849 by Rev. John S. Martin

Hornn, George Wesley Hartman, son of William and Tabitha Hornn, b. 20 Oct 1840, bapt. 5 Jan 1841 by Rev. Charles B. Tippett

Horse, Rosanna and William Stokes m. 13 Dec 1849 by Rev. Dr. George C. M. Roberts [Ed. Note: Her last name was given as "Horstman" in their Baltimore Sun marriage notice.]

Hosinow, William and Ann E. Garish m. 19 Sep 1847 by Rev. Stephen A. Roszel, lic. dated 13 Sep 1847

Houck, Ann and Abijah B. Smith m. 10 Mar 1841 by Rev. Wesley Stevenson

Houck, George H. and Elizabeth Arnold m. 7 Dec 1848 by Rev. Isaac P. Cook

Houck, Henry T. and Eleanor Williams m. 9 Jun 1840 by Rev. John Bear

Hough, Edward, son of Edward S. and Susan A. Hough, b. 13 Dec 1839, bapt. 26 Dec 1845 by Rev. Dr. George C. M. Roberts

Hough, Elizabeth Ann and Henry A. Barling m. 28 Dec 1843 by Rev. Isaac P. Cook

Hough, George Roberts, son of Edward S. and Susan A. Hough, b. 20 May 1843, bapt. 5 Jun 1845 by Rev. Dr. George C. M. Roberts

Hough, Henry, son of Edward S. and Susan A. Hough, b. 10 Aug 1842, bapt. 5 Jun 1845 by Rev. Dr. George C. M. Roberts

Hough, Louis Coale, son of Edward S. and Susan A. Hough, b. 1849, bapt. 26 Mar 1850 by Rev. Dr. George C. M. Roberts

House, Jesse and Elizabeth A. Harford m. 11 Jan 1844 by Rev. Isaac P. Cook

Houseman, Elizabeth and John Anderson m. 22 Jun 1843 by Rev. Dr. George C. M. Roberts

Houston, Coupland and Mary S. Johnson m. 18 Oct 1846 by Rev. Samuel Keppler (date of lic. not recorded)

Houston, Sarah Jane and Charles Henry Byron m. 10 Jun 1847 by Rev. Dr. George C. M. Roberts

Hovell (Hevell?), Catharine and Lemuel Durham m. 13 May 1843 by Rev. Wesley Stevenson

Howard, Asa and Sophia J. Dickson m. ---- [no date given] by Rev. John Miller, lic. dated 17 Dec 1850 [Ed. Note: Their marriage notice in the Baltimore Sun stated they married on 19 Dec 1850.]

Howard, Benjamin and Augusta Eubanks m. 18 Nov 1845 by Rev. Dr. George C. M. Roberts

Howard, James and Mary Elizabeth Cramer m. 3 Dec 1840 by Rev. Joseph Shane

Howard, Mary and Reubin Zepp m. 18 Aug 1844 by Rev. Joseph Shane

Howard, Sarah Ann and Thomas Trepp m. 2 Nov 1843 by Rev. Joseph Shane

Howe, Alexander D. and Emily Youngman m. 14 Apr 1842 by Rev. Job Guest, lic. dated 8 Feb 1842

Howe, William and Ann Rogers m. 13 Aug 1842 by Rev. Joseph Shane

Howell, Ruth, d. circa 1850 (exact date not given in Record of Members) [Ed. Note: Death notice in the Baltimore Sun stated that Ruth B. Howell, wife of George H. Howell, d. 11 Jun 1850.]

Howes, Sarah and Elijah Dove m. 21 Nov 1849 by Rev. Isaac P. Cook

Hubart, James Nelson, son of James and Ann Hubart, b. 24 Jan 1838, bapt. 27 Aug 1840 by Rev. Dr. George C. M. Roberts

Hubbard, Elizabeth Ellen and William H. Denney m. 9 Sep 1845 by Rev. James Sewell, lic. dated 8 Sep 1845 [Ed. Note: Their marriage notice in the Baltimore Sun stated that William H. Denny and Elizabeth E. Hubbard m. 8 Sep 1845.]

Hubbard, Henry and Elizabeth Trego m. 2 Apr 1843 by Rev. Henry Slicer, lic. dated 1 Mar 1843

Hubbard, Samuel, son of William and Sarah Ann Hubbard, b. 21 May 1839, Fells Point, Baltimore City, bapt. 21 Sep 1840 by Rev. Samuel Keppler

Hubbard, William and Lavinia Briscoe m. 29 Mar 1847 by Rev. Dr. George C. M. Roberts

Hudson, Edward and Harriet Hadaway m. 5 Apr 1847 by Rev. Dr. George C. M. Roberts

Hudson, James and Rebecca Webb, both of Baltimore County, m. 10 Feb 1846 by Rev. George Hildt, lic. dated same day

Hudson, Thomas and Keturrah Jury m. 20 Jan 1842 by Rev. Dr. George C. M. Roberts

Hues, John Harrison, son of John and Henrietta Hues, aged 1 year and 25 days, bapt. 27 Aug 1841 by Rev. Gerard Morgan

Hugg, Ann, d. 1844 (exact date not given in Record of Members) [Ed. Note: Death notice in the Baltimore Sun stated that Anna M. Hugg, widow of Charles Hugg, d. 10 Dec 1844.]

Hugg, Charles, see "Ann Hugg," q.v.

Hugg, John and Avarilla G. Knapp m. 27 Jul 1840 by Rev. Samuel Keppler, lic. dated same day

Hugg, Mary Elizabeth, dau. of Richard and Adaline Hugg, b. 20 Sep 1840, bapt. 29 Sep 1840 by Rev. Charles B Tippett

Huggins, Mary Ann, dau. of William and Lucinda Huggins, b. -- Feb 1840, bapt. 28 Jan 1841 by Rev. Thomas Myers

Hughes, Ann Eliza, dau. of Elijah and Rebecca Hughes, b. 29 Sep 1841, bapt. 22 Mar 1845 by Rev. Dr. George C. M. Roberts

Hughes, George Scott, son of Scott and Rebecca Hughes, b. 7 May 1839, Fells Point, Baltimore City, bapt. 19 Feb 1840 by Rev. Samuel Keppler

Hughes, James Upton, son of Elijah and Rebecca Hughes, b. 26 Dec 1839, bapt. 15 Jun 1840 by Rev. Dr. George C. M. Roberts

Hughes, Michael and Margaret A. Lowther m. 20 Jun 1849 by Rev. Aquila A. Reese, lic. dated 19 Jun 1849

Hughes, Rebecca Ellen, dau. of Elijah and Rebecca Hughes, b. 29 Jul 1843, bapt. 22 Mar 1845 by Rev. Dr. George C. M. Roberts

Hughes, Sarah Elizabeth, dau. of Elijah and Rebecca Hughes, b. 10 Mar 1845, bapt. 22 Mar 1845 by Rev. Dr. George C. M. Roberts

Hughes, Thomas, d. circa 1844 (death noted in Class List)

Huisler, John and Mary Mitchell, both of Baltimore County, m. 25 Jun 1840 by Rev. Bernard H. Nadal

Hull, William and Mahala Penrose m. 11 Dec 1849 by Rev. Aquila A. Reese, lic. dated 10 Dec 1849

Hulse, Harriet Jane and James S. Sparks m. 26 Dec 1843 by Rev. Dr. George C. M. Roberts

Humes, John H. and Caroline Curren (Curven?) m. 20 Mar 1845 by Rev. Dr. George C. M. Roberts

Humphreys, James J. and Louisa Gray m. 29 Sep 1848 by Rev. Joseph Shane

Humphreys, Owen T. and Eliza Jane Eldred m. 2 Aug 1841 by Rev. Dr. George C. M. Roberts

Humphries, Abner and Margaret Hoffman m. 3 Sep 1843 by Rev. Henry Slicer, lic. dated 2 Sep 1843

Humphries, Mary, d. circa 1847-1850 (exact date not given in Record of Members)

Hunt, Eliza and John C. Hennick m. 27 Feb 1845 by Rev. Dr. George C. M. Roberts

Hunt, Eliza and Nathaniel G. Cobb m. 9 Apr 1840 by Rev. Samuel Keppler, lic. dated same day

Hunt, Judson W. and Elizabeth A. Hinton m. 10 Jan 1850 by Rev. Aquila A. Reese, lic. dated 9 Jan 1850

Hunt, Maria, d. circa 1840 (death noted in Class List)

Hunt, Walamina M. and Lewis Beard m. 15 Jan 1845 by Rev. Dr. George C. M. Roberts

Hunter, Ann, d. circa 1845-1847 (exact date not given in Record of Members)

Hunter, Anne M. and Nicholas Lynch m. 2 Jul 1845 by Rev. James Sewell, lic. dated same day

Hurley, Harriet and Isaac Lankford m. 16 May 1842 by Rev. Joseph Shane

Hurley, Mordecai, d. circa 1840 (exact date not given in Record of Members) [Ed. Note: Death notice in the Baltimore Sun stated that Mordecai Hurley d. 8 Dec 1840.]

Hurley, Sarah, d. 1844 (exact date not given in Record of Members) [Ed. Note: Death notice in the Baltimore Sun stated that Sarah Hurley, widow of Mordecai Hurley and dau. of George and Margery Timanus, d. 2 Apr 1844.]

Hursh, John and Margaret Scott m. 12 Apr 1848 by Rev. William Hirst

Hurst, Alphonso Roberts, son of Rev. William and Eliza Hurst, b. 1850, bapt. 1 Jan 1851 by Rev. Dr. George C. M. Roberts

Hurst, Rebecca, d. circa 1847 (death noted in Class List) [*Ed. Note:* Death notice in the *Baltimore Sun* stated that Rebecca Hurst d. 12 Mar 1848.]

Hush, Samuel C. and Hannah M. Skillman m. 10 Jun 1845 by Rev. Dr. George C. M. Roberts

Hush, Samuel Conrad, son of Samuel O. and Hannah Maria Hush, b. 10 Apr 1845, bapt. 19 Apr 1846 by Rev. Dr. George C. M. Roberts

Hush, William Josiah, son of Samuel C. and Hannah M. Hush, b. 17 Sep 1847, bapt. 24 Sep 1847 by Rev. Dr. George C. M. Roberts

Hutchins, Amelia A. and William R. Jackson m. 7 Nov 1841 by Rev. Dr. George C. M. Roberts

Hutchins, Rebecca S. and Joshua P. Disney m. 20 Dec 1849 by Rev. Isaac P. Cook

Hutchinson, Emily J. and Charles A. Talbott m. 10 Apr 1849 by Rev. Isaac P. Cook

Hutson, Robert and Caroline Darrington m. 29 Apr 1840 by Rev. Samuel Keppler, lic. dated 28 Apr 1840

Hutton, Agnes and William Sley m. 15 Jul 1844 by Rev. James Sewell, lic. dated same day

Huzza, Columbus and Susanna A. Church m. 14 Jan 1845 by Rev. Dr. George C. M. Roberts

Hyatt, Richard H. and Mary Traverse m. 12 Nov 1849 by Rev. William Hirst, lic. dated same day

Hymann, Horace, son of Henry F. and Susan Hymann, b. 3 Jan 1840, bapt. 26 Apr 1840 by Rev. Dr. George C. M. Roberts

Hynes, Caleb B. and Mary Pool m. 13 Sep 1846 by Rev. Isaac P. Cook

Hyson, Mary R. and Samuel Caskey m. 28 Jul 1841 by Rev. Dr. George C. M. Roberts

Hytaffer, Mary F. and John Smith m. 29 Oct 1850 by Rev. Henry Slicer, lic. dated same day

Iiams, William and Sarah A. Kinzie, both of Baltimore County, m. 16 Apr 1840 by Rev. Bernard H. Nadal

Ijams, William L. and Jane Sorter m. 12 Jun 1845 by Rev. Dr. George C. M. Roberts [*Ed. Note:* His last name was spelled "Jiams" or "Iiams" in the church register, but their marriage notice in the *Baltimore Sun* gave his name as "Ijams."]

Ing, Elias Daley, son of Edward and Ann Ing, b. ---- [blank], bapt. 15 Jun 1844 by Rev. Isaac P. Cook

Ing, Mary Elizabeth and Edward A. Cassell m. 11 Oct 1848 by Rev. Dr. George C. M. Roberts

Inloes, David and Bridget Gosloe m. 26 Jul 1841 by Rev. Isaac P. Cook

Inloes, Rebecca Sank, dau. of James and Sarah Inloes, b. 10 May 1841, bapt. 29 Sep 1841 by Rev. Dr. George C. M. Roberts

Inloes, Sarah Emma, dau. of Henry A. and Priscilla P. Inloes, b. 16 May 1846, bapt. 17 Sep 1846 by Rev. Samuel Keppler

Ireland, John and Charlotte Weivelle m. 27 Jul 1843 by Rev. Dr. George C. M. Roberts

Ireland, Margaret B. and Joseph H. Day m. 15 Apr 1845 by Rev. Dr. George C. M. Roberts

Irvin, Mary E. and William Broom m. 4 Jun 1845 by Rev. James Sewell, lic. dated same day

Irvine, Sarah, d. circa 1849-1850 (death noted in Class List) [*Ed. Note:* Death notice in the *Baltimore Sun* stated that Sarah L. Irvin d. 29 Aug 1850.]

Irving, Virginia and George W. Buck m. 24 Aug 1848 by Rev. James H. Brown, lic. dated 24 May 1848

Irving, William Henry, son of William Henry and Georgianna Irving, b. 2 Aug 1846, bapt. 27 Aug 1846 by Rev. Samuel Keppler

Irwin, Edward F. and Henrietta Ballow m. 24 Jun 1846 by Rev. Wesley Stevenson

Irwin, Edward William, son of Henry J. and Mary Ann Irwin, b. 28 Feb 1850, bapt. 6 Jan 1852 by Rev. Dr. George C. M. Roberts

Irwing(?), Sally E. and Caleb C. Shaw, both of Baltimore County, m. 5 Nov 1846 by Rev. George Hildt, lic. dated 16 Oct 1846

Isaacs, Rachel and Edmund Bull m. 16 Jun 1846 by Rev. Littleton F. Morgan, lic. dated same day

Israel, Anna, d. circa 1846-1847 (exact date not given in Record of Members) [*Ed. Note:* Death notice in the *Baltimore Sun* stated that Anna Israel, wife of J. Robert Israel and dau. of Thomas Flint, d. 14 Jul 1846.]

Israel, Arall, child of John Robert and Anna Israel, b. 22 Aug 1841, bapt. 16 Dec 1845 by Rev. Dr. George C. M. Roberts

Israel, John Robert, son of John Robert and Anna Israel, b. 10 Jun 1843, bapt. 16 Dec 1845 by Rev. Dr. George C. M. Roberts

Israel, Mary Janes and George R. A. Hiss m. 15 Jan 1850 at the house of her mother in Baltimore by Rev. Beverly Waugh, lic. dated 14 Jan 1850

Israel, Thomas Beale and Elizabeth Rodgers Hiss m. 11 May 1848 by Rev. James H. Brown, lic. dated 10 May 1848

Ivans, Anna and John Davis m. 20 Nov 1848 by Rev. Dr. George C. M. Roberts

Ives, Nelson, son of William and Ann Ives, b. 13 Mar 1844, bapt. 28 Oct 1844 by Rev. Isaac P. Cook

Izard, Susan Catherine, dau. of George and Ann Izard, b. 13 Jul 1840, bapt. 6 Jun 1840 *[sic]* by Rev. Dr. George C. M. Roberts

Jackson, A. I. W., see "Hester A. Jackson," q.v.

Jackson, Andrew Thomas, son of Thomas and Sarah Jackson, aged 3 weeks, bapt. 1 Feb 1845 by Rev. Wesley Stevenson

Jackson, Elisha and Carey Ann Thompson m. 13 Jun 1848 by Rev. Isaac P. Cook

Jackson, Hester A., d. circa 1840-1847 (exact date not given in Record of Members) [*Ed. Note:* She was possibly the H. Jackson, wife of A. I. W. Jackson, whose death notice in the *Baltimore Sun* stated that she d. 10 Jan 1844.]

Jackson, Isaac Henry and Caroline Johnson m. 19 Nov 1843 by Rev. Dr. George C. M. Roberts

Jackson, James F. and Almira Priscilla Lauder m. 7 Aug 1843 by Rev. Henry Slicer, lic. dated same day

Jackson, Mary A. and Charles Baker m. 3 Oct 1842 by Rev. Henry Slicer, lic. dated same day

Jackson, Mary Jane, dau. of William H. and Amanda M. Jackson, b. 31 Aug 1848, bapt. 24 Sep 1848 by Rev. Dr. George C. M. Roberts

Jackson, William L. and Leah Chalk m. 6 Nov 1843 by Rev. Wesley Stevenson

Jackson, William R. and Amelia A. Hutchins m. 7 Nov 1841 by Rev. Dr. George C. M. Roberts

Jackson, William and Julia Taylor m. 5 Apr 1848 by Rev. Stephen A. Roszel, lic. dated 3 Apr 1848

Jacob, Mary C. and Joseph F. Clark m. 30 Jun 1842 by Rev. Isaac P. Cook

Jacob, Sarah Jane and John R. Black m. 18 Feb 1847 by Rev. Isaac P. Cook

Jacobs, Julien and Margaret K. Lane m. 22 Oct 1845 by Rev. Samuel Keppler (date of lic. not recorded)

James, Elizabeth and William B. Jones m. 19 Nov 1840 by Rev. Samuel Keppler, lic. dated same day

James, Elizabeth, d. 1849 (death noted in Class List) [*Ed. Note:* Death notice in the *Baltimore Sun* stated that Elizabeth James, widow of Levi James, d. 24 Oct 1849.]

James, John and Ann Dunning m. 1 Oct 1842 by Rev. Wesley Stevenson

James, Levi, see "Elizabeth James," q.v.

James, Susan A. and John E. Warrington m. 18 Nov 1846 by Rev. Dr. George C. M. Roberts

Jameson, Andrew (Rev.) and Mary Ann Clark m. 28 Mar 1850 by Rev. Isaac P. Cook

Jameson, Charles M. and Elizabeth Smith, both of Baltimore County, m. ---- [date not given] by Rev. George D. Chenoweth, lic. dated 31 Jan 1842

Jamieson, ---- [blank], child of ---- [blank], b. -- Jun 1848, bapt. 25 Jul 1849 by Rev. John S. Martin

Jarboe, Catharine Eugenia, dau. of John R. and Catharine Jarboe, b. 18 Jan 1842, bapt. 2 Jun 1842 by Rev. Isaac P. Cook

Jarboe, Vernon Cook, son of John R. and Catherine Jarboe, b. 6 Feb 1840, bapt. 22 Dec 1840 by Rev. Isaac P. Cook

Jarrett, Henry Clay and Wilhemina J. Johnson m. 8 May 1849 at Light Street Church in Baltimore by Rev. Beverly Waugh, lic. dated 7 May 1849

Jarrett, Jesse and Julia Ann Downey m. 3 Oct 1850 by Rev. Henry Slicer, lic. dated same day

Jarrett, John and Mahela Shorter m. 16 Jul 1845 by Rev. Dr. George C. M. Roberts

Jarrett, William and Mary Jones, both of Baltimore County, m. 25 Oct 1845 by Rev. William Hamilton

Jarvis, Joseph, d. circa 1844-1845 (exact date not given in Record of Members) [*Ed. Note:* Death notice in the *Baltimore Sun* stated that Joseph Jarvis d. 3 Jul 1845.]

Jarvis, Martha Ann and William Morris m. 16 Aug 1841 by Rev. Wesley Stevenson

Jarvis, Rebecca and William Raywood m. 29 Jun 1847 by Rev. Stephen A. Roszel, lic. dated same day

Jarvis, Rosetta and John R. Trenton m. 20 Apr 1843 by Rev. Joseph Shane

Jarvis, Sarah, d. circa 1840 (exact date not given in Class Record) [*Ed. Note:* Death notice in the *Baltimore Sun* stated that Sarah Jarvis d. 10 Oct 1840.]

Jay, Ann, d. "last year" (exact date not given; death noted in Record of Members in 1844) [*Ed. Note:* Death notice in the *Baltimore Sun* stated that Ann Jay, wife of Joseph W. Jay, d. 16 Apr 1843.]

Jay, John Williams, son of Thomas W. and Elizabeth Jay, b. 1 Mar 1839, bapt. 2 Mar 1840 by Rev. Dr. George C. M. Roberts

Jay, Joseph W., d. circa 1850 (exact date not given in Record of Members) [Ed. Note: Death notice in the Baltimore Sun stated that Joseph W. Jay d. 9 Sep 1850. See "Ann Jay," q.v.

Jay, Mary, d. circa 1847-1850 (exact date not given in Record of Members)

Jay, Mary Josephine, dau. of Thomas W. and Elizabeth Jay, b. 2 Oct 1840, bapt. 13 Apr 1840 [sic] by Rev. Dr. George C. M. Roberts

Jay, Peter A., see "Sarah A. Dawson," q.v.

Jay, William Henry, son of Thomas W. and Elizabeth Jay, b. 10 Sep 1842, bapt. 19 Sep 1845 by Rev. Dr. George C. M. Roberts

Jeans, Elizabeth and Isaac P. Beaumount, both of Baltimore County, m. ---- [date not given] by Rev. George Hildt, lic. dated 2 May 1846 [Ed. Note: Their marriage notice in the Baltimore Sun indicated Isaac Beaumont and Elizabeth Jean m. 2 May 1846.]

Jeffers, Elizabeth, dau. of Joseph and Barbara Jeffers, b. 5 Aug 1820, bapt. 3 Dec 1840 by Rev. Dr. George C. M. Roberts

Jefferson, Harriet Ann and George Wesley Ayres m. 5 Mar 1848 by Rev. Stephen A. Roszel, lic. dated 4 Mar 1848

Jefferson, Lydia and John Ball m. 1 Jan 1850 by Rev. John S. Martin (date of lic. not recorded)

Jeffres, John R. and Susanna C. Embret m. 26 Oct 1847 by Rev. Dr. George C. M. Roberts

Jeffrey, Benjamin and Caroline Hamilton m. 3 Dec 1846 by Rev. Isaac P. Cook

Jeffrey, Thomas and Alice M. Spillman m. 3 Mar 1846 by Rev. Isaac P. Cook

Jeffries, John and Elizabeth E. Shaffer m. 17 Aug 1843 by Rev. Joseph Shane

Jeffry, Samuel and Elizabeth Ann Turner m. ---- [blank] by Rev. John S. Martin, lic. dated 15 Apr 1850

Jemison, Mary A. and Nicholas Tredway m. 16 Feb 1843 by Rev. Isaac P. Cook

Jenkins, Ann and George Scott m. 4 Feb 1840 by Rev. Samuel Keppler (date of lic. not recorded)

Jenkins, Ann Rebecca and Roderick Arnold m. 26 Mar 1850 by Rev. Joseph Shane

Jenkins, Eleanora and Henry Strobel m. 23 Nov 1848 by Rev. Stephen A. Roszel, lic. dated 22 Nov 1848

Jenkins, James T. and Martha Pickering m. 16 Jun 1847 by Rev. Stephen A. Roszel, lic. dated 10 Jun 1847

Jenkins, John Francis, son of Joseph and Ellen Jenkins, b. 23 Sep 1846, Baltimore, bapt. 11 Feb 1847 by Rev. Samuel Keppler

Jenkins, Joseph, son of Joseph and Ellen Jenkins, b. 22 Mar 1844, Baltimore, bapt. 11 Feb 1847 by Rev. Samuel Keppler

Jenkins, Joseph and Elizabeth Diggs m. 10 Aug 1845 by Rev. Joseph Shane

Jenkins, Julia Ann and David Alexander Jones m. 26 Nov 1840 by Rev. Samuel Keppler (date of lic. not recorded)

Jenkins, Louisa and Isaac T. Basford m. 18 Apr 1847 by Rev. Littleton F. Morgan, lic. dated 17 Apr 1847

Jenkins, Mary and Richard Mitchell m. 16 Apr 1840 by Rev. Samuel Keppler, lic. dated same day

Jenkins, Mary A. and Samuel Stewart m. 22 Oct 1846 by Rev. Joseph Shane

Jenkins, Richard E. and Anna E. Edwards m. 21 Mar 1848 by Rev. Benjamin F. Brooke

Jenkins, Sarah Ann, dau. of William and Patience Jenkins, b. 20 Mar 1838, bapt. 26 Sep 1840 by Rev. Joseph Shane

Jenkins, Thomas and Mary Ellen Shaw m. 9 Jul 1850 by Rev. John S. Martin, lic. dated 8 Jul 1850

Jessop, William and Charlotte Duval, both of Baltimore County, m. 22 Jan 1841 by Rev. John Rice, lic. dated 21 Jan 1841

Jewett, Diantha E. and George G. Green m. 4 Sep 1848 by Rev. Dr. George C. M. Roberts

Johnson, Addison and Isabella Stansbury, both of Baltimore County, m. ---- [date not given] by Rev. George Hildt, lic. dated 14 Oct 1845

Johnson, Ann, d. circa 1840 (exact date not given in Class Record) [Ed. Note: Death notice in the Baltimore Sun stated that Ann M. Johnson, wife of James Johnson, d. 18 Nov 1840.]

Johnson, Ann and Abraham Ellis m. 22 Sep 1841 by Rev. Gerard Morgan, lic. dated 20 Sep 1841

Johnson, Ann and Scott Ewing m. 18 Dec 1842 by Rev. Henry Slicer, lic. dated 17 Dec 1842

Johnson, Ann and Charles Griswold m. 29 Aug 1844 by Rev. Isaac P. Cook

Johnson, Arley Ann (colored) and William Williams (colored) m. 3 Mar 1842 by Rev,. Gerard Morgan (date of lic. not recorded)

Johnson, Caroline and Isaac Henry Jackson m. 19 Nov 1843 by Rev. Dr. George C. M. Roberts

Johnson, Caroline, dau. of Arthur L. and Margaret Johnson, b. 19 Nov 1840, bapt. 17 Nov 1845 by Rev. Dr. George C. M. Roberts

Johnson, Cassa H., d. circa 1847-1850 (exact date not given in Record of Members)

Johnson, Cato (colored) and Rachel Jones (colored) m. 23 Feb 1841 by Rev. Samuel Keppler (date of lic. not recorded)

Johnson, Edward, son of William and Sarah Johnson, b. 16 Feb 1842, bapt. 29 May 1842 by Rev. Henry Slicer

Johnson, Eleanor and Jacob Miller m. 16 Sep 1840 by Rev. Joseph Shane

Johnson, Eliza, d. circa 1845 (death noted in Class List) [Ed. Note: She was possibly the Eliza Johnson whose death notice in the Baltimore Sun stated that she d. 16 Jan 1847.]

Johnson, Ellen, dau. of Arthur L. and Margaret Johnson, b. 9 Nov 1845, bapt. 17 Nov 1845 by Rev. Dr. George C. M. Roberts

Johnson, Francis and Mary Ann Flyn m. 23 Apr 1840 by Rev. John Bear

Johnson, George (colored) and Elizabeth Grinnage (colored) m. 2 Jul 1846 by Rev. Samuel Keppler

Johnson, George W. and Sarah Ann Welling m. 19 Jul 1849 by Rev. Dr. George C. M. Roberts

Johnson, Hannah and Joseph Brass m. 6 Oct 1847 by Rev. Benjamin F. Brooke

Johnson, Henrietta Hope, dau. of Joseph T. and Ann S. Johnson, b. 9 Jan 1848, bapt. 22 Sep 1850 by Rev. Dr. George C. M. Roberts

Johnson, James, see "Ann Johnson," q.v.

Johnson, James and Sarah Cathwood m. 1 Apr 1844 by Rev. Dr. George C. M. Roberts

Johnson, Jeremiah and Eliza Ann Young m. 28 Sep 1845 by Rev. Dr. George C. M. Roberts

Johnson, John Frith, son of William and Sarah Johnson, b. 12 Dec 1838, bapt. 29 May 1842 by Rev. Henry Slicer

Johnson, John J. and Mary Ann Reaves, both of Baltimore County, m. ---- [date not given] by Rev. George Hildt, lic. dated 11 Nov 1845

Johnson, John J. and Mary E. Stevenson m. 28 Dec 1847 by Rev. Dr. George C. M. Roberts

Johnson, John M. and Margaret McCormick m. 11 Sep 1845 by Rev. Samuel Keppler (date of lic. not recorded)

Johnson, Joseph T. and Ann S. Harvey m. 23 Dec 1841 by Rev. Dr. George C. M. Roberts

Johnson, Joshua and Jane Kerrick m. 22 Dec 1850 by Rev. Isaac P. Cook

Johnson, Laura, dau. of Arthur L. and Margaret Johnson, b. 15 Dec 1842, bapt. 17 Nov 1845 by Rev. Dr. George C. M. Roberts

Johnson, Mary and William J. McClatchie m. 28 May 1846 by Rev. Dr. George C. M. Roberts

Johnson, Mary E. and George W. Zeigler m. 4 Mar 1845 at the house of B. Waugh in Baltimore by Rev. Beverly Waugh, lic. dated 3 Mar 1845

Johnson, Mary Jane and Samuel L. Barton m. 13 Apr 1847 by Rev. Stephen A. Roszel, lic. dated same day

Johnson, Mary S. and Coupland Houston m. 18 Oct 1846 by Rev. Samuel Keppler (date of lic. not recorded)

Johnson, Philip and Sarah Wisner m. 14 Nov 1850 by Rev. Henry Slicer, lic. dated 22 Oct 1850

Johnson, Priscilla and Elijah Sterret m. 10 Mar 1842 by Rev. Joseph Shane

Johnson, Rebecca, dau. of Arthur L. and Margaret Johnson, b. 18 Mar 1838(?), bapt. 17 Nov 1845 by Rev. Dr. George C. M. Roberts

Johnson, Samuel Augustus, son of Joseph T. and Ann S. Johnson, b. 13 Apr 1849, bapt. 22 Sep 1850 by Rev. Dr. George C. M. Roberts

Johnson, Susan Elizabeth, dau. of Samuel and Susanna C. Johnson, b. 20 Feb 1839, bapt. 8 Mar 1840 by Rev. Dr. George C. M. Roberts

Johnson, Susan S. and Henry S. King m. 14 Dec 1848 by Rev. Dr. George C. M. Roberts

Johnson, Theodore, son of William and Susanna Johnson, aged 2 years and 2 months [b. 1840], bapt. 7 Mar 1842 by Rev. Wesley Stevenson

Johnson, Wilhemina J. and Henry Clay Jarrett m. 8 May 1849 at Light Street Church in Baltimore by Rev. Beverly Waugh, lic. dated 7 May 1849

Johnson, William and Eliza Saddler m. ---- [blank] by Rev. John S. Martin, lic. dated 27 May 1850

Johnson, William O. and Sarah Ann Price m. 25 Sep 1845 by Rev. James Sewell, lic. dated 26 Sep 1845 [sic]

Johnson, William T. and Mary Ann Rogers m. 24 Jul 1849 by Rev. Dr. George C. M. Roberts

Johnston, Amelia J. B. and Charles T. Morris m. 22 Dec 1840 by Rev. Samuel Keppler, lic. dated 21 Dec 1840

Johnston, Andrew Jackson, son of John J. and Sarah Johnston, b. 12 Mar 1844, bapt. 10 Sep 1844 by Rev. Isaac P. Cook

Johnston, John Jefferson, son of John J. and Sarah Johnston, b. 4 Oct 1842, bapt. 19 Jan 1843 by Rev. Isaac P. Cook

Johnston, Mary Ann and William A. Sauerwein, both of Baltimore County, m. 4 Jan 1843 by Rev. Nelson Head

Johnston, Mary Jane and James B. Street m. 7 Oct 1847 by Rev. James H. Brown, lic. dated 6 Oct 1847

Jolley, George Thomas, son of John and Mary Ann Jolley, b. 13 May 1830, bapt. 12 Jun 1844 by Rev. James Sewell

Jolley, Mary Lettetta, dau. of John and Elizabeth Jolley, b. 10 May 1843, bapt. 12 Jun 1844 by Rev. James Sewell

Jolley, Robert Henry, son of John and Elizabeth Jolley, b. ---- [blank], bapt. 12 Jun 1844 by Rev. James Sewell

Jolly, Elizabeth, d. 1845 (death noted in Class List) [Ed. Note: Death notice in the Baltimore Sun stated that Elizabeth Jolly d. 19 Jul 1845.]

Jones, Alexander and Isabella C. Shaw m. ---- [blank] by Rev. John S. Martin, lic. dated 5 Mar 1850 [Ed. Note: Their marriage notice in the Baltimore Sun stated Alexander Shaw m. Isabella C. Shaw, dau. of William Shaw, on 7 Mar 1850.]

Jones, Amelia Sophia, dau. of Hamilton and Ann Maria Jones, b. 15 Apr 1840, bapt. 26 Sep 1840 by Rev. Joseph Shane

Jones, Ann and Joshua Jones m. 26 Aug 1845 by Rev. Dr. George C. M. Roberts

Jones, Barzella and Mary J.(S.?) Sumwalt m. 1 Jun 1847 by Rev. Wesley Stevenson

Jones, Charlotte M. and John W. Ward m. 30 Jul 1844 by Rev. James Sewell, lic. dated same day

Jones, David Alexander and Julia Ann Jenkins m. 26 Nov 1840 by Rev. Samuel Keppler (date of lic. not recorded)

Jones, Elizabeth and James McBride m. 19 Jul 1846 by Rev. Joseph Shane

Jones, Elizabeth J. and Joseph Sadler m. 26 Jul 1849 by Rev. Joseph Shane

Jones, Emily Catherine and Thomas Munn m. 13 Jan 1845 by Rev. Joseph Shane

Jones, Esther, dau. of John and Elizabeth Jones, b. 4 Apr 1841, bapt. 6 Jun 1840 [sic] by Rev. Dr. George C. M. Roberts

Jones, Henry and Maria Folgar m. 8 Oct 1840 by Rev. Samuel Keppler, lic. dated 6 Oct 1840

Jones, Henry and Henrietta G. Cross, both of Baltimore County, m. 26 Sep 1840 by Rev. Bernard H. Nadal

Jones, Henry A. Inloes, son of William and Caroline Jones, aged 3 years and 1 month [b. 1839], bapt. 26 Jun 1842 by Rev. Joseph Merriken

Jones, Henry Aisquith, son of Joseph and Martha Jones, b. 15 Apr 1840, bapt. 20 Nov 1840 by Rev. Charles B. Tippett

Jones, Hester A. E. and Charles Allen m. 25 Aug 1845 by Rev. Joseph Shane

Jones, Isaac and Mary Pickett m. 14 Oct 1842 by Rev. Joseph Shane

Jones, Isabel and Thomas A. Bean m. 9 Oct 1844 by Rev. James Sewell, lic. dated 8 Oct 1844

Jones, James W. and Rose A. Wingert m. 27 May 1849 by Rev. John S. Martin, lic. dated 26 May 1849

Jones, Jane H. and Andrew D. White m. 3 May 1849 by Rev. Joseph Shane

Jones, John, see "Hannah Skinner," q.v.

Jones, John and Catharine Gardner m. 15 Apr 1847 by Rev. Stephen A. Roszel, lic. dated 13 Apr 1847

Jones, John Joseph, son of Joseph and Martha Jones, b. 15 Sep 1834, bapt. 20 Nov 1840 by Rev. Charles B. Tippett

Jones, John S. and Sophia Griffith m. 21 Mar 1849 by Rev. William Hirst

Jones, Joshua and Ann Jones m. 26 Aug 1845 by Rev. Dr. George C. M. Roberts

Jones, Justinea Ann, dau. of Ezekiel and Sophia Jones, aged 16 months [b. 1840], bapt. 1 Dec 1841 by Rev. Gerard Morgan

Jones, Leah, d. after 1840 (exact date not given in Record of Members) [*Ed. Note:* Death notice in the *Baltimore Sun* stated that Leah Jones d. 10 Nov 1842.]

Jones, Leven and Jenet Bohen, both of Baltimore, MD, m. 24 Dec 1840

Jones, Levin and Ann Elizabeth Harrison m. 7 Jan 1849 by Rev. Stephen A. Roszel, lic. dated 6 Jan 1849

Jones, Lewis and Mary Ann Doxson m. 3 Aug 1842 by Rev. Dr. George C. M. Roberts

Jones, Malachi and Elizabeth Knox m. 22 Nov 1845 by Rev. Dr. George C. M. Roberts

Jones, Maria Ann and Henry Shanter m. 2 Dec 1840 by Rev. Samuel Keppler, lic. dated same day

Jones, Martha E. and John H. Case m. 13 Dec 1849 by Rev. Dr. George C. M. Roberts

Jones, Mary and William Jarrett, both of Baltimore County, m. 25 Oct 1845 by Rev. William Hamilton

Jones, Mary and William G. Davis m. 26 May 1848 by Rev. Joseph Shane

Jones, Mary Ann and Israel Ortlip m. 26 Jul 1846 by Rev. Wesley Stevenson

Jones, Mary Ann and Ephraim Pierce m. 21 Dec 1843 by Rev. Joseph Shane

Jones, Mary E., dau. of Lemuel and Elizabeth Jones, aged 16 months [b. 1839], bapt. 20 Jul 1840 by Rev. Gerard Morgan

Jones, Mary Elizabeth and Thomas James Edwards m. 2 Jan 1843 by Rev. Job Guest, lic. dated same day

Jones, Mary Elizabeth, dau. of Hamilton and Ann Maria Jones, b. 27 Feb 1837, bapt. 26 Sep 1840 by Rev. Joseph Shane

Jones, Rachel (colored) and Cato Johnson (colored) m. 23 Feb 1841 by Rev. Samuel Keppler (date of lic. not recorded)

Jones, Rebecca, d. circa 1847-1850 (exact date not given in Record of Members)

Jones, Reese and Jane Losquem m. 25 Jun 1844 by Rev. James Sewell, lic. dated same day

Jones, Robert Henry, son of Robert and Mary Jones, b. 29 Jun 1839, New York, bapt. 2 Mar 1840, Baltimore, by Rev. Samuel Keppler

Jones, Ruth and William Burgess m. 15 Sep 1844 by Rev. Joseph Shane

Jones, Sarah Jane, dau. of Capt. W. B. and Sarah Ann Jones, b. 21 Mar 1847, bapt. 10 Apr 1847 by Rev. Dr. George C. M. Roberts

Jones, Sarah M., dau. of John and Elizabeth Jones, b. 5 Dec 1846, bapt. 29 Sep 1849 by Rev. John S. Martin

Jones, Stephen Fuller, son of Margaret Jones, aged 6 years [b. 1850 or 1851] bapt. 1 Jun 1857 by Rev. William A. Snively

Jones, Susanna, dau. of Hamilton and Ann Maria Jones, b. 17 Jul 1838, bapt. 26 Sep 1840 by Rev. Joseph Shane

Jones, Susannah and James Williams Marshall m. 28 Oct 1841 by Rev. Gerard Morgan, lic. dated same day

Jones, Teresa and Henry L. Fouse m. 24 Oct 1847 by Rev. Stephen A. Roszel, lic. dated 23 Oct 1847

Jones, Wesley and Ellen Woods m. 12 Aug 1841 by Rev. Dr. George C. M. Roberts

Jones, William B. and Elizabeth James m. 19 Nov 1840 by Rev. Samuel Keppler, lic. dated same day

Jones, William H. and Mary McCormick m. 20 Nov 1844 by Rev. James Sewell, lic. dated 10 Nov 1844

Jones, William Henry, son of Margaret Jones, aged 9 years [b. 1848], bapt. 1 Jun 1857 by Rev. William A. Snively

Jones, William Henry, son of John and Elizabeth Jones, b. 28 Sep 1849, bapt. 29 Sep 1849 by Rev. John S. Martin

Jones, William Humphrey, son of William H. and Martha Jones, b. 9 Oct 1849, bapt. 4 Mar 1849 by Rev. Dr. George C. M. Roberts

Jones, William Thomas, son of Capt. W. B. and Sarah Ann Jones, b. 21 Mar 1847, bapt. 10 Apr 1847 by Rev. Dr. George C. M. Roberts

Jordan, John B. and Martha Ann Townsend m. 1 Jan 1840 by Rev. John Bear

Jordan, John B. and Mary E. Rengrose (Ringrose) m. 5 Oct 1847 by Rev. Stephen A. Roszel, lic. dated 4 Oct 1847

Jorden, Jemima Jane, dau. of William and Elizabeth Jorden, b. 30 Jul 1837, Fells Point, Baltimore City, bapt. 17 May 1840 by Rev. Samuel Keppler

Jordon, Sophia and John W. Pollard m. 13 Jan 1848 by Rev. Benjamin F. Brooke

Joy, Sarah Catherine, dau. of James F. and Catherine Joy, b. 27 Feb 1831, bapt. 30 Jun 1844 by Rev. James Sewell

Joy, William Edwin, son of James F. and Catherine Joy, b. 21 May 1844, bapt. 30 Jun 1844 by Rev. James Sewell

Joyce, George H. and Eliza Greenly m. 8 Oct 1843 by Rev. Dr. George C. M. Roberts

Jubb, Elizabeth, d. 1849 (death noted in Class List)

Jubb, Margaret Ann and William J. Watkins m. 28 Jun 1846 by Rev. Joseph Shane

Jubb, Reuben and Jane Foster m. 25 Oct 1840 by Rev. Samuel Keppler, lic. dated 24 Oct 1840

Jump, Emily, d. circa 1850 (exact date not given in Record of Members) [Ed. Note: She was possibly the Emeline Jump, wife of Francis E. Jump, whose death notice in the Baltimore Sun stated that she d. 22 May 1850.]

Junnock, Susan E. and Joseph B. Wolford m. 6 Jan 1848 by Rev. Dr. George C. M. Roberts

Jury, George and Ann Stauter m. 11 Mar 1845 by Rev. Dr. George C. M. Roberts

Jury, Keturrah and Thomas Hudson m. 20 Jan 1842 by Rev. Dr. George C. M. Roberts

Jury, William M. and Barbary A. Tracy m. 29 May 1844 by Rev. James Sewell, lic. dated same day

Justice, Mahlon and Nancy Shipley m. 13 May 1847 by Rev. James H. Brown, lic. dated 8 May 1847

Justice, Sarah and David Banks m. 5 Sep 1841 by Rev. Gerard Morgan, lic. dated 3 Sep 1841

Kane, Amanda, an orphan in the Female Asylum in Mulberry Street, b. 27 Jul 1834, bapt. 4 Oct 1840 by Rev. Thomas Myers

Kane, Mary and James Watkins m. 17 Jun 1845 by Rev. James Sewell, lic. dated 16 Jun 1845

Kane, Virginia, an orphan in the Female Asylum in Mulberry Street, b. 4 May 1836, bapt. 4 Oct 1840 by Rev. Thomas Myers

Karny, James and Emily J. West m. 26 Dec 1845 by Rev. Dr. George C. M. Roberts

Kauf, Elizabeth, dau. of William and Catherine M. Kauf, b. 1 May 1847, bapt. 27 May 1847 by Rev. Dr. George C. M. Roberts

Kauffman, Catherine and Samuel Wood m. 9 Oct 1842 by Rev. Joseph Shane

Kauffman, Henry and Ann Driver m. 10 Dec 1848 by Rev. Joseph Shane

Kay, Margaret Jane and Charles S. Morse m. 24 Jun 1850 by Rev. Dr. George C. M. Roberts

Keatly, Richard, d. 1841 (death noted in Class List)

Keen, George V. and Georgeanna Haggerty m. 1 Jan 1845 by Rev. Dr. George C. M. Roberts

Keener, Eliza, d. circa 1840 (exact date not given in Class Record)

Keenor, Sarah B. and William M. Dunnington, both of Baltimore County, m. 7 Jan 1846 by Rev. William Hamilton

Keiffer, John and Mary Zeigler m. 29 Sep 1846 by Rev. Dr. George C. M. Roberts

Keirle, Talitha A. and Thomas B. Busk m. 5 Apr 1843 at the house of her father Joshua Dryden in Baltimore by Rev. Beverly Waugh, lic. dated 2 Apr 1843

Keith, Robert and Ann Walker m. 26 Dec 1844 by Rev. James Sewell, lic. dated 13 Dec 1844

Kell, George and Eveline Cunningham m. 29 Dec 1847 by Rev. Stephen A. Roszel, lic. dated 23 Dec 1847

Keller, Hugh and Susan Parsons m. 11 Feb 1850 by Rev. Aquila A. Reese, lic. dated 10 Feb 1850

Keller, Sarah Jane and Henry Decoursey m. 2 Nov 1848 by Rev. Stephen A. Roszel, lic. dated same day

Kelley, Mary J. and Samuel Shaw m. 25 Mar 1849 by Rev. Isaac P. Cook

Kelly, John and Mary Jane Malloney m. 12 Feb 1850 by Rev. Aquila A. Reese, lic. dated 11 Feb 1850

Kelly, Patrick and Mary Durkee m. 14 Jan 1849 by Rev. Dr. George C. M. Roberts

Kelly, William H. and Nancy Hancock m. 18 Jan 1846 by Rev. Dr. George C. M. Roberts

Kelman, Angeline and John L. Baker m. 26 Dec 1849 by Rev. William Hirst, lic. dated same day

Kemp, Warren P. and Virginia Bockman m. 7 May 1846 by Rev. Dr. George C. M. Roberts

Kemp, William, son of William and Sarah Ann Kemp, b. 4 Mar 1840, bapt. 29 Jul 1840 by Rev. Joseph Shane

Kemp, William A. and Caroline L. Holmes m. 27 Oct 1846 by Rev. Benjamin F. Brooke

Kempton, Henrietta E. and Upton A. Stephens, both of Baltimore County, m. 21 May 1844 by Rev. William Hamilton

Kempton, Moses and Maria L. Bird m. 29 aug 1848 by Rev. Dr. George C. M. Roberts

Kendall, Mary and James Sutton m. 29 Oct 1843 by Rev. Isaac P. Cook

Kendall, Thomas W. and Ann L. Vickers m. 2 May 1849 by Rev. Joseph Shane

Kennedy, Amelia Roberts, dau. of William W. and Catherine E. Kennedy, b. 9 Sep 1850, bapt. 15 Sep 1850 by Rev. Dr. George C. M. Roberts

Kennedy, Catherine E., b. ---- [blank], bapt. 31 Jan 1841 by Rev. Dr. George C. M. Roberts [*Ed. Note:* A later entry in the register stated she was bapt. 5 Feb 1841.]

Kennedy, Catherine Estelle, dau. of William W. and Catherine E. Kennedy, b. 18 Oct 1848, bapt. 13 Nov 1848 by Rev. Dr. George C. M. Roberts

Kennedy, Emma Louisa, dau. of William W. and Catherine E. Kennedy, b. 2 Jan 1843, bapt. 19 Sep 1845 by Rev. Dr. George C. M. Roberts

Kennedy, Henry Hoffman, son of William W. and Catherine E. Kennedy, b. 22 Mar 1847, bapt. 3 Apr 1847 by Rev. Dr. George C. M. Roberts

Kennedy, John Williams, son of William W. and Catherine E. Kennedy, b. 19 Sep 1845, bapt. same day by Rev. Dr. George C. M. Roberts

Kennell, Henrietta and John Forrester m. 5 Dec 1844 by Rev. Joseph Shane

Kent, Sally and James Edward Watson m. 29 Jun 1841 by Rev. Job Guest, lic. dated same day

Kepbron, Ann Elizabeth and Colin F. Hollingsworth m. 15 Sep 1846 by Rev. Dr. George C. M. Roberts

Kephart (Rephart?), Elizabeth, dau. of Lewis and Elizabeth Kephart Rephart(?), b. 15 Jun 1840, bapt. same day by Rev. Dr. George C. M. Roberts

Keppler, Eliza, d. 1847 (death noted in Class List) [*Ed. Note:* Death notice in the *Baltimore Sun* stated that Eliza Keppler, sister of Samuel Keppler, d. 3 Nov 1847.]

Keppler, Mary Jane, d. 1841 (death noted in Class List) [*Ed. Note:* Death notice in the *Baltimore Sun* stated that Mary J. Keppler, wife of Samuel Keppler and dau. of Basil and Elizabeth Waring, d. 4 Jun 1841.]

Keppler, Samuel (Rev.), of the Baltimore Annual Conference, and Miss Permelia Davidson, of Anne Arundel County, m. ---- [date not given], lic. dated 15 Apr 1846. See "Eliza Keppler" and "Mary Jane Keppler," q.v.

Kerlinger, Catherine and David Van Fossen m. 27 Mar 1849 by Rev. Aquila A. Reese, lic. dated 26 Mar 1849

Kerr, Alexander and Elizabeth Bell m. 8 Jan 1850 by Rev. Aquila A. Reese, lic. dated 7 Jan 1850

Kerrick, Jane and Joshua Johnson m. 22 Dec 1850 by Rev. Isaac P. Cook

Kerster(?), William Shaer, son of Charles and Sarah Kerster(?), b. 5 Jul 1846, bapt. 11 Aug 1846 by Rev. Dr. George C. M. Roberts

Kervil, Mary H. and Alvin A. Chickering m. 27 Jul 1847 by Rev. Dr. George C. M. Roberts

Kevans, Isabella, d. 1845 (death noted in Class List)

Keys, John and Ann Maria Thorn m. 5 Aug 1847 by Rev. Dr. George C. M. Roberts

Keys, John J. and Elizabeth A. Buck m. 12 May 1842 by Rev. Joseph Shane

Kidd, Pencilla Ann and Samuel McK. Read m. ---- [blank] by Rev. John S. Martin, lic. dated 25 Nov 1850 [*Ed. Note:* Their marriage notice in the *Baltimore Sun* stated Samuel M. Read m. Pencilla A. Kidd on 26 Nov 1850.]

Kidwell, Elizabeth and John B. Rignor m. 23 Dec 1847 by Rev. Dr. George C. M. Roberts

Kilbourn, Ann E. and Charles H. Shott m. 9 Jun 1850 by Rev. Henry Slicer, lic. dated 7 Jun 1850

Kilbourn, Elbridge G. and Elizabeth Ann Hall m. 6 Nov 1849 at the house of her mother in Baltimore by Rev. Beverly Waugh, lic. dated same day

Kilburn, Matilda (adult), b. ---- [blank], bapt. 8 Sep 1841 by Rev. Gerard Morgan
Killmon, Thomas W. and Charlotte M. Foster m. 20 May 1849 by Rev. John S. Martin, lic. dated 15 May 1849 by Rev. John S. Martin, lic. dated [*Ed. Note:* Their marriage notice in the *Baltimore Sun* gave his name as Thomas W. Killmon even though it looked more like Thomas St. Killmon in the church register.]
Kilty, Elizabeth Jane, dau. of William and Matilda Kilty, b. 28 Aug 1840, bapt. ---- 184- [page torn] by Rev. ---- (name not indicated) [*Ed. Note:* Information was written on a piece of paper and inserted in the church register.]
Kimberly, George Stansbury, son of Jeremiah McK. and Olivia Kimberly, b. 10 Dec 1845, bapt. 27 May 1847 by Rev. Dr. George C. M. Roberts
King, Adaline, of Baltimore, MD, and Albert R. Bolour m. 11 Oct 1840 by Rev. John A. Hening
King, Elizabeth Ann, dau. of Samuel and Elizabeth King, b. 17 Nov 1850, bapt. 3 Apr 1851 by Rev. Dr. George C. M. Roberts
King, Henry, son of Henry S. and Susan S. King, b. 24 Dec 1849, bapt. 26 Jan 1852 by Rev. Dr. George C. M. Roberts
King, Henry S. and Susan S. Johnson m. 14 Dec 1848 by Rev. Dr. George C. M. Roberts
King, Jacob, d. -- Mar 1844 (death noted in Record of Members) [*Ed. Note:* Death notice in the *Baltimore Sun* stated that Jacob King d. 13 Mar 1844.]
King, John, d. 1847 (death noted in Probationers Book) [*Ed. Note:* Death notice in the *Baltimore Sun* stated that John King d. 30 Mar 1847.]
King, Lucy Ann, d. 1841 (death noted in Class List)
King, Sarah Catharine, dau. of Jared and Eliza King, aged 1 year, bapt. 12 Sep 1841 by Rev. Robert Emory
King, Sarah Ellen, dau. of John and Eliza King, b. 13 Mar 1846, Baltimore, bapt. 27 Jun 1847 by Rev. Stephen A. Roszel
Kinnman, Margaret Ann and Samuel Harris m. 16 Apr 1844 by Rev. Joseph Merriken
Kinzendolff, Rosina and Benjamin Whittle m. 9 Jul 1844 by Rev. Joseph Shane
Kinzie, Sarah A. and William Iiams, both of Baltimore County, m. 16 Apr 1840 by Rev. Bernard H. Nadal
Kipp, Albert, son of John W. and Margaret L. Kipp, b. 25 May 1850, bapt. 17 Jul 1850 by Rev. Dr. George C. M. Roberts
Kipp, John Gist, son of John William and Margaret Louisa Kipp, b. 18 Jul 1842, bapt. 13 Jan 1844 by Rev. Dr. George C. M. Roberts
Kipp, Mary Ecleston, dau. of John William and Margaret Louisa Kipp, b. 4 Jul 1840, bapt. 13 Jan 1844 by Rev. Dr. George C. M. Roberts
Kipp, William Henry, son of John William and Margaret Louisa Kipp, b. 8 Dec 1843, bapt. 13 Jan 1844 by Rev. Dr. George C. M. Roberts
Kirby, Allen and Martha A. Farringer m. 26 Apr 1845 by Rev. James Sewell, lic. dated 8 May 1845 [*sic*]
Kirby, Ann, d. circa 1847 (death noted in Class List) [*Ed. Note:* Death notice in the *Baltimore Sun* stated that Ann E. Kirby d. 31 Jan 1848.]
Kirby, Elizabeth, dau. of ---- [blank] and Mary Kirby, b. 5 Oct 1839, bapt. 28 Apr 1840 by Rev. Dr. George C. M. Roberts
Kirby, John, see "Sarah Kirby," q.v.

Kirby, Mary and Thomas Walker m. 11 Jun 1849 by Rev. Dr. George C. M. Roberts

Kirby, Mary Ellen and Robert B. Meads m. 4 Jul 1847 by Rev. Stephen A. Roszel, lic. dated 3 Jul 1847

Kirby, Sarah, d. 1845 (death noted in Class List) [*Ed. Note:* Death notice in the *Baltimore Sun* stated that Sarah Kirby, widow of John Kirby, d. 13 Aug 1845

Kirby, Sarah, d. circa 1847 (death noted in Class List)

Kirby, Sarah J. and Charles F. Crisp m. 31 Jul 1842 by Rev. Henry Slicer, lic. dated 29 Jul 1842

Kirby, Susan and William Flannigan m. 12 Apr 1848 by Rev. Dr. George C. M. Roberts

Kirkland, David and Mary Ann Miller m. 17 Jun 1845 by Rev. James Sewell, lic. dated same day

Kirkland, Margaret and John S. Weeks m. 16 Oct 1850 at the house of her father in Baltimore by Rev. Beverly Waugh, lic. dated 14 Oct 1850

Kirkley, Thomas and Sarah Ann Uppercoe m. 20 Aug 1846 by Rev. Littleton F. Morgan, lic. dated same day

Kirkwood, William H. and Catherine A. Elliott m. 30 Jun 1846 by Rev. Dr. George C. M. Roberts

Kirwan, John R. and Jane Agel m. 13 Sep 1845 by Rev. Dr. George C. M. Roberts

Klein, Martha Ann and James Lee m. 9 Jan 1845 by Rev. Dr. George C. M. Roberts

Kline, Frances Augusta and Eugene Ahern m. 28 Sep 1844 by Rev. Isaac P. Cook

Kline, Frederick and Sarah A. Martin m. 1 Aug 1850 by Rev. Henry Slicer, lic. dated same day

Kline, Margaret T. and Barnet K. Merryman m. 23 Apr 1846 by Rev. Dr. George C. M. Roberts

Klockgelter, Amelia and Edward William Brown m. 9 Aug 1841 by Rev. Job Guest, lic. dated same day

Knapp, Avarilla G. and John Hugg m. 27 Jul 1840 by Rev. Samuel Keppler, lic. dated same day

Knapp, Henry Moore, son of Josiah and Mary C. Knapp (residents of New York), b. 12 Dec 1845, bapt. 30 Aug 1846 by Rev. Dr. George C. M. Roberts

Knapp, Mary Emma, dau. of Josiah and Mary C. Knapp (residents of New York), b. 11 Aug 1843, bapt. 30 Aug 1846 by Rev. Dr. George C. M. Roberts

Knapp, Rebecca, d. circa 1847 (death noted in Class List) [*Ed. Note:* Death notice in the *Baltimore Sun* stated that Rebecca Knap d. 13 Feb 1848.]

Knauf, Phillip Hiss, son of William and Catherine M. Knauf, b. 10 Aug 1848, bapt. 7 Oct 1848 by Rev. Dr. George C. M. Roberts

Knight, Almira and John Debow, Jr. m. 10 Jan 1847 by Rev. Dr. George C. M. Roberts

Knight, Amelia and Anthony Cross m. 26 Feb 1843 by Rev. Job Guest, lic. dated 25 Feb 1843

Knight, Clara Ann and Robert Liddle m. 3 Jun 1845 by Rev. Isaac P. Cook

Knight, Comfort, d. circa 1840 (exact date not given in Class Record)

Knight, Ellen and George W. Crisall m. 9 Jul 1846 by Rev. Dr. George C. M. Roberts

Knight, George Henry, son of Henry N. and Mary Ellen Knight, b. 14 Feb 1850, bapt. 15 May 1851 by Rev. Dr. George C. M. Roberts

Knight, John and Elmira Sheppard m. 9 Jun 1845 by Rev. Wesley Stevenson

Knight, Mary Elizabeth and Jacob F. McClean m. 21 Aug 1848 by Rev. Dr. George C. M. Roberts

Knight, Orman and Sarah Ann Durham m. 28 Sep 1848 by Rev. Joseph Shane

Knight, Susan M. and William Parks m. 3 Nov 1845 by Rev. Dr. George C. M. Roberts

Knighton, John Oliver Parker, son of John Wesley and Sarah Jane Knighton, b. 6 Sep 1844, bapt. 15 Nov 1845 by Rev. Dr. George C. M. Roberts

Knighton, Mary Margaretta, dau. of John W. and Sarah L. Knighton, b. 27 Sep 1843, bapt. 4 Oct 1843 by Rev. Dr. George C. M. Roberts

Knipe, William M. and Ann R. Rankin m. 15 Jun 1848 by Rev. Stephen A. Roszel, lic. dated 13 Jun 1848

Knowles, George Henry, son of Thomas and Sarah Knowles, b. 7 Jul 1842, bapt. 27 Jul 1842 by Rev. Elisha D. Owen

Knowles, Thomas Franklin, son of Thomas and Sarah Knowles, b. 1 Dec 1840, bapt. 27 Jul 1842 by Rev. Elisha D. Owen

Knox, Elizabeth and Malachi Jones m. 22 Nov 1845 by Rev. Dr. George C. M. Roberts

Kone, Henry and Mary Gamble m. 1 Sep 1843 by Rev. Joseph Shane

Kraft, George C. M. Roberts, son of Jacob and Christiana S. Kraft, b. 24 Aug 1850, bapt. 6 Aug 1851 by Rev. Dr. George C. M. Roberts

Kraft, Jacob and Christianna S. Kraft, b. 23 Aug 1849, bapt. 3 Sep 1849 by Rev. Dr. George C. M. Roberts

Kraft, Jacob Henry, son of Jacob and Christiana S. Kraft, b. 6 Aug 1847, bapt. 14 Aug 1847 by Rev. Dr. George C. M. Roberts

Kraft, Sophia Sevilla, dau. of Jacob and Christiana S. Kraft, b. 4 Mar 1846, bapt. 17 Mar 1846 by Rev. Dr. George C. M. Roberts

Krager, Mary J. and Benjamin F. Harris, both of Baltimore County, m. ---- [date not given] by Rev. George Hildt, lic. dated 25 Mar 1846

Kramer, Clara Virginia Cookman, dau. of Samuel and Rebecca Kramer, b. 16 Jul 1847, bapt. 2 Nov 1847 by Rev. Dr. George C. M. Roberts

Kramer, Clarissa, d. circa 1850 (exact date not given in Record of Members) [Ed. Note: Death notice in the Baltimore Sun stated that Clarissa Kramer, mother of Samuel Kramer, d. 25 Jul 1850.]

Kramer, Samuel, see "Clarissa Kramer," q.v.

Kramer, William Roberts, son of Samuel and Rebecca Kramer, b. 11 Aug 1841, bapt. 3 Oct 1841 by Rev. Dr. George C. M. Roberts

Krebbs (Kribbs), Caroline, d. after 1841 (death noted in Class List) [Ed. Note: Death notice in the Baltimore Sun stated that Caroline Krebs, wife of Jacob Krebs, d. 19 Apr 1843.]

Krebbs, George, d. circa 1842-1844 (exact date not given in Record of Members) [Ed. Note: Death notice in the Baltimore Sun stated that George Krebs d. 1 Apr 1843.]

Krebs, Jacob, see "Caroline Krebbs," q.v.

Krebs, John William, son of Nathaniel and Martha Krebs, b. 10 Jan 1841, bapt. 29 Sep 1841 by Rev. Dr. George C. M. Roberts

Kretch, Samuel and Elizabeth, see "Ann Walton," q.v.

Kriel, Caroline and Jacob H. Medairy m. 18 Jan 1844 by Rev. Dr. George C. M. Roberts

Kruse, Charles J. and Margaret Elizabeth Wilson m. 8 Sep 1850 by Rev. Isaac P. Cook

Kunds, Henry and Ann Myers m. 10 Aug 1845 by Rev. Joseph Shane

Labdyer, Nicholas and Mary Sharp m. 20 Sep 1847 by Rev. Dr. George C. M. Roberts

Lafferty, Sarah J. and John W. Delcher m. 9 Oct 1842 by Rev. Henry Slicer, lic. dated 8 Oct 1842

Laird, Thomas and Rachel Bond m. 17 Sep 1843 by Rev. Phillip B. Reese (date of lic. not recorded)

Lamb, Ann, d. 1849 (death noted in Class List) [*Ed. Note:* Death notice in the *Baltimore Sun* stated that Ann Lamb, mother of William D. Harris, d. 19 Mar 1849.]

Lambdin, Charles W. and Aleathea Mewshaw m. 15 Apr 1847 by Rev. Benjamin F. Brooke

Lambdin, John W. and Sarah E. Tilghman m. 29 Nov 1849 by Rev. Dr. George C. M. Roberts [*Ed. Note:* Her last name was misspelled "Tilgman" in the marriage register.]

Lamben, John R. and E. H. Bennett m. 4 May 1849 by Rev. William Hirst

Lamberson, Rixin Leveret, son of John and Margaret Lamberson, b. 27 Sep 1844, bapt. 20 Apr 1845 by Rev. Dr. George C. M. Roberts

Lambert, Margaretta and Charles French m. 9 Jul 1850 by Rev. Dr. George C. M. Roberts

Landis, Edmund (Dr.) and Hannah P. Robinson m. 30 Oct 1845 by Rev. Samuel Keppler (date of lic. not recorded)

Landon, Elizabeth K. and William C. Matthews m. 27 Apr 1848 by Rev. Isaac P. Cook

Landon, Mary W. and Richard P. Sherwood m. 16 Feb 1841 by Rev. Isaac P. Cook

Landstreet, Ann Verlinda and Upton Slingluff m. 15 Mar 1842 at the house of her father in Baltimore by Rev. Beverly Waugh, lic. dated same day

Landstreet, Lucy, dau. of Samuel and Maria Anna Landstreet, b. 1 Apr 1843, bapt. 23 Apr 1843 by Rev. Dr. George C. M. Roberts

Lane, Margaret K. and Julien Jacobs m. 22 Oct 1845 by Rev. Samuel Keppler (date of lic. not recorded)

Lane, Sarah Ann and John S. Hoofnogle m. 22 Dec 1842 by Rev. Dr. George C. M. Roberts

Lane, Sewell F. and Virginia A. Twiford m. 24 Mar 1843 by Rev. Isaac P. Cook

Langford, Ann Rebecca, dau. of William and Mary A. Langford, b. 8 Jun 1836, bapt. 3 Jun 1842 by Rev. Elisha D. Owen

Langford, Eliza Jane, dau. of William and Mary A. Langford, b. 22 Oct 1837, bapt. 3 Jun 1842 by Rev. Elisha D. Owen

Langford, Elizabeth R., dau. of William and Elizabeth Langford, b. -- Oct 1842, bapt. 17 Jan 1843 by Rev. Elisha D. Owen

Langford, Samuel T., son of William and Mary A. Langford, b. 2 Jul 1839, bapt. 3 Jun 1842 by Rev. Elisha D. Owen

Langley, Ann E. and J. A. Dunbar, both of Baltimore County, m. 10 Sep 1840 by Rev. Bernard H. Nadal [*Ed. Note:* Her first name was misspelled "Aan" in the marriage register.]

Langston, Elizabeth Catherine, b. 5 Apr 1813, bapt. 10 Feb 1849 by Rev. Dr. George C. M. Roberts

Langston, Frances Ann, dau. of Lawrence and Elizabeth C. Langston, b. 1 Dec 1848, bapt. 10 Feb 1849 by Rev. Dr. George C. M. Roberts

Langwell, Ann E. and Joseph Gibbons m. 16 Aug 1846 by Rev. Samuel Keppler (date of lic. not recorded)

Lankford, Elizabeth, d. circa 1850 (death noted in Class List) [*Ed. Note:* Death notice in the *Baltimore Sun* stated that Elizabeth Lankford, wife of William Lankford, d. 17 Dec 1850.]

Lankford, Hesther and John Wood m. ---- [blank] by Rev. John S. Martin, lic. dated 5 Oct 1850 [*Ed. Note:* Their marriage notice in the *Baltimore Sun* stated that John Woods m. Hester Lankford on 6 Oct 1850.]

Lankford, Isaac and Harriet Hurley m. 16 May 1842 by Rev. Joseph Shane

Lankford, Mary J. and Marcellus R. Hitch m. 21 May 1845 by Rev. James Sewell, lic. dated 20 May 1845

Lankford, Robert Henry, son of ---- [blank], b. 13 Jul 1849, bapt. 3 Sep 1849 by Rev. John S. Martin

Lankford, William, see "Elizabeth Lankford," q.v.

Lannahan, John (Rev.) and Mary E. Andrews m. ---- [blank] by Rev. Littleton F. Morgan, lic. dated 13 May 1846

Lansdale, Cassandra B. and Edwin L. Parker m. 31 Aug 1840 by Rev. Wesley Stevenson

Lansdale, Isaac W. and Jane D. Tomblinson m. 14 Nov 1848 by Rev. Wesley Stevenson

Larimer, Mary and Joseph G. Wade m. 17 Dec 1843 by Rev. Phillip B. Reese (date of lic. not recorded)

Larkin, Susan A. and Frederick H. Ditterich m. 19 Dec 1847 by Rev. Dr. George C. M. Roberts

Latham, Edward and Amanda Melvina Hopkins m. 31 Dec 1840 by Rev. Samuel Keppler, lic. dated 30 Dec 1840

Latham, Joseph and Martha Clark m. 24 Sep 1846 by Rev. Dr. George C. M. Roberts

Lauder, Almira Priscilla and James F. Jackson m. 7 Aug 1843 by Rev. Henry Slicer, lic. dated same day

Lauderman, Georgiana, dau. of ---- [blank], b. 8 Dec 1834, bapt. -- Jun 1844 by Rev. James Sewell

Lauderman, Henry Barnes, son of ---- [blank], b. 15 Dec 1843, bapt. -- Jun 1844 by Rev. James Sewell

Lauderman, James Shep, son of ---- [blank], b. 5 Feb 1835, bapt. -- Jun 1844 by Rev. James Sewell

Laughlin, Mary Lavinia, dau. of Thomas and Margaret Laughlin, b. 14 Apr 1838, bapt. 20 Apr 1841 by Rev. Robert Emory

Laughlin, Thomas Henry Harrison, son of Thomas and Margaret Laughlin, b. 30 Aug 1839, bapt. 20 Apr 1841 by Rev. Robert Emory

Laurenson, Robert J. and Mary Ann Shanks, both of Baltimore County, m. 28 May 1844 by Rev. William Hamilton

Lawrence, ---- [blank] and M. A. Booth m. 1 May 1849 by Rev. William Hirst [*Ed. Note:* Their marriage notice in the *Baltimore Sun* gave their names as Matthew A. Booth and Anna L. Lawrence.]

Lawrence, Charles J. and Ellen Scharff m. 23 Nov 1848 by Rev. William Hirst

Lawrence, Margaret, d. circa 1840-1847 (exact date not given in Record of Members)

Lawrenson, John W. and Sophia Smiley, both of Baltimore County, m. 14 Apr 1845 by Rev. William Hamilton, lic. dated 4 Apr 1845

Lawson, Henry S. and Harriet M. Barker m. 13 Jan 1848 by Rev. Stephen A. Roszel, lic. dated same day

Lawson, Sarah and George W. Young, both of Baltimore County, m. 18 May 1843 by Rev. S. S. Roszel, lic. dated same day

Leach, Charles and Sophia Ailman m. 10 Aug 1847 by Rev. Stephen A. Roszel, lic. dated same day

Leach, Charlotte F. and Haman Battow m. 10 Mar 1845 by Rev. James Sewell, lic. dated 2 Mar 1845

Leach, Sarah J., dau. of Benedict and Harriot Leach, b. 19 Sep 1842, bapt. 28 Nov 1842 by Rev. William Prettyman

Leakin, Hannah, of Baltimore County, and Isaac Collins, of Frederick County, MD, m. 4 Jul 1843 by Rev. S. S. Roszel, lic. dated same day

Leary, Basil W. and Caroline Goulden m. 5 Oct 1845 by Rev. Samuel Keppler (date of lic. not recorded)

Leary, Elizabeth and John Benjamin Andrews m. 28 Aug 1850 by Rev. John S. Martin, lic. dated 24 Aug 1850

Leary, Rebecca Ann and James J. Darrington m. 12 Nov 1844 by Rev. James Sewell, lic. dated 9 Nov 1844

Leatch, Elizabeth A. and George W. Earheart, both of Baltimore County, m. 8 Feb 1843 by Rev. Nelson Head

Leatherbury, Margaret S. and Thomas W. Evans m. 27 Jan 1848 by Rev. Dr. George C. M. Roberts

Leaville, Sarah and Samuel Hollingshead m. 11 Jun 1846 by Rev. Dr. George C. M. Roberts

Lebrun, Ambrose and Maria Thireon m. 30 Apr 1844 by Rev. Dr. George C. M. Roberts

Lechler, Adeline Seggrave and James Alexander Anderson m. 27 May 1840 by Rev. Samuel Keppler, lic. dated same day

Leddy, Barney and Elizabeth Ellen Lednum m. 20 Nov 1845 by Rev. Samuel Keppler (date of lic. not recorded)

Ledley, Agnes and John Moltz m. 17 Jun 1841 by Rev. Joseph Shane

Ledman, Sarah Ann, dau. of John and Julia Ann Ledman, b. -- Aug 1840, bapt. 20 Sep 1840 by Rev. Thomas Myers

Lednum, Elizabeth Ellen and Barney Leddy m. 20 Nov 1845 by Rev. Samuel Keppler (date of lic. not recorded)

Lednum, Mary J. and William W. Thorrington m. 25 May 1843 by Rev. Isaac P. Cook

Ledsinger, Rebecca and Jeremiah Paul m. 29 Apr 1845 by Rev. James Sewell, lic. dated 22 Apr 1845

Lee, Ann M. D. and Henry F. Byrne m. 18 Nov 1847 by Rev. Dr. George C. M. Roberts

Lee, Elizabeth and Philip Rigby m. 10 May 1842 by Rev. Dr. George C. M. Roberts

Lee, James and Martha Ann Klein m. 9 Jan 1845 by Rev. Dr. George C. M. Roberts

Lee, John R. and Elizabeth A. Oursler m. 21 Jun 1849 by Rev. Isaac P. Cook

Lee, Mary and George Steers m. 25 Oct 1841 by Rev. Joseph Shane

Lee, Mary and William Frazier m. 12 Jul 1846 by Rev. Joseph Shane

Lee, Mary A. and Levi Pearce m. 23 Dec 1841 by Rev. Joseph Shane

Lee, Mary Elizabeth, dau. of John and Sarah Lee, b. 18 Nov 1840, bapt. 23 Jul 184-
[page torn] by Rev. ---- (name not indicated) [*Ed. Note:* Information was
written on a piece of paper and inserted in the church register.]

Lefevre, Alice King, dau. of David and Comfort Lefevre, b. 12 Jan 1850, bapt. 9
Mar 1852 by Rev. Dr. George C. M. Roberts

Lefevre, John Wesley, son of Charles and Anna Maria Lefevre, b. 1 Jan 1835, bapt.
16 Jul 1844 by Rev. Dr. George C. M. Roberts

Lefevre, Mary Ann, dau. of Charles and Anna Maria Lefevre, b. 1 Jun 1839, bapt.
16 Jul 1844 by Rev. Dr. George C. M. Roberts

Legar, Eliza Jane, see "Eliza Jane Egarrer" q.v.

Legard, Joseph and Elizabeth Oor *[sic]* m. 2 Jan 1844 by Rev. Henry Slicer, lic.
dated same day

Legg, James W. and Mary Ann Lenox m. 22 May 1845 by Rev. Isaac P. Cook

Legg, John Thomas and Sarah Ann Williams m. 5 Jul 1849 by Rev. John S. Martin,
lic. dated same day

Legoe, Cornelia and John A. Walsh m. 18 Jul 1843 by Rev. Henry Slicer, lic. dated
same day

Leguin, John F. and Mary E. Simonson m. 7 Nov 1843 by Rev. Dr. George C. M.
Roberts

Lehman, Sophia and Alexander Duncan m. 3 Sep 1850 by Rev. Dr. George C. M.
Roberts

Lehmen, Jacob and Mary E. Waters m. 30 Apr 1846 by Rev. Littleton F. Morgan,
lic. dated 27 Apr 1846

Leightner, Frances Jane, dau. of William Penn and Jane Leightner, b. 4 Sep 1846,
bapt. 27 May 1847 by Rev. Dr. George C. M. Roberts

Leme, Isabelle and Antonio Barros m. 4 May 1849 by Rev. John S. Martin, lic.
dated same day

Lemmon, Caroline F. and Francis Carter m. 16 Sep 1849 by Rev. Aquila A. Reese,
lic. dated 15 Sep 1849

Lemmon, Catherine and John Campbell m. 19 Jan 1842 by Rev. Joseph Shane

Lennon, Sarah, d. 1845 (death noted in Class List)

Lennox, Thomas A. and Julia Ann Voice m. 4 May 1843 by Rev. Dr. George C. M.
Roberts

Lenox, George, an adopted son of James and Sophia Lenox, b. 7 May 1835, bapt.
30 Dec 1842 by Rev. Henry Slicer

Lenox, Mary Ann and James W. Legg m. 22 May 1845 by Rev. Isaac P. Cook

Lenox, Virginia, dau. of James and Sophia Lenox, b. 6 Mar 1840, bapt. 30 Dec
1842 by Rev. Henry Slicer

Lentz, Louis H. and Catharine E. Dorsey m. 21 Nov 1841 by Rev. Gerard Morgan,
lic. dated 20 Nov 1841

Leonard, Ann Jerome, dau. of Joseph and Mary Leonard, aged 7 months [b. 1841],
bapt. 9 Nov 1841 by Rev. Gerard Morgan

Leonard, Mary A., d. 1845 (death noted in Class List)

Letsinger, Emeline and George Fray m. 24 Dec 1843 by Rev. Henry Slicer, lic.
dated 22 Dec 1843

Lewis, Francis, son of Joseph W. and Priscilla E. Lewis, b. 3 Jan 1844, bapt. 1 Jul 1844 by Rev. Dr. George C. M. Roberts

Lewis, John and Margarett Carroll m. 7 Jun 1840 by Rev. Joseph Shane

Lewis, John and Maria Duckworth m. 7 Oct 1849 by Rev. Aquila A. Reese, lic. dated 6 Oct 1849

Lewis, Joseph B. and Jane A. Scott m. 21 Jan 1846 by Rev. Wesley Stevenson [*Ed. Note:* Their marriage notice in the *Baltimore Sun* gave his last name as "Lewis" even though it looked more like "Seems" in the marriage register.]

Lewis, Joseph N., son of Joseph and Priscilla Lewis, b. ---- [blank], bapt. 27 Feb 1840 by Rev. Thomas Myers

Lewis, Mary and W. Ruark m. 10 Jul 1848 by Rev. William Hirst

Lewis, Paca Smith, son of Joseph and Priscilla Lewis, b. ---- [blank], bapt. 27 Feb 1840 by Rev. William B. Edwards

Lewis, William J. and Elvira E. Reeder m. 27 Oct 1846 by Rev. Joseph Shane

Lewis, William and Sarah Petticord, both of Baltimore County, m. ---- [date not given] by Rev. George Hildt, lic. dated 26 Dec 1845

Libbart, Catherine and Martin White m. 2 Nov 1845 by Rev. James Sewell, lic. dated 1 Nov 1845

Liddard, Hester Ann, dau. of Moses and Eliza Liddard (residents of Patapsco Neck in Baltimore County), b. 16 Jan 1829, bapt. 11 Oct 1841 by Rev. Isaac P. Cook

Liddle, Joseph and Ann Rebecca Curmine m. 19 Mar 1840 by Rev. Joseph Shane

Liddle, Robert and Clara Ann Knight m. 3 Jun 1845 by Rev. Isaac P. Cook

Lightner, William P. and Jane Algie m. 8 Dec 1845 by Rev. Dr. George C. M. Roberts

Liley, Sarah Ann and Robert Rengrose (Ringrose) m. 28 Sep 1847 by Rev. Stephen A. Roszel, lic. dated same day

Lilly, Evan and Margaret A. McCartner m. 27 Jan 1842 by Rev. Dr. George C. M. Roberts

Lilly, Robert and Martha McCurrister m. 29 Feb 1840 by Rev. Joseph Shane

Lindenberger, Mary O. and Robert Maxwell m. 22 Jun 1847 by Rev. Stephen A. Roszel, lic. dated 1 Jun 1847

Ling, Robert M. and Susannah Hayes m. 14 Jun 1844 by Rev. James Sewell, lic. dated 13 Jun 1844

Lingan, Susan, d. 16 Oct 1844, aged 87 (death noted in Record of Members)

Lingril, Catharine P. and William H. Biggins m. 22 Dec 1844 by Rev. Isaac P. Cook

Linsey, Stephen and Rachel Cooper m. 7 Aug 1842 by Rev. Henry Slicer, lic. dated 6 Aug 1842

Linten, Mary and Noah Sterling m. 8 Dec 1842 by Rev. Samuel Brison

Linthicum, Rebecca and Robert J. Ross m. 19 Jan 1847 by Rev. Samuel Keppler (date of lic. not recorded)

Lippey, Elizabeth McCafferty, dau. of Jesse and Margaret Lippey, aged 4 months [b. 1841], bapt. 12 Sep 1841 by Rev. Robert Emory

Lirmon, George Washington, son of Isaac and Priscilla Lirmon, aged about 7 years [b. 1835 or 1836], bapt. 21 Feb 1843 by Rev. Henry Slicer

Litchfield, William and Lydia Ann Shoemaker m. 13 Oct 1842 by Rev. Samuel Brison

Littig, Margaret E. and Abraham Woodward m. 30 Apr 1844 by Rev. James Sewell, lic. dated 29 Apr 1844

Littig, Maria Dorsey, dau. of Philip and Jane L. Littig, b. 17 May 1848, bapt. 8 Jul 1848 by Rev. Dr. George C. M. Roberts

Little, Dorcas, d. circa 1844 (exact date not given in Record of Members) [Ed. Note: Death notice in the Baltimore Sun stated that Dorcas Little d. 6 Jun 1843.]

Little, George H. and Mary J. Crapster m. 25 Jul 1850 by Rev. Henry Slicer, lic. dated same day

Little, John and Elizabeth Metzdorff m. 20 Jun 1840 by Rev. Joseph Shane

Little, Mary R. and Charles S. Cutler m. 19 Dec 1850 by Rev. Dr. George C. M. Roberts

Little, William and Catharine Emory, both of Baltimore County, m. 24 Dec 1840 by Rev. Bernard H. Nadal

Livingston, Eliza and James Henry Connoway m. 10 Apr 1849 by Rev. Dr. George C. M. Roberts

Livingston, Elizabeth A. and William Merriken m. 11 Feb 1846 by Rev. Dr. George C. M. Roberts

Lloyd, James and Mary Towes m. 3 May 1842 by Rev. Henry Slicer, lic. dated 2 May 1842

Lloyd, Jane and David N. Wiley m. 6 Jun 1840 by Rev. John Bear

Lloyd, John Thomas and Margaret Ann Harris m. 11 Jul 1842 by Rev. Samuel Brison

Lloyd, Mary Ann and Robert E. Hogg m. 24 Aug 1847 by Rev. Dr. George C. M. Roberts

Lloyd, Thomas and Rebecca Plummer m. 15 Jun 1847 by Rev. Stephen A. Roszel, lic. dated same day

Loane, James R. and Elizabeth Adams m. 27 Aug 1849 by Rev. Isaac P. Cook

Loc, William J. (colored) and Mary A. Reed (colored) m. 2 Nov 1841 by Rev. Gerard Morgan, lic. dated 28 Oct 1841

Locke, Sarah, d. circa 1850 (exact date not given in Record of Members) [Ed. Note: Death notice in the Baltimore Sun stated that Sarah Locke d. 14 Oct 1850.]

Loflin, Margaret and Nicholas Pamphilion m. 30 Jul 1844 by Rev. Joseph Shane

Logan, Adeline and Noble G. Watkins m. 10 Dec 1848 by Rev. Joseph Shane

Logan, Alexander and Mary Patterson m. 28 May 1841 by Rev. John Rice, lic. dated 27 May 1841

Logan, James H., "aged 35 years on 23 Jun 1842," bapt. 25 Sep 1842 by Rev. Benjamin H. Crever

Logan, Maria and James T. Griffith m. 13 Jun 1850 by Rev. Henry Slicer, lic. dated 29 May 1850

Logan, Sarah and George Marshall m. 1 Jul 1849 by Rev. Aquila A. Reese, lic. dated same day

Logue, Mary A. and Robert Harrington m. 14 Dec 1848 by Rev. Stephen A. Roszel, lic. dated 13 Dec 1848

Loman, Ann Eliza, dau. of Emory and Catherine Loman, b. -- Mar 1822, bapt. 3 Dec 1840 by Rev. Dr. George C. M. Roberts

Loman, John and Ellen Pumphry m. 16 Apr 1840 by Rev. Joseph Shane

Long, David W. and Mary Catharine Gilman m. 19 Jan 1847

Long, Drucilla and John Whittington, both of Baltimore County, m. 18 Mar 1845 by Rev. William Hamilton

Long, Eliza S., d. 1845 (death noted in Class List)

Long, Elizabeth and John A. Lusk m. 21 Mar 1850 by Rev. Isaac P. Cook

Long, Lyttleton N. B. and Virginia C. Chiverell m. ---- [blank] by Rev. John S. Martin, lic. dated 8 Jul 1850 [*Ed. Note:* Their marriage notice in the *Baltimore Sun* stated Littleton N. B. Long and Virginia C. Chiverfill *[sic]* m. 9 Jul 1850, even though his last name looked more like "Laig" or "Lang" in the church register.]

Long, Mary Ann Bainbridge and Oliver Perry Merryman m. 15 Dec 1841 by Rev. Gerard Morgan, lic. dated 13 Dec 1841

Long, Parthenia, d. circa 1847 (death noted in Class List) [*Ed. Note:* Death notice in the *Baltimore Sun* stated that Parthenia Long, wife of John D. Long, d. 17 Mar 1848.]

Long, Thomas T., son of William and Rebecca Long, b. 24 Sep 1842, bapt. 8 Oct 1842 by Rev. Elisha D. Owen

Longe, Amanda and Daniel Wyatt m. 21 May 1849 by Rev. Joseph Shane

Longley, Eliza and Caleb Roden m. 7 Sep 1841 by Rev. Dr. George C. M. Roberts

Longly, Eleanora and Alexander Williams m. 11 Mar 1849 by Rev. Joseph Shane

Longmoore, Sarah and William O'Hara m. 2 Jul 1842 by Rev. Wesley Stevenson

Lory, Josephine and Jesse Bromly m. 19 Nov 1843 by Rev. Dr. George C. M. Roberts

Losquem, Jane and Reese Jones m. 25 Jun 1844 by Rev. James Sewell, lic. dated same day

Louderman, Ann L. and Nathaniel B. Wells m. 23 Apr 1850 by Rev. Henry Slicer, lic. dated same day

Loury, Elizabeth Amelia and Hamilton Galaspie m. 14 Oct 1846 by Rev. Joseph Shane

Love, Elvira and George Washington Hammond m. 11 Apr 1843 by Rev. Samuel Brison

Love, Monemia and James H. Fulton m. 21 Jun 1849 by Rev. Dr. George C. M. Roberts

Lovell, Henry V. and Caroline Pritchard, both of Baltimore County, m. 7 Feb 1843 by Rev. Nelson Head

Lowe, Levi B. and Elizabeth A. Peregoy m. 21 Dec 1843 by Rev. Henry Slicer, lic. dated 20 Dec 1843

Lowman, Ann and John Hood m. 11 Feb 1841 by Rev. Joseph Shane

Lowman, Margery and Samuel Wood m. 12 Sep 1848 by Rev. Joseph Shane

Lowrey, Ellen and Louis H. Browning m. 1 Mar 1841 by Rev. Wesley Stevenson

Lowrey, Mary E. and William H. Darrington m. 9 Apr 1848 by Rev. Stephen A. Roszel, lic. dated 7 Apr 1848

Lowry, Mary Elizabeth Hopkins, dau. of Stephen and Elizabeth H. Lowry, b. 7 Feb 1845, bapt. 31 Jul 1848 by Rev. Dr. George C. M. Roberts

Lowry, William Prettyman, son of John and Mary Lowry, b. 28 Dec 1841, bapt. -- Apr 1842 by Rev. William Prettyman

Lowther, Margaret and Michael Hughes m. 20 Jun 1849 by Rev. Aquila A. Reese, lic. dated 19 Jun 1849

Lowther, William and Emily Robinson, both of Baltimore County, m. 6 May 1840 by Rev. Thomas Myers, lic. dated same day

Lucas, Catherine and Robert Haynes m. 24 Apr 1845 by Rev. James Sewell, lic. dated same day

Lucas, Mary Jane, dau. of Edward and Sarah Lucas, b. 4 Jul 1842, bapt. 17 Aug 1843 by Rev. Isaac P. Cook

Lucas, Thomas W. and Caroline Harlow m. 2 Jan 1844 by Rev. Henry Slicer, lic. dated same day

Luke, Francis and Catharine Stout m. 3 Jul 1843 by Rev. Isaac P. Cook

Lusby, Ann and William Stewart m. 13 Aug 1846 by Rev. Samuel Keppler (date of lic. not recorded)

Lusby, Mary and John Elliot m. 5 Aug 1841 by Rev. Dr. George C. M. Roberts

Lusk, John A. and Elizabeth Long m. 21 Mar 1850 by Rev. Isaac P. Cook

Lutz, John, son of Charles F. and Susan Ann Lutz, b. 13 Apr 1842, bapt. 6 May 1842 by Rev. Henry Slicer

Lutz, Mary Elizabeth, dau. of Charles F. and Susan Ann Lutz, b. 16 Sep 1839, bapt. 6 May 1842 by Rev. Henry Slicer

Luwth, Hannah and Jacob Olivier m. 29 Apr 1844 by Rev. Joseph Merriken

Lydicker, Sarah (adult), bapt. 26 Dec 1841 by Rev. Charles B. Tippett

Lydnam, Sarah Ann Elizabeth, dau. of William and Ann Lydnam, aged 8 weeks, b. Baltimore City, bapt. 1841 (exact date not given) by Rev. Gerard Morgan

Lyles, Joseph and Margaret Brooks m. 2 Jan 1850 by Rev. Aquila A. Reese, lic. dated same day

Lynch, John, d. circa 1847-1848 (exact date not given in Record of Members) [Ed. Note: Death notice in the Baltimore Sun stated that John Lynch d. 15 Jan 1848.] See "Naomi Lynch," q.v.

Lynch, Margaret and William Baker m. 21 Apr 1844 by Rev. Dr. George C. M. Roberts

Lynch, Naomi, d. circa 1840 (exact date not given in Record of Members) [Ed. Note: Death notice in the Baltimore Sun stated that Naomi Lynch, wife of John Lynch, d. 19 Jan 1840.]

Lynch, Nicholas and Anne M. Hunter m. 2 Jul 1845 by Rev. James Sewell, lic. dated same day

Lyons, Andrew J. and Alverda Taylor m. 7 May 1850 by Rev. Henry Slicer, lic. dated 6 May 1850

Lyons, Henry R. and Rebecca H. Davis m. 21 Feb 1844 by Rev. Samuel Brison

Lyons, William and Frances Wadlow m. 18 Apr 1848 by Rev. Stephen A. Roszel, lic. dated same day

Lytle, Thomas and Matilda Andrews m. 19 Mar 1844 by Rev. Isaac P. Cook

Lyus, Elizabeth and Jesse C. Bennett m. 5 May 1841 by Rev. Joseph Shane

"M.... O. J.... and U.... L...., G. H.... offd." m. 4 Oct 1848, lic. dated 25 Oct [sic] 1848 [Ed. Note: This was written, as shown here with the incomplete names, among the marriages performed by Rev. Stephen A. Roszel.]

Maben, Nancy, dau. of John and Mary Maben, b. ---- [blank], bapt. 4 Aug 1840 by Rev. John Rice

Maccubbin, Samuel and Susan Amanda Turner m. 14 Mar 1849 by Rev. Isaac P. Cook

Mace, Caroline and George Wolfe m. 11 Jun 1846 by Rev. Joseph Shane

Macemore, Ariel and Grafton E. Marshall m. 24 Oct 1850 by Rev. Isaac P. Cook

Macey, Anna Maria, dau. of Mrs. Susan Macey, b. 23 Feb 1837, Fells Point, Baltimore City, bapt. 5 Mar 1840 by Rev. Samuel Keppler

Macey, Elizabeth Folger, dau. of Mrs. Susan Macey, b. 16 Jul 1827, Fells Point, Baltimore City, bapt. 5 Mar 1840 by Rev. Samuel Keppler

Macey, John Robert, son of Mrs. Susan Macey, b. 12 Jan 1834, Fells Point, Baltimore City, bapt. 5 Mar 1840 by Rev. Samuel Keppler

Macgill, George T. and Catharine Collins m. 24 Dec 1844 by Rev. Isaac P. Cook

Macher, Benjamin, son of John S. and Frances Macher, b. 9 Oct 1843, bapt. 4 Feb 1846 by Rev. Dr. George C. M. Roberts

Macher, George Roberts, son of John S. and Frances Macher, b. 6 May 1850, bapt. 15 Aug 1852 by Rev. Dr. George C. M. Roberts

Macher, James Poole, son of John S. and Frances Macher, b. 24 Jun 1845, bapt. 4 Feb 1846 by Rev. Dr. George C. M. Roberts

Macher, Margaret Jane, dau. of J. S. and Frances Macher, b. 21 Nov 1841, bapt. 11 May 1843 by Rev. Dr. George C. M. Roberts

Macher, Susanna and Joseph Shane m. 25 Oct 1842 by Rev. Dr. George C. M. Roberts

Macintosh, Joseph, d. circa 1847-1850 (exact date not given in Record of Members)

Mackall, Frances Ellen, dau. of Samuel and Frances Mackall, b. 19 Jul 1840, bapt. 24 Aug 1840 by Rev. Charles B. Tippett

Mackelfresh, Mary and Henry Baker, both of Baltimore County, m. ---- [date not given] by Rev. George Hildt, lic. dated 3 Jun 1845

Mackentosh, Joseph and Rebecca Ann Robinson m. 29 Jun 1846 by Rev. Littleton F. Morgan, lic. dated same day

Mackey, William H. (coloured), son of William and Mary Mackey, b. 7 May 1842, bapt. 15 Jan 1843 by Rev. Isaac P. Cook

Macking, George Washington, son of Thomas and Sarah Meek Marking, b. 18 Dec 1840, bapt. 12 Aug 184- [page torn] by Rev. ---- (name not indicated) [*Ed. Note:* Information was written on a piece of paper and inserted in the church register.]

Maclay, John (Rev.) and Georgiana Griffith m. 19 Apr 1849 by Rev. Dr. George C. M. Roberts

Madeiry, Annie, dau. of Alexander R. and Lavinia A. Madeiry, b. 26 Sep 1847, bapt. 16 Apr 1848 by Rev. Dr. George C. M. Roberts

Madeiry, Florence Elizabeth, dau. of Jacob H. and Caroline Madeiry, b. 24 Dec 1847, bapt. 3 Apr 1848 by Rev. Dr. George C. M. Roberts

Madeiry, John, son of Jacob H. and Caroline Madeiry, b. 23 May 1850, bapt. 31 Jul 1850, by Rev. Dr. George C. M. Roberts

Madeiry, Joseph Whitney, son of Jacob H. and Caroline Madeiry, b. 23 Aug 1846, bapt. 3 Apr 1848 by Rev. Dr. George C. M. Roberts

Madeiry, Rachel Russel, dau. of Jacob H. and Caroline Madeiry, b. 23 Jan 1849, bapt. 16 Aug 1849 by Rev. Dr. George C. M. Roberts

Maffitt, Amanda, d. circa 1845-1847 (exact date not given in Record of Members)

Magers, Mary Elizabeth, dau. of Elias and Mary Magers, b. 25 Jun 1840, bapt. 27 Oct 1840 by Rev. Charles B. Tippett

Magnes, George Roberts, son of Zacharia and Acsha Magnes, aged 3 years [b. 1837 or 1838], bapt. 21 Feb 1841 by Rev. John A. Hening

Magnes, Thomas M., son of Zacharia and Acsha Magnes, aged 5 months [b. 1840], bapt. 21 Feb 1841 by Rev. John A. Hening

Magness, Charles E. and Mary Jane Whiteford m. 15 Oct 1848 by Rev. Stephen A. Roszel, lic. dated 14 Oct 1848

Maguire, Anne and Edward Mullen m. 3 Sep 1848 by Rev. Stephen A. Roszel, lic. dated 29 Aug 1848

Magurgans, Rosana M. and Levin D. Ridgely m. 10 Mar 1840 by Rev. Joseph Shane

Mahoney, John Edward (colored), son of George W. and Sophia Mahoney, b. 22 Feb 1839, bapt. 30 Jul 1840 by Rev. Dr. George C. M. Roberts

Maidlow, Charles and Sarah Care m. 21 Apr 1846 by Rev. Littleton F. Morgan, lic. dated 17 Apr 1846

Mainard, Elizabeth and Henry Arthur m. ---- [date not given] by Rev. George D. Chenoweth, lic. dated 10 Jan 1842 [*Ed. Note:* Their marriage notice in the *Baltimore Sun* stated Henry Arthur and Elizabeth Maynard m. 12 Jan 1842.]

Makibben, James G. and Ellen Jane Anderson m. 25 Oct 1846 by Rev. Littleton F. Morgan, lic. dated 5 Oct 1846

Malchar, George Wilson, son of Charles and Margaret Malchar, b. 6 Apr 1842, bapt. 26 Jun 1842 by Rev. Henry Slicer

Malloney, Mary Jane and John Kelly m. 12 Feb 1850 by Rev. Aquila A. Reese, lic. dated 11 Feb 1850

Malone, Mary Ann and William J. Sawyer m. 15 Aug 1844 by Rev. James Sewell, lic. dated 14 Aug 1844

Malone, Moses and Rachel Hopkins m. -- Mar 1846 [page torn] by Rev. James Sewell, lic. dated 18 Mar 1846

Mangan, Eliza Ann, see "J. T. Bishop," q.v.

Mangles, Martha A. and Richard E. Davis m. 29 Aug 1845 by Rev. James Sewell, lic. dated 27 Aug 1845

Mann, Mary Jane and Henry Stromberger m. 22 Jun 1845 by Rev. James Sewell, lic. dated 21 Jun 1845

Manning, Margaret A. and Thomas Crogan m. 12 Sep 1843 by Rev. Samuel Brison

Mansfield, Rebecca, d. circa 1845 (exact date not given in Record of Members) [*Ed. Note:* Death notice in the *Baltimore Sun* stated that Rebecca Mansfield d. 21 Jul 1845.]

March, Philip and Ellen Taylor m. 10 Nov 1845 by Rev. Joseph Shane

Mardy, Samuel and Mary Boures m. 21 Sep 1848 by Rev. William Hirst

Marfield, Mary and Gover S. Billington m. 7 Sep 1848 by Rev. Stephen A. Roszel, lic. dated same day

Markland, James H. and Mary E. Matthews m. 28 Aug 1842 by Rev. Dr. George C. M. Roberts

Markland, Richard Thomas, son of John T. and Elizabeth Ann Markland, b. 27 Mar 1840, bapt. 7 Jul 1840 by Rev. Dr. George C. M. Roberts

Marley, John and Elizabeth E. Clark m. 7 Dec 1843 by Rev. Isaac P. Cook

Marr, George, son of John and Ann Marr, b. ---- [blank], Fells Point, Baltimore City, bapt. 14 Jul 1840 by Rev. Samuel Keppler

Marr, Robert, son of John and Ann Marr, b. ---- [blank], Fells Point, Baltimore City, bapt. 14 Jul 1840 by Rev. Samuel Keppler

Marselas, John J. and Elizabeth W. Ward m. 4 Sep 1843 by Rev. Henry Slicer, lic. dated same day

Marshall, Amanda and James Tier m. ---- [blank] by Rev. John S. Martin, lic. dated 17 Sep 1850 [*Ed. Note:* Their marriage notice in the *Baltimore Sun* stated James C. Tier m. Mary A. Marshall on 17 Sep 1850.]

Marshall, Caroline T. and Obed M. Coffin m. 14 Mar 1844 by Rev. Joseph Shane

Marshall, Eleanor and William Childs m. 14 Jul 1840 by Rev. Samuel Keppler, lic. dated 13 Jul 1840

Marshall, Elizabeth A. and Thomas C. Pinkind m. 4 Oct 1842 by Rev. Henry Slicer, lic. dated same day

Marshall, George and Sarah Logan m. 1 Jul 1849 by Rev. Aquila A. Reese, lic. dated same day

Marshall, Grafton E. and Ariel Macemore m. 24 Oct 1850 by Rev. Isaac P. Cook

Marshall, James Williams and Susannah Jones m. 28 Oct 1841 by Rev. Gerard Morgan, lic. dated same day

Marshall, Sarah Ann and Robert C. Winks m. ---- [blank] by Rev. John S. Martin, lic. dated 19 Sep 1850 [*Ed. Note:* Their marriage notice in the *Baltimore Sun* stated they married on 19 Sep 1850.]

Marston, Frederick W. and Mary Chaytor m. 13 Feb 1844 at the house of Mrs. Chaytor in Baltimore by Rev. Beverly Waugh, lic. dated same day

Martin, Ann, d. circa 1840-1847 (exact date not given in Record of Members) [*Ed. Note:* She was possibly the Ann M. Martin, wife of Lenox Martin, whose death notice in the *Baltimore Sun* stated that she d. 24 Nov 1843, or she was possibly the Ann E. C. Martin, dau. of David and Catherine Martin, whose death notice in the *Baltimore Sun* stated that she d. 18 Aug 1847.]

Martin, Ann and William Parlett m. 3 Oct 1850 by Rev. Henry Slicer, lic. dated 30 Sep 1850

Martin, Charles Henry and Eliza Jane Cook m. 21 Nov 1841 by Rev. Isaac P. Cook

Martin, David and Catherine, see "Ann Martin," q.v.

Martin, Edward and Ann Horney m. 21 Apr 1843 by Rev. Joseph Shane

Martin, Elizabeth, dau. of William and Anne Martin, b. 15 Apr 1818, bapt. 29 Jun 1840 by Rev. Dr. George C. M. Roberts

Martin, John and Helen McCoy m. 1 Aug 1843 by Rev. Dr. George C. M. Roberts

Martin, Lenox, see "Ann Martin," q.v.

Martin, Louisa C. and George Franton m. 16 Jul 1844 by Rev. Dr. George C. M. Roberts

Martin, Luisa [*sic*] Rebecca, dau. of Samuel and Susanna Martin, b. 24 Jan 1841, bapt. 26 Mar 1843 by Rev. John Smith

Martin, Mary and Charles Folsum m. 16 Jan 1844 by Rev. Samuel Brison

Martin, Mary Virginia, dau. of Samuel and Susannah Martin, aged 1 week, bapt. -- May 1845 by Rev. J. Hoffman Waugh

Martin, Millicent, aged 28, b. Baltimore City, bapt. 20 Jul 1840 by Rev. Gerard Morgan

Martin, Samuel and Martha E. Robinson m. 5 Aug 1841 by Rev. Dr. George C. M. Roberts

Martin, Samuel, son of Ephraim and Rachel Martin, b. 13 Apr 1850, bapt. 28 Jul 1850 by Rev. Dr. George C. M. Roberts

Martin, Samuel Thomas, son of Samuel and Susanna Martin, b. 1 Jan 1843, bapt. 26 Mar 1843 by Rev. John Smith

Martin, Sarah A. and Frederick Kline m. 1 Aug 1850 by Rev. Henry Slicer, lic. dated same day

Martin, Sarah Ellen, dau. of Samuel and Susanna Martin, b. 17 Apr 1836, bapt. 26 Mar 1843 by Rev. John Smith

Martin, Susanna Georgianna, dau. of Samuel and Susanna Martin, b. 14 Nov 1838, bapt. 26 Mar 1843 by Rev. John Smith

Martinborn, George and Elizabeth Shields m. 26 Jul 1844 by Rev. James Sewell, lic. dated 15 Jul 1844

Mason, Almira and John Poulson m. 30 Jan 1848 by Rev. Joseph Shane

Mason, Amanda and William H. Downs m. 22 Jan 1850 by Rev. Aquila A. Reese, lic. dated 21 Jan 1850

Mason, Caroline M. and Joseph Hiss m. 28 Sep 1845 by Rev. Dr. George C. M. Roberts

Mason, Catherine A. (adult), b. ---- [blank], bapt. 30 Sep 1840 by Rev. Samuel Keppler; d. 1840 (death noted in Class List) [*Ed. Note:* She was possibly the Catherine Masson, dau. of William Masson, whose death notice in the *Baltimore Sun* stated that she d. 21 Nov 1840.]

Mason, Edgcomb G., son of Mr. and Mrs. Mason, b. 1838, bapt. 10 Jan 1843 by Rev. Philip B. Reese

Mason, Mary E., dau. of Mr. and Mrs. Mason, b. 1840, bapt. 10 Jan 1843 by Rev. Philip B. Reese

Mason, Samuel F. and Margaret J. Pindel m. 19 Aug 1850 by Rev. Isaac P. Cook

Mason, Sarah, d. 1841 (death noted in Class List) [*Ed. Note:* Death notice in the *Baltimore Sun* stated that Sarah Masson d. 23 Dec 1841.]

Mason, Temperance and James Smith m. 22 Feb 1849 by Rev. Wesley Stevenson

Mason (Masson), William, see "Catherine Mason," q.v.

Mason, William and Ann M. Bechum m. 17 Apr 1845 at the house of B. Waugh in Baltimore by Rev. Beverly Waugh, lic. dated 16 Apr 1845

Mason, William C., son of Mr. and Mrs. Mason, b. 1836, bapt. 10 Jan 1843 by Rev. Philip B. Reese

Massey, Mary Olivia, dau. of ---- [blank] Massey, aged 9 months [b. 1842], bapt. 15 Nov 1842 by Rev. Benjamin H. Crever

Massey, Nathan Webster and Mary Ellen Thompson, both of Baltimore County, m. 20 Feb 1841 by Rev. John Rice

Matchett, James and Elizabeth McCarter m. 24 Dec 1843 by Rev. Dr. George C. M. Roberts

Matheny, Emily France *[sic]*, dau. of Isaac and Eliza Ann Matheny, b. 1 Apr 1840, bapt. 23 Aug 1840 by Rev. Charles B. Tippett

Matthews, Harriet Elizabeth (coloured), dau. of Mary Matthews, aged 9, bapt. 26 May 1857 by Rev. William A. Snively

Matthews, Mary E. and James H. Markland m. 28 Aug 1842 by Rev. Dr. George C. M. Roberts

Matthews (Mathews), Phebe, d. circa 1840-1844 (exact date not given in Record of Members) [*Ed. Note:* Death notice in the *Baltimore Sun* stated that Phebe K. Matthews d. 25 Oct 1842.]

Matthews, William C. and Elizabeth K. Landon m. 27 Apr 1848 by Rev. Isaac P. Cook

Mattox, Daniel James, son of Daniel and Susan Mattox, b. 26 Aug 1841, bapt. 10 Jun 1842 by Rev. William Prettyman

Mattox, Rachel and William M. Olmstead m. 15 Apr 1846 by Rev. Dr. George C. M. Roberts

Maurace (Manrace?), John W. and Mary Elizabeth White m. 2 Dec 1847 by Rev. Dr. George C. M. Roberts

Maxwell, Margaret Eugenia, dau. of George and Mary Ann Maxwell, b. 15 Feb 1846, Baltimore, bapt. 7 Mar 1847 by Rev. Samuel Keppler

Maxwell, Marshal D. and Elizabeth C. Brown m. 4 Feb 1843 by Rev. Job Guest, lic. dated 3 Feb 1843

Maxwell, Mary Ann Lavinia(?), dau. of ---- [blank], b. 28 Aug 1848, bapt. -- Jul 1849 by Rev. John S. Martin

Maxwell, Mary Catherine, dau. of ---- [blank], b. 30 Apr 1848, bapt. -- Jul 1849 by Rev. John S. Martin

Maxwell, Robert and Mary O. Lindenberger m. 22 Jun 1847 by Rev. Stephen A. Roszel, lic. dated 1 Jun 1847

Maxwell, Sarah and John Shannon m. ---- [blank] by Rev. John S. Martin, lic. dated 14 Nov 1850

Maybury, Frances Ann (colored), dau. of John and Sarah Maybury, b. -- Mar 1840, bapt. 22 Sep 1840 by Rev. Thomas Myers

Maydwell, Theodore Frelinghuysen, son of William and M. A. Maydwell, b. 25 Apr 1845, bapt. 25 Sep 1845 by Rev. Isaac P. Cook

Maynard, Elizabeth and Henry Arthur m. 12 Jan 1842 by Rev. Job Guest, lic. dated 10 Jan 1842

Maynard, James Bohen, son of William and Eliza Maynard, b. 25 Apr 1842, bapt. 4 May 1842 by Rev. Dr. George C. M. Roberts

Mayo, Eleanor Susanna Alverda, dau. of John and Ann E. Mayo, b. 27 Mar 1834, bapt. 20 May 1850 by Rev. Dr. George C. M. Roberts

Mayo, Elizabeth G. and Richard A. Harwood m. 16 Mar 1848 by Rev. Dr. George C. M. Roberts

Mayo, Georgianna Octavia Maria Virginia, dau. of John and Ann E. Mayo, b. 26 Jul 1840, bapt. 20 May 1850 by Rev. Dr. George C. M. Roberts

Mayo, James, son of John and Ann E. Mayo, b. 10 Mar 1826, bapt. 20 May 1850 by Rev. Dr. George C. M. Roberts

Mayo, Josephine Elvira Adelaide Ophera(?), dau. of John and Ann E. Mayo, b. 26 Jul 1840, bapt. 20 May 1850 by Rev. Dr. George C. M. Roberts

Mayo, Mary Emma Alexalia, dau. of John and Ann E. Mayo, b. 1 Feb 1837, bapt. 20 May 1850 by Rev. Dr. George C. M. Roberts

Mayo, Sarah Ann and William Roberts m. 5 Dec 1843 by Rev. Samuel Brison

McAlbers, Sophia and Peter Rose m. 3 Jun 1847 by Rev. Dr. George C. M. Roberts

McAlister, Kate, dau. of Robert A. and Alice R. McAlister, b. ---- [blank], bapt. 23 Sep 1849 by Rev. John S. Martin

McAllister, Alexander and Mary Jane Dew m. 14 Dec 1841 by Rev. Dr. George C. M. Roberts

McAllister, Mary Jane and Samuel Holland m. 7 Oct 1847 by Rev. Stephen A. Roszel, lic. dated 4 Oct 1847

McBee, Harriot, d. circa 1840, lost at sea (exact date not given in Class Record)

McBride, James and Elizabeth Jones m. 19 Jul 1846 by Rev. Joseph Shane

McCabe, George W. C. and Roseana Vernon m. 11 Feb 1842 by Rev. Joseph Shane

McCabe, Henry H. and Martha Eddy French m. 15 Dec 1840 by Rev. Joseph Shane

McCall, Mary and Thomas Fitzpatrick m. 18 May 1846 by Rev. Dr. George C. M. Roberts

McCann, James and Jane Campbell m. 29 Nov 1840 by Rev. Joseph Shane

McCannon, Ann, d. by 1840 (exact date not given in Class Record) [*Ed. Note:* Death notice in the *Baltimore Sun* stated that Ann McCannon, widow of James McCannon, d. 31 Oct 1838.]

McCanty, Ann M. E., see "Ann M. E. Gill," q.v.

McCarter, Elizabeth and James Matchett m. 24 Dec 1843 by Rev. Dr. George C. M. Roberts

McCartner, Margaret A. and Evan Lilly m. 27 Jan 1842 by Rev. Dr. George C. M. Roberts

McCarty, Temperance and William Osborne m. 14 Dec 1846 by Rev. Dr. George C. M. Roberts

McCaslind, Robert and Elizabeth Adams m. 28 Jan 1847 by Rev. Joseph Shane

McCassell, Rachel and Nelson Rosher, both of Baltimore County, m. ---- [date not given] by Rev. George Hildt, lic. dated 25 Aug 1845

McCauley, Harriet and Robert M. Walmsley m. 28 Oct 1841 by Rev. Dr. George C. M. Roberts

McCauley, Rachel and John W. Turner m. 24 Dec 1846 by Rev. Dr. George C. M. Roberts

McCauley, Thomas and Henry [sic] Wheeler m. 28 Dec 1847 by Rev. Joseph Shane

McClamar, John L. S. and Jane Ann Adeline Clark m. 14 Dec 1840 by Rev. Samuel Keppler, lic. dated same day

McClannagan, John, d. 1841 (death noted in Class List)

McClary, George Brown, son of James and Julia McClary, b. 18 Sep 1846, bapt. 26 Sep 1846 by Rev. Dr. George C. M. Roberts

McClatchie, William J. and Mary Johnson m. 28 May 1846 by Rev. Dr. George C. M. Roberts

McClean, Jacob F. and Mary Elizabeth Knight m. 21 Aug 1848 by Rev. Dr. George C. M. Roberts

McClean, James Latimer, son of Louis and Catherine McClean, b. 2 Sep 1834, bapt. 16 Feb 1841 by Rev. Dr. George C. M. Roberts

McClean, Lydia Milligan, dau. of Louis and Catherine McClean, b. 31 Jan 1822, bapt. 16 Feb 1841 by Rev. Dr. George C. M. Roberts

McClean, Robert and Margaret Watchman m. 16 Apr 1850 by Rev. Dr. George C. M. Roberts

McClean, Sarah Jones, dau. of Louis and Catherine McClean, b. 28 Sep 1820, bapt. 16 Feb 1841 by Rev. Dr. George C. M. Roberts

McCleester, David and Sarah A. Coleman m. 2 Jun 1844 by Rev. James Sewell, lic. dated 31 May 1844

McCleester, David, d. circa 1849-1850 (exact date not given in Record of Members) [Ed. Note: Death notice in the Baltimore Sun stated that David McCleester d. 8 Dec 1849.] -

McClellen, Julia, dau. of Thomas and Julia McClellen, b. 8 Mar 1846, bapt. 18 Jun 1846 by Rev. Samuel Keppler

McClenaghan, Edward Sturgeon, son of James and Amanda McClenaghan, b. 22 Sep 1847, bapt. 8 Dec 1847 by Rev. Dr. George C. M. Roberts

McClure, Mary, d. circa 1845-1847 (exact date not given in Record of Members) [Ed. Note: Death notice in the Baltimore Sun stated that Mary A. McClure, widow of John McClure, d. 12 Mar 1846.]

McCollum, Catharine and Peter G. Schlosser, both of Carroll County, MD, m. 9 Oct 1844 by Rev. William Hamilton

McComas, Stephen O. and Angeline Parlett m. 9 Sep 1849 by Rev. Isaac P. Cook

McConkey, Mary and Howard H. Hopkins, both of Baltimore County, m. 25 Nov 1844 by Rev. William Hamilton

McCormick, Margaret and John M. Johnson m. 11 Sep 1845 by Rev. Samuel Keppler (date of lic. not recorded)

McCormick, Mary and William H. Jones m. 20 Nov 1844 by Rev. James Sewell, lic. dated 10 Nov 1844

McCormick, Mary C. and James B. Buck m. 17 May 1849 by Rev. Isaac P. Cook

McCoy, Helen and John Martin m. 1 Aug 1843 by Rev. Dr. George C. M. Roberts

McCracken, Jeanette and George W. Shoemaker m. 15 Jun 1848 by Rev. Dr. George C. M. Roberts

McCrea, Mary and Thomas McCrea m. 6 Apr 1841 by Rev. Job Guest, lic. dated 1 Apr 1841

McCrea, Thomas and Mary McCrea m. 6 Apr 1841 by Rev. Job Guest, lic. dated 1 Apr 1841

McCready, Harvey J. and Mary Louisa Dickson m. 18 Nov 1847 by Rev. Littleton F. Morgan, lic. dated same day

McCrone, Ann E. and James H. Hahn m. 19 Apr 1849 by Rev. Isaac P. Cook

McCulley, Catherine and Jacob F. Morris m. 21 Dec 1849 by Rev. Dr. George C. M. Roberts [Ed. Note: Another entry in the church register stated Catherine McCulley and Jacob Morris m. 21 Jun 1850 by Rev. Dr. George C. M. Roberts.]

McCulley, James and Sarah Spence m. 29 Jul 1841 by Rev. Dr. George C. M. Roberts [Ed. Note: His name was written "James McCulley, Sol." in the marriage register.]

McCulloh, Mary Jane and Charles Debaugh m. 25 Jan 1844 by Rev. Isaac P. Cook

McCurdy, Ellenora, dau. of James and Mary McCurdy (residents of Elkridge Landing), aged 6 months [b. 1840], bapt. 20 Sep 1840 by Rev. Isaac P. Cook

McCurley, Charles, son of Jacob and Susan McCurley, b. 5 Jul 1841, bapt. 11 Dec 1841 by Rev. Dr. George C. M. Roberts

McCurley, James and Rachel Aler m. 23 Jan 1848 by Rev. Joseph Shane

McCurrister, Martha and Robert Lilly m. 29 Feb 1840 by Rev. Joseph Shane

McCussht(?), David Hamilton, son of David and Rebecca McCussht(?), b. 29 Dec 1848, bapt. 30 Jan 1849 by Rev. Dr. George C. M. Roberts

McCutchen, James G. and Sarah J. Ward m. 29 Feb 1844 by Rev. Joseph Shane

McDonnel, Alexander and Mary Jane Ramsay m. 8 Sep 1840 by Rev. Samuel Keppler, lic. dated same day

McDowall, Francis and Johanna S. McPherson m. 10 May 1849 by Rev. Aquila A. Reese, lic. dated 9 May 1849 [Ed. Note: Their marriage notice in the Baltimore Sun gave their names as Francis McDowell and Joanna McPherson, dau. of William.]

McEwen(?), Mary Ellen, dau. of William and Cecelia McEwen(?), aged 4 years [b. 1836], bapt. 12 Jul 1840 by Rev. John Rice

McFaddon, Cornelius and Mary Dillon m. 12 Mar 1840 by Rev. Joseph Shane

McGinnis, Maria, dau. of Richard and Maria McGinnis, b. -- Aug 1838, bapt. 8 Feb 1841 by Rev. Thomas Myers

McGinnis, Richard, son of Richard and Maria McGinnis, b. 1834, bapt. 8 Feb 1841 by Rev. Thomas Myers

McGlone, Sarah A. and Stephen A. Morse m. 19 Jul 1847 by Rev. Dr. George C. M. Roberts

McGlue, Henry Slicer, son of George Theodore and Hester McGlue, b. 18 Sep 1839, bapt. 5 Jan 1841 by Rev. Charles B. Tippett

McGow, John (adult), b. ---- [blank], bapt. 30 Aug 1840 by Rev. Isaac P. Cook

McIlvaney, Catherine and George J. Smallwood m. 14 Sep 1850 by Rev. Joseph Shane

McIntire, Henry W. and Jane Wilkinson m. 1 Jun 1841 by Rev. Dr. George C. M. Roberts

McIntire, Joshua G. and Sarah A. L. Coates m. 18 Oct 1846 by Rev. Dr. George C. M. Roberts

McJilton, Anna Neville, dau. of Thomas A. and Susan R. McJilton, b. 5 May 1848, bapt. 7 Jun 1848 by Rev. Dr. George C. M. Roberts

McJilton, John Forley, son of William Wesley and Elizabeth McJilton, b. 26 Aug 1845, bapt. 9 Jul 1846 by Rev. Dr. George C. M. Roberts

McKee, Arthur and Martha Campbell m. 19 Aug 1844 by Rev. Joseph Shane

McKeldin, Edward A. and Sophia Wolf m. 13 Nov 1845 by Rev. Joseph Shane

McKenley, William R. and Rebecca Fort m. 5 Mar 1850 by Rev. Isaac P. Cook

McKenney, Mary and Charles H. Crugin, both of Georgetown, District of Columbia, m. 2 Oct 1845 by Rev. William Hamilton, lic. dated 1 Oct 1845

McKenny, Elizabeth and Benjamin Tucker m. 17 Oct 1841 by Rev. Dr. George C. M. Roberts

McKeys, Henry Bailey, son of Joseph J. and Ruth McKeys, b. 9 Aug 1846, bapt. 3 Feb 1847 by Rev. Dr. George C. M. Roberts

McKinsey, Mary Louiza, dau. of Evan and Eliza McKinsey, b. 20 Sep 1839, bapt. 24 Aug 1840 by Rev. Charles B. Tippett

McLar, John T., son of John and Adeline McLar, b. 10 Jun 1842, bapt. 3 Nov 1842 by Rev. William Prettyman

McLaughlin, James and Ann Maria Blade m. 15 Oct 1849 by Rev. Aquila A. Reese, lic. dated 14 Oct 1849

McLaughlin, Mary, d. 1 Mar 1848 (death noted in Record of Members)

McLaughlin, Rosa Ann and Alfried P. Moffitt m. 22 Jun 1846 by Rev. Dr. George C. M. Roberts

McLean, Mary E., dau. of Samuel and Ann M. McLean, b. 14 Mar 1841, bapt. 29 Jun 1842 by Rev. William Prettyman

McLeane, Eliza J. and George Skillman m. 11 Apr 1842 by Rev. Dr. George C. M. Roberts

McLease, Patrick and Catharine A. Bishop m. 10 Jun 1847 by Rev. Stephen A. Roszel, lic. dated 8 Jun 1847

McMachen, Wesley and Ellinor Boyd m. 3 Jan 1850 by Rev. Aquila A. Reese, lic. dated 2 Jan 1850

McMackin, Thomas and Elizabeth Binley m. 21 Mar 1844 by Rev. Isaac P. Cook

McManus, Ann and William W. F. Bailey m. 7 Sep 1842 by Rev. Dr. George C. M. Roberts

McMullen, Martha Jane, dau. of John and Mary Ann McMullen, aged 3 months [b. 1840], bapt. 21 Feb 1841 by Rev. John A. Hening

McNeal, Archibald and Kezia Ann Bosley m. 28 Sep 1843 by Rev. Samuel Brison

McNeal, Kezia Ann and William B. Rimby m. 31 Aug 1847 by Rev. Isaac P. Cook

McNeal, Sarah A., d. circa 1840 (death noted in Class List)

McNelly, Eleanor and Robert Davis m. 3 Sep 1850 by Rev. Henry Slicer, lic. dated 2 Sep 1850

McNelly, Margaret B., d. circa 1849-1850 (exact date not given in Record of Members) [*Ed. Note:* Death notice in the *Baltimore Sun* stated that Margaret McNelly d. 5 Aug 1849.]

McNier, Thomas S. and Emily R. Schurar, both of Annapolis, m. 1 Mar 1842 at Annapolis by Rev. Job Guest, lic. dated same day [*Ed. Note:* Marriage records of Anne Arundel County indicate Thomas S. McNeir and Emily R. Schwarar obtained a license on 12 Feb 1842.]

McPhail, Amanda Millenberger, dau. of J. L. and ---- [blank] McPhail, b. ---- [blank], bapt. 1845 (exact date not given) by Rev. George Hildt

McPhail, Daniel Henry, son of J. L. and ---- [blank] McPhail, b. ---- [blank], bapt. 1845 (exact date not given) by Rev. George Hildt

McPhail, Emily Louisa and Thomas T. Nelson m. 1 Sep 1846 by Rev. Littleton F. Morgan, lic. dated 31 Aug 1846

McPhail, James Lawrence and Margaret Ann Harman, both of Baltimore County, m. 5 Nov 1840 by Rev. Thomas Myers, lic. dated same day

McPhail, Mary Ann, dau. of J. L. and ---- [blank] McPhail, b. ---- [blank], bapt. 1845 (exact date not given) by Rev. George Hildt

McPhail, Mary Jane and Garrett Smith, both of Baltimore County, m. 19 May 1840 by Rev. Thomas Myers, lic. dated same day

McPherson, Johanna and Francis McDowall m. 10 May 1849 by Rev. Aquila A. Reese, lic. dated 9 May 1849 [*Ed. Note:* Their marriage notice in the *Baltimore Sun* gave their names as Francis McDowell and Joanna McPherson, dau. of William.]

McPherson, Mary Elizabeth, dau. of John and Margaret McPherson, b. 8 Mar 1840, bapt. 20 Oct 1840 by Rev. Charles B. Tippett

McVay, Martha Elizabeth, dau. of John W. and Elizabeth McVay, b. 30 May 1840, bapt. 29 Jul 1840 by Rev. Dr. George C. M. Roberts

McWilliams, Elizabeth, dau. of Robert and Agness McWilliams, b. 18 Mar 1843, bapt. 21 May 1843 by Rev. Henry Slicer

McWilliams, Jane, dau. of Edward and Jane McWilliams, b. 27 Jan 1843, bapt. 1 Feb 1843 by Rev. Henry Slicer

McWilliams, Mary Jane, dau. of Robert and Agness McWilliams, aged 4 weeks, bapt. 5 Dec 1841 by Rev. Gerard Morgan

Mead, Rebecca, d. circa 1840 (exact date not given in Class Record)

Meads, Robert B. and Mary Ellen Kirby m. 4 Jul 1847 by Rev. Stephen A. Roszel, lic. dated 3 Jul 1847

Meakin, Ann S. and John Moore m. 4 Jul 1849 by Rev. Aquila A. Reese, lic. dated 3 Jul 1849

Meconnekin, Elisha and Laura M. Richardson, both of Baltimore County, m. 23 Dec 1845 by Rev. William Hamilton

Medairy, Alexander R. and Lavinia A. Hardy m. 15 Jul 1847 by Rev. Stephen A. Roszel, lic. dated 13 Jul 1847

Medairy, Jacob H. and Caroline Kriel m. 18 Jan 1844 by Rev. Dr. George C. M. Roberts

Medairy, Lavinia, dau. of Jacob H. and Caroline Medairy, b. 13 Apr 1850, bapt. 26 Apr 1852 by Rev. Dr. George C. M. Roberts

Medairy, Sarah Donaldson, dau. of Alexander R. and Lavinia Ann Medairy, b. 6 Jul 1843, bapt. 1 Feb 1855 by Rev. Dr. George C. M. Roberts

Medinger, John Repart(?), son of John G. and Hannah L.(?) Medinger, b. 9 Jul 1845, bapt. 19 Jul 1845 by Rev. Dr. George C. M. Roberts

Meeks, Elizabeth, dau. of William and Louisa Meeks, b. 4 Feb 1836, bapt. 15 Jun 1840 by Rev. Joseph Shane

Meeks, Louisa, dau. of William and Louisa Meeks, b. 24 Apr 1839, bapt. 15 Jun 1840 by Rev. Joseph Shane

Megrue, William A., son of John and Mary J. Megrue, b. 9 Sep 1841, bapt. 29 Jun 1842 by Rev. William Prettyman

Mellon, George W. and Rachel Gosnell m. 21 May 1845 by Rev. Joseph Shane

Mellor, Anna and Josiah Christopher m. 21 Apr 1844 by Rev. Joseph Merriken

Mellville, Samuel and Eliza Jane Stephens m. 25 May 1848 by Rev. Isaac P. Cook

Mennick, John M. E. and Agnes A. Bailey m. 25 Jun 1846 by Rev. Littleton F. Morgan, lic. dated same day

Merchant, John William and Mary Baldwin Beacham m. 2 Dec 1845 by Rev. James Sewell, lic. dated same day

Merridith, Mary, d. "3 years ago" (death noted in Record of Members in 1847) [Ed. Note: Death notice in the Baltimore Sun stated that Mary Meredith d. 7 Nov 1845.]

Merriken, George and Priscilla W. Smith m. 22 Feb 1849 at Light Street Church in Baltimore by Rev. Beverly Waugh, lic. dated 21 Feb 1849

Merriken, Joseph Roberts, son of Rev. Joseph and Elizabeth Merriken, b. 17 Sep 1844, bapt. 25 Nov 1844 by Rev. Dr. George C. M. Roberts

Merriken, Leah Josephine, dau. of Joseph S. and Alfonso [sic] Merriken, b. -- Oct 1832, bapt. 5 Aug 1840 by Rev. John Bear

Merriken, Peter Livingston, son of William and Elizabeth A. Merriken, b. 2 Jan 1849, bapt. 16 Jan 1849 by Rev. Dr. George C. M. Roberts

Merriken, William and Elizabeth A. Livingston m. 11 Feb 1846 by Rev. Dr. George C. M. Roberts

Merritt, Joseph C. and Elizabeth C. Ross m. 9 Jan 1849 by Rev. Stephen A. Roszel, lic. dated 8 Jan 1849

Merryman, Barnet K. and Margaret T. Kline m. 23 Apr 1846 by Rev. Dr. George C. M. Roberts

Merryman, Margaret Ann, dau. of Philomen and Ann Maria Merryman, b. 25 Feb 1840, bapt. 25 Jul 1841 by Rev. Dr. George C. M. Roberts

Merryman, Oliver Perry and Mary Ann Bainbridge Long m. 15 Dec 1841 by Rev. Gerard Morgan, lic. dated 13 Dec 1841

Methanay, Daniel and Louisa Priscilla Morris m. 2 Dec 1840 by Rev. Samuel Keppler, lic. dated same day

Mette, Amelia Catherine and George W. L. Carnalier (Cavnalier?) m. 8 Sep 1846 by Rev. Job Guest being then in Alexandria D. C., lic. dated 7 Sep 1846

Mettee, Charles A. and Mary A. Frisby m. 23 Jun 1844 by Rev. Joseph Shane

Mettee, Mr., see "Rev. James Gamble," q.v.

Metz, Martha and Marion DeKalb Galloway m. 29 Feb 1848 by Rev. Stephen A. Roszel, lic. dated 28 Feb 1848

Metzdorff, Catherine and Herman Spence m. 24 Mar 1844 by Rev. Joseph Shane

Metzdorff, Elizabeth and John Little m. 20 Jun 1840 by Rev. Joseph Shane

Metzdorff, Frederick, son of Henry and Eliza Metzdorff, b. 15 Jan 1840, bapt. 18 Aug 1840 by Rev. Joseph Shane

Metzdorff, Rachel Ann, dau. of Henry and Eliza Metzdorff, b. 20 Mar 1838, bapt. 18 Aug 1840 by Rev. Joseph Shane

Mewshaw, Aleathea and Charles W. Lambdin m. 15 Apr 1847 by Rev. Benjamin F. Brooke

Mewshaw, Ann Eliza, dau. of Joseph and Sarah A. Mewshaw (residents of Elkridge Landing), b. 27 Aug 1835, bapt. 28 Jun 1840 by Rev. Isaac P. Cook

Mewshaw, Dennis and Jemima Earpe m. 7 Oct 1841 by Rev. Isaac P. Cook

Mewshaw, James and Maria Wondersford m. 25 Mar 1845 by Rev. Joseph Shane

Mewshaw, Mary Ann, dau. of Joseph and Sarah A. Mewshaw (residents of Eldridge Landing), b. 19 Aug 1837, bapt. 28 Jun 1840 by Rev. Isaac P. Cook

Mewshaw, William, see "William Mushaw," q.v.

Michaels, Francis W. and Sarah J. Stallens m. 8 Feb 1849 by Rev. Dr. George C. M. Roberts [Ed. Note: Their marriage notice in the Baltimore Sun gave their names as Francis W. Michael and Sarah J. Stalings.]

Michall, Mamiel [sic] H. and Mary Ann Price m. 11 Sep 1843 by Rev. Dr. George C. M. Roberts

Milburn, Elizabeth and Jesse Cain m. 15 Oct 1846 by Rev. Littleton F. Morgan, lic. dated 14 Oct 1846

Miles, Albert Leander, son of Isaac H. and Elizabeth A. Miles, b. 23 Mar 1849, bapt. 1860 (exact date not given) by Rev. William R. Mills

Miles, Georgeanna Alford, dau. of Isaac H. and Elizabeth A. Miles, b. 3 Jan 1843, bapt. 1860 (exact date not given) by Rev. William R. Mills

Miles, Jane, d. circa 1842-1844 (exact date not given in Record of Members) [Ed. Note: Death notice in the Baltimore Sun stated that Jane Miles, widow of Joshua Miles and mother-in-law of Leonard J. Quinlan, d. 6 Feb 1843.]

Miles, Joshua, see "Jane Miles," q.v.

Miles, Mary E. Cornelia, dau. of Isaac H. and Elizabeth A. Miles, b. 2 Mar 1841, bapt. 1860 (exact date not given) by Rev. William R. Mills

Miles, Rebecca Frances, dau. of Isaac H. and Elizabeth A. Miles, b. 8 Feb 1847, bapt. 1860 (exact date not given) by Rev. William R. Mills

Miller, Ann and Edmond Turner m. 17 Jun 1844 by Rev. James Sewell, lic. dated 10 Jun 1844

Miller, Ann and Ralph H. Palmer m. 20 Sep 1843 by Rev. Samuel Brison

Miller, Araminta, d. circa 1840-1844 (exact date not given in Record of Members) [Ed. Note: Death notice in the Baltimore Sun stated that Araminta Miller, widow of Lewis Miller, d. 28 Oct 1842.]

Miller, Asbury (colored) and Ann Newman (colored) m. 13 Feb 1841 by Rev. Samuel Keppler (date of lic. not recorded)

Miller, Decatur Howard, son of Decatur H. and Eliza C. Miller, b. 20 Jan 1850, bapt. same day by Rev. Dr. George C. M. Roberts

Miller, Elizabeth Ann, dau. of Jacob F. and Margaret Miller, b. 16 Apr 1842, bapt. 27 Nov 1842 by Rev. Henry Slicer

Miller, Enoch and Lydia A. Royston, both of Baltimore County, m. 7 Dec 1843 by Rev. S. S. Roszel, lic. dated same day

Miller, Frisby (colored) and Hannah Nichols (colored) m. 27 Feb 1843 by Rev. Henry Slicer (date of lic. not recorded)

Miller, George E., son of ---- [blank], b. 28 Oct 1836, bapt. 30 Jan 1842 by Rev. Gerard Morgan

Miller, George Henry, son of Conrad and Sarah Miller, b. 5 Feb 1842, bapt. 11 Aug 1842 by Rev. Henry Slicer

Miller, Irving Campbell, son of Decatur H. and Eliza C. Miller, b. 10 Jul 1848, bapt. 20 Jan 1850 by Rev. Dr. George C. M. Roberts

Miller, Jacob and Eleanor Johnson m. 16 Sep 1840 by Rev. Joseph Shane

Miller, James H., see "Margaret Miller," q.v.

Miller, John and Catharine Hitchcock m. 14 Jan 1841 by Rev. John Bear

Miller, Joseph and Harriet Wilson m. 1 Jun 1843 by Rev. Joseph Shane

Miller, Joshua and Emily Moore, both of Baltimore County, m. 20 Apr 1845 by Rev. William Hamilton, lic. dated 19 Apr 1845

Miller, Lewis, see "Araminta Miller," q.v

Miller, Margaret, d. 1844 (death noted in Class List) [*Ed. Note:* Death notice in the *Baltimore Sun* stated that Margaret Miller, mother of James H. Miller, d. 11 Feb 1844.]

Miller, Margaret and Elias Clampitt, both of Baltimore County, m. ---- [date not given] by Rev. George Hildt, lic. dated 21 Aug 1845 [*Ed. Note:* Their marriage notice in the *Baltimore Sun* stated they married on 21 Aug 1845.]

Miller, Margaret Ann, dau. of John and Ann M. Miller, b. 18 Feb 1834, bapt. ---- 184- [page torn] by Rev. ---- (name not indicated) [*Ed. Note:* Information was written on a piece of paper and inserted in the church register.]

Miller, Maria, d. 1841 (death noted in Class List)

Miller, Marion, son of Joshua M. and Susan Miller, b. 24 Jul 1839, bapt. 2 Apr 1840 by Rev. John Bear

Miller, Martha C. and Michael Miller m. 28 Oct 1847 by Rev. Dr. George C. M. Roberts

Miller, Mary Ann and Andrew Glinnin, both of Baltimore County, m. ---- [date not given] by Rev. George D. Chenoweth, lic. dated 3 Feb 1842

Miller, Mary Ann and David Kirkland m. 17 Jun 1845 by Rev. James Sewell, lic. dated same day

Miller, Michael and Martha C. Miller m. 28 Oct 1847 by Rev. Dr. George C. M. Roberts

Miller, Nehemiah and Louisa A. Hardesty m. 16 Dec 1845 by Rev. Dr. George C. M. Roberts

Miller, Samuel, son of Mr. & Mrs. Miller, aged 40 years, bapt. 31 Jan 1841 by Rev. Dr. George C. M. Roberts [*Ed. Note:* A later entry in the register stated he was b. 1800 and bapt. 5 Feb 1841.]

Million, Sophia E. and Samuel Stansbury m. 26 Apr 1849 by Rev. Dr. George C. M. Roberts

Mills, Elizabeth, d. circa 1847-1848 (exact date not given in Record of Members) [*Ed. Note:* Death notice in the *Baltimore Sun* stated that Elizabeth Mills, wife of Levin Mills, d. before 7 Sep 1848.]

Mills, Emily Virginia, dau. of Rev. Francis M. and Mary H. Mills, b. 20 Oct 1845, bapt. 25 Sep 1846 by Rev. Dr. Edwin Dorsey

Mills, George W. and Charlotte Dunn m. 4 Jan 1848 by Rev. Stephen A. Roszel, lic. dated 31 Dec 1847

Mills, Henry G. and Agnes C. Anderson m. 21 Apr 1847 by Rev. Benjamin F. Brooke

Mills, Levin, see "Elizabeth Mills," q.v.

Mills, William P. and Ann Buchanan m. 6 Dec 1842 by Rev. Benjamin H. Crever, lic. dated same day

Milroy, John and Mary Ann Abigail m. 14 Aug 1843 by Rev. Dr. George C. M. Roberts

Minnick, Conrad Albert and Elizabeth Reed m. 23 Jan 1848 by Rev. Stephen A. Roszel, lic. dated same day

Minnick, Helen, dau. of George W. and Maria Anna Minnick, b. 29 Oct 1847, bapt. 20 [sic] Oct 1847 by Rev. Dr. George C. M. Roberts

Mister, Abraham, see "Margaret Mister," q.v.

Mister, Emily, d. circa 1847-1850 (exact date not given in Record of Members)

Mister, Julianna, dau. of Abraham and Margaret Mister, b. 22 Oct 1839, bapt. -- Nov 1840 by Rev. John A. Hening

Mister, Margaret, d. circa 1847 (exact date not given in Record of Members) [Ed. Note: Death notice in the Baltimore Sun stated that Margaret Mister, wife of Abraham Mister, d. 26 Jun 1847.]

Mister, Sarah F. and William A. Fardwell m. 10 Sep 1850 by Rev. Henry Slicer, lic. dated 28 May 1850

Mitchel, Caroline A., dau. of John and Henrietta Mitchel, b. 13 Sep 1841, bapt. 12 Sep 1842 by Rev. Elisha D. Owen

Mitchel, Henry N., son of John and Henrietta Mitchel, b. 8 Jun 1840, bapt. 12 Sep 1842 by Rev. Elisha D. Owen

Mitchel, Uriah and Elizabeth Adare m. 1 Jun 1843 by Rev. Joseph Shane

Mitchell, Edwin Lewis, son of John and Rebecca Mitchell, b. 28 Dec 1842, bapt. 27 Mar 1844 by Rev. Dr. George C. M. Roberts

Mitchell, Elizabeth and John Walker m. 16 Dec 1841 by Rev. Dr. George C. M. Roberts

Mitchell, James and Julia Ann Mitchell m. ---- [blank] by Rev. John S. Martin, lic. dated 14 Nov 1849

Mitchell, Laura E. and George A. Ford m. 9 Nov 1848 by Rev. Dr. George C. M. Roberts

Mitchell, Mary, d. 1840 (death noted in Class List)

Mitchell, Mary and John Huisler, both of Baltimore County, m. 25 Jun 1840 by Rev. Bernard H. Nadal

Mitchell, Perry G. and Ann Maria Beckley, both of Baltimore County, m. 19 May 1840 by Rev. Bernard H. Nadal

Mitchell, Richard and Mary Jenkins m. 16 Apr 1840 by Rev. Samuel Keppler, lic. dated same day

Mitchell, Samuel Cole, son of John H. and Henrietta McC. Mitchell, b. 10 Dec 1850, bapt. 18 Nov 1854 by Rev. Dr. George C. M. Roberts

Mitchell, Sarah C.(?) and John P. Edmonson m. 30 Nov 1847 by Rev. Benjamin F. Brooke

Mitchell, Sarah J. and William Tolman m. 2 Jun 1844 by Rev. Dr. George C. M. Roberts

Mitchell, Virginia Rebecca, dau. of John and Rebecca Mitchell, b. 9 Nov 1846, bapt. 7 Mar 1847 by Rev. Dr. George C. M. Roberts

Mitchell, William and Drucilla Wilson m. 16 May 1844 by Rev. Dr. George C. M. Roberts

Mitchell, William H. and Elizabeth Waller m. 31 Oct 1849 by Rev. William Hirst, lic. dated same day

Mittan, Amanda, dau. of John and Mary Mittan, b. 3 Feb 1837(?), bapt. 5 Jul 1840 by Rev. Charles B. Tippett

Mobery, Ann Elizabeth and Robert Elliott m. 16 Jan 1848 by Rev. Stephen A. Roszel, lic. dated 15 Jan 1848 [Ed. Note: Their marriage notice in the Baltimore Sun gave her name as Ann E. Mowbray.]

Moffitt, Alfried P. and Rosa Ann McLaughlin m. 22 Jun 1846 by Rev. Dr. George C. M. Roberts

Molestead, Eliza A. and Christopher Taylor m. 22 Jun 1844 by Rev. James Sewell, lic. dated 14 Jun 1844

Moltz, John and Agnes Ledley m. 17 Jun 1841 by Rev. Joseph Shane

Monk, George and Susan Ellis m. 21 Mar 1844 by Rev. Isaac P. Cook

Montague, Augustus F. and Eliza Gregory m. 2 Jul 1844 by Rev. Dr. George C. M. Roberts

Montgarret, John and Susan Deer m. 3 Jul 1846 by Rev. Joseph Shane

Moon, William D. and Angeline Doyle m. 18 Jun 1844 by Rev. Joseph Shane

Moore, Amelia, d. circa 1840 (death noted in Class List)

Moore, Emily and Joshua Miller, both of Baltimore County, m. 20 Apr 1845 by Rev. William Hamilton, lic. dated 19 Apr 1845

Moore, George Washington, son of George and Margaret Moore, aged 14 months [b. 1840], bapt. 28 Oct 1841 by Rev. Gerard Morgan

Moore, Henry W. and Frances Harvey m. 7 Jan 1849 by Rev. Dr. George C. M. Roberts

Moore, John and Ann S. Meakin m. 4 Jul 1849 by Rev. Aquila A. Reese, lic. dated 3 Jul 1849

Moore, Mary and John H. Renaud, both of Baltimore County, m. 4 Nov 1844 by Rev. William Hamilton

Moore, Stephen and Rose Devalin m. 4 Jan 1848 by Rev. Stephen A. Roszel, lic. dated same day

Moore, William, son of Thomas and Ellen Moore, b. 10 Aug 1844, bapt. 1 Apr 1845 by Rev. Dr. George C. M. Roberts

Moores, Mary and John Wilson m. 27 Feb 1844 by Rev. Samuel Brison

Morford, James, of Baltimore County, and Ruth Ann Bidderson, of Baltimore City, m. 13 Oct 1840 by Rev. John A. Hening

Morgan, Elizabeth and Benjamin Tracy m. 31 Oct 1846 by Rev. Wesley Stevenson

Morgan, Lowraine and Thomas Corprell m. 11 Oct 1849 by Rev. John S. Martin, lic. dated 10 Oct 1849 [Ed. Note: Their marriage notice in the Baltimore Sun gave their names as Thomas Corprew and Lowraine Morgan.]

Morgan, Rebecca and Nelson R. Sheckles, both of Baltimore County, m. 28 Dec 1840 by Rev. Bernard H. Nadal

Morgan, Samuel (colored) and Amelia Pollard (colored) m. 6 Jul 1849 by Rev. Dr. George C. M. Roberts

Morgan, Susan and Alonzo Welsh m. 28 Feb 1849 by Rev. Joseph Shane

Morgan, Virginia, d. circa 1847-1850 (exact date not given in Record of Members)

Morris, Charles T. and Amelia J. B. Johnston m. 22 Dec 1840 by Rev. Samuel Keppler, lic. dated 21 Dec 1840

Morris, Jacob F. and Catherine McCulley m. 21 Dec 1849 by Rev. Dr. George C. M. Roberts [Ed. Note: Another entry in the church register stated Catherine McCulley and Jacob Morris m. 21 Jun 1850 by Rev. Dr. George C. M. Roberts.]

Morris, Jacob S., see "Jeremiah Frazier," q.v.

Morris, James, see "John Wesley Morris," q.v.

Morris, John Wesley (coloured), son of James and Lavinia Morris, b. 17 Jan 1840, Fells Point, Baltimore City, bapt. 1 Aug 1840 by Rev. Samuel Keppler

Morris, Joseph S. (Rev.) and Sarah Ann Turner, both of Baltimore County, m. 1 Oct 1840 by Rev. Thomas Myers, lic. dated 29 Sep 1840

Morris, Louisa Priscilla and Daniel Methanay m. 2 Dec 1840 by Rev. Samuel Keppler, lic. dated same day

Morris, Mary, d. circa 1845-1847 (exact date not given in Record of Members)

Morris, Owen and Annette Fowler m. 22 Jun 1843 by Rev. Isaac P. Cook

Morris, Rachel and Samuel Wanel m. 24 Jul 1843 by Rev. Dr. George C. M. Roberts

Morris, William and Martha Ann Jarvis m. 16 Aug 1841 by Rev. Wesley Stevenson

Morrison, Ann Demelia (adult), b. ---- [blank], bapt. 4 Jul 1841 by Rev. Robert Emory

Morrow, Eleanor C., d. circa 1847-1848 (exact date not given in Record of Members; her name was listed as Elenora Morrow in another record) [Ed. Note: Death notice in the Baltimore Sun stated that Eleanora C. Morrow, wife of John Morrow and dau. of Benjamin Berry, d. 12 Mar 1848.]

Morrow, James William, son of John and Elenora C. Morrow, b. 14 Jan 1848, bapt. 24 May 1848 by Rev. Dr. George C. M. Roberts

Morrow, John, see "Eleanor C. Morrow," q.v.

Morrow, John and Harriet Brunner m. 9 Apr 1850 by Rev. Dr. George C. M. Roberts

Morrow, Mary Hester, dau. of John and Elenora Morrow, b. 5 Jun 1845, bapt. 15 Jun 1845 by Rev. Dr. George C. M. Roberts

Morse, Charles S. and Margaret Jane Kay m. 24 Jun 1850 by Rev. Dr. George C. M. Roberts

Morse, Loren, aged 24 years [b. 1817], bapt. 29 Aug 1841 by Rev. John A. Hening

Morse, Mary A. and John W. Winks m. 21 Oct 1847 by Rev. Stephen A. Roszel, lic. dated 19 Oct 1847

Morse, Stephen A. and Sarah A. McGlone m. 19 Jul 1847 by Rev. Dr. George C. M. Roberts

Morsell, Hetty, d. circa 1850 (exact date not given in Record of Members) [Ed. Note: Death notice in the Baltimore Sun stated that Hetty Morsell, widow of Benjamin Morsell, d. 10 Jul 1850.]

Mortimer, John and Margaret A. Taylor m. 30 May 1847 by Rev. Isaac P. Cook

Mortimer, Thomas and Arneda Busey m. 14 Dec 1841 by Rev. Joseph Shane

Morton, John H. T. and Ann Maria Tindell m. 7 Jan 1844 by Rev. Dr. George C. M. Roberts

Moss, Caroline and Edward W. Curlett m. 23 May 1849 by Rev. John S. Martin, lic. dated same day

Moss, Isaac and Mary Holt m. 14 Apr 1844 by Rev. Joseph Shane

Mothland, Robert and Mary Ann Bennet m. 14 Jan 1845 by Rev. James Sewell, lic. dated 13 Jan 1845

Mott, Abraham G. and Mary E. G. Thompson m. 4 May 1843 by Rev. Henry Slicer, lic. dated same day

Mountgarett, Mary A. and Frederick Holtz m. 6 Apr 1845 by Rev. Dr. George C. M. Roberts

Mowbray, Alexandria *[sic]* and Mary Ann Nash m. 22 Aug 1841 by Rev. Gerard Morgan, lic. dated 19 Aug 1841

Mowbray, Elizabeth A. and John North m. 14 Dec 1848 by Rev. William Hirst

Mowbray, John and Euphemia E. Tapman m. 11 Dec 1849 by Rev. William Hirst, lic. dated 10 Dec 1849

Mowbray, Mary A. and John A. W. Bryan m. 27 Mar 1849 at Light Street Church in Baltimore by Rev. Beverly Waugh, lic. dated 26 Mar 1849

Moxley, Caleb Henry, son of Walter and Cornelia Moxley, b. 23 Dec 1842, bapt. 30 May 1844 by Rev. James Sewell

Moxley, Cecelia F., dau. of Walter and Cornelia Moxley, b. 11 Oct 1840, bapt. 30 May 1844 by Rev. James Sewell

Moxley, Mary Ann, dau. of William and Sarah J. Moxley, b. 19 Mar 1841, bapt. 9 Apr 1841 by Rev. John A. Hening

Moxley, Sarah, d. circa 1847 (exact date not given in Record of Members) *[Ed. Note:* Death notice in the *Baltimore Sun* stated that Sarah J. Moxley, wife of William Moxley, d. 14 Aug 1847.]

Moxley, William, see "Sarah Moxley," q.v.

Muir, James N. and Elizabeth A. Grieves m. 28 Jun 1842 by Rev. Henry Slicer, lic. dated same day

Mullen, Edward and Anne Maguire m. 3 Sep 1848 by Rev. Stephen A. Roszel, lic. dated 29 Aug 1848

Muller, James Nicholas, son of James N. and Mary Muller, aged 20 months [b. 1840], bapt. 1 Mar 1842 by Rev. Gerard Morgan

Mulligan, Julia Ann and Christian Sybrant m. 24 Jul 1843 by Rev. Dr. George C. M. Roberts

Mulligan, Mary J. and Francis B. Hart m. 7 Feb 1850 by Rev. Aquila A. Reese, lic. dated same day

Mullin, Mary and James Duling m. 26 Nov 1844 by Rev. James Sewell, lic. dated 25 Nov 1844

Munder, Lewis F. and Elizabeth C. Robinson m. 4 Feb 1850 by Rev. Dr. George C. M. Roberts

Munder, Mary Louisa Jeannette, dau. of Henry W. and Mary E. Munder, b. 14 Dec 1850, bapt. 18 Jun 1851 by Rev. Dr. George C. M. Roberts

Mungan, Elizabeth Ann and J. T. Bishop m. 30 Dec 1841 by Rev. Wesley Stevenson *[Ed. Note:* However, another entry in the marriage register stated John T. Bishop and Eliza Ann Mangan m. 4 Jan 1842 by Rev. Wesley Stevenson; perhaps the first date was the date of license. No marriage notice was found in the *Baltimore Sun* newspaper.]

Munn, Thomas and Emily Catherine Jones m. 13 Jan 1845 by Rev. Joseph Shane

Munotten, John and Charlotte Chapman m. 15 Jun 1841 by Rev. Gerard Morgan, lic. dated 31 May 1841

Murdoch, Ellen E. and Nathan Parker m. 22 Jun 1847 by Rev. Dr. George C. M. Roberts

Murdoch, Samuel and Jemima J. Henry m. 15 Nov 1846 by Rev. Littleton F. Morgan, lic. dated 9 Nov 1846

Murdock, William and Fanny M. Evans m. 17 Oct 1849 by Rev. John S. Martin, lic. dated 16 Oct 1849

Murkley, Mary Elizabeth, dau. of George and Caroline Murkley, aged 8 months [b. 1839], bapt. 1 Mar 1840 by Rev. William B. Edwards

Murphy, Elizabeth Ann and John S. Beacham m. 5 May 1846 by Rev. Samuel Keppler (date of lic. not recorded)

Murphy, Levinia, d. circa 1849-1850 (exact date not given in Record of Members) [*Ed. Note:* Death notice in the *Baltimore Sun* stated that Lavinia P. Murphy, dau. of John N. Murphy, d. 18 Dec 1849.]

Murray, Ellen and George W. Chase m. 9 Jun 1847 by Rev. James H. Brown, lic. dated 8 Jun 1847

Murray, Julia Ann and James Cordry m. 17 Oct 1844 by Rev. James Sewell, lic. dated same day

Murray, Margaret Ann and George M. Hammock m. 3 Jun 1847 by Rev. Stephen A. Roszel, lic. dated 2 Jun 1847

Murray, Sarah, d. 1847 (death noted in Class List) [*Ed. Note:* Death notice in the *Baltimore Sun* stated that Sarah Murray, mother-in-law of Robert Dutton, m. 6 Jun 1847.]

Murray, Thomas and Ann Combus m. 28 Jan 1850 by Rev. William Hirst, lic. dated 26 Jan 1850

Murry, John and Julia Dunsford m. 27 Oct 1842 by Rev. Henry Slicer, lic. dated same day

Murry, William and Elizabeth Cox m. 29 May 1847 by Rev. Littleton F. Morgan, lic. dated same day

Musgrave, Maria, d. circa 1840 (death noted in Class List)

Mushaw, William and Sophia Hook m. 17 Jan 1850 by Rev. John S. Martin, lic. dated 16 Jan 1850

Myers, Ann and Henry Kunds m. 10 Aug 1845 by Rev. Joseph Shane

Myers, James Edwin, son of Edward S. and Rebecca Myers, b. 15 Oct 1840, bapt. 8 May 1841 by Rev. Robert Emory

Myers, John J. and Margaret H. Amoss m. 14 Jan 1840 at John Haskitt's house in Baltimore by Rev. Beverly Waugh, lic. dated 13 Jan 1840

Myers, Joshua W. and Sarah A. Woolford m. 12 Jul 1841 by Rev. Gerard Morgan, lic. dated same day

Myers, Maria, d. circa 1840-1842 (exact date not given in Record of Members) [*Ed. Note:* Death notice in the *Baltimore Sun* stated that Maria A. Myers d. 26 Dec 1841.]

Myers, Maria L. and William C. Wilson m. 16 Jul 1843 by Rev. Henry Slicer, lic. dated 15 Jul 1843

Myers, Martha Ann and William Louis Delacour, both of Baltimore County, m. 8 Oct 1842 by Rev. Nelson Head

Myers, Mary Elizabeth (coloured), dau. of Daniel and Charlotte Myers, b. 15 May 1840, Fells Point, Baltimore City, bapt. 3 Jan 1841 by Rev. Samuel Keppler

Myers, Robert and Eliza Triger m. 24 Dec 1840 by Rev. John Bear

Myers, Thomas (Rev.) and Sarah Ann Norris m. 24 Feb 1842 at the house of her brother in Baltimore by Rev. Beverly Waugh, lic. dated 22 Feb 1842

Myres, Amelia, dau. of William and Ellen Myres, b. 6 Jan 1840, bapt. 4 Jul 1842 by Rev. Elisha D. Owen

Myres, Jacob, son of William and Ellen Myres, b. 9 Mar 1842, bapt. 4 Jul 1842 by Rev. Elisha D. Owen

Myres, Mary Ann and Joshua Eagleston m. 27 Oct 1842 by Rev. Dr. George C. M. Roberts

Myrtz, Catherine and George J. Holton m. 7 Jun 1842 by Rev. Henry Slicer, lic. dated 6 Jun 1842

Nace, Mary and Jackson Wyman m. 6 May 1846 by Rev. Isaac P. Cook

Nagel, George A. and Emily Brooks m. 5 Jan 1844 by Rev. Dr. George C. M. Roberts

Nash, James and Elizabeth Jane Culley m. 2 Oct 1846 by Rev. Joseph Shane

Nash, John Thomas, son of John Wesley and Elizabeth Ann Nash, b. 16 Jan 1849, bapt. 20 Jan 1849 by Rev. Dr. George C. M. Roberts

Nash, John W. and Elizabeth A. Taylor m. 25 Oct 1846 by Rev. Dr. George C. M. Roberts

Nash, Mary Ann and Alexandria [sic] Mowbray m. 22 Aug 1841 by Rev. Gerard Morgan, lic. dated 19 Aug 1841

Neal, James, d. circa 1847-1850 (exact date not given in Record of Members)

Neal, John Abbott, son of James Z. and Sarah Elizabeth Neal, b. 26 Aug 1840, bapt. 2 Sep 1841 by Rev. Dr. George C. M. Roberts

Neale, Sarah Frances, dau. of Henry and Susanna Neale, b. 6 Mar 1837, bapt. 18 Jun 1840 by Rev. Dr. George C. M. Roberts

Neighoof, Jacob T. and Mary M. Bodensick m. 23 Nov 1848 by Rev. Isaac P. Cook

Neilson, William H. and Ellen E. Edwards m. 27 Jan 1848 by Rev. Stephen A. Roszel, lic. dated same day

Nelson, Jane and Frederick Fefel m. 25 May 1843 by Rev. Dr. George C. M. Roberts

Nelson, John F. and Martha Peterson m. 3 aug 1848 by Rev. Stephen A. Roszel, lic. dated 2 Aug 1848

Nelson, Joseph P. and Emeline Reynolds m. 7 Jun 1849 by Rev. Aquila A. Reese, lic. dated 6 Jun 1849

Nelson, Thomas T. and Emily Louisa McPhail m. 1 Sep 1846 by Rev. Littleton F. Morgan, lic. dated 31 Aug 1846

Nevet, Mary, d. circa 1841 (death noted in Class List) [Ed. Note: She may possibly be the Mary A. Nevette whose death notice in the Baltimore Sun stated that she d. 2 Oct 1843.]

Nevicker, Peter J. and Mary Catherine Shaeffer m. 27 Jul 1848 by Rev. Joseph Shane

Nevil, Sarah Sophia and Thomas Jefferson Britton m. 2 Jul 1845 by Rev. James Sewell, lic. dated same day

Newell, Peter and Sarah Worrell m. 17 Jan 1841 by Rev. John Bear

Newell, Samuel T. and Maria Harrington m. 23 Jul 1844 by Rev. Dr. George C. M. Roberts

Newlin, Daniel and Achsah Arnold m. 6 Nov 1842 by Rev. Joseph Shane

Newman, Amelia Morris, dau. of Thomas and Mary Elizabeth Newman, b. 26 May 1843, bapt. 3 Jun 1844 by Rev. James Sewell

Newman, Ann (colored) and Asbury Miller (colored) m. 13 Feb 1841 by Rev. Samuel Keppler (date of lic. not recorded)

Newman, Cloressa Ann, dau. of Thomas and Mary Elizabeth Newman, b. 10 Jan 1840, bapt. 3 Jun 1844 by Rev. James Sewell

Newman, Harriot, d. circa 1840 (exact date not given in Class Record) [Ed. Note: Death notice in the Baltimore Sun stated that Harriet L. Newman, wife of Joseph Newman, d. 19 May 1839.]

Newman, Joseph, see "Harriot Newman," q.v.

Newman, Sarah Jane Kemp, dau. of Thomas and Mary E. Newman, b. 5 Jun 1836, Baltimore City, bapt. 30 May 1841 by Rev. Gerard Morgan

Newman, Thomas, d. circa 1848 (death noted in Probationers Book)

Newman, Virginia Emily, dau. of Thomas and Mary Elizabeth Newman, b. 25 Mar 1838, bapt. 3 Jun 1844 by Rev. James Sewell

Newton, Eliza J. and George W. Handy, both of Baltimore County, m. 19 Mar 1846 by Rev. J. Hoffman Waugh, lic. dated same day

Nichol, David and Sarah Ann Farlow m. 24 Dec 1840 by Rev. Samuel Keppler, lic. dated same day

Nichols, Hannah (colored) and Frisby Miller (colored) m. 27 Feb 1843 by Rev. Henry Slicer (date of lic. not recorded)

Nichols, Mary and Edward Oxborrow m. 23 Oct 1845 by Rev. Dr. George C. M. Roberts

Nichols, Virginia Florinda, dau. of Charles and Eliza Nichols, b. 9 Aug 1840, bapt. 13 Aug 1842 by Rev. Henry Slicer

Nicholson, Alexander and Sophia H. Rowe m. 12 Apr 1843 by Rev. Henry Slicer, lic. dated same day

Nicholson, Ellen, d. circa 1844-1847 (exact date not given in Record of Members)

Nicholson, James and Lavinia Fultz m. 12 Nov 1846 by Rev. Isaac P. Cook

Nicholson, James A. K., son of Edward and Ann Eliza Nicholson, aged 4 years [b. 1836, Baltimore City], bapt. 1840 (exact date not given) by Rev. Gerard Morgan

Nicholson, Martha A. and George Herling m. 12 Dec 1844 by Rev. Dr. George C. M. Roberts [*Ed. Note:* His last name was initially written as "Hawling" but it was lined out and "Herling" was written above it.]

Nicholson, Mary Ann and Isaac T. Ramsey m. 29 Mar 1846 by Rev. James Sewell, lic. dated same day

Nicholson, Mary Ellen, dau. of Joseph H. and Ann C. Nicholson, b. -- Mar 1841, bapt. 14 Oct 1844 by Rev. Dr. George C. M. Roberts

Nicholson, Thomasine Hopper Emory, dau. of Joseph H. and Ann C. Nicholson, b. 7 Nov 1847, bapt. 9 Jun 1849 by Rev. Dr. George C. M. Roberts

Nicholson, William H. and Ann S. Rodney m. 11 Oct 1848 by Rev. William Hirst

Nicoll, Frances Dorsey, son of William D. and Catherine Ann Nicoll, b. 23 Dec 1847, bapt. 13 Nov 1848 by Rev. Dr. George C. M. Roberts

Nicoll, William James, son of William D. and Catherine Ann Nicoll, b. 23 Aug 1845, bapt. 13 Nov 1848 by Rev. Dr. George C. M. Roberts

Night, Henry N. and Mary Ellen Davis m. 14 Jan 1849 by Rev. Dr. George C. M. Roberts

Noble, David and Lavenia Gregory m. 28 Dec 1848 by Rev. Joseph Shane

Noble, Franklin Alexander, son of ---- [blank], b. 5 Oct 1846, bapt. 1849 (exact date not given) by Rev. John S. Martin

Noble, John Napoleon, son of ---- [blank], b. 23 Dec 1847, bapt. -- Jul 1849 by Rev. John S. Martin

Noble, Margaret, d. circa 1845-1847 (exact date not given in Record of Members)

Noble, Rachael J., dau. of ---- [blank], b. ---- [blank], bapt. -- Jul 1849 by Rev. John S. Martin

Noble, Sarah Ann and John H. Cook m. 4 Aug 1844 by Rev. Isaac P. Cook

Noblet, Anthony, see "Mary Cook," q.v.

Noblet, Eliza and John L. Wields m. 1 Apr 1849 by Rev. John S. Martin, lic. dated
    31 Mar 1849
Norfolk, Eliza J. and Daniel Hardesty m. 5 Aug 1845 by Rev. Dr. George C. M.
    Roberts
Norfolk, Thomas and Mary A. Seward m. 8 Mar 1843 by Rev. Henry Slicer, lic.
    dated same day
Norris, Elizabeth and William Chase m. 8 May 1849 by Rev. Aquila A. Reese, lic.
    dated 7 May 1849
Norris, James H. and Josephine Frances Patrick m. 20 Dec 1841 by Rev. Gerard
    Morgan, lic. dated same day
Norris, Joseph Tucker, son of Isaac H. and Sarah A. Norris, b. 21 Dec 1842, bapt.
    24 Jan 1843 by Rev. Henry Slicer
Norris, Sarah Ann and Rev. Thomas Myers m. 24 Feb 1842 at the house of her
    brother in Baltimore by Rev. Beverly Waugh, lic. dated 22 Feb 1842
Norris, Sydney Stephen, son of Isaac H. and Sarah Ann Norris, b. 27 Jan 1840,
    Fells Point, Baltimore City, bapt. 14 Jul 1840 by Rev. Gerard Wood
Norte, Sarah Ann and Edward Perkins m. 1 Jan 1848 by Rev. Benjamin F. Brooke
North, John and Elizabeth A. Mowbray m. 14 Dec 1848 by Rev. William Hirst
North, Mary and James Walker m. 6 Sep 1843 by Rev. Henry Slicer, lic. dated
    same day
Norvell, John T. and Sarah Clark m. 22 Aug 1841 by Rev. Dr. George C. M.
    Roberts
Norwood, Ariann and Joseph Barlow, both of Baltimore County, m. 2 Feb 1841 by
    Rev. Bernard H. Nadal
Norwood, Caroline Sophia and Thomas Cowan m. 10 Sep 1846 by Rev. Littleton
    F. Morgan, lic. dated same day
Norwood, Edward S. and Elizabeth Richards m. 9 Mar 1848 by Rev. Isaac P. Cook
Noyes, Dr., see "Thomas Cromwell," q.v.
Noyes, Sarah E. and Thomas Cromwell m. 27 Apr 1843 at the house of Dr. Noyes
    in Baltimore by Rev. Beverly Waugh, lic. dated 26 Apr 1843
Nunemaker, George and Mary Ann Gildea m. 23 Mar 1840 by Rev. Joseph Shane
O'Brien, Edwin Harrison, son of Matthew and Hannah C. O'Brien, b. 13 May 1843,
    bapt. 14 Mar 1852 by Rev. Dr. George C. M. Roberts
O'Brien, Hannah Lavinia, dau. of Matthew and Hannah C. O'Brien, b. 19 Nov 1847,
    bapt. 14 Mar 1852 by Rev. Dr. George C. M. Roberts
O'Brien, John and Elizabeth Fisher m. 28 Jun 1845 by Rev. Wesley Stevenson
O'Brien, Mary Elizabeth, dau. of Matthew and Hannah C. O'Brien, b. 22 Aug 1845,
    bapt. 14 Mar 1852 by Rev. Dr. George C. M. Roberts
O'Hara, John So [sic], son of William and Sarah O'Hara, aged 3 weeks, bapt. 14
    May 1843 by Rev. Wesley Stevenson
O'Hara, Mary and James S. Piper, both of Baltimore, m. 2 Aug 1841 by Rev. John
    A. Hening
O'Hara, William and Sarah Longmoore m. 2 Jul 1842 by Rev. Wesley Stevenson
O'Laughlin, David and Matilda A. Habner m. 9 Nov 1842 by Rev. Isaac P. Cook
O'Neal, William and Keziah Spencer m. 4 Jun 1848 by Rev. James H. Brown, lic.
    dated 3 Jun 1848
Ogden, Elizabeth and Claas Tholen m. 19 Dec 1849 by Rev. Aquila A. Reese, lic.
    dated 18 Dec 1849

Oldham, Elizabeth J. and Andrew J. Reeder m. 29 Sep 1841 by Rev. Dr. George C. M. Roberts

Oldham, Jacob, d. circa 1840 (exact date not given in Class Record)

Olen, Alexander M. and Margaret S. Brannaman, both of Baltimore County, m. 18 May 1842 by Rev. Nelson Head

Olivet, Francis and Ann Abbert m. 1 Jun 1843 by Rev. Henry Slicer, lic. dated same day

Olivier, Jacob and Hannah Luwth m. 29 Apr 1844 by Rev. Joseph Merriken

Olmstead, William M. and Rachel Mattox m. 15 Apr 1846 by Rev. Dr. George C. M. Roberts

Onell, Arthar [sic] and Margaret Walker m. ---- [no date given] by Rev. John Miller, lic. dated 19 Jun 1850

Oor [sic], Elizabeth and Joseph Legard m. 2 Jan 1844 by Rev. Henry Slicer, lic. dated same day

Orchard, Angelina and John Campbell m. 23 Jan 1849 by Rev. Dr. George C. M. Roberts

Orem, James H., son of William G. and Keziah Orem, b. 24 Jun 1841, bapt. 6 Jul 1841 by Rev. John A. Hening

Orem, James and Eugenia Chase, both of Baltimore County, m. ---- [date not given] by Rev. George D. Chenoweth, lic. dated 14 Jan 1842

Orem, James W. and Hannah Talbott m. 13 May 1850 by Rev. Joseph Shane [Ed. Note: Their marriage notice in the Baltimore Sun gave her name as Hannah E. Tolbert.]

Orem, James W. and Mary E. Day m. 21 Aug 1847 by Rev. Isaac P. Cook

Orendoff, John H., d. circa 1847-1850 (exact date not given in Record of Members)

Orme, Rebecca, d. circa 1840-1847 (exact date not given in Record of Members)

Orrick, Daniel, d. circa 1847-1850 (exact date not given in Record of Members)

Ortlip, Israel and Mary Ann Jones m. 26 Jul 1846 by Rev. Wesley Stevenson

Osborne, John Henry and Mary Jane Wilson m. 8 Dec 1846 by Rev. Isaac P. Cook

Osborne, William and Temperance McCarty m. 14 Dec 1846 by Rev. Dr. George C. M. Roberts

Osbourn, John Gassaway, son of William and Minerva Osbourn, b. 13 Mar 1840, bapt. 29 May 1840 by Rev. Joseph Shane

Osbourn, Mary Ellen, dau. of Mary Mahala Osbourn, b. 28 Dec 1836, bapt. 29 May 1840 by Rev. Joseph Shane

Oscuby, Charlotte and Hamilton Foster, both of Baltimore County, m. 24 Dec 1844 by Rev. William Hamilton [Ed. Note: Their marriage notice in the Baltimore Sun gave her name as Charlotte Osgodby.]

Otto, Alice Susanna, dau. of Andrew and Rachel Otto, b. 5 Feb 1842, bapt. 26 Jun 1842 by Rev. Joseph Merriken

Oursler, Elizabeth A. and John R. Lee m. 21 Jun 1849 by Rev. Isaac P. Cook

Owen, Eleanor and John H. Baron m. 5 Jan 1843 by Rev. Dr. George C. M. Roberts

Owen, Read S. and Elizabeth Bond m. 28 Dec 1845 by Rev. Dr. George C. M. Roberts

Owens, Anna and Ephraim Hare m. 18 Nov 1848 by Rev. Joseph Shane

Owens, Charlotte W. and Philip R. Reiter m. 25 Jun 1844 by Rev. James Sewell, lic. dated same day

Owens, Edward Thomas and Susan Green Buck m. 15 Dec 1840 by Rev. Samuel Keppler, lic. dated same day

Owens, Francis and Mary Ann Gibson, both of Baltimore County, m. ---- [date not given] by Rev. George D. Chenoweth, lic. dated 3 Feb 1842

Owens, Mary, dau. of Sarah Owens, b. 22 Dec 1833, bapt. 22 Nov 1840 by Rev. Joseph Shane

Owens, Sally E. and Stephen B. Dorsey, both of Baltimore County, m. 24 Nov 1842 by Rev. Nelson Head

Owens, Sarah Ann and John P. Sheahan m. 2 Sep 1847 by Rev. Stephen A. Roszel, lic. dated same day

Owens, Thomas A. and Simerimis Camm m. 18 Feb 1845 by Rev. James Sewell, lic. dated same day

Owens, Young and Ann E. Williamson Travillo m. 17 Dec 1850 by Rev. Henry Slicer, lic. dated 16 Dec 1850

Owings, Achsah and Alexander Stinchcomb m. 31 Mar 1842 by Rev. Joseph Shane

Owings, Charles R. and Eleanora Small, both of Baltimore County, m. 24 Nov 1840 by Rev. Thomas Myers, lic. dated 23 Nov 1840

Owings, Hannah, d. circa 1840 (exact date not given in Class Record)

Owings, Joshua and Anna Maria Grimes m. 4 Dec 1849 by Rev. Joseph Shane

Owings, Theodore and Ann E. Worthington m. 31 Jul 1849 by Rev. Aquila A. Reese, lic. dated 30 Jul 1849

Oxborrow, Edward and Mary Nichols m. 23 Oct 1845 by Rev. Dr. George C. M. Roberts

Paddy, John R. and Priscilla Hardestie m. 14 Oct 1845 by Rev. James Sewell, lic. dated 23 Aug 1845

Page, Amanda L. and George W. Cullison m. 28 Apr 1847 by Rev. Stephen A. Roszel, lic. dated same day

Page, Lucian S. and Miss Sarah Painter, both of Baltimore County, m. ---- [date not given] by Rev. George Hildt, lic. dated 15 Jul 1845

Palmer, Catharine, d. circa 1847-1850 (exact date not given in Record of Members)

Palmer, David Keener, son of William C. and Harriet Palmer, b. 20 Mar 1844, bapt. 22 May 1844 by Rev. Dr. George C. M. Roberts

Palmer, Edward Trippe, son of William and Harriet Palmer, b. 20 Feb 183- [blank], bapt. 25 Dec 1841 by Rev. Dr. George C. M. Roberts

Palmer, Elizabeth, dau. of William and Harriet Palmer, b. 10 Mar 1838, bapt. 25 Dec 1841 by Rev. Dr. George C. M. Roberts

Palmer, Elizabeth Barney, dau. of William and Harriet Palmer, b. ---- [blank], bapt. 6 Nov 1840 by Rev. Dr. George C. M. Roberts

Palmer, Mr., see "Hannah Eliza Duncan," q.v.

Palmer, Ralph H. and Ann Miller m. 20 Sep 1843 by Rev. Samuel Brison

Palmer, William Preston, son of William and Harriet Palmer, b. 14 Nov 1841, bapt. 25 Dec 1841 by Rev. Dr. George C. M. Roberts

Pamer, Elizabeth and John Wever m. 2 Sep 1847 by Rev. Stephen A. Roszel, lic. dated same day

Pamphilion, Margaret (Martha?) and Joshua Robinson m. 17 Jan 1842 by Rev. Joseph Shane [Ed. Note: Her name was listed as Martha Pampelin in the church register, but their marriage notice in the Baltimore Sun gave her name as Margaret Pamphillion.]

Pamphilion, Nicholas and Margaret Loflin m. 30 Jul 1844 by Rev. Joseph Shane

Pamphilion, Susan, d. circa 1850 (exact date not given in Record of Members) [*Ed. Note:* Death notice in the *Baltimore Sun* stated that Susan Pampillion d. 1 Apr 1850.]

Parden, James and Mary Ann Batson, both of Baltimore, m. ---- [date not given] by Rev. John A. Hening, lic. dated 10 Sep 1841

Parker, Catherine and Washington Hamilton m. 8 Apr 1849 by Rev. Aquila A. Reese, lic. dated 7 Apr 1849

Parker, Edwin L. and Cassandra B. Lansdale m. 31 Aug 1840 by Rev. Wesley Stevenson

Parker, Margaret Hughes, dau. of Hugh and Maria C. Parker (residents of Charleston, S.C.), b. 9 Nov 1839, bapt. 30 Nov 1843 by Rev. Isaac P. Cook

Parker, Mary E. and George William Smith m. 30 Jan 1849 by Rev. Dr. George C. M. Roberts

Parker, Nathan, son of Oliver and Mary Parker, b. 3 Jun 1843, bapt. 4 Oct 1843 by Rev. Dr. George C. M. Roberts

Parker, Nathan and Ellen E. Murdoch m. 22 Jun 1847 by Rev. Dr. George C. M. Roberts

Parker, Rebecca and Daniel D. Hobbs m. 13 Aug 1850 by Rev. Isaac P. Cook

Parks, Alexina, dau. of Alexander and Sarah Parks, b. 31 Dec 1842, bapt. 10 May 1845 by Rev. Dr. George C. M. Roberts

Parks, Archibald, d. circa 1841 (death noted in Class List) [*Ed. Note:* Death notice in the *Baltimore Sun* stated that Archibald Parks d. 3 Jan 1842.]

Parks, Edward Furlong, son of Madison M. and Laura M. Parks, b. 7 Jul 1848, bapt. 9 Aug 1851 by Rev. Dr. George C. M. Roberts

Parks, Laura Elizabeth, dau. of Madison M. and Laura M. Parks, b. 1 Feb 1850, bapt. 9 Aug 1851 by Rev. Dr. George C. M. Roberts

Parks, Mary Roberts, dau. of Alexander and Sarah Parks, b. 23 Oct 1844, bapt. 10 May 1845 by Rev. Dr. George C. M. Roberts

Parks, Rebecca and George W. Cost m. 12 Sep 1850 by Rev. John S. Martin, lic. dated 11 Sep 1850

Parks, Rosanna and Robert K. Reddish m. 9 Nov 1847 by Rev. Dr. George C. M. Roberts

Parks, William and Susan M. Knight m. 3 Nov 1845 by Rev. Dr. George C. M. Roberts

Parlett, Angeline and Stephen O. McComas m. 9 Sep 1849 by Rev. Isaac P. Cook

Parlett, William and Ann Martin m. 3 Oct 1850 by Rev. Henry Slicer, lic. dated 30 Sep 1850

Parr, Mary F., dau. of John and Louisa Parr, b. 20 Jan 1843, bapt. 22 Feb 1843 by Rev. Elisha D. Owen

Parrott, Ann, d. 1840 (death noted in Class List) [*Ed. Note:* Death notice in the *Baltimore Sun* stated that Anne E. Parrott d. 25 Apr 1840.]

Parson, Joseph and Priscilla Hardesty m. 23 Dec 1849 by Rev. William Hirst, lic. dated 22 Dec 1849

Parsons, Charles Emory, son of Jonathon and Mary Ann Parsons, b. 28 May 1841, bapt. 4 Mar 1842 by Rev. Robert Emory

Parsons, George Gideon (adult), aged 21, bapt. 10 May 1857 by Rev. William A. Snively

Parsons, Hester, d. circa 1845 (death noted in Class List)

Parsons, Jemima and Solomon Hodges, both of Baltimore County, m. 9 Jan 1843 by Rev. Nelson Head

Parsons, Susan and Hugh Keller m. 11 Feb 1850 by Rev. Aquila A. Reese, lic. dated 10 Feb 1850

Pate, Isabel Elizabeth and William T. Shreck m. 17 Oct 1850 by Rev. John S. Martin, lic. dated 16 Oct 1850

Patrick, Josephine Frances and James H. Norris m. 20 Dec 1841 by Rev. Gerard Morgan, lic. dated same day

Patterson, Jacob and Ann Maria Troxall m. 28 Jun 1849 by Rev. Aquila A. Reese, lic. dated 27 Jun 1849

Patterson, James, son of James and Ann Mariah Patterson, b. 16 Jul 1840, Baltimore City, bapt. 20 Jul 1840 by Rev. Gerard Morgan

Patterson, Margaret J. and Francis W. Bennett m. 10 Dec 1845 by Rev. Dr. George C. M. Roberts

Patterson, Mary and Alexander Logan m. 28 May 1841 by Rev. John Rice, lic. dated 27 May 1841

Patterson, Mary Ann and William Anthony m. 28 Nov 1842 by Rev. Job Guest, lic. dated same day

Patterson, Rebecca and Talbot Bosley m. 5 Mar 1843 by Rev. Dr. George C. M. Roberts

Patterson, Thomas (colored) and Sophia Bowser (colored) m. 4 Nov 1841 by Rev. Gerard Morgan, lic. dated 28 Oct 1841

Patterson, William, d. circa 1847 (exact date not given in Record of Members) [Ed. Note: He may possibly be the William Patterson whose death notice in the Baltimore Sun stated that he d. 6 Jan 1846.]

Patterson, William C., d. circa 1847-1850 (exact date not given in Record of Members)

Patterson, William E. and Rebecca Jane Barren, both of Baltimore County, m. 4 Nov 1845 by Rev. William Hamilton

Patton, Elizabeth Melissa, dau. of Thomas H. and Melissa Patton, b. 24 Jun 1847, bapt. 2 Aug 1847 by Rev. Dr. George C. M. Roberts

Paul, Aschah Ann and John S. Ford m. 2 Jan 1845 by Rev. Dr. George C. M. Roberts

Paul, Jeremiah and Rebecca Ledsinger m. 29 Apr 1845 by Rev. James Sewell, lic. dated 22 Apr 1845

Paul, William and Eliza Ann Gill m. 27 Jan 1840 in Baltimore by Rev. Beverly Waugh, lic. dated 13 Jan 1840

Pausen, Sarah, d. circa 1847-1850 (exact date not given in Record of Members)

Peacock, Elizabeth and Christopher Gardner m. 23 Jun 1841 by Rev. Dr. George C. M. Roberts

Peacock, M. E. and Arnold N. Pennington m. 5 Jun 1848 by Rev. William Hirst [Ed. Note: Their names were listed as Arnold N. Penington and M. E. Pecock in the church register.]

Peacock, Samuel and Elizabeth Walker m. 12 Jan 1843 by Rev. Job Guest, lic. dated same day

Peal, Margaret A. and John H. Waggner m. 10 Nov 1844 by Rev. James Sewell, lic. dated 9 Nov 1844

Peale, Martha Ann and Henry Collier m. 2 Dec 1849 by Rev. John S. Martin, lic. dated 1 Dec 1849

Pearce, Anna Maria Athelbert Jedediah, dau. of Stephen A. and Catherine H.
Pearce, b. 21 Nov 1837, bapt. 28 Apr 1840 by Rev. Thomas Myers
Pearce, Francis and Anna Downs m. 31 May 1841 by Rev. Dr. George C. M.
  Roberts
Pearce, Levi and Mary A. Lee m. 23 Dec 1841 by Rev. Joseph Shane
Pearson, Charles Edwin, dau. of Solomon and Elizabeth Pearson, b. 14 Nov 1849,
  bapt. 3 Feb 1850 by Rev. Dr. George C. M. Roberts
Pearson, Clara Elizabeth, dau. of Solomon and Elizabeth Pearson, b. 4 Jan 1846,
  bapt. 3 Feb 1850 by Rev. Dr. George C. M. Roberts
Peck, Alverta and James F. Tucker, both of Baltimore County, m. 7 May 1846 by
  Rev. George Hildt, lic. dated 18 Apr 1846
Peck, Stephen and Harriet Adams m. 9 May 1849 by Rev. Joseph Shane
Peddicord, Julian A. and William Betts m. 13 Jan 1842 by Rev. Joseph Shane
Pedicord, Catherine and Henry Shipley m. 1 Oct 1844 by Rev. Joseph Shane
Penn, John and Sarah L. Gaither m. 4 Jun 1850 by Rev. Henry Slicer, lic. dated 27
  May 1850
Pennington, Arnold N. and M. E. Peacock m. 5 Jun 1848 by Rev. William Hirst
  [Ed. Note: Their names were listed as Arnold N. Penington and M. E. Pecock
  in the church register.]
Pennington, Mary and William Hackett m. 11 Apr 1844 by Rev. James Sewell, lic.
  dated same day
Pennington, Nathan, d. circa 1845-1847 (exact date not given in Record of
  Members) [Ed. Note: Death notice in the Baltimore Sun stated that Nathan
  Pennington d. 31 May 1846.]
Pennington, William A. and Elizabeth Ann Clement m. 25 Feb 1844 by Rev. Isaac
  P. Cook
Pennington, William James and Emeline Swan m. 6 Sep 1848 by Rev. Stephen A.
  Roszel, lic. dated same day
Penrose, Mahala and William Hull m. 11 Dec 1849 by Rev. Aquila A. Reese, lic.
  dated 10 Dec 1849
Pentz, Catharine and Charles W. Botler, Jr., both of Baltimore County, m. 8 Mar
  1840 by Rev. Bernard H. Nadal
Peregoy, Caroline and Jacob Tweedy m. 17 Jan 1850 by Rev. Joseph Shane
Peregoy, Elizabeth A. and Levi B. Lowe m. 21 Dec 1843 by Rev. Henry Slicer, lic.
  dated 20 Dec 1843
Peregoy, Joseph M. and Mary Ann Saulsbury m. 15 Feb 1848 by Rev. Dr. George
  C. M. Roberts
Peregoy, Rachel Ann and William Rose m. 14 Jun 1849 by Rev. Aquila A. Reese,
  lic. dated 13 Jun 1849
Peregoy, Samuel F. and Anna M. Sauner m. 26 Sep 1850 by Rev. Dr. George C. M.
  Roberts
Perine, Richard and Sophia Brown, both of Baltimore County, m. 18 Nov 1842 by
  Rev. Nelson Head
Perkins, Edward and Sarah Ann Norte m. 1 Jan 1848 by Rev. Benjamin F. Brooke
Perkins, John B. and Mary J. Tucker m. 2 Jun 1845 by Rev. James Sewell, lic.
  dated same day
Perkins, John R. and Priscilla Travers m. 19 Dec 1848 by Rev. Dr. George C. M.
  Roberts

Perkins, John Travers, son of John R. and Priscilla Perkins, b. 7 Oct 1849, bapt. 19 Dec 1849 by Rev. Dr. George C. M. Roberts

Perkins, Mary F., d. circa 1844-1847 (exact date not given in Record of Members)

Perrian, John and Ann Hamilton m. 24 Nov 1840 by Rev. Samuel Keppler, lic. dated same day

Perrigo, Joseph, see "Temperance Briggs," q.v.

Perry, James B. and Priscilla S. Travers m. 2 1 Oct 1 847 by Rev. Littleton F. Morgan, lic. dated same day

Perry, Jane and Henry E. H. Reese m. 26 Oct 1843 by Rev. Phillip B. Reese (date of lic. not recorded)

Perry, Jeremiah, d. after 1841 (death noted in Class List) [Ed. Note: Death notice in the Baltimore Sun stated that Jeremiah Perry d. 9 Jan 1843.]

Perry, Mary Ann and Joseph K. T. White m. 25 Jan 1842 by Rev. Isaac P. Cook

Perry, William Henry, son of Thomas and Rachel Perry, b. 7 Dec 1839, bapt. 18 Aug 1840 by Rev. Joseph Shane

Personett, Lovern M. and Margaret Ann Vanderford m. 6 Jul 1840 by Rev. Joseph Shane

Pervis, Ella Maria, dau. of James F. and Maria L. Pervis, b. 14 Jan 1846, bapt. 24 Jan 1846 by Rev. Dr. George C. M. Roberts

Peterson, Fredericka and Henry Erpenbeck m. 8 Jul 1845 by Rev. Dr. George C. M. Roberts [Ed. Note: Their marriage notice in the Baltimore Sun gave her name as Fredericker Petersen.]

Peterson, Martha and John F. Nelson m. 3 aug 1848 by Rev. Stephen A. Roszel, lic. dated 2 Aug 1848

Peterson, Mary and John Craif m. 9 Jul 1845 by Rev. Dr. George C. M. Roberts

Peterson, Mary, dau. of Louis and Catherine Peterson, b. 24 Oct 1843, bapt. 9 Jul 1845 by Rev. Dr. George C. M. Roberts

Peterson, William, d. after 1841 (death noted in Class List) [Ed. Note: He may possibly be the William N. Peterson whose death notice in the Baltimore Sun stated that he d. 1 Nov 1842.]

Petted, Alfred T. and Lucinda B. Stephens m. ---- [no date given] by Rev. John Miller, lic. dated 14 May 1850 [Ed. Note: Their marriage notice in the Baltimore Sun stated A. T. Pettit and L. B. Stephens married on 14 May 1850.]

Petticord, Sarah and William Lewis, both of Baltimore County, m. ---- [date not given] by Rev. George Hildt, lic. dated 26 Dec 1845

Pettit, Mary L. and John Brooks Smith m. 19 Sep 1850 by Rev. Isaac P. Cook

Pew, James and Margaret Butcher m. 11 May 1841 by Rev. Isaac P. Cook

Peyton, Andrew and Julian Thompson m. 18 Feb 1841 by Rev. John Bear

Peyton, Charles Henry Mott, son of Charles Henry and Charlotte A. Peyton, b. 27 Sep 1844, bapt. 1 Mar 1845 by Rev. Dr. George C. M. Roberts

Pflieger, Sarah Ann, dau. of Charles and Ann Pflieger, b. 27 Aug 1840, bapt. 13 Nov 1840 by Rev. Charles B. Tippett

Phelan, Elizabeth and David Sanks m. 5 Feb 1850 by Rev. Joseph Shane

Phelps, William and Angeline Chaney m. 14 Dec 1843 by Rev. Joseph Shane

Philips, James, son of Thomas Philips, b. ---- [blank], Fells Point, Baltimore City, bapt. 12 Jul 1840 by Rev. Philip Rescorl

Philips, Marcella A. and Bernard Carroll m. 20 Jul 1850 by Rev. Dr. George C. M. Roberts, lic. dated 17 Jul 1850

Philips, Mary Elizabeth, dau. of Thomas Philips, b. ---- [blank], Fells Point, Baltimore City, bapt. 12 Jul 1840 by Rev. Philip Rescorl

Philips, Mary V., dau. of William and Mary J. Philips, b. 24 Dec 1839, bapt. 29 Jun 1842 by Rev. William Prettyman

Phillips, Ann R., d. 1845 (exact date not given in Record of Members)

Phillips, Edwin and Caroline Wright m. 14 Aug 1846 by Rev. Joseph Shane

Phillips, Elizabeth and John T. White m. 28 Mar 1848 by Rev. Stephen A. Roszel, lic. dated 24 Mar 1848

Phillips, Sarah Ann and Samuel Cameron m. 30 Jan 1849 by Rev. Dr. George C. M. Roberts

Philpot, Joseph Alexander, son of Joseph and Veronica Philpot, b. 20 Jan 1840, bapt. 7 Jun 1840 by Rev. Dr. George C. M. Roberts

Pickering, Martha and James T. Jenkins m. 16 Jun 1847 by Rev. Stephen A. Roszel, lic. dated 10 Jun 1847

Pickett, Mary and Isaac Jones m. 14 Oct 1842 by Rev. Joseph Shane

Pierce, Ephraim and Mary Ann Jones m. 21 Dec 1843 by Rev. Joseph Shane

Pierce, George C. and Margaret Ann Cissel, both of Montgomery County, MD, m. 15 Sep 1840 by Rev. Thomas Myers, lic. dated 13 Sep 1840

Pindel, Margaret J. and Samuel F. Mason m. 19 Aug 1850 by Rev. Isaac P. Cook

Pindell, Jane, d. 1840 (death noted in Class List) [*Ed. Note:* Death notice in the *Baltimore Sun* stated that Jane Pindell, wife of Richard Pindell, d. 23 Feb 1840.]

Pinkind, Thomas C. and Elizabeth A. Marshall m. 4 Oct 1842 by Rev. Henry Slicer, lic. dated same day

Piper, James S. and Mary O'Hara, both of Baltimore, m. 2 Aug 1841 by Rev. Bernard H. Nadal

Pitcher, William H. and Mary Jane Reese m. 20 Feb 1850 by Rev. Aquila A. Reese, lic. dated 19 Feb 1850

Pitcock, Sarah E. and John Price m. 12 Apr 1847 by Rev. Stephen A. Roszel, lic. dated same day

Pitt, Catherine Jane Creagh, dau. of Charles F. and Catherine C. Pitt, b. 10 Jan 1848, bapt. 20 Aug 1848 by Rev. Dr. George C. M. Roberts

Pittinger, Joseph, son of Richard and Elizabeth Pittinger, b. 13 Sep 1842, bapt. 23 Feb 1843 by Rev. Elisha D. Owen

Pitts, Charles H. and Elizabeth Reynolds, both of Baltimore County, m. 28 Jun 1844 by Rev. Dr. Thomas E. Bond, lic. dated same day

Placide, Alice, dau. of Henry S. and Susan E. Placide, b. 28 Feb 1850, bapt. 1 Mar 1850 by Rev. Dr. George C. M. Roberts

Plant, Louisa and Ezekiel Badger, both of Baltimore, m. 25 Oct 1841 by Rev. John A. Hening

Platt, John F. and Emma E. Rusk m. 7 Apr 1850 by Rev. Henry Slicer, lic. dated 5 Apr 1850

Plummer, Elizabeth, d. before 1844 (exact date not given in Record of Members) [*Ed. Note:* Death notice in the *Baltimore Sun* stated that Elizabeth Plummer, widow of Samuel Plummer, d. 29 Dec 1842.]

Plummer, James H. and Mary Viney m. 12 Aug 1849 by Rev. Dr. George C. M. Roberts

Plummer, Mary G. and Cloud Carter, both of Baltimore County, m. 27 Apr 1840 by Rev. Thomas Myers, lic. dated same day

Plummer, Rebecca and Thomas Lloyd m. 15 Jun 1847 by Rev. Stephen A. Roszel, lic. dated same day

Plummer, Robert M. and Susanna Daddz m. 5 Nov 1850 by Rev. Dr. George C. M. Roberts [Ed. Note: Their marriage notice in the Baltimore Sun gave their names as Robert Plumer and Susanna Dadds.]

Plummer, Samuel, son of Samuel and Elizabeth Plummer, b. 1839, bapt. 25 Jun 1840 by Rev. Dr. George C. M. Roberts

Plummer, Samuel, d. circa 1840-1842 (exact date not given in Record of Members) [Ed. Note: Death notice in the Baltimore Sun stated that Samuel Plummer d. 29 Dec 1842.] See "Elizabeth Plummer," q.v.

Plyman, John Joseph (colored), son of John and Susanna Plyman, b. 13 Nov 1844, bapt. 27 May 1845 by Rev. Dr. George C. M. Roberts

Pocock, Postilana, child of ---- [blank] Pocock, aged 11 years [b. 1833], bapt. 27 Oct 1844 by Rev. Isaac P. Cook

Poe, Harriet and Henry Bishop m. 8 Mar 1849 by Rev. Joseph Shane

Poits, Rebecca and Thomas L. Hall m. 26 Oct 1843 at the house of her mother Mrs. Chaytor in Baltimore by Rev. Beverly Waugh, lic. dated 26 Oct 1843 [Ed. Note: Their marriage notice in the Baltimore Sun gave her name as Rebecca P. Chaytor.]

Pollard, Amelia (colored) and Samuel Morgan m. 6 Jul 1849 by Rev. Dr. George C. M. Roberts

Pollard, Catherine P. and Chatham C. Flowers, both of Baltimore County, m. 15 May 1846 by Rev. George Hildt, lic. dated same day

Pollard, John W. and Sophia C. Jordon m. 13 Jan 1848 by Rev. Benjamin F. Brooke

Ponder, Mary Julia, dau. of George W. and Martha Ponder, b. 15 Apr 1850, bapt. 31 Jul 1850 by Rev. Dr. George C. M. Roberts

Pontz, Ann and William Bateman m. 21 May 1846 by Rev. Samuel Keppler (date of lic. not recorded)

Pool, Angelina, d. circa 1845-1847 (exact date not given in Record of Members)

Pool, George T. and Sarah Burke m. 1 Sep 1846 by Rev. Littleton F. Morgan, lic. dated same day

Pool, Mary and Caleb B. Hynes m. 13 Sep 1846 by Rev. Isaac P. Cook

Pool, Mary E. and Charles H. Dany (Dairy?) m. 11 May 1843 by Rev. Dr. George C. M. Roberts

Pool, Thomas and Elizabeth Wilkinson m. 14 Mar 1850 by Rev. Isaac P. Cook

Poole, Henry and Sally A. Davis m. 15 Nov 1849 by Rev. Aquila A. Reese, lic. dated 14 Nov 1849

Poole, Joseph Frey, son of Rezin and Eliza Poole, b. 15 Jan 1840, bapt. 26 Jan 1841 by Rev. Dr. George C. M. Roberts

Popplein, Franklin, son of Nicholas and Susanna Popplein, b. 20 Sep 1850, bapt. 11 Aug 1852 by Rev. Dr. George C. M. Roberts

Popplein, John Thompson, son of Nicholas and Susanna Popplein, b. 7 Nov 1846, bapt. 11 Aug 1852 by Rev. Dr. George C. M. Roberts

Popplein, Joseph, son of Nicholas and Susanna Popplein, b. 21 Aug 1848, bapt. 11 Aug 1852 by Rev. Dr. George C. M. Roberts

Popplein, Maria Margaretta, dau. of Nicholas and Susanna Popplein, b. 2 Mar 1845, bapt. 11 Aug 1852 by Rev. Dr. George C. M. Roberts

Porter, Catherine, d. 1847 (death noted in Class List)

Porter, Edward P. and Martha A. Stallings m. 25 Jul 1846 by Rev. Joseph Shane

Porter, Eliza and Richard Porter m. 7 Feb 1841 by Rev. Joseph Shane

Porter, Rebecca Jane and Henry Horace Sprigg m. 4 Apr 1844 by Rev. Dr. George C. M. Roberts

Porter, Richard and Eliza Porter m. 7 Feb 1841 by Rev. Joseph Shane

Porter, Thomas and Catherine A. Sinclair m. 24 Dec 1843 by Rev. Henry Slicer, lic. dated 23 Dec 1843

Porter, William and Amanda M. Alexander m. 1 Feb 1848 by Rev. Dr. George C. M. Roberts

Posey, Mary Jane and John Foreman, both of Baltimore County, m. 31 Dec 1840 by Rev. Bernard H. Nadal

Potee, George N. and Sarah Roach m. 19 May 1850 by Rev. Joseph Shane

Poteet, Ann Maria and George W. Fitzgerald m. 16 Jan 1844 by Rev. Joseph Shane

Poteet, Isaac Clare and Ann Maria Wolf m. 7 Dec 1846 by Rev. Joseph Shane

Potter, Mary and Samuel Dales m. 15 Feb 1842 by Rev. Joseph Shane

Poulson, John and Almira Mason m. 30 Jan 1848 by Rev. Joseph Shane

Poultner, Charles and Mary Twigg m. 27 Mar 1845 by Rev. Joseph Shane

Powell, Mary Ann, dau. of Robert and Priscilla Powell, b. 16 Mar 1840, Fells Point, Baltimore City, bapt. 14 Jul 1840 by Rev. Samuel Keppler

Powell, Sidney A. and John F. Adams m. 10 May 1848 by Rev. Dr. George C. M. Roberts

Powers, Josiah T. and Caroline Commine m. 14 Jun 1847 by Rev. Stephen A. Roszel, lic. dated same day

Powers, Mancy [sic] and William W. Powers m. 7 Dec 1846 by Rev. George Hildt, lic. dated same day

Powers, William W. and Mancy [sic] Powers m. 7 Dec 1846 by Rev. George Hildt, lic. dated same day

Pressley, Hester J. and William A. Dell m. 3 Oct 1850 by Rev. Henry Slicer, lic. dated same day

Preston, George and Elizabeth Trott m. 30 Dec 1841 by Rev. Joseph Shane

Preston, Lavinia, d. circa 1847-1850 (exact date not given in Record of Members)

Preston, Mary J. (colored) and Isaac Hawkins (colored) m. 27 Dec 1842 by Rev. Henry Slicer (date of lic. not recorded)

Preston, William Henry, son of William and Elizabeth Preston, b. 20 Aug 1840, bapt. 6 Jun 1840 [sic] by Rev. Dr. George C. M. Roberts

Pretlove, Sarah, d. 1847 (death noted in Class List)

Price, David Thomas, son of Richard and Elizabeth A. Price, b. 18 Sep 1841, bapt. 10 Sep 1845 by Rev. Dr. George C. M. Roberts

Price, Eliza, d. circa 1847-1850 (exact date not given in Record of Members)

Price, Eliza Jane and Charles Turner, both of Baltimore County, m. ---- [date not given] by Rev. George D. Chenoweth, lic. dated 17 Feb 1842 [Ed. Note: Their marriage notice in the Baltimore Sun stated they were married on 17 Feb 1842.]

Price, Elizabeth Ann, dau. of Richard and Elizabeth A. Price, b. 1 Mar 1845, bapt. 10 Sep 1845 by Rev. Dr. George C. M. Roberts

Price, Emily, d. circa 1840-1847 (exact date not given in Record of Members)

Price, John and Sarah E. Pitcock m. 12 Apr 1847 by Rev. Stephen A. Roszel, lic. dated same day

Price, Mary Ann and Mamiel *[sic]* H. Michall m. 11 Sep 1843 by Rev. Dr. George C. M. Roberts

Price, Richard, son of Richard and Elizabeth A. Price, b. ---- [blank], bapt. 10 Sep 1845 by Rev. Dr. George C. M. Roberts [*Ed. Note:* It appears that 18 Sep 1841 was initially entered in the register as his birth date, but it was subsequently erased.]

Price, Richard and Elizabeth Ann Thomas m. 21 Jul 1840 at Light Street Church in Baltimore by Rev. Beverly Waugh, lic. dated 18 Jul 1840

Price, Richard William, son of Richard and Elizabeth A. Price, b. 26 Jun 1843, bapt. 10 Sep 1845 by Rev. Dr. George C. M. Roberts

Price, Sarah Ann and William O. Johnson m. 25 Sep 1845 by Rev. James Sewell, lic. dated 26 Sep 1845 *[sic]*

Price, Sophia Grauff(?), of Baltimore County, and Rev. John W. Tongue, of the Baltimore Annual Conference, m. 13 May 1846 by Rev. George Hildt, lic. dated 12 May 1846

Price, William and Rachel B. Draper m. 16 Jan 1840 by Rev. John Bear

Price, William and Sarah Donaldson m. 29 Oct 1843 by Rev. Isaac P. Cook

Price, William and Sarah Cassey m. 19 Jan 1841 by Rev. Samuel Keppler, lic. dated same day

Prill (Price?), Rebecca A. and Robert J. Hall, both of Baltimore County, m. 26 Feb 1846 by Rev. William Hamilton

Prince, Ann Barbara and John W. Constantine m. 24 Jan 1850 by Rev. Wesley Stevenson

Prior, Mary, d. circa 1845-1847 (exact date not given in Record of Members) [*Ed. Note:* Death notice in the *Baltimore Sun* stated that Mary Prior, wife of Joseph B. Prior, d. 17 Sep 1846.]

Pritchard, Caroline and Henry V. Lovell, both of Baltimore County, m. 7 Feb 1843 by Rev. Nelson Head

Prueitt, Severn, see "Elizabeth W. Pruitt," q.v.

Pruett, Henry and Sarah C. Wilkinson m. 7 Mar 1850 by Rev. Isaac P. Cook

Pruitt, Elizabeth W. and William H. Fleming m. 26 Mar 1843 by Rev. Dr. George C. M. Roberts [*Ed. Note:* Their marriage notice in the *Baltimore Sun* stated that William H. Flemming m. Elizabeth W. Prueitt, dau. of Severn Prueitt.]

Pruitt, Sarah and William Carter m. 31 Mar 1845 by Rev. Dr. George C. M. Roberts

Pryor, George W. and Jauelda(?) Catharine Bruiman (Bwiman?) m. 24 Oct 1848 by Rev. Stephen A. Roszel, lic. dated same day

Pugh, William and Mary Jane Applegarth m. 10 Jan 1850 by Rev. John S. Martin, lic. dated 8 Jan 1850

Pulley, Elvey Ann and John Bailey m. 11 Sep 1845 by Rev. Samuel Keppler (date of lic. not recorded)

Pulley, Robert and Elizabeth Duncan m. 24 Jul 1843 by Rev. Henry Slicer, lic. dated same day

Pulley, William and Harriet E. Young m. 16 Nov 1845 by Rev. Dr. George C. M. Roberts

Pullins, Randall (adult), b. ---- [blank], Baltimore City, bapt. 1840 (exact date not given) by Rev. Gerard Morgan

Pullins, Ugena, dau. of Randall Pullins, aged 11 years [b. 1829, Baltimore City], bapt. 1840 (exact date not given) by Rev. Gerard Morgan

Pumphrey, George Shipley, son of George S. and Mary Ann Pumphrey, b. 21 Oct 1842, bapt. 8 Apr 1843 by Rev. Dr. George C. M. Roberts

Pumphrey, Vachel R. and Lydia Wilson m. 24 Dec 1843 by Rev. Isaac P. Cook

Pumphry, Ellen and John Loman m. 16 Apr 1840 by Rev. Joseph Shane

Purner, Sarah and Phillip Bacon m. 26 Dec 1850 by Rev. Joseph Shane

Purper, Julia Ann, dau. of John and Treasy Purper, b. 20 Feb 1839, bapt. 29 Jul 1840 by Rev. Joseph Shane

Pursell, Hugh and Jane B. Eltonhead m. 13 Jun 1844 by Rev. Isaac P. Cook

Pyle, Isaac C. and Elizabeth Skinner m. 19 Dec 1844 by Rev. Dr. George C. M. Roberts

Pyne, Kate M. and John H. Sterling m. 1 Sep 1847 by Rev. Stephen A. Roszel, lic. dated 31 Aug 1847

Quarley, Frances E. and Elizabeth M. Warrington m. 19 Feb 1844 by Rev. Samuel Brison

Quay, Charles Gillet, son of John M. and Sarah Ann Quay, b. 11 Dec 1839, Fells Point, Baltimore City, bapt. 11 Jul 1840 by Rev. Samuel Keppler

Quay, James Y. Peyton, son of J. C. and Mary Ann Quay, b. 25 May 1840, bapt. 19 Jul 1840 by Rev. John Bear

Quick, John William and Mary Jane Disney m. 30 May 1848 by Rev. Isaac P. Cook

Quinlan, Leonard J., see "Jane Miles," q.v.

Quinn, Julia Ann, d. circa 1845-1847 (exact date not given in Record of Members)

Rampineyer, Charles and Mary Schmedes m. 15 Mar 1847 by Rev. Isaac P. Cook

Ramsay, Isaac, see "Mary Ramsey," q.v.

Ramsay, Mary Jane and Alexander McDonnel m. 8 Sep 1840 by Rev. Samuel Keppler, lic. dated same day

Ramsey, Isaac T. and Mary Ann Nicholson m. 29 Mar 1846 by Rev. James Sewell, lic. dated same day

Ramsey, John and Eliza Smith m. 22 Feb 1849 by Rev. Joseph Shane

Ramsey, Mary, d. 1844 (death noted in Class List) [Ed. Note: Death notice in the Baltimore Sun stated that Mary Ramsay, wife of Isaac Ramsay, d. 11 Jul 1844.]

Randolph, James T. and Agness C. Boyd m. 8 Oct 1840 by Rev. Samuel Keppler, lic. dated 6 Oct 1840

Randolph, Thompson, son of James T. and Agness Randolph, b. 2 Aug 1841, bapt. 26 Jun 1842 by Rev. Henry Slicer

Raney, Amelia, d. circa 1840-1847 (exact date not given in Record of Members)

Rankin, Ann R. and William M. Knipe m. 15 Jun 1848 by Rev. Stephen A. Roszel, lic. dated 13 Jun 1848

Ransdall, Ann, d. circa 1847-1850 (exact date not given in Record of Members)

Rarick, George Washington, son of John and Mary Rarick, b. 1 Mar 1839, bapt. 30 Aug 1840 by Rev. Isaac P. Cook

Rash, Martin and Catherine Bennett m. 2 Jul 1846 by Rev. Dr. George C. M. Roberts

Ratcliff, Elizabeth and Thomas Hall m. 22 Jul 1843 by Rev. Joseph Shane

Ratcliff, William, d. circa 1847-1850 (exact date not given in Record of Members)

Ravenset, George and Elezina Goshell m. 17 Apr 1845 by Rev. James Sewell, lic. dated same day [Ed. Note: Their marriage notice in the Baltimore Sun gave their names as George Ravenot and Elezine Goshell.]

Rawlings, Adeline Elizabeth, dau. of George A. and Almira F. Rawlings, b. 11 Oct 1847, bapt. 24 Apr 1848 by Rev. Dr. George C. M. Roberts

Rawlings, Amelia Betson, dau. of George A. and Almira F. Rawlings, b. 23 Nov 1848, bapt. 13 Jul 1849 by Rev. Dr. George C. M. Roberts

Rawlings, George and Almira F. Woodcock m. 20 Jan 1847 by Rev. Dr. George C. M. Roberts

Rawlings, Susanna Matilda, dau. of James and Angeline Rawlings, b. 5 Mar 1840, bapt. 22 Oct 1840 by Rev. Dr. George C. M. Roberts

Rawlings, William John, son of James and Mary Rawlings, aged 15 months [b. 1841], bapt. 4 Feb 1842 by Rev. Wesley Stevenson

Ray, Alfred and Caroline Martha Seymour m. 2 Mar 1848 by Rev. Stephen A. Roszel, lic. dated 24 Feb 1848

Ray, Francis and Susan Tipton m. 16 Mar 1841 by Rev. Joseph Shane

Rayns, Lewis and Martha A. Baker m. 13 Mar 1844 by Rev. Dr. George C. M. Roberts

Raywood, William and Rebecca Jarvis m. 29 Jun 1847 by Rev. Stephen A. Roszel, lic. dated same day

Rea, Hannah, d. circa 1840-1844 (exact date not given in Record of Members) [*Ed. Note:* Death notice in the *Baltimore Sun* stated that Hannah Rea, wife of John H. Rea, d. 10 Sep 1842.]

Read, Anna M. and Charles L. Bruff m. 3 Sep 1846 by Rev. Dr. George C. M. Roberts

Read, Robert, see "Robert Reed," q.v.

Read, Samuel McK. and Pencilla Ann Kidd m. ---- [blank] by Rev. John S. Martin, lic. dated 25 Nov 1850 [*Ed. Note:* Their marriage notice in the *Baltimore Sun* stated that Samuel M. Read m. Pencilla A. Kidd on 26 Nov 1850.]

Reaney, Isabella, dau. of Richard W. and Louisa J. Reaney, b. 2 Sep 1845, bapt. 10 Sep 1845 by Rev. Dr. George C. M. Roberts

Reaney, James, son of Richard W. and Louisa Jane Reaney, b. 13 Oct 1843, bapt. 1 Sep 1844 by Rev. Dr. George C. M. Roberts [*Ed. Note:* The name was misspelled "Reeney" in the church register.]

Reaves, Mary Ann and John J. Johnson, both of Baltimore County, m. ---- [date not given] by Rev. George Hildt, lic. dated 11 Nov 1845

Reay, Martha, d. 1845 (death noted in Class List)

Reddish, James and Lucretia Starr m. 25 Jun 1843 by Rev. Dr. George C. M. Roberts

Reddish, Robert K. and Rosanna Parks m. 9 Nov 1847 by Rev. Dr. George C. M. Roberts

Redman, Charlotte and Maxwell Hamilton m. 5 Sep 1841 by Rev. Joseph Shane

Redman, George C. and Sarah Bosley m. 31 May 1846 by Rev. Joseph Shane

Redman, William C. and Susan French m. 8 Jul 1841 by Rev. Joseph Shane

Reece, Ann (colored) and Joseph Williams (colored) m. 9 Sep 1841 by Rev. Gerard Morgan, lic. dated same day

Reece, Mary A. and Charles N. Brown m. 24 May 1848 by Rev. Joseph Shane

Reed, Elizabeth, d. circa 1840-1847 (exact date not given in Record of Members) [*Ed. Note:* Death notices in the *Baltimore Sun* stated that three women named Elizabeth Reed died during this time period: one d. 28 Jul 1840, wife of William Reed; one d. 28 Feb 1842, wife of Samuel Reed; and, one d. 1 Apr 1846, widow of John Reed.]

Reed, Elizabeth and Conrad Albert Minnick m. 23 Jan 1848 by Rev. Stephen A. Roszel, lic. dated same day

Reed, Emeline, see "Mary Frances Reed," q.v.

Reed, John, see "Elizabeth Reed" and "William H. Reed," q.v.

Reed, Mary A. (colored) and William J. Loc (colored) m. 2 Nov 1841 by Rev. Gerard Morgan, lic. dated 28 Oct 1841

Reed, Mary Frances, dau. of Emeline Reed (colored), b. 27 Feb 1847, bapt. 14 Mar 1852 by Rev. Dr. George C. M. Roberts

Reed, Noah and Rosanna Seebright m. 10 Apr 1849 by Rev. Aquila A. Reese, lic. dated 9 Apr 1849

Reed, Rebecca and Edward Richards m. 24 Oct 1850 by Rev. Isaac P. Cook

Reed, Robert, d. 1849 (death noted in Class List) [Ed. Note: Death notice in the Baltimore Sun stated that Robert Read d. 8 May 1849.]

Reed, Samuel, see "Elizabeth Reed," q.v.

Reed, Samuel D. and Cynthia Ann Baker m. 28 Nov 1844 by Rev. Isaac P. Cook

Reed, Sarah Elizabeth and Abraham P. Hilgar m. 30 May 1848 by Rev. Isaac P. Cook

Reed, William, see "Elizabeth Reed," q.v.

Reed, William Henry, son of John and Margaret Reed, b. 9 Feb 1838, bapt. 12 Sep 1841 by Rev. Robert Emory

Reeder, Andrew J. and Elizabeth J. Oldham m. 29 Sep 1841 by Rev. Dr. George C. M. Roberts

Reeder, Elvira E. and William J. Lewis m. 27 Oct 1846 by Rev. Joseph Shane

Reese, Alexander Disney, son of William and Elizabeth Reese, b. -- Feb 1842, bapt. 29 Oct 1841 [sic] by Rev. Dr. George C. M. Roberts

Reese, Alice, d. 1844 (death noted in Class List)

Reese, Ann and William Graham m. 10 Jul 1843 by Rev. Isaac P. Cook

Reese, Anna Lucy, dau. of John E. and Sarah E. Reese, b. 8 Apr 1845, bapt. 30 Jun 1846 by Rev. Dr. George C. M. Roberts

Reese, Catherine and William Coleman m. 13 May 1850 by Rev. Joseph Shane

Reese, Cordelia Fillmore, dau. of William D. and Alexina Reese, b. 24 Oct 1848, bapt. 29 Oct 1848 by Rev. Dr. George C. M. Roberts

Reese, D. E., see "Ruth Reese," q.v.

Reese, Emma Susanna, dau. of William D. and Alexina Reese, b. 17 Dec 1845, bapt. 29 Oct 1848 by Rev. Dr. George C. M. Roberts

Reese, Henry E. H. and Jane Perry m. 26 Oct 1843 by Rev. Phillip B. Reese (date of lic. not recorded)

Reese, Horatio Berry, son of John Evan and Sarah E. Reese, b. 26 May 1831, bapt. 22 Apr 1840 by Rev. Dr. George C. M. Roberts

Reese, Jacob, d. circa 1849-1850 (death noted in Class List) [Ed. Note: Death notice in the Baltimore Sun stated that Jacob Reese, father-in-law of Benjamin F. Tear, d. 5 Aug 1850.]

Reese, James, see "Josephine Reese," q.v.

Reese, John A. and Anna L. Bailey m. 12 Dec 1849 by Rev. Aquila A. Reese, lic. dated 11 Dec 1849

Reese, John Evan, son of John and Ann Reese, b. 15 Aug 1799, bapt. 22 Apr 1840 by Rev. Dr. George C. M. Roberts. See "Anna L. Reese" and "Horatio B. Reese" and "John E. Reese, Jr." and "Mary E. Reese" and "Matthew F. Reese" and "Sarah A. Reese" and "William H. Reese," q.v.

Reese, John Evan Jr., son of John Evan and Sarah E. Reese, b. 12 May 1833, bapt. 22 Apr 1840 by Rev. Dr. George C. M. Roberts

Reese, John Wesley, son of William and Elizabeth Reese, b. ---- [blank], bapt. 10 Jan 1844 by Rev. Dr. George C. M. Roberts

Reese, Josephine, dau. of James Edward and Mary Ann Reese, b. 28 Jan 1843, bapt. 8 Feb 1843 by Rev. Dr. George C. M. Roberts

Reese, Margaretta and Thomas Davis m. 26 Feb 1848 by Rev. Dr. George C. M. Roberts

Reese, Martha, see "William H. Reese," q.v.

Reese, Martha Ann, dau. of William and Elizabeth Reese, b. ---- [blank], bapt. 27 Jan 1842 by Rev. Dr. George C. M. Roberts

Reese, Mary, d. circa 1844 (exact date not given in Record of Members) [*Ed. Note:* Death notice in the *Baltimore Sun* stated that Mary A. Reese d. 31 Dec 1843.]

Reese, Mary Elizabeth and Charles Edward Gray m. 3 Feb 1848 by Rev. Isaac P. Cook

Reese, Mary Elizabeth, dau. of John Evan and Sarah E. Reese, b. 20 Oct 1836, bapt. 22 Apr 1840 by Rev. Dr. George C. M. Roberts

Reese, Mary Jane and Joseph H. Boyd, both of Baltimore County, m. 2 Sep 1845 by Rev. J. Hoffman Waugh, lic. dated same day

Reese, Mary Jane and William H. Pitcher m. 20 Feb 1850 by Rev. Aquila A. Reese, lic. dated 19 Feb 1850

Reese, Matthew Forney, son of John Evan and Sarah E. Reese, b. 22 Sept 1838, bapt. 22 Apr 1840 by Rev. Dr. George C. M. Roberts

Reese, Rebecca Susanna, dau. of James E. and Mary Reese, b. 4 Jan 1841, bapt. 9 Dec 1841 by Rev. Dr. George C. M. Roberts

Reese, Ruth, d. circa 1840-1842 (exact date not given in Record of Members) [*Ed. Note:* Death notice in the *Baltimore Sun* stated that Ruth Reese, wife of D. E. Reese, d. 23 Feb 1842.]

Reese, Sarah E., see "Anna L. Reese" and "Horatio B. Reese" and "John E. Reese, Jr." and "Mary E. Reese" and "Matthew F. Reese" and "Sarah A. Reese" and "William H. Reese," q.v.

Reese, Susan and John Bradford, both of Baltimore County, m. ---- [date not given] by Rev. George Hildt, lic. dated 20 Dec 1845 [*Ed. Note:* Their marriage notice in the *Baltimore Sun* stated they married on 21 Dec 1845.]

Reese, Sarah Ann, dau. of John Evan and Sarah E. Reese, b. 30 Dec 1830, bapt. 22 Apr 1840 by Rev. Dr. George C. M. Roberts

Reese, Thomas and Rebecca Blade m. 16 Oct 1844 by Rev. James Sewell, lic. dated same day

Reese, William, see "Alexander D. Reese" and "John W. Reese" and "Martha A. Reese" and William H. Reese, q.v.

Reese, William D., see "Cordelia F. Reese" and "Emma D. Reese," q.v.

Reese, William Henry, son of John Evan and Sarah E. Reese, b. 4 Oct 1840, bapt. 15 May 1840 *[sic]* by Rev. Dr. George C. M. Roberts

Reese, William Henry, son of William and Martha Reese, b. 8 Jul 1841, bapt. 13 Mar 1842 by Rev. Dr. George C. M. Roberts

Reeve, Ursula and David A. Gardner m. 30 Apr 1845 by Rev. James Sewell, lic. dated same day

Register, Robert W. and Susanna Evans, both of Baltimore, MD, m. 10 Nov 1840 by Rev. John A. Hening

Reiley, Ann Rebecca, dau. of John and Mary Ann Reiley, b. 6 Jun 1840, Fells Point, Baltimore City, bapt. 14 Jul 1840 by Rev. Samuel Keppler

Reiter, Philip R. and Charlotte W. Owens m. 25 Jun 1844 by Rev. James Sewell, lic. dated same day

Reith, Margaret and William Bryan m. 7 Apr 1846 by Rev. Dr. George C. M. Roberts

Relm, Joseph, son of Mr. and Mrs. Relm, b. ---- [blank], bapt. 16 Aug 1843 by Rev. Philip B. Reese

Remington, Jesse, son of Jesse and Avarilla T. Remington, b. 24 Dec 1839, Baltimore City, bapt. 21 Jan 1841 by Rev. Samuel Keppler

Renaud, John H. and Mary Moore, both of Baltimore County, m. 4 Nov 1844 by Rev. William Hamilton

Rengrose (Ringrose), Mary E. and John B. Jordan m. 5 Oct 1847 by Rev. Stephen A. Roszel, lic. dated 4 Oct 1847

Rengrose (Ringrose), Robert and Sarah Ann Liley m. 28 Sep 1847 by Rev. Stephen A. Roszel, lic. dated same day

Reno, William H. and Martha L. Bramble m. 25 Oct 1848 by Rev. Dr. George C. M. Roberts

Rephart (Kephart?), Elizabeth, dau. of Lewis and Elizabeth Rephart Kephart(?), b. 15 Jun 1840, bapt. same day by Rev. Dr. George C. M. Roberts

Reynolds, Benjamin, see "Juliet Reynolds," q.v.

Reynolds, Catharine A. and Henry Rose m. 13 Jul 1842 by Rev. Wesley Stevenson

Reynolds, Elizabeth and Charles H. Pitts, both of Baltimore County, m. 28 Jun 1844 by Rev. Dr. Thomas E. Bond, lic. dated same day

Reynolds, Emeline and Joseph P. Nelson m. 7 Jun 1849 by Rev. Aquila A. Reese, lic. dated 6 Jun 1849

Reynolds, George Washington, son of Goven and Mary Reynolds, b. 20 Jan 1839, bapt. 21 Aug 1840 by Rev. Joseph Shane

Reynolds, Goven, see "George W. Reynolds" and "Mary A. Reynolds," q.v.

Reynolds, Isaac, d. circa 1847-1850 (exact date not given in Record of Members)

Reynolds, Jemima and John, see "Thomas Reynolds," q.v.

Reynolds, John W. and Louisa E. Scott m. 30 May 1845 by Rev. Wesley Stevenson

Reynolds, Juliet, dau. of Benjamin and Salena Reynolds, b. 13 Oct 1839, bapt. 27 Aug 1840 by Rev. Dr. George C. M. Roberts

Reynolds, Laura S. and Charles L. Askew m. 30 Apr 1848 by Rev. Dr. George C. M. Roberts

Reynolds, Mary, see "George W. Reynolds" and "Mary A. Reynolds," q.v.

Reynolds, Mary Ann and Sylvester H. Stevens, both of Baltimore County, m. ---- [date not given] by Rev. George Hildt, lic. dated 7 Nov 1845

Reynolds, Mary Arrabella, dau. of Goven and Mary Reynolds, b. 18 May 1836, bapt. 21 Aug 1840 by Rev. Joseph Shane

Reynolds, Salena, see "Juliet Reynolds," q.v.

Reynolds, Thomas, son of John and Jemima Reynolds, b. 26 May 1840, bapt. 31 Aug 1840 by Rev. Joseph Shane

Rhea, Robert Bruce, son of Capt. Allen and Mary Ann Rhea, b. 22 Feb 1843, bapt. 1 Mar 1843 by Rev. Dr. George C. M. Roberts

Rhea, William Wallace, son of Capt. Allen and Mary Ann Rhea, b. 1 Feb 1841, bapt. 1 Mar 1843 by Rev. Dr. George C. M. Roberts

Rhodes, Catharine and Dixon Brown, both of Baltimore County, m. 8 Nov 1840 by Rev. Bernard H. Nadal

Rhodes, Elizabeth, d. circa 1840 (exact date not given in Class Record)

Rhodes, Mary Ann, dau. of John R. and Mary A. Rhodes, b. 5 Aug 1839, bapt. 7 Jun 1840 by Rev. Isaac P. Cook

Richards, Edward and Rebecca Reed m. 24 Oct 1850 by Rev. Isaac P. Cook

Richards, Elizabeth and Edward S. Norwood m. 9 Mar 1848 by Rev. Isaac P. Cook

Richards, Joshua H. and Sarah E. Richards m. 2 Mar 1845 by Rev. James Sewell, lic. dated 1 Mar 1845

Richards, Mary and Michael Connors m. 10 Nov 1840 by Rev. Samuel Keppler, lic. dated same day

Richards, Randolph and Ann Catharine Burns m. 1 Sep 1847 by Rev. Isaac P. Cook

Richards, Sarah E. and Joshua H. Richards m. 2 Mar 1845 by Rev. James Sewell, lic. dated 1 Mar 1845

Richards, William Jr. and Eliza A. Tucker m. 16 Nov 1848 by Rev. Joseph Shane

Richardson, Benjamin, see "Elizabeth Richardson," q.v.

Richardson, E lizabeth, d. c irca 1 847-1849 ( exact d ate n ot g iven i n R ecord o f Members) [*Ed. Note:* Death notice in the *Baltimore Sun* stated that Elizabeth Richardson, wife of Benjamin Richardson, d. 3 Nov 1848.]

Richardson, Jane E. and George J. Sanner m. 24 Dec 1848 by Rev. Stephen A. Roszel, lic. dated 23 Dec 1848

Richardson, Laura M. and Elisha Meconnekin, both of Baltimore County, m. 23 Dec 1845 by Rev. William Hamilton

Richardson, Levin, of Dorchester County, MD, and Eleanor Collison, of Baltimore, m. 28 Oct 1841 by Rev. Bernard H. Nadal, lic. dated 25 Oct 1841

Richardson, Mary E. and E. Clinton C hickering m. 16 Mar 1848 by Rev. Dr. George C. M. Roberts

Richardson, Miranda and Thomas C. Ruckle m. 17 Oct 1843 by Rev. Dr. George C. M. Roberts

Richardson, Robert and Sarah J. Robinson, both of Baltimore County, m. 13 Apr 1844 by Rev. William Hamilton

Riddell, John A. and Sarah A. Harp m. 11 Aug 1847 by Rev. Stephen A. Roszel, lic. dated same day

Riddle, John W. and Susan J. Simpson m. 13 Aug 1850 by Rev. Isaac P. Cook

Ridgaway, Emma Augusta, dau. of Samuel C. and Rachel Ann Ridgaway, b. 25 Dec 1832 [*sic*], bapt. 7 Jun 1846 by Rev. Dr. George C. M. Roberts [*Ed. Note:* It should be noted that another entry stated Emma Ridgeway, dau. of Samuel C. and Rachel Ridgeway, b. 23 Jul 1840 [*sic*], bapt. 19 Apr 1840 [*sic*] by Rev. Dr. George C. M. Roberts. This is an obvious error that requires additional research.]

Ridgaway, Samuel Clark, son of Samuel C. and Rachel Ann Ridgaway, b. 25 Jul 1845, bapt. 7 Jun 1846 by Rev. Dr. George C. M. Roberts

Ridgely, Daniel, see "Mary Ridgely" and "Elizabeth Sangston," q.v.

Ridgely (Ridgley), David and Mary R. Glanville m. 4 Aug 1846 by Rev. Isaac P. Cook

Ridgely, Emily Louisa, dau. of William H. and Catherine R. Ridgely, b. 25 Jun 1839, bapt. 29 Jan 1840 by Rev. Dr. George C. M. Roberts

Ridgely, Levin D. and Rosana M. Magurgans m. 10 Mar 1840 by Rev. Joseph Shane

Ridgely (Ridgeley), Mary, d. 1840 (exact date not given in Record of Members) [*Ed. Note:* Death notice in the *Baltimore Sun* stated that Mary Ridgely, widow of Daniel B. Ridgely, d. 26 Jun 1840.]

Ridick, Adeline and William G. Stratton m. 16 Sep 1847 by Rev. Littleton F. Morgan, lic. dated 15 Sep 1847

Rieman, Samuel, d. after 1840 (death noted in Probationers Book) [*Ed. Note:* Death notice in the *Baltimore Sun* stated that Samuel Rieman d. 25 Jan 1841.]

Rigby, Ann, d. 1845 (death noted in Class List) [*Ed. Note:* Death notice in the *Baltimore Sun* stated that Ann Rigby, widow of James J. Rigby, d. 25 Jun 1845.]

Rigby, Frances Elizabeth, dau. of Oliver P. and Elizabeth Rigby, b. 23 Jan 1840, bapt. 4 Mar 1840 by Rev. Thomas Myers

Rigby, James J., see "Ann Rigby," q.v.

Rigby, Oliver, see "Frances E. Rigby," q.v.

Rigby, Philip and Elizabeth Lee m. 10 May 1842 by Rev. Dr. George C. M. Roberts

Riggins, Mary M. and Hezekiah M. Everett m. 25 Nov 1845 by Rev. Dr. George C. M. Roberts

Riggs, Daniel P. and Sarah Ann Creighton m. 17 May 1849 by Rev. William Hirst, lic. dated 14 May 1849

Riggs, Edward and Margaret Wallace m. 13 Dec 1848 by Rev. Stephen A. Roszel, lic. dated same day

Riggs (Rigs), Lucy, d. circa 1840 (exact date not given in Class Record)

Rignor, John B. and Elizabeth Kidwell m. 23 Dec 1847 by Rev. Dr. George C. M. Roberts

Riley, Ann Eliza and George W. Smith m. 27 Jun 1847 by Rev. Stephen A. Roszel, lic. dated 26 Jun 1847

Riley, Elizabeth and Benjamin F. Green m. 20 Sep 1841 by Rev. Isaac P. Cook

Riley, Elizabeth and Joseph Shipley m. 19 May 1842 by Rev. Joseph Shane

Riley, Elizabeth and John, see "Matilda Riley," q.v.

Riley, John and Margaret Hogans m. 28 May 1845 by Rev. Joseph Shane

Riley, Martha Ann and Creighton W. Brant m. ---- [no date given] by Rev. John Miller, lic. dated 31 Dec 1850

Riley, Mary Ann and Edward Hackett m. 15 Jun 1848 by Rev. Isaac P. Cook

Riley, Matilda, dau. of John and Elizabeth Riley, b. 27 Jan 1845, bapt. 29 Jun 1845 by Rev. Isaac P. Cook

Riley, William Henry and Ann Jane Younger m. 23 Oct 1841 by Rev. Wesley Stevenson

Rimage, Elizabeth, d. circa 1847-1850 (exact date not given in Record of Members)

Rimby, Jacob and Helen L. Bobeth m. 10 Dec 1846 by Rev. Isaac P. Cook

Rimby, Rhoda and Thomas Hobbs, both of Baltimore, MD, m. 11 Oct 1840 by Rev. John A. Hening [*Ed. Note:* Her name was misspelled "Rimbe" in the church register.]

Rimby, William B. and Ann Tilton m. 17 Sep 1844 by Rev. Isaac P. Cook

Rimby, William B. and Kezia Ann McNeal m. 31 Aug 1847 by Rev. Isaac P. Cook

Rin, Mary, dau. of William and Eliza Rin, b. 13 May 1844, bapt. 13 May 1844 by Rev. James Sewell

Ringgold, James B. and Rebecca H. Harris, both of Baltimore County, m. 8 Dec 1845 by Rev. J. Hoffman Waugh, lic. dated 6 Dec 1845

Ringleb, Henry and Mary Ann Smith m. 11 Aug 1850 by Rev. Isaac P. Cook

Ringrose, Mary E., see "Mary E. Rengrose," q.v.

Ringrose, Robert, see "Robert Rengrose," q.v.

Rippey, William A. and Rebecca S. Valiant m. ---- [blank] by Rev. John S. Martin, lic. dated 28 Jan 1850 [*Ed. Note:* Their marriage notice in the *Baltimore Sun* stated that William A. Rippey m. Rebecca S. Valiant, dau. of John Valiant, on 28 Jan 1850.]

Risteau, Elizabeth A. and Carlton T. Brown m. 10 Apr 1843 by Rev. Henry Slicer, lic. dated same day

Roach, Amelia Virginia, dau. of John and Elizabeth Sarah Roach, b. 5 Mar 1843, bapt. 5 Dec 1843 by Rev. Dr. George C. M. Roberts

Roach, Catherine, dau. of Charles J. and Sarah Roach, b. 27 May 1843, bapt. 7 Apr 1844 by Rev. Dr. George C. M. Roberts

Roach, Charles Henry, son of ---- [blank], b. 31 May 1849, bapt. -- Jul 1849 by Rev. John S. Martin

Roach, Sarah and George N. Potee m. 19 May 1850 by Rev. Joseph Shane

Roads, William and Margaret Skinner m. 11 Oct 1849 by Rev. William Hirst, lic. dated same day

Robb, Cornelia, dau. of James and Sarah Ann Robb, b. 8 Feb 1842, bapt. -- Jun 1842 by Rev. William Prettyman

Robbson, Francis and Rebecca Jane Fowler, of Baltimore County, m. 4 Apr 1841 by Rev. John Rice, lic. dated 3 Apr 1841

Roberts, Charles and Catharine Bodensick m. 30 Nov 1843 by Rev. Isaac P. Cook

Roberts, Charles E., see "Theresa L. Roberts," q.v.

Roberts, Elizabeth, d. circa 1840 (exact date not given in Record of Members)

Roberts, John B. and Ann Rebecca Amos m. 29 Jan 1848 by Rev. James H. Brown, lic. dated same day

Roberts, Jonathan, see "Henrietta Waugh," q.v.

Roberts, Joseph and Mary Gregory m. 7 Aug 1842 by Rev. Henry Slicer, lic. dated 6 Aug 1842

Roberts, Joseph, son of Joseph and Mary Roberts, b. 12 Jul 1846 (twin of Mary Ellen Roberts), Baltimore, bapt. 25 Jul 1847 by Rev. William M. D. Ryan. See "Mary Ellen Roberts," q.v.

Roberts, Joseph Jr. and Eliza Jane Egarrer m. 13 May 1849 by Rev. Dr. George C. M. Roberts [*Ed. Note:* Her last name was given as "Legar" in their *Baltimore Sun* marriage notice.]

Roberts, Mary Ellen, dau. of Joseph and Mary Roberts, b. 12 Jul 1846 (twin of Joseph Roberts), Baltimore, bapt. 25 Jul 1847 by Rev. William M. D. Ryan. See "Joseph Roberts," q.v.

Roberts, Mary Cornelia, dau. of Matthias and Cornelia Roberts, b. 26 May 1847, bapt. 26 May 1848 by Rev. Dr. George C. M. Roberts

Roberts, Matthias, see "Mary C. Roberts," q.v.

Roberts, Samuel, d. 1845 (death noted in Class List)

Roberts, Theresa LePage, dau. of Charles E. and Virginia H. Roberts, b. ---- [blank], bapt. 26 Mar 1850 by Rev. Dr. George C. M. Roberts

Roberts, William and Sarah Ann Mayo m. 5 Dec 1843 by Rev. Samuel Brison

Robin, Emiley A., dau. of Mr. and Mrs. Reoben [*sic*], b. 12 Feb 1842, bapt. 18 Sep 1843 by Rev. Philip B. Reese

Robinson, Agnes A. and Joseph Goodfellow m. 10 Jul 1849 by Rev. John S. Martin, lic. dated 9 Jul 1849

Robinson, Alexander and Ann Maria Appold, both of Baltimore County, m. 17 Nov 1840 by Rev. Bernard H. Nadal

Robinson, Ann, d. 1847 (death noted in Class List) [*Ed. Note:* Death notice in the *Baltimore Sun* stated that Ann Robinson, widow of Samuel Robinson, d. 6 Apr 1847.]

Robinson, Catherine and James G. W. Baunner m. 7 Oct 1850 by Rev. Dr. George C. M. Roberts

Robinson, Elizabeth C. and Lewis F. Munder m. 4 Feb 1850 by Rev. Dr. George C. M. Roberts

Robinson, Emily and William Lowther, both of Baltimore County, m. 6 May 1840 by Rev. Thomas Myers, lic. dated same day

Robinson, George, see "Jane Robinson," q.v.

Robinson, George and Brittania Chival m. 12 Dec 1843 by Rev. Isaac P. Cook

Robinson, Hannah P. and Dr. Edmund Landis m. 30 Oct 1845 by Rev. Samuel Keppler (date of lic. not recorded)

Robinson, Jane, d. circa 1840 (exact date not given in Class Record) [*Ed. Note:* Death notice in the *Baltimore Sun* stated that Jane Robinson, mother of George Robinson, d. 11 Jan 1839.]

Robinson, Joseph J., son of Joseph J. and Emily M. Robinson, b. 14 Feb 1850, bapt. 1860 (exact date not given) by Rev. William R. Mills

Robinson, Joshua and Margaret (Martha?) Pamphilion m. 17 Jan 1842 by Rev. Joseph Shane [*Ed. Note:* Her name was listed as Martha Pampelin in the church register, but their marriage notice in the *Baltimore Sun* gave her name as Margaret Pamphillion.]

Robinson, Martha E. and Samuel Martin m. 5 Aug 1841 by Rev. Dr. George C. M. Roberts

Robinson, Mary A. and John W. Seidenstricker m. 19 Oct 1847 by Rev. Stephen A. Roszel, lic. dated same day

Robinson, Rebecca Ann and Joseph Mackentosh m. 29 Jun 1846 by Rev. Littleton F. Morgan, lic. dated same day

Robinson, Richard J. and Hariot [*sic*] Denney m. 26 Jul 1844 by Rev. James Sewell, lic. dated 25 Jul 1844

Robinson, Roda [*sic*] S. and John Crookshanks m. 28 Oct 1846 by Rev. Benjamin F. Brooke

Robinson, Samuel, see "Ann Robinson," q.v.

Robinson, Sarah J. and Robert Richardson, both of Baltimore County, m. 13 Apr 1844 by Rev. William Hamilton

Robinson, William H. and Sarah W. Ballow(?) m. 22 Oct 1843 by Rev. Isaac P. Cook

Robison, John and Susan Turfle, both of Baltimore County, m. 17 Jan 1843 by Rev. Nelson Head

Roden, Caleb and Eliza Longley m. 7 Sep 1841 by Rev. Dr. George C. M. Roberts

Rodney, Ann S. and William H. Nicholson m. 11 Oct 1848 by Rev. William Hirst

Rogers, Albert Perry, son of John H. and Ann E. Rogers, b. 1 Nov 1849, bapt. 25 Mar 1850 by Rev. Dr. George C. M. Roberts

Rogers, Ann and William Howe m. 13 Aug 1842 by Rev. Joseph Shane

Rogers, Annie, dau. of George M. and Mary F. Rogers, b. 20 Sep 1849, bapt. 30 Jun 1851 by Rev. Dr. George C. M. Roberts

Rogers, Daniel Roszel, son of Isaac and Catharine Rogers, b. 16 Oct 1846, Baltimore, bapt. 25 Jul 1847 by Rev. Stephen A. Roszel

Rogers, Edward Spedden, son of John H. and Ann E. Rogers, b. 13 Feb 1847, bapt. 25 Mar 1850 by Rev. Dr. George C. M. Roberts

Rogers, Elizabeth, d. 1849 (death noted in Class List) [*Ed. Note:* Death notice in the *Baltimore Sun* stated that Elizabeth Rogers, wife of George Rogers, d. 27 Mar 1849.]

Rogers, Elizabeth, d. 12 May 1840 (death noted in Record of Members) [*Ed. Note:* Death notice in the *Baltimore Sun* stated that Elizabeth Rogers, wife of Jacob Rogers, d. 12 May 1840.]

Rogers, George, see "Annie Rogers" and "Elizabeth Rogers" and "Mary B. Rogers," q.v.

Rogers, Isaac, see "Daniel R. Rogers," q.v.

Rogers, Jacob, d. circa 1840-1842 (exact date not given in Record of Members) [*Ed. Note:* Death notice in the *Baltimore Sun* stated that Jacob Rogers d. 10 Apr 1842.] See "Elizabeth Rogers," q.v.

Rogers, John, d. circa 1845-1847 (exact date not given in Record of Members) [*Ed. Note:* Death notice in the *Baltimore Sun* stated that John Rogers d. 12 Jun 1846.]

Rogers, John H., see "Albert P. Rogers" and "Edward S. Rogers," q.v.

Rogers, Mary Ann and William T. Johnson m. 24 Jul 1849 by Rev. Dr. George C. M. Roberts

Rogers, Mary Ann Green, dau. of William and Catherine Ann Rogers, b. 23 Sep 1843, bapt. 8 Oct 1843 by Rev. Dr. George C. M. Roberts

Rogers, Mary Brewer, dau. of George M. and Mary F. Rogers, b. 29 Jan 1847, bapt. 30 Jun 1851 by Rev. Dr. George C. M. Roberts

Rogers, William, see "Mary Ann Green Rogers," q.v.

Rollins, Laura Louiza R., dau. of James and Mary Ann Rollins, b. 12 Nov 1838, bapt. 5 Jul 1840 by Rev. Charles B. Tippett

Rollins, Mary Jane, dau. of James and Mary Ann Rollins, b. 24 Aug 1836, bapt. 5 Jul 1840 by Rev. Charles B. Tippett

Roney, Josephine, dau. of Charles and Mary Ann Roney, b. 8 Feb 1840, Fells Point, Baltimore City, bapt. 21 Sep 1840 by Rev. Samuel Keppler

Ronsaville, David C. and Sarah Whitson, both of Baltimore City, m. 15 Apr 1841 by Rev. Robert Emory

Rooke, Elizabeth, d. 1845 (death noted in Class List) [*Ed. Note:* Death notice in the *Baltimore Sun* stated that Elizabeth Rook, mother-in-law of James C. Davis, d. 18 Oct 1845.]

Rookes, Mary Ann Priscilla, dau. of Samuel and Mary Ann Rookes, b. 10 Jul 1841, bapt. 13 Nov 1842 by Rev. Benjamin H. Crever

Rorback, Josephine and Thomas R. Dunnington m. 29 Jan 1843 by Rev. Job Guest, lic. dated 28 Jan 1843

Rose, Elizabeth D. and James J. Stranley m. 12 Aug 1845 by Rev. Samuel Keppler (date of lic. not recorded)

Rose, Francis A. and Hannah E. Woolcott m. 15 May 1845 by Rev. Dr. George C. M. Roberts

Rose, Henry and Catharine A. Reynolds m. 13 Jul 1842 by Rev. Wesley Stevenson

Rose, Peter and Sophia McAlbers m. 3 Jun 1847 by Rev. Dr. George C. M. Roberts

Rose, William and Rachel Ann Peregoy m. 14 Jun 1849 by Rev. Aquila A. Reese, lic. dated 13 Jun 1849

Rosher, Nelson and Rachel McCassell, both of Baltimore County, m. ---- [date not given] by Rev. George Hildt, lic. dated 25 Aug 1845

Ross, Catherine and Henry Faithful m. 14 Sep 1842 by Rev. Joseph Shane

Ross, Elizabeth C. and Joseph C. Merritt m. 9 Jan 1849 by Rev. Stephen A. Roszel, lic. dated 8 Jan 1849

Ross, Leroy C. and Charlotte Gildea m. 3 Mar 1842 by Rev. Isaac P. Cook

Ross, Margaret and John Bennett m. 21 Aug 1845 by Rev. Samuel Keppler (date of lic. not recorded)

Ross, Robert J. and Rebecca Linthicum m. 19 Jan 1847 by Rev. Samuel Keppler (date of lic. not recorded)

Ross, Rosanna and William Sindell m. 18 May 1845 by Rev. Dr. George C. M. Roberts

Rothrock, Mary Catherine, dau. of Rieman Stewart and Mary Rothrock, b. 17 Jul 1840, bapt. 22 Nov 1840 by Rev. Joseph Shane

Rountree, Charles Edward, son of John and Sophia H. Rountree, b. 1 Jan 1850, bapt. 7 Oct 1851 by Rev. Dr. George C. M. Roberts

Rowe, Julia Ann and Rev. James Gamble m. 21 Feb 1843 at the house of Mr. Mettee in Baltimore by Rev. Beverly Waugh, lic. dated 20 Feb 1843

Rowe, Sophia and Alexander Nicholson m. 12 Apr 1843 by Rev. Henry Slicer, lic. dated same day

Rowe, William N. and Elizabeth H. Havenner m. 28 Apr 1842 in Washington City by Rev. Henry Slicer, lic. dated same day

Royston, Caleb, see "Mary Eliza Royston," q.v.

Royston, Joshua, see "Mary Virginia Royston," q.v.

Royston, Lydia A. and Enoch Miller, both of Baltimore County, m. 7 Dec 1843 by Rev. S. S. Roszel, lic. dated same day

Royston, Mary Eliza, d. circa 1844-1846 (exact date not given in Record of Members) [Ed. Note: Death notice in the Baltimore Sun stated that Mary Royston, wife of Caleb Royston, d. 5 Jun 1845.]

Royston, Mary Virginia, dau. of Joshua and Ellen Royston, b. 8 Dec 1845, bapt. 25 Dec 1845 by Rev. Dr. George C. M. Roberts

Royston, Mr., see "Wesley ---- (colored)," q.v.

Ruark, W. and Mary Lewis m. 10 Jul 1848 by Rev. William Hirst

Ruckle, Eleanor, d. circa 1844-1847 (exact date not given in Record of Members)

Ruckle, Galileo Sebastian, son of Thomas C. and Miranda J. Ruckle, b. 8 Nov 1846, bapt. 20 May 1847 by Rev. Dr. George C. M. Roberts

Ruckle, Oliver Paul, son of Joseph N. and Louisa Ruckle, b. 24 Feb 1840, bapt. 2 Mar 1840 by Rev. Dr. George C. M. Roberts

Ruckle, Paul, d. circa 1847-1850 (exact date not given in Record of Members)

Ruckle, Thomas C. and Miranda Richardson m. 17 Oct 1843 by Rev. Dr. George C. M. Roberts

Ruckle, Thomas Coke Cassell, son of Thomas C. and Miranda Ruckle, b. 9 Mar 1849, bapt. 11 Nov 1850 by Rev. Dr. George C. M. Roberts

Ruddach, James Maxwell, son of David and Lucy H. Ruddach, b. 11 Jun 1839, bapt. 16 Jul 1840 by Rev. Dr. George C. M. Roberts

Ruff, Elizabeth, d. circa 1847-1850 (exact date not given in Record of Members)

Ruff, Henrietta M. and John Armstrong m. 22 Dec 1842 by Rev. Job Guest, lic. dated 6 Dec 1842

Ruff, Richard H. and Ann M. Seigler m. 16 Feb 1845 by Rev. Isaac P. Cook

Ruley, Samuel Harrison, son of Benjamin and Matilda Ruley, b. 7 Feb 1842, bapt. 27 Aug 1842 by Rev. Elisha D. Owen

Ruley, Samuel W. and Emma Elizabeth Shields m. 30 Jun 1850 by Rev. John S. Martin, lic. dated 29 Jun 1850

Rumney, Emily Jane, dau. of Robert and Henrietta Rumney, aged 8 months [b. 1840], bapt. 20 Apr 1841 by Rev. Robert Emory

Rurick, George Washington, son of John and Mary Rurick, b. 1 Mar 1839, Fells Point, Baltimore City, bapt. 7 Jan 1841 by Rev. Isaac P. Cook

Rusides, John, son of James and Rusides, b. 7 Dec 1838, bapt. 18 Aug 1840 by Rev. Joseph Shane

Rusk, Caroline and George Whiteman, both of Baltimore County, m. 6 Jan 1845 by Rev. William Hamilton

Rusk, Emma E. and John F. Platt m. 7 Apr 1850 by Rev. Henry Slicer, lic. dated 5 Apr 1850

Rusk, Hester Ann and William H. H. Turner m. 15 Nov 1843 by Rev. Henry Slicer, lic. dated 13 Nov 1843

Russel, James Blair, son of James and Sarah Russel, aged 8 months [b. 1840], bapt. 11 Mar 1841 by Rev. John A. Hening

Russell, Lavenia and James H. Wood m. 3 Jun 1846 by Rev. Dr. George C. M. Roberts

Russell, Mary A., d. circa 1840 (exact date not given in Class Record)

Rutter, John and Ann Maria Wright m. 30 Sep 1847 by Rev. Stephen A. Roszel, lic. dated 27 Sep 1847

Rutter, John H. and Harriett A. Elkington m. 14 Feb 1841 by Rev. John Bear

Rutter, John Henry, son of John and Barbary Rutter, aged 5 days, bapt. 13 Nov 1841 by Rev. Gerard Morgan

Rutter, Mary and John L. Benson m. 13 May 1848 by Rev. William Hirst

Sabell, Andrew Jackson and Sarah Seward m. 9 Jul 1849 by Rev. John S. Martin, lic. dated 7 Jul 1849

Saddler, Eliza and William Johnson m. ---- [blank] by Rev. John S. Martin, lic. dated 27 May 1850

Sadler, Joseph and Elizabeth J. Jones m. 26 Jul 1849 by Rev. Joseph Shane

Sadtler, Elenora and William F. Ungerer m. ---- [blank] by Rev. John S. Martin, lic. dated 20 Apr 1849 [Ed. Note: Their marriage notice in the Baltimore Sun stated that William T. Ungerer m. Eleanora Sadler on 20 Apr 1849.]

Salger, Caroline and William B. Stone m. 19 Jul 1849 by Rev. Dr. George C. M. Roberts

Salisbury, Ann Elizabeth and Samuel Bushman m. 2 Aug 1847 by Rev. Dr. George C. M. Roberts

Salisbury, James and Laura L. Dryden m. 31 Oct 1848 by Rev. James H. Brown, lic. dated 30 Oct 1848

Salter, Eliza, dau. of John and Ellen Salter, b. 3 Mar 1841, bapt. 31 Oct 1841 by Rev. Dr. George C. M. Roberts

Salvador, Eliza and Francis Crawford m. 4 Oct 1846 by Rev. Dr. George C. M. Roberts

Sammon, James and Maria Foster m. 10 Feb 1840 by Rev. Joseph Shane

Sanbourn, Isaiah G. and Maria S. Dawson m. 20 May 1840 at her father's house in Baltimore by Rev. Beverly Waugh, lic. dated same day

Sanders, Charlotte (colored) and Benjamin Duges (colored) m. 11 Aug 1847 by Rev. Dr. George C. M. Roberts

Sanders, Diana and Jacob Cridler m. 14 Jan 1846 by Rev. Dr. George C. M. Roberts

Sanders, John S. and Mary Fowler, both of Baltimore County, m. ---- [date not given] by Rev. George Hildt, lic. dated 18 Dec 1845

Sanders, Mary C. and Joseph Carson m. 2 Sep 1843 by Rev. Henry Slicer, lic. dated 27 Aug 1843

Sands, Washington, d. after 1847 (death noted in Class List) [*Ed. Note:* Death notice in the *Baltimore Sun* stated that Washington Sands d. 5 Jan 1849.]

Sangston, Elizabeth, d. circa 1841 (exact date not given in Record of Members) [*Ed. Note:* Death notice in the *Baltimore Sun* stated that Elizabeth D. Sangston, wife of James A. Sangston and dau. of Daniel Ridgely, d. 4 Sep 1841.]

Sank, Eliza P. and John J. Groves m. 25 Oct 1847 by Rev. Dr. George C. M. Roberts [*Ed. Note:* Their marriage notice in the *Baltimore Sun* gave their names as Eliza Sank and John T. Groves.]

Sanks, David and Elizabeth Phelan m. 5 Feb 1850 by Rev. Joseph Shane

Sanks, Eleanor, d. circa 1841 (death noted in Class List)

Sanks, James and Harriet Ann Timanus m. 27 Feb 1850 by Rev. Aquila A. Reese, lic. dated 26 Feb 1850

Sanks, John Wesley, son of John Philip and Hannah Sanks, b. 20 Sep 1831, bapt. 29 Sep 1841 by Rev. Dr. George C. M. Roberts

Sanks, Priscilla, d. circa 1840 (exact date not given in Class Record)

Sanner, George J. and Jane E. Richardson m. 24 Dec 1848 by Rev. Stephen A. Roszel, lic. dated 23 Dec 1848

Sanner, William Roberts, son of Sylvester and Ann E. Sanner, b. 16 Nov 1841, bapt. 4 Nov 1841 by Rev. Dr. George C. M. Roberts

Sapp, James and Ann Carter m. 13 Sep 1846 by Rev. Dr. George C. M. Roberts

Sapp, William and Mary Cann m. 29 Aug 1845 by Rev. James Sewell, lic. dated same day

Sappington, Mary Bartol, dau. of Thomas and Mary A. E. Sappington, aged 4 years [b. 1837], bapt. 30 Apr 1841 by Rev. Robert Emory

Sappington, Otis Bartol, son of Thomas and Mary A. E. Sappington, aged 7 years [b. 1834], bapt. 30 Apr 1841 by Rev. Robert Emory

Saucer, John H., son of ---- [blank], b. 24 Aug 1848, bapt. -- Jul 1849 by Rev. John S. Martin

Sauerwein, William A. and Mary Ann Johnston, both of Baltimore County, m. 4 Jan 1843 by Rev. Nelson Head

Saulsbury, Eugene Leon, son of Andrew and Mary A. Saulsbury, b. 29 Mar 1845, bapt. 3 Apr 1845 by Rev. Dr. George C. M. Roberts

Saulsbury, Mary Ann and Joseph M. Peregoy m. 15 Feb 1848 by Rev. Dr. George C. M. Roberts

Sauner, Anna M. and Samuel F. Peregoy m. 26 Sep 1850 by Rev. Dr. George C. M. Roberts

Sauner, John Abel, son of Capt. Joseph A. and Martha Sauner, b. 25 Sep 1840, bapt. 27 Sep 1844 by Rev. Dr. George C. M. Roberts

Sawyer, William J. and Mary Ann Malone m. 15 Aug 1844 by Rev. James Sewell, lic. dated 14 Aug 1844

Sayward, Marinda and William K. Gardner m. 18 Feb 1844 by Rev. Henry Slicer, lic. dated 17 Feb 1844

Schaffer, Margaret C. and Daniel L. Grove m. 19 Jan 1843 by Rev. Dr. George C. M. Roberts

Scharff, Ellen and Charles J. Lawrence m. 23 Nov 1848 by Rev. William Hirst

Scheerer, John A. and Ann Maria Hale m. 2 Sep 1845 by Rev. Dr. George C. M. Roberts

Schley, Caroline and James W. Aburn m. 29 Jul 1849 by Rev. John S. Martin, lic. dated 27 Jul 1849

Schlosser, Peter G. and Catharine McCollum, both of Carroll County, MD, m. 9 Oct 1844 by Rev. William Hamilton

Schmedes, Mary and Charles Rampineyer m. 15 Mar 1847 by Rev. Isaac P. Cook

Scholl, William Lewis, son of Lewis and Ann E. Scholl, b. 17 Jan 1842, bapt. 26 Jun 1842 by Rev. Joseph Merriken

Schoolfield, Thomas S., d. after 1841 (death noted in Class List) [*Ed. Note:* Death notice in the *Baltimore Sun* stated that Thomas S. Schoolfield d. 1 Aug 1842.]

Schrote, Eliza Ann and John R. Black, both of Baltimore County, m. 26 Nov 1840 by Rev. Thomas Myers, lic. dated 25 Nov 1840

Schrote, Eveline, d. circa 1840 (exact date not given in Class Record)

Schults, Catherine and Joseph Barbine m. 22 Dec 1850 by Rev. Dr. George C. M. Roberts

Schultz, Ann S. and Nathan Tutchton m. 9 Mar 1843 by Rev. Henry Slicer, lic. dated 8 Mar 1843

Schumacher, Conrad and Louisa Polk Disney m. 25 Jul 1850 by Rev. Dr. George C. M. Roberts

Schumacher, Edward, son of Fred and Mary Schumacher, b. 18 Jun 1844, bapt. 28 May 1846 by Rev. Dr. George C. M. Roberts

Schumacher, Mary Roberts, dau. of Fred and Mary Schumacher, b. 13 Jan 1841, bapt. 28 May 1846 by Rev. Dr. George C. M. Roberts

Schumacher, Rudolphe, child of Fred and Mary Schumacher, b. 28 May 1845, bapt. 28 May 1846 by Rev. Dr. George C. M. Roberts

Schurar, Emily R. and Thomas S. McNier, both of Annapolis, m. 1 Mar 1842 at Annapolis by Rev. Job Guest, lic. dated same day [*Ed. Note:* Marriage records of Anne Arundel County indicate Thomas S. McNeir and Emily R. Schwarar obtained a license on 12 Feb 1842.]

Schwatkas, Pamelia and Henry Sinclair m. 3 May 1849 by Rev. Aquila A. Reese, lic. dated 2 May 1849

Schwitzer, John S. and Amelia M. Elliott m. 21 Jun 1849 by Rev. Aquila A. Reese, lic. dated 20 Jun 1849

Scott, Ann, see "Ann Maria Scott" and "Elizabeth Scott," q.v.

Scott, Ann Maria, dau. of Joseph and Ann Scott, b. 13 Mar 1842, bapt. 14 Jun 1842 by Rev. Elisha D. Owen

Scott, Elizabeth, dau. of Joseph and Ann Scott, b. 25 Apr 1839(?), bapt. 14 Jun 1842 by Rev. Elisha D. Owen

Scott, Ellen and William Burroughs m. 23 Sep 1844 by Rev. James Sewell, lic. dated same day

Scott, George and Ann Jenkins m. 4 Feb 1840 by Rev. Samuel Keppler (date of lic. not recorded)

Scott, George (colored) and Elisabeth Brady (colored) m. 5 Aug 1841 by Rev. Gerard Morgan, lic. dated 4 Aug 1841

Scott, Henrietta E. and William H. Allen m. 31 Jan 1844 by Rev. Joseph Shane

Scott, Jane A. and Joseph B. Lewis m. 21 Jan 1846 by Rev. Wesley Stevenson [*Ed. Note:* Their marriage notice in the *Baltimore Sun* gave his last name as "Lewis" even though it looked more like "Seems" in the marriage register.]

Scott, John R. and A. Juliet Craig m. 25 Dec 1842 by Rev. Henry Slicer, lic. dated 22 Dec 1842

Scott, Joseph, see "Ann Maria Scott" and "Elizabeth Scott," q.v.

Scott, Louisa E. and John W. Reynolds m. 30 May 1845 by Rev. Wesley Stevenson

Scott, Margaret and John Hursh m. 12 Apr 1848 by Rev. William Hirst

Scott, Mary, dau. of Joseph and Ann Scott, b. 19 Oct 1837, bapt. 14 Jun 1842 by Rev. Elisha D. Owen

Scotti, John Wesley, son of John and Frances Scotti, b. 7 Nov 1840, bapt. 21 Dec 1840 by Rev. Dr. George C. M. Roberts

Scribner, Sarah, d. 1849 (death noted in Class List) [*Ed. Note:* Death notice in the *Baltimore Sun* stated that Sarah Scribner, widow of Nathan Scribner, d. 18 Jul 1849.]

Sears, Amanda, dau. of ---- [blank], b. 12 Jan 1841, bapt. 17 Mar 1841, by Rev. Robert Emory

Sears, Ann Matilda and Pilkington C. Codd m. 21 Nov 1841 by Rev. Dr. George C. M. Roberts

Sears, John L. and Arianna A. Auld m. 6 Dec 1843 by Rev. Dr. George C. M. Roberts

Secord, George C. M. Roberts, son of Dr. Van Courtland and Marion Ann Secord, b. 15 Mar 1850, bapt. 1 Jun 1850 by Rev. Dr. George C. M. Roberts

Secord, Van Courtland and Marion A. Thompson m. 6 Jun 1849 by Rev. Dr. George C. M. Roberts

Seebright, Rosanna and Noah Reed m. 10 Apr 1849 by Rev. Aquila A. Reese, lic. dated 9 Apr 1849

Seeman, John and Rosina Bocree m. 7 Jun 1849 by Rev. Dr. George C. M. Roberts

Seems, Joseph B., see "Joseph B. Lewis," q.v.

Seers, Sarah Elizabeth, dau. of Thomas and Violetta Seers, b. 15 Oct 1840, bapt. 21 Dec 1840 by Rev. Dr. George C. M. Roberts

Seidenstricker, John W. and Mary A. Robinson m. 19 Oct 1847 by Rev. Stephen A. Roszel, lic. dated same day

Seigler, Ann M. and Richard H. Ruff m. 16 Feb 1845 by Rev. Isaac P. Cook

Selby, Harriet, d. circa 1847-1850 (exact date not given in Record of Members)

Selby, Mary Clare Watkins, dau. of John S. and Margaret Ann Selby, b. 18 Sep 1846, bapt. 26 Sep 1847 by Rev. Dr. George C. M. Roberts

Semon, Catherine and Adam W. Deems m. 23 Jun 1846 by Rev. Joseph Shane

Severson, Elizabeth M. and Charles A. Emich m. 27 Jul 1847 by Rev. Dr. George C. M. Roberts

Seward, Mary A. and Thomas Norfolk m. 8 Mar 1843 by Rev. Henry Slicer, lic. dated same day

Seward, Sarah and Andrew Jackson Sabell m. 9 Jul 1849 by Rev. John S. Martin, lic. dated 7 Jul 1849

Sewell, Amelia Rebecca and William Ellis Hopkins m. 4 Feb 1847 at Light Street Church in Baltimore by Rev. Beverly Waugh, lic. dated 2 Feb 1847

Sewell, Elizabeth Virginia, dau. of Thomas and Mary Jane Sewell, b. 31 Mar 1843, bapt. 17 Jun 1844 by Rev. James Sewell

Sewell, Rachel E. and Solomon Williams m. 27 Dec 1848 by Rev. Stephen A. Roszel, lic. dated 23 Dec 1848

Sewell, Thomas, see "Elizabeth V. Sewell," q.v.

Seymour, Caroline Martha and Alfred Ray m. 2 Mar 1848 by Rev. Stephen A. Roszel, lic. dated 24 Feb 1848

Seymour, Elizabeth, d. 1844 (death noted in Class List) [*Ed. Note:* Death notice in the *Baltimore Sun* stated that Elizabeth Seymour d. 18 Aug 1844.]

Seymour, Sophia, d. 1840 (death noted in Class List) [*Ed. Note:* Death notice in the *Baltimore Sun* stated that Sophia Seymour d. 9 Feb 1840.]

Shaeffer, Mary Catherine and Peter J. Nevicker m. 27 Jul 1848 by Rev. Joseph Shane

Shaffer, Allen G. and Mary Aler m. 29 May 1845 by Rev. Isaac P. Cook

Shaffer, Ann Emma and William A. Welch m. 10 Jun 1845 by Rev. Samuel Keppler (date of lic. not recorded)

Shaffer, Elizabeth E. and John Jeffries m. 17 Aug 1843 by Rev. Joseph Shane

Shaffer. F. L., see "Hellen L. Shaffer," q.v.

Shaffer, Frederick, d. 1844 (death noted in Class List) [*Ed. Note:* Death notice in the *Baltimore Sun* stated that Frederick Shaffer d. 17 Mar 1844.]

Shaffer, George E. and Sarah A. White m. 9 Dec 1845 by Rev. James Sewell, lic. dated 8 Dec 1845

Shaffer, Hellen Littig, dau. of F. L. and C. A. L. Shaffer, b. 2 Aug 1846, bapt. 27 Sep 1846 by Rev. Dr. Edwin Dorsey

Shaffer, Mary and Charles Yager m. 31 Dec 1844 by Rev. Wesley Stevenson

Shaffer, Rachel Littig and Theodore Corner m. 26 Oct 1848 by Rev. Stephen A. Roszel, lic. dated 25 Oct 1848

Shakespeare, Benjamin F. and Catharine E. Hatchison m. 22 Jul 1847 by Rev. Stephen A. Roszel, lic. dated 20 Jul 1847

Shamburg, Margaret L. and Stephen George m. 4 Mar 1845 by Rev. Dr. George C. M. Roberts

Shane, Elizabeth, d. circa 1849-1850 (exact date not given in Record of Members) [*Ed. Note:* Death notice in the *Baltimore Sun* stated that Elizabeth Shane, wife of Joseph Shane, d. 1 Oct 1849.]

Shane, Joseph and Susanna Macher m. 25 Oct 1842 by Rev. Dr. George C. M. Roberts

Shanks, Mary Ann and Robert J. Laurenson, both of Baltimore County, m. 28 May 1844 by Rev. William Hamilton

Shannon, John and Sarah Maxwell m. ---- [blank] by Rev. John S. Martin, lic. dated 14 Nov 1850

Shanter, Henry and Maria Ann Jones m. 2 Dec 1840 by Rev. Samuel Keppler, lic. dated same day

Sharp, Mary and Nicholas Labdyer m. 20 Sep 1847 by Rev. Dr. George C. M. Roberts

Shaw, Ann and William Hennaman m. 5 May 1842 by Rev. Henry Slicer, lic. dated 4 May 1842

Shaw, Caleb C. and Sally E. Irwing(?), both of Baltimore County, m. 5 Nov 1846 by Rev. George Hildt, lic. dated 16 Oct 1846

Shaw, Cecelia and John Harp m. 13 Sep 1842 by Rev. Henry Slicer, lic. dated 12 Sep 1842

Shaw, Daniel Edgar, son of William F. and Sarah Jane Shaw, b. 14 Dec 1845, Baltimore, bapt. 25 Jul 1847 by Rev. Stephen A. Roszel

Shaw, Edward Owens, son of Ruel and Eliza Ann Shaw, b. 9 May 1839, bapt. 4 Apr 1846 by Rev. Dr. George C. M. Roberts

Shaw, Eliza Ellen, dau. of William S. and Jane Shaw, b. 29 Dec 1843, bapt. 13 Jan 1844 by Rev. Dr. George C. M. Roberts

Shaw, George Henry, son of Ruel and Eliza Ann Shaw, b. 16 Mar 1846, bapt. 4 Apr 1846 by Rev. Dr. George C. M. Roberts

Shaw, Isabella C. and Alexander Jones m. ---- [blank] by Rev. John S. Martin, lic. dated 5 Mar 1850 [Ed. Note: Their marriage notice in the Baltimore Sun stated Alexander Shaw m. Isabella C. Shaw, dau. of William Shaw, on 7 Mar 1850.]

Shaw, Joseph M. and Mary Ann Brown m. 10 Feb 1841 by Rev. Samuel Keppler, lic. dated 9 Feb 1841

Shaw, Martha Jane, dau. of William and Jane Shaw, b. 13 Jun 1846, bapt. 22 Jun 1846 by Rev. Dr. George C. M. Roberts

Shaw, Mary Ellen and Thomas Jenkins by Rev. John S. Martin, lic. dated 8 Jul 1850

Shaw, Peter and Susan Townshend m. 12 May 1847 by Rev. Stephen A. Roszel, lic. dated same day

Shaw, Ruel, see "George Henry Shaw" and "Edward Owens Shaw," q.v.

Shaw, Samuel and Mary J. Kelley m. 25 Mar 1849 by Rev. Isaac P. Cook

Shaw, Sarah Rebecca, dau. of Ruel and Eliza Ann Shaw, b. 20 Jun 1842, bapt. 4 Apr 1846 by Rev. Dr. George C. M. Roberts

Shaw, William, see "Isbella C. Shaw," q.v.

Shaw, William T. and Jane Bowdle m. 11 Dec 1842 by Rev. Dr. George C. M. Roberts

Shawn, Martha Ann and Alfred Smith Gees m. 4 Oct 1846 by Rev. Littleton F. Morgan, lic. dated 1 Oct 1846 [Ed. Note: Their marriage notice in the Baltimore Sun gave their names as Alfred S. Geer and Martha A. Shoon.]

Sheahan, John P. and Sarah Ann Owens m. 2 Sep 1847 by Rev. Stephen A. Roszel, lic. dated same day

Shear, Charlotte Ann, d. circa 1840 (exact date not given in Class Record)

Sheckells, Samuel K. and Mary A. Gibson m. 1 Jun 1847 by Rev. Dr. George C. M. Roberts

Sheckle, Vincent Rixan, son of Benjamin and Mary Sheckle, b. 20 Mar 1841, bapt. 7 Jun 1846 by Rev. Dr. George C. M. Roberts

Sheckles, Nelson R. and Rebecca Morgan, both of Baltimore County, m. 28 Dec 1840 by Rev. Bernard H. Nadal

Shedrick, Richard Henry and Permelia Jane Taylor m. 14 Nov 1847 by Rev. Stephen A. Roszel, lic. dated 8 Nov 1847

Shelder (Sheldon), James and Sarah J. Burrick m. 22 Aug 1850 by Rev. Dr. George C. M. Roberts [Ed. Note: Their marriage notice in the Baltimore Sun gave their names as James Sheldon and Sarah J. Barrick.]

Sheldon, William and Mary Ann Chisall m. 24 Jul 1843 by Rev. Dr. George C. M. Roberts

Shelly, John Thomas, son of William and Mary A. Shelly, b. 29 Sep 1842, bapt. 31 Oct 1842 by Rev. Elisha D. Owen

Shepherd, Frederick and Margaret Gross m. 24 Jun 1849 by Rev. Joseph Shane

Sheppard, Elmira and John Knight m. 9 Jun 1845 by Rev. Wesley Stevenson

Sherington, Isabella E. S. and Thomas Grooms m. 20 Sep 1846 by Rev. Samuel Keppler (date of lic. not recorded)

Sherlock, Nathan and Sarah Blades m. 28 Sep 1843 by Rev. Dr. George C. M. Roberts

Sherry, Elizabeth and Samuel Collins, both of Baltimore County, m. 5 Dec 1844 by Rev. William Hamilton

Sherwood, Emily, d. 1849 (death noted in Class List) [Ed. Note: Death notice in the Baltimore Sun stated that Emily Sherwood, wife of Francis A. Sherwood, d. 20 Jul 1849.]

Sherwood, Francis, see "Emily Sherwood," q.v.

Sherwood, Philip and Susanna Gosnell m. 24 Sep 1840 by Rev. Samuel Keppler, lic. dated same day

Sherwood, Richard P. and Mary W. Landon m. 16 Feb 1841 by Rev. Isaac P. Cook

Sherwood, Robert Howell, son of Robert and Susan L. Sherwood, b. 4 Jul 1839, bapt. 4 Apr 1846 by Rev. Dr. George C. M. Roberts

Shields, Absalom B. and Margaret Slater m. 14 Aug 1849 by Rev. Dr. George C. M. Roberts

Shields, Elizabeth and George Martinborn m. 26 Jul 1844 by Rev. James Sewell, lic. dated 15 Jul 1844

Shields, Emma Elizabeth and Samuel W. Ruley m. 30 Jun 1850 by Rev. John S. Martin, lic. dated 29 Jun 1850

Shillingbag, Caroline Elizabeth, dau. of Samuel and Mary Ann Shillingbag, aged 6(?) years [b. c1834], bapt. 23 Sep 1840 by Rev. Charles B. Tippett

Shillingbag, Margaretta, dau. of Samuel and Mary Ann Shillingbag, b. 22 Sep 1836, bapt. 23 Sep 1840 by Rev. Charles B. Tippett

Shillingbag, Mary, dau. of Samuel and Mary Ann Shillingbag, b. 13 Sep 1839, bapt. 23 Sep 1840 by Rev. Charles B. Tippett

Shillingberger, Henry and Charlotte Wolf m. 1 Nov 1847 by Rev. Joseph Shane

Shiningham, George Washington and Catharine Walmsley m. 25 Jul 1848 by Rev. Stephen A. Roszel, lic. dated 24 Jul 1848

Shipley, Henry and Catherine Pedicord m. 1 Oct 1844 by Rev. Joseph Shane

Shipley, Joseph and Elizabeth A. Riley m. 19 May 1842 by Rev. Joseph Shane

Shipley, Lucinda and John B. Hackett m. 31 Jan 1850 by Rev. Isaac P. Cook

Shipley, Mary Elizabeth, dau. of Washington and Elizabeth Shipley, b. 20 Oct 1839, bapt. 29 May 1840 by Rev. Joseph Shane

Shipley, Nancy and Mahlon Justice m. 13 May 1847 by Rev. James H. Brown, lic. dated 8 May 1847

Shipley, Rachel E. and Plummer Donaldson m. 16 Jul 1848 by Rev. William Hirst

Shipley, Rezin and Margarett Wells m. 28 Apr 1844 by Rev. Joseph Shane

Shipley, Robert H. and Sophia Hains m. 28 May 1846 by Rev. Littleton F. Morgan, lic. dated same day

Shoemacker, Johanna and Julius Devitch m. 20 Dec 1841 by Rev. Dr. George C. M. Roberts

Shoemaker, Alverda and John S. Ford m. ---- [no date given] by Rev. John Miller, lic. dated 22 Oct 1850 [Ed. Note: Their marriage notice in the Baltimore Sun stated that John S. Ford and Alverda Shoemaker, dau. of George Shoemaker, m. 22 Oct 1850.]

Shoemaker, Edwin B. Slicer, son of William S. and Rebecca A. Shoemaker, aged 10 months [b. 1841], bapt. 28 Jun 1842 by Rev. Henry Slicer

Shoemaker, George W. and Jeanette McCracken m. 15 Jun 1848 by Rev. Dr. George C. M. Roberts

Shoemaker, Lewis W., son of Joseph and Elizabeth Shoemaker, b. 27 Dec 1824, bapt. 23 Oct 1842 by Rev. Henry Slicer

Shoemaker, Lydia Ann and William Litchfield m. 13 Oct 1842 by Rev. Samuel Brison

Shoemaker, William (adult), b. ---- [blank], Baltimore City, bapt. 1840 (exact date not given) by Rev. Gerard Morgan

Shoon, Martha A., see "Martha Ann Shawn," q.v.

Shorb, Andrew, see "Elizabeth Hitzelberger," q.v.

Short, Elizabeth and Peter Wolf m. 8 Dec 1844 by Rev. Joseph Shane

Short, William Hutson, son of Hutson and Ann Short, b. 24 Oct 1841, bapt. 31 Jul 1842 by Rev. William Prettyman

Shorter, Mahela and John Jarrett m. 16 Jul 1845 by Rev. Dr. George C. M. Roberts

Shott, Charles H. and Ann E. Kilbourn m. 9 Jun 1850 by Rev. Henry Slicer, lic. dated 7 Jun 1850

Shreck, William T. and Isabel Elizabeth Pate m. 17 Oct 1850 by Rev. John S. Martin, lic. dated 16 Oct 1850

Shuck, William, son of Adam and Julia Shuck, b. 3 Nov 1841, bapt. 15 Feb 1842 by Rev. Isaac P. Cook

Shueman, Sarah E. and William T. Doyle m. 4 Dec 1845 by Rev. Dr. George C. M. Roberts

Shumler, William K. and Mary J. Ashley m. 9 Jun 1846 by Rev. Dr. George C. M. Roberts

Shutts, Mary Elizabeth, dau. of Augustus P. and Mary A. Shutts, b. 12 Nov 1843, bapt. 6 Dec 1843 by Rev. Isaac P. Cook

Sicoden(?), William F. and Sarah B. Benoreti(?) m. 2 Apr 1843 by Rev. Job Guest, lic. dated 1 Apr 1843

Silk, Ann Maria, dau. of Thomas and Elizabeth Silk, b. 5 Oct 1841, bapt. 29 Dec 1842 by Rev. Elisha D. Owen

Silva, Susan and James R. Hervey m. 16 Dec 1841 by Rev. Gerard Morgan, lic. dated same day

Simmering, Daniel and Mary Ann Adams m. 5 Jan 1846 by Rev. Dr. George C. M. Roberts

Simmond, Matthew and Susannah, see "Susanna Simmons," q.v.

Simmonds, Alice and John M. Durham m. 8 Dec 1850 by Rev. Isaac P. Cook

Simmonds, Edward and Elizabeth Ann Franklin m. 25 Jul 1847 by Rev. Stephen A. Roszel, lic. dated 21 Jul 1847

Simmonds, Emma, dau. of John A. and Susan Simmonds, b. 14 Jan 1842, bapt. 22 Feb 1842 by Rev. Job Guest

Simmons, Catherine Ann (coloured), dau. of James and Patience Simmons, b. 31 Mar 1840, Baltimore County, bapt. 12 Sep 1840 by Rev. Samuel Keppler

Simmons, John Thomas, son of John and Mary Simmons, aged "some 9 or 10 months" [b. 1841], bapt. 11 Sep 1842 by Rev. Benjamin H. Crever

Simmons, Sophia A. and Robert G. Greerson m. 12 (13?) [ink smudged] Dec 1848 by Rev. William Hirst

Simmons, Susanna, d. circa 1844 (exact date not given in Record of Members) [*Ed. Note:* She may possibly be the Susannah Simmond, widow of Matthew Y. Simmond, whose death notice in the *Baltimore Sun* stated that she d. 28 Feb 1843.]

Simms, Elizabeth and William Williams m. 6 May 1844 by Rev. Joseph Shane

Simms, Mary Jane and Isaac Wyman m. 28 Sep 1848 by Rev. Stephen A. Roszel, lic. dated 7 Sep 1848 by Rev. Stephen A. Roszel, lic. dated

Simone, John and Sarah Haney m. 21 Aug 1842 by Rev. Joseph Shane

Simons, Benjamin Franklin, son of Levi and Miranda Simons, b. 6 Oct 1843, bapt. 17 Oct 1843 by Rev. Isaac P. Cook

Simonson, John and Rachel Eagen m. 3 Apr 1845 by Rev. Dr. George C. M. Roberts

Simonson, Mary E. and John F. Leguin m. 7 Nov 1843 by Rev. Dr. George C. M. Roberts

Simonson, Susanna and William Armstrong m. 25 Aug 1847 by Rev. Dr. George C. M. Roberts

Simpson, Eliza Ann, dau. of Rezin B. and Jane Simpson, b. 8 Feb 1823, bapt. 17 Jun 1840 by Rev. Dr. George C. M. Roberts

Simpson, Eliza J. and Charles H. Hartlove m. 12 Sep 1844 by Rev. Dr. George C. M. Roberts

Simpson, John W. and Eliza Ann Downes m. 24 Sep 1844 by Rev. Dr. George C. M. Roberts

Simpson, Mary Elizabeth, dau. of James F. and Ann Maria Simpson, b. 14 Dec 1846, bapt. 21 Jul 1847 by Rev. Dr. George C. M. Roberts

Simpson, Melvina and James Stanley, both of Baltimore County, m. 16 Jun 1842 by Rev. Nelson Head

Simpson, Susan J. and John W. Riddle m. 13 Aug 1850 by Rev. Isaac P. Cook

Simpson, William and Mary Ann Turner m. 13 May 1845 by Rev. Samuel Keppler (date of lic. not recorded)

Sinclair, Catherine A. and Thomas Porter m. 24 Dec 1843 by Rev. Henry Slicer, lic. dated 23 Dec 1843

Sinclair, Henry and Pamelia Schwatkas m. 3 May 1849 by Rev. Aquila A. Reese, lic. dated 2 May 1849

Sindell, William and Rosanna Ross m. 18 May 1845 by Rev. Dr. George C. M. Roberts

Sinners, Alice Grillet, dau. of Elijah R. and Mary Ann Sinners, b. 20 Jun 1848, bapt. 3 Apr 1849 by Rev. Dr. George C. M. Roberts

Sinners, Elijah R. and Mary Girlett m. 15 Aug 1847 by Rev. Isaac P. Cook

Sipe, George and Maria Elizabeth Griffith m. 14 Jan 1849 by Rev. Joseph Shane

Siscoe, Mary Jane and William Charles Welsh m. 28 Sep 1845 by Rev. Isaac P. Cook

Skillman, George and Eliza J. McLeane m. 11 Apr 1842 by Rev. Dr. George C. M. Roberts

Skillman, Hannah M. and Samuel C. Hush m. 10 Jun 1845 by Rev. Dr. George C. M. Roberts

Skillman, Hannah Maria, dau. of Josiah and Catherine Skillman, b. 27 Sep 1825, bapt. 19 Apr 1846 by Rev. Dr. George C. M. Roberts

Skillman, Joseph F. and Lucretia A. Welsh m. 24 Sep 1849 by Rev. William Hirst, lic. dated same day

Skilman, Rebecca C. and Samuel G. Hopkins m. 3 Feb 1843 by Rev. Joseph Shane

Skinner, Elizabeth and Isaac C. Pyle m. 19 Dec 1844 by Rev. Dr. George C. M. Roberts

Skinner, Hannah, d. circa 1845-1847 (exact date not given in Record of Members) [*Ed. Note:* Death notice in the *Baltimore Sun* stated that Hannah Skinner, wife of Zachariah Skinner and dau. of John Jones, d. 18 Jun 1846.]

Skinner, Joseph and Sarah J. Cameron m. 2 Jul 1846 by Rev. Dr. George C. M. Roberts

Skinner, Margaret and William Roads m. 11 Oct 1849 by Rev. William Hirst, lic. dated same day

Skinner, Mary Emiline, d. circa 1847-1850 (exact date not given in Record of Members)

Skinner, Zachariah, see "Hannah Skinner," q.v.

Slagel, John W. and Sarah E. Yearly m. 25 Jun 1846 by Rev. Dr. George C. M. Roberts

Slagell, Mary, dau. of John W. and Sarah E. Slagell, b. 17 Jun 1847, bapt. 17 Aug 1847 by Rev. Dr. George C. M. Roberts

Slate, William and Arianna Valiant m. 24 Jan 1840 by Rev. Joseph Shane

Slater, Amelia Ann, dau. of Henry Slater, aged 5, b. East Baltimore, bapt. 25 Jul 1841 by Rev. William Prettyman

Slater, Charles Wesley, son of Henry and Joanna Slater, b. 9 Jul 1844, bapt. 28 Jun 1846 by Rev. Samuel Keppler

Slater, Margaret and Absalom B. Shields m. 14 Aug 1849 by Rev. Dr. George C. M. Roberts

Slater, Mary Elona, dau. of Henry Slater, aged 7, b. East Baltimore, bapt. 25 Jul 1841 by Rev. William Prettyman

Slater, Thomas Benton, son of Henry Slater, aged 3, b. East Baltimore, bapt. 25 Jul 1841 by Rev. William Prettyman

Slater, William Henry, son of Henry Slater, aged 9, b. East Baltimore, bapt. 25 Jul 1841 by Rev. William Prettyman

Sley, William and Agnes Hutton m. 15 Jul 1844 by Rev. James Sewell, lic. dated same day

Slicer, Thomas Roberts, son of Rev. Henry and Eliza C. Slicer, b. ---- [blank], bapt. ---- [blank] by Rev. Dr. George C. M. Roberts [*Ed. Note:* This baptism was listed between 10 Oct and 20 Oct 1847.]

Slingluff, Anna Verlinder, dau. of Upton and Anna Verlinder Slingluff, b. 1 Nov 1847, bapt. 2 Nov 1847 by Rev. Dr. George C. M. Roberts

Slingluff, Helen, dau. of Upton and Anna Verlinder Slingluff, b. 30 Nov 1842, bapt. 2 Nov 1847 by Rev. Dr. George C. M. Roberts

Slingluff, John Landstreet, son of Upton and Anna Verlinder Slingluff, b. 7 May 1845, bapt. 2 Nov 1847 by Rev. Dr. George C. M. Roberts

Slingluff, Upton and Ann Verlinda Landstreet m. 15 Mar 1842 at the house of her father in Baltimore by Rev. Beverly Waugh, lic. dated same day

Sloan, William and Matilda A. Wright m. ---- [blank] by Rev. John S. Martin, lic. dated 1 Mar 1850 [*Ed. Note:* Their marriage notice in the *Baltimore Sun* stated they were married on 2 Mar 1850.]

Small, David E. and Mary A. Fulton m. 13 Jun 1849 by Rev. Wesley Stevenson

Small, Edward, d. circa 1849-1850 (exact date not given in Record of Members) [*Ed. Note:* Death notice in the *Baltimore Sun* stated that Edward Small, son of John Small, d. 13 Aug 1849.]

Small, Eleanor and Charles R. Owings, both of Baltimore County, m. 24 Nov 1840 by Rev. Thomas Myers, lic. dated 23 Nov 1840

Small, John, see "Edward Small," q.v.

Smallwood, George J. and Catherine McIlvaney m. 14 Sep 1850 by Rev. Joseph Shane

Smarden, Elizabeth and John Collins m. 5 Dec 1843 by Rev. Samuel Brison

Smiley, Sophia and John W. Lawrenson, both of Baltimore County, m. 14 Apr 1845 by Rev. William Hamilton, lic. dated 4 Apr 1845

Smith, Abijah B. and Ann Houck m. 10 Mar 1841 by Rev. Wesley Stevenson

Smith, Ada, dau. of Charles A. and Clementina V. Smith, b. 11 Feb 1850, bapt. 15 Dec 1850 by Rev. Dr. George C. M. Roberts

Smith, Ann Maria and Jacob Harney m. 27 Jul 1843 by Rev. Joseph Shane

Smith, Anna Amelia, dau. of John T. and Isabella Smith, b. 9 Nov 1848, bapt. 25 Mar 1850 by Rev. Dr. George C. M. Roberts

Smith, Anna Rebecca, dau. of John Alexander and Mary Ann Smith, b. 20 Sep 1844, bapt. 27 Sep 1844 by Rev. Dr. George C. M. Roberts

Smith, Charles A., see "Ada Smith," q.v.

Smith, Charles Tippitt, son of John and Margaret Smith, b. 25 Mar 1842, bapt. 10 Oct 1842 by Rev. William Prettyman

Smith, Clementina, see "Ada Smith," q.v

Smith, Daniel, see "Hannah Smith," q.v.

Smith, David W., d. circa 1840 (exact date not given in Class Record) [*Ed. Note:* Death notice in the *Baltimore Sun* stated that David W. Smith d. 12 Jul 1838.]

Smith, Eliza and John Ramsey m. 22 Feb 1849 by Rev. Joseph Shane

Smith, Elizabeth and Charles M. Jameson, both of Baltimore County, m. ---- [date not given] by Rev. George D. Chenoweth, lic. dated 31 Jan 1842

Smith, Elizabeth and James Bond, Jr. m. 15 Nov 1842 by Rev. Henry Slicer, lic. dated 14 Nov 1842

Smith, Elizabeth and Gilbert Carcaud m. 1 Oct 1850 by Rev. Henry Slicer, lic. dated same day

Smith, Elizabeth C., see "George J. Smith," q.v.

Smith, Emily Jane and Johnson B. Aburn m. 16 May 1849 by Rev. John S. Martin, lic. dated 15 May 1849

Smith, Emma Louisa Clay, dau. of James and Sophia Smith, b. 16 Feb 1845, bapt. 15 Sep 1845 by Rev. Isaac P. Cook

Smith, Frederick, see "Leonard J. Smith," q.v.

Smith, Garrett and Mary Jane McPhail, both of Baltimore County, m. 19 May 1840 by Rev. Thomas Myers, lic. dated same day

Smith, George, d. 1847 (death noted in Class List)

Smith, George and Elizabeth Collins m. 10 Sep 1840 by Rev. John Bear

Smith, George and Catherine Casey m. 30 May 1841 by Rev. Joseph Shane

Smith, George Inlows, son of Mr. and Mrs. Smith, b. ---- [blank], bapt. 19 Jul 1843 by Rev. Philip B. Reese

Smith, George James, son of John R. and Elizabeth C. Smith, b. 30 May 1850, bapt. 27 May 1850 by Rev. Dr. George C. M. Roberts

Smith, George W. and Ann Eliza Riley m. 27 Jun 1847 by Rev. Stephen A. Roszel, lic. dated 26 Jun 1847

Smith, George William and Mary E. Parker m. 30 Jan 1849 by Rev. Dr. George C. M. Roberts

Smith, Hammilton, d. 1842 (death noted in Probationers Book)

Smith, Hannah, d. 1840 (death noted in Class List) [*Ed. Note:* Death notice in the *Baltimore Sun* stated that Hannah Smith, widow of Daniel Smith, d. 6 Feb 1840.]

Smith, Harriet, see "Millard F. Smith," q.v.

Smith, Henry Clay and Isabella E. Chalmers m. 25 Jul 1850 by Rev. Isaac P. Cook

Smith, Henry J., son of Mr. and Mrs. Smith, b. ---- [blank], bapt. 19 Jul 1843 by Rev. Philip B. Reese

Smith, Isabell, dau. of John and Laura Smith, aged 6 months [b. 1842], bapt. 19 Feb 1843 by Rev. Wesley Stevenson

Smith, Isabella, see "Anna A. Smith" and "Isabella B. Smith," q.v.

Smith, Isabella Briscoe, dau. of John T. and Isabella Smith, b. 11 Jun 1847, bapt. 1 Jul 1847 by Rev. Dr. George C. M. Roberts

Smith, James, b. 1815, bapt. 1841, aged 26 (exact date not given) by Rev. Gerard Morgan

Smith, James, see "Emma L. Smith," q.v.

Smith, James, d. circa 1847-1850 (exact date not given in Record of Members) [*Ed. Note:* Death notice in the *Baltimore Sun* stated that a James Smith d. 25 Jun 1848.]

Smith, James and Temperance Mason m. 22 Feb 1849 by Rev. Wesley Stevenson

Smith, James Elias and Sarah Elizabeth Smith m. 28 Oct 1840 by Rev. Samuel Keppler, lic. dated 23 Oct 1840

Smith, James L., see "Sarah Smith" and "Mary Ann Smith," q.v.

Smith, James P. and Eliza Brian, both of Baltimore County, m. ---- [date not given] by Rev. George D. Chenoweth, lic. dated 21 Mar 1842

Smith, Job, see "Rachel Smith," q.v.

Smith, John, see "Charles T. Smith" and "Isabell Smith" and "Millard F. Smith" and "Walter G. Smith" and "William G. Smith," q.v.

Smith, John and Elizabeth Collins m. 28 Mar 1847 by Rev. Joseph Shane

Smith, John and Mary Ann Louisa Harman m. 24 Sep 1849 by Rev. Aquila A. Reese, lic. dated 23 Sep 1849

Smith, John and Mary F. Hytaffer m. 29 Oct 1850 by Rev. Henry Slicer, lic. dated same day

Smith, John A. and Mary Ann Adams m. 29 Nov 1843 by Rev. Dr. George C. M. Roberts. See "Anna R. Smith," q.v.

Smith, John Brooks and Mary L. Pettit m. 19 Sep 1850 by Rev. Isaac P. Cook

Smith, John J., see "William F. Smith," q.v.

Smith, John R., see "George J. Smith," q.v.

Smith, John T., see "Anna A. Smith" and "Isabella B. Smith," q.v.

Smith, Josiah K. and Susan Ann Clash m. 19 Aug 1844 by Rev. Dr. George C. M. Roberts

Smith, Juliah Ann (adult), b. ---- [blank], Baltimore City, bapt. 1840 (exact date not given) by Rev. Gerard Morgan

Smith, Julian, see "Leonard J. Smith," q.v.

Smith, Laura, see "Isabell Smith," q.v.

166

Smith, Laura, dau. of James and Sophia Smith, b. 27 Oct 1842, bapt. 10 Jan 1843 by Rev. Isaac P. Cook

Smith, Laura V., dau. of Samuel C. and Elizabeth Smith, b. 10 Feb 1842, bapt. 8 Oct 1842 by Rev. Elisha D. Owen

Smith, Leonard Joines, son of Frederick and Julian Smith, aged 8 months [b. 1840], bapt. 21 Jun 1841 by Rev. John A. Hening

Smith, Margaret, see "Charles T. Smith" and "William G. Smith," q.v.

Smith, Margaret, d. circa 1847-1849 (exact date not given in Record of Members) [*Ed. Note:* Death notice in the *Baltimore Sun* stated that Margaret Smith, widow of Nicholas Smith, d. 28 Dec 1847.]

Smith, Margaret and Charles Andrews m. 3 Oct 1850 by Rev. Dr. George C. M. Roberts

Smith, Margaret and Thomas V. Brundidge, both of Baltimore County, m. 21 Jul 1842 by Rev. Nelson Head

Smith, Mary, d. circa 1847-1850 (exact date not given in Record of Members)

Smith, Mary, d. circa 1840 (exact date not given in Class Record)

Smith, Mary A., see "Anna R. Smith," q.v.

Smith, Mary Ann and Henry Ringleb m. 11 Aug 1850 by Rev. Isaac P. Cook

Smith, Mary Ann E. G., dau. of James and Sophia Smith, b. 27 Jun 1840, bapt. ---- "date lost" *[sic]* by Rev. Isaac P. Cook [*Ed. Note:* Her name was listed with the baptisms in 1843.]

Smith, Mary C. and James S. Collins m. 11 Jan 1844 by Rev. Henry Slicer, lic. dated 10 Jan 1844

Smith, Mary E. and George H. West m. 15 Jan 1845 by Rev. James Sewell, lic. dated 13 Jan 1845

Smith, Mary E. and Joseph Hebb m. 15 Dec 1847 by Rev. Stephen A. Roszel, lic. dated same day

Smith, Mary M. and William P. Earpe m. 13 Aug 1846 by Rev. Isaac P. Cook

Smith, Maryanna, d. circa 1847-1850 (exact date not given in Record of Members)

Smith, Millard Fillmore, son of John and Harriet Smith (colored), b. 21 Dec 1850, bapt. 13 Oct 1851 by Rev. Dr. George C. M. Roberts

Smith, Nicholas, see "Margaret Smith," q.v.

Smith, Priscilla W. and George Merriken m. 22 Feb 1849 at Light Street Church in Baltimore by Rev. Beverly Waugh, lic. dated 21 Feb 1849

Smith, Rachel, d. 6 Nov 1840 (death noted in Record of Members) [*Ed. Note:* Death notice in the *Baltimore Sun* stated that Rachel Smith, wife of Job Smith, d. 6 Nov 1840.]

Smith, Rebecca, d. circa 1840 (exact date not given in Class Record)

Smith, Rebecca B. and Charles B. White m. 4 Nov 1841 by Rev. Dr. George C. M. Roberts

Smith, Richard E. and Sarah E. Adams m. 5 Jun 1845 by Rev. James Sewell, lic. dated same day

Smith, Ringold, see "Walter D. Smith," q.v.

Smith, Samuel A. and Susan Bargar m. 2 Jan 1850 by Rev. Aquila A. Reese, lic. dated same day

Smith, Samuel C., see "Laura V. Smith," q.v.

Smith, Samuel H. and Rebecca Essex m. 16 Jan 1844 by Rev. Joseph Shane

Smith, Sarah, d. 1849 (death noted in Class List) [*Ed. Note:* Death notice in the *Baltimore Sun* stated that Sarah Smith, wife of James L. Smith, d. 3 Nov 1849.]

Smith, Sarah and Jabez S. Wilkinson m. 24 Sep 1843 by Rev. Dr. George C. M. Roberts

Smith, Sarah and John Depo m. 21 Aug 1842 by Rev. Henry Slicer, lic. dated same day

Smith, Sarah Elizabeth and James Elias Smith m. 28 Oct 1840 by Rev. Samuel Keppler, lic. dated 23 Oct 1840

Smith, Sophia, see "Emma Smith" and "Mary Ann Smith," q.v.

Smith, Syney [sic] V., of Baltimore County, and John Douglass, John, of Washington City, m. 21 Jun 1845 by Rev. William Hamilton

Smith, Walter Dorsey, son of Ringold and Elizabeth Smith, b. 29 Sep 1839, bapt. 10 Mar 1840 by Rev. Dr. George C. M. Roberts

Smith, Walter George, son of John and Laura Smith, aged 3 years [b. 1839 or 1840], bapt. 19 Feb 1843 by Rev. Wesley Stevenson

Smith, William Francis, son of John J. and Ann O. Smith, b. 5 Dec 1840, bapt. 10 Jan 1841 by Rev. Dr. George C. M. Roberts

Smith, William Glasgow McClure, son of John and Margaret Smith, b. 9 Oct 1839, bapt. 24 Aug 1840 by Rev. Charles B. Tippett

Smith, William Henry and Mary Jane Espey m. 2 Mar 1848 by Rev. Stephen A. Roszel, lic. dated 1 Mar 1848

Smithson, Henry Clay, son of Thomas and Clarissa Smithson, b. 3 Dec 1841, bapt. 9 Apr 1853 by Rev. Dr. George C. M. Roberts

Smythe, Emily C. and William C. Brown m. 2 May 1850 by Rev. Joseph Shane

Snook, William and Ann Vickers m. 27 Dec 1843 by Rev. Dr. George C. M. Roberts

Snow, William Freeman, son of William Freeman and Anna C. Snow, b. 25 Nov 1850, bapt. 6 May 1851 by Rev. Dr. George C. M. Roberts

Snyder, Edwin, son of Benjamin B. and Rebecca C. Snyder, b. 21 Apr 1843, bapt. 4 Oct 1843 by Rev. Dr. George C. M. Roberts

Snyder, John, d. 1845 (death noted in Class List)

Snyder, Mary, d. 1841 (death noted in Class List)

Snyder, Susan, d. 1849 (death noted in Class List)

Sohn, Johannes and Margaret Spear m. 26 Feb 1850 by Rev. Isaac P. Cook

Sollers, Eliza, d. 1847 (death noted in Class List) [Ed. Note: Death notice in the Baltimore Sun stated that Elizabeth Sollers, widow of John Sollers, d. 27 May 1847.]

Sollers, John, d. after 1841 (death noted in Class List) [Ed. Note: Death notice in the Baltimore Sun stated that John Sollers d. 18 Apr 1842.]

Soper, Henry Brackin, son of Samuel J. and Anna Maria Soper, b. 23 May 1850, bapt. 2 Jan 1853 by Rev. Dr. George C. M. Roberts

Sorter, Jane and William L. Ijams m. 12 Jun 1845 by Rev. Dr. George C. M. Roberts [Ed. Note: His last name was spelled "Jiams" or "Iiams" in the church register, but their marriage notice in the Baltimore Sun gave his name as "Ijams."]

Sottle, Elizabeth, dau. of James and Elizabeth P. Sottle, b. 7 Dec 1850, bapt. 27 Oct 1851 by Rev. Dr. George C. M. Roberts

Southcomb, Alexandria Layfayet, child of Thomas and Elisabeth Southcomb, b. 28 Dec 1835, bapt. -- Aug 1841 by Rev. Gerard Morgan

Southgate, Mary Elizabeth, dau. of Walter Fuller and Mary Elizabeth Southgate, b. 29 Jun 1840, Baltimore City, bapt. 5 Feb 1841 by Rev. Samuel Keppler

Sparks, James S. and Harriet Jane Hulse m. 26 Dec 1843 by Rev. Dr. George C. M. Roberts

Sparrow, Elijah Abigail, dau. of John and Hannah Sparrow, b. ---- [blank], bapt. 12 Apr 1846 by Rev. Dr. George C. M. Roberts

Spear, Barclay and Louisa E. Creighton m. 18 Dec 1849 by Rev. William Hirst, lic. dated 10 Dec 1849

Spear, Margaret and Johannes Sohn m. 26 Feb 1850 by Rev. Isaac P. Cook

Spence, Herman and Catherine Metzdorff m. 24 Mar 1844 by Rev. Joseph Shane

Spence, Martha Ann, dau. of John and Lydia Spence, b. 21 Oct 1840, bapt. 11 Apr 1841 by Rev. Isaac P. Cook

Spence, Sarah and James McCulley m. 29 Jul 1841 by Rev. Dr. George C. M. Roberts [Ed. Note: His name was written as "James McCulley, Sol." in the marriage register.]

Spencer, Abel, see "William Spencer," q.v.

Spencer, Charlotte J. and James A. G. Watters, both of Baltimore County, m. 23 Feb 1843 by Rev. Nelson Head

Spencer, Dorothy and William W. Woodward m. 25 Sep 1845 by Rev. Dr. George C. M. Roberts

Spencer, George Washington, son of Hugh and Susan Spencer, b. 8 Oct 1839, bapt. 18 Jun 1840 by Rev. Dr. George C. M. Roberts

Spencer, Henry B., son of John and Rosanna Spencer, b. 1 Apr 1842, bapt. 12 Sep 1842 by Rev. Elisha D. Owen

Spencer, Hugh, see "George W. Spencer" and "Hugh S. Spencer" and "Richard P. Spencer," q.v.

Spencer, Hugh Samuel, son of Hugh and Susan Spencer, b. 4 Sep 1846, bapt. 5 Aug 1847 by Rev. Dr. George C. M. Roberts

Spencer, John, see "Henry B. Spencer," q.v.

Spencer, Keziah and William O'Neal m. 4 Jun 1848 by Rev. James H. Brown, lic. dated 3 Jun 1848

Spencer, Mary Ann and James T. Gorman m. 14 Dec 1847 by Rev. Stephen A. Roszel, lic. dated 9 Dec 1847

Spencer, Richard Perry, son of Hugh and Susan Spencer, b. 13(?) Jun 1840, bapt. 18 Jun 1840 by Rev. Dr. George C. M. Roberts

Spencer, Rosanna, see "Henry B. Spencer," q.v.

Spencer, Sarah Ann, dau. of John and Mary Spencer, b. 2 Sep 1824, bapt. 29 Aug 1841 by Rev. Dr. George C. M. Roberts

Spencer, Susan, see "George W. Spencer" and "Hugh S. Spencer" and "Richard P. Spencer," q.v.

Spencer, William, son of Abel Spencer, b. 8 Aug 1809, bapt. 10 Sep 1843 by Rev. Isaac P. Cook

Spies, William T. and Susan Vinsen m. 6 Jan 1850 by Rev. William Hirst, lic. dated 4 Jan 1850

Spillman, Alice and Thomas Jeffrey m. 3 Mar 1846 by Rev. Isaac P. Cook

Spillman, Jane and William Fowler m. 6 May 1849 by Rev. Joseph Shane

Sprigg, Henry Horace and Rebecca Jane Porter m. 4 Apr 1844 by Rev. Dr. George C. M. Roberts

Sprinkle, Charles H., son of Charles and Margaret Sprinkle, b. 18 Jul 1841, bapt. 3 Oct 1842 by Rev. William Prettyman

Sprinkle, Margaret J., dau. of Charles and Margaret Sprinkle, b. 14 Jul 1843, bapt. 20 Apr 1844 by Rev. James Sewell

Sprinkle, Mary E., dau. of Charles and Margaret Sprinkle, aged 13 months [b. 1840], bapt. 1841 (exact date not given) by Rev. Gerard Morgan [*Ed. Note:* The last name was spelled "Sprinckel" in the church register.]

Spry, David Jr. and Mary Rosetta Spry m. 29 Nov 1846 by Rev. Dr. George C. M. Roberts

Spry, Mary Rosetta and David Spry, Jr. m. 29 Nov 1846 by Rev. Dr. George C. M. Roberts

Staines, Mary, d. circa 1840 (death noted in Class List)

Stallens, Sarah J. and Francis W. Michaels m. 8 Feb 1849 by Rev. Dr. George C. M. Roberts [*Ed. Note:* Their marriage notice in the *Baltimore Sun* gave their names as Francis W. Michael and Sarah J. Stalings.]

Stalling, John, son of Samuel and Sarah Ann Stalling, b. 4 Oct 1840, bapt. 20 Nov 1840 by Rev. Joseph Shane

Stallings, Martha A. and Edward P. Porter m. 25 Jul 1846 by Rev. Joseph Shane

Stallings, William C. and Emily Asparkin m. 9 Oct 1844 by Rev. Dr. George C. M. Roberts

Stanley, James and Melvina Simpson, both of Baltimore County, m. 16 Jun 1842 by Rev. Nelson Head

Stanley, William D. and Elizabeth Thompson, both of Baltimore County, m. ---- [date not given] by Rev. George D. Chenoweth, lic. dated 13 Mar 1842 [*Ed. Note:* Their marriage notice in the *Baltimore Sun* stated that William D. Stanley m. Elizabeth A. Thomson on 31 Mar 1850.]

Stansberry, Elizabeth, d. 1840 (death noted in Class List) [*Ed. Note:* Death notice in the *Baltimore Sun* stated that Elizabeth Stansbury, wife of Joseph Stansbury, d. 6 Nov 1840.]

Stansberry, William and Harriett Tregg m. 22 Aug 1841 by Rev. Job Guest, lic. dated 21 Aug 1841

Stansbury, Ann Josephene, dau. of John and Mary Stansbury, b. 14 Jul 1842, bapt. 15 Oct 1842 by Rev. Elisha D. Owen

Stansbury, Assenith, d. circa 1844-1845 (exact date not given in Record of Members) [*Ed. Note:* Death notice in the *Baltimore Sun* stated that Azenath Stansbury, dau. of Thomas Stansbury and sister of Lemuel Stansbury, d. 18 Oct 1844.]

Stansbury, Clementine and Philip Bridener m. 20 Oct 1847 by Rev. James H. Brown, lic. dated same day

Stansbury, Elizabeth A. and Christopher L. Grafflin m. 25 Apr 1850 by Rev. Henry Slicer, lic. dated same day

Stansbury, Isabella and Addison Johnson, both of Baltimore County, m. ---- [date not given] by Rev. George Hildt, lic. dated 14 Oct 1845

Stansbury, Joseph, see "Elizabeth Stansberry," q.v.

Stansbury, Lemuel, see "Assenith Stansbury," q.v.

Stansbury, Samuel and Sophia E. Million m. 26 Apr 1849 by Rev. Dr. George C. M. Roberts

Stansbury, Thomas, see "Assenith Stansbury," q.v.

Stansbury, Tobias and Sarah E. Thomas m. 16 Sep 1842 by Rev. Henry Slicer, lic. dated same day

Stansbury, William E. and Christiana Taylor m. 16 Apr 1844 at the house of her father Isaac Taylor in Baltimore County by Rev. Beverly Waugh, lic. dated 15 Apr 1844

Starr, Amos Gregory, son of Solomon R. and Lydia Starr, b. 3 Jan 1843, bapt. 14 Oct 1843 by Rev. Dr. George C. M. Roberts

Starr, Ann E. and Joseph J. Treakle m. 24 Dec 1850 by Rev. Henry Slicer, lic. dated 23 Dec 1850

Starr, Edward Grimes, son of Edward G. and Cecelia Ann Starr, b. 25 Jan 1850, bapt. 1 Feb 1850 by Rev. Dr. George C. M. Roberts

Starr, Helen Phillipi, dau. of Robert T. and Caroline Starr, b. 3 Nov 1843, bapt. 15 Nov 1843 by Rev. Dr. George C. M. Roberts

Starr, Henry, son of Edward G. and Cecelia Ann Starr, b. 18 Oct 1845, bapt. 25 Oct 1845 by Rev. Dr. George C. M. Roberts

Starr, John James, son of Edward G. and Cecelia A. Starr, b. 8 Jun 1843, bapt. 10 Jan 1844 by Rev. Dr. George C. M. Roberts

Starr, Lucretia and James Reddish m. 25 Jun 1843 by Rev. Dr. George C. M. Roberts

Starr, Marion, son of Robert and Caroline Starr, b. 21 Nov 1840, bapt. 14 Dec 1841 by Rev. Dr. George C. M. Roberts

Stating, Joseph and Ann Barrett m. 13 Jul 1845 by Rev. Dr. George C. M. Roberts

Stauter, Ann and George Jury m. 11 Mar 1845 by Rev. Dr. George C. M. Roberts

Steers, George and Mary Lee m. 25 Oct 1841 by Rev. Joseph Shane

Steever, Francis and Jane Stever m. 9 Feb 1843 by Rev. Dr. George C. M. Roberts

Steever, Georgiana R. and Uriah Coleman m. 17 Jul 1848 by Rev. Stephen A. Roszel, lic. dated 26 Jun 1848

Steever, Sarah Alexina, dau. of Daniel and Ann Eliza Steever, b. 25 May 1848, bapt. 11 Jan 1859 by Rev. Dr. George C. M. Roberts

Steiner, Imogene, dau. of James and Matilda Ann Steiner, b. 21 Oct 1844, bapt. 14 Jun 1845 by Rev. Dr. George C. M. Roberts

Steiver, Christian and Emeline Wheeler m. 31 Dec 1848 by Rev. Joseph Shane

Stembler, Emily and Benjamin Davis m. 18 Mar 1849 by Rev. Aquila A. Reese, lic. dated 17 Mar 1849

Stephens, Achsa, d. 1844 (exact date not given in Record of Members) [Ed. Note: Death notice in the Baltimore Sun stated that Achsah Stevens, widow of John Stevens, d. 20 Sep 1844.]

Stephens, Ann Rebecca, dau. of John A. and Sarah Ann V. Stephens, aged 2 years and 3 months [b. 1839], bapt. 10 Oct 1841 by Rev. John A. Hening

Stephens, Eliza Jane and Samuel Mellville m. 25 May 1848 by Rev. Isaac P. Cook

Stephens, Lucinda B. and Alfred T. Petted m. ---- [no date given] by Rev. John Miller, lic. dated 14 May 1850 [Ed. Note: Their marriage notice in the Baltimore Sun gave their names as A. T. Pettit and L. B. Stephens and their marriage date as 14 May 1850.]

Stephens, Sarah E. and William J. Hopper, both of Baltimore County, m. 27 May 1844 by Rev. William Hamilton

Stephens, Upton A. and Henrietta E. Kempton, both of Baltimore County, m. 21 May 1844 by Rev. William Hamilton

Stephenson, John H. Evans, son of Robert and Sarah J. Stephenson, b. 29 Jan 1841, bapt. 30 Oct 1842 by Rev. Henry Slicer

Stephenson, Rebecca, d. after 1840 (exact date not given in Class Record) [*Ed. Note:* Death notice in the *Baltimore Sun* stated that a Rebecca Stevenson, wife of John Stevenson, d. 4 Aug 1844.]

Sterling, John H. and Kate M. Pyne m. 1 Sep 1847 by Rev. Stephen A. Roszel, lic. dated 31 Aug 1847

Sterling, Noah and Mary Linten m. 8 Dec 1842 by Rev. Samuel Brison

Sterret, Elijah and Priscilla Johnson m. 10 Mar 1842 by Rev. Joseph Shane

Sterrett, Emily and John Brian, both of Baltimore County, m. ---- [date not given] by Rev. George Hildt, lic. dated 1 Nov 1845 [*Ed. Note:* Their marriage notice in the *Baltimore Sun* stated they married on 2 Nov 1845.]

Stevens, Achsah, see "Achsa Stephens," q.v.

Stevens, Anna Kempton, dau. of Capt. H. and Henrietta E. Stevens, b. 20 Mar 1845, bapt. 16 Jun 1846 by Rev. Dr. George C. M. Roberts

Stevens, Caroline and Joseph S. Boston m. 19 Jan 1845 by Rev. Dr. George C. M. Roberts

Stevens, Henrietta, see "Anna K. Stevens," q.v.

Stevens, John, see "Achsa Stephens," q.v.

Stevens, John Wesley and Mary Jane Beacham m. 6 Dec 1848 by Rev. Dr. George C. M. Roberts

Stevens, Sylvester H. and Mary Ann Reynolds, both of Baltimore County, m. ---- [date not given] by Rev. George Hildt, lic. dated 7 Nov 1845

Stevenson, Hannah P. and William E. Hopkins m. 16 Jun 1847 by Rev. Isaac P. Cook

Stevenson, James and Elizabeth Hewens m. 26 Jun 1843 by Rev. Henry Slicer, lic. dated 23 Jun 1843

Stevenson, John, see "Rebecca Stephenson," q.v.

Stevenson, John, d. "3 years ago" (death noted in Record of Members in 1847)

Stevenson, Mary and David Buckley m. 28 Aug 1842 by Rev. Dr. George C. M. Roberts

Stevenson, Mary E. and John J. Johnson m. 28 Dec 1847 by Rev. Dr. George C. M. Roberts

Stevenson, Rebecca, see "Rebecca Stephenson," q.v.

Stever, Jane and Francis Steever m. 9 Feb 1843 by Rev. Dr. George C. M. Roberts

Steward, John (colored) and Margaret Forman (colored) m. 13 Dec 1842 by Rev. Henry Slicer (date of lic. not recorded)

Stewart, Abraham and Francis Thompson m. 1 Sep 1847 by Rev. James H. Brown, lic. dated 14 Aug 1847

Stewart, Charles and Margaret Holt m. 24 Dec 1840 by Rev. Joseph Shane

Stewart, Francis, see "George F. Stewart," q.v.

Stewart, George Franklin, son of Francis and Mary Ann Stewart, b. 2 Mar 1846, bapt. 19 Jun 1846 by Rev. Samuel Keppler

Stewart, George L., see "John T. B. Stewart," q.v.

Stewart, Glendi, see "John J. Stewart," q.v.

Stewart, Harriot A., dau. of Henry and Mary A. Stewart, b. 28 Mar 1838, bapt. 1842 (exact date not given) by Rev. William Prettyman

Stewart, Henrietta, see "John T. B. Stewart," q.v.

Stewart, Henry, see "Harriot A. Stewart" and "William H. Stewart," q.v.

Stewart, John J., son of Glendi and Isabella Stewart, b. 25 Aug 1840, bapt. 29 Jun 1842 by Rev. William Prettyman

Stewart, John Thomas Benton, son of George L. and Henrietta Stewart, aged 11 months [b. 1842], bapt. 29 Jan 1843 by Rev. Henry Slicer

Stewart, Louisa, d. circa 1840 (exact date not given in Class Record)

Stewart, Lydia R., see "Michael S. Stewart," q.v.

Stewart, Mary A., see "George F. Stewart" and "Harriot A. Stewart" and William H. Stewart," q.v.

Stewart, Mary F. and Henry T. Barrow m. 14 Jul 1842 by Rev. Henry Slicer, lic. dated same day

Stewart, Michael Shellman, son of William H. and Lydia R. Stewart, b. 5 Dec 1846, bapt. 27 Feb 1847 by Rev. Dr. George C. M. Roberts

Stewart, Robert and Elmira A. Bowers m. 28 May 1845 by Rev. Dr. George C. M. Roberts

Stewart, Samuel and Mary A. Jenkins m. 22 Oct 1846 by Rev. Joseph Shane

Stewart, William, d. circa 1847-1850 (exact date not given in Record of Members)

Stewart, William and Ann Lusby m. 13 Aug 1846 by Rev. Samuel Keppler (date of lic. not recorded)

Stewart, William H., see "Michael S. Stewart," q.v.

Stewart, William H., son of Henry and Mary A. Stewart, b. 29 Apr 1840, bapt. 25 Dec 1842 by Rev. Henry Slicer

Stinchcomb, Alexander and Achsah Owings m. 31 Mar 1842 by Rev. Joseph Shane

Stiner, Matilda A. and Moses L. Edmondson m. 1 Jan 1850 by Rev. William Hirst, lic. dated 31 Dec 1849 [*Ed. Note:* Their marriage notice in the *Baltimore Sun* gave their names as Moses Edmonson and Matilda A. Steiner.]

Stirling, Elizabeth and Peter M. Dulany m. 2 Sep 1846 by Rev. Samuel Keppler (date of lic. not recorded)

Stites, John Alexander, son of William and Elizabeth Stites, b. 18 Dec 1842, bapt. 6 Jan 1843 by Rev. William Prettyman

Stiver, Sarah A. E. and Eugene Devline m. 7 Aug 1849 by Rev. Joseph Shane [*Ed. Note:* Their marriage notice in the *Baltimore Sun* gave their names as Eugene Devlin and Sarah A. E. Stivers.]

Stocksdale, Dolly and Thomas A. Conaway m. 25 Jul 1850 by Rev. Henry Slicer, lic. dated same day

Stockton, William C. and Martha M. Brusster m. 12 May 1842 by Rev. Henry Slicer, lic. dated same day

Stokes, William and Rosanna Horse m. 13 Dec 1849 by Rev. Dr. George C. M. Roberts [*Ed. Note:* Her last name was given as "Horstman" in their *Baltimore Sun* marriage notice.]

Stone, Adaline and Jacob O. Hickner m. 18 Jun 1846 by Rev. Littleton F. Morgan, lic. dated 15 Jun 1846

Stone, William B. and Caroline Salger m. 19 Jul 1849 by Rev. Dr. George C. M. Roberts

Stonnan(?), William H. and Sarah R. Bonssell m. 11 Nov 1841 by Rev. Job Guest, lic. dated 8 Nov 1841

Stouffer, Ann, d. circa 1847-1848 (exact date not given in Record of Members) [*Ed. Note:* Death notice in the *Baltimore Sun* stated that Ann Stouffer, widow of Henry Stouffer, d. 18 Oct 1848.]

Stout, Catharine and Francis Luke m. 3 Jul 1843 by Rev. Isaac P. Cook

Stover (Storer?), James J. and Sarah Ann Hopkins m. 17 Jun 1849 by Rev. John S. Martin, lic. dated 16 Jun 1849

Stran, Hannah Ann, dau. of William H. and Ann Maria Stran, b. 10 Jul 1846, bapt. 27 Sep 1846 by Rev. Dr. Edwin Dorsey

Stranley, James J. and Elizabeth D. Rose m. 12 Aug 1845 by Rev. Samuel Keppler (date of lic. not recorded)

Stratton, William G. and Adeline Ridick m. 16 Sep 1847 by Rev. Littleton F. Morgan, lic. dated 15 Sep 1847

Strebeck, Harriet Elizabeth, dau. of John and Elizabeth Strebeck, b. 4 Feb 1845, bapt. 27 Aug 1846 by Rev. Samuel Keppler

Street, James B. and Mary Jane Johnston m. 7 Oct 1847 by Rev. James H. Brown, lic. dated 6 Oct 1847

Strider, Thomas and Jane E. Grant m. 17 Jan 1843 by Rev. Isaac P. Cook

Strobel, Henry and Eleanora Jenkins m. 23 Nov 1848 by Rev. Stephen A. Roszel, lic. dated 22 Nov 1848

Stromberger, Henry and Mary Jane Mann m. 22 Jun 1845 by Rev. James Sewell, lic. dated 21 Jun 1845

Strong, Lawrence M. and Angeline A. Hoffman m. 21 Dec 1846 by Rev. Dr. George C. M. Roberts

Strong, Lawrence Miller, son of Lawrence M. and Angeline A. Strong, b. 23 Oct 1847, bapt. 7 Jun 1848 by Rev. Dr. George C. M. Roberts

Stroud, Rebecca, d. circa 1840-1847 (exact date not given in Record of Members)

Stuart, Mary Charlotta, dau. of Dr. Hammond and J. Maria Stuart, b. 7 Oct 1849, bapt. 18 Nov 1854 by Rev. Dr. George C. M. Roberts

Stuart, William Patterson, son of James and Ellen Stuart, b. 5 Dec 1848, bapt. 4 Mar 1849 by Rev. Dr. George C. M. Roberts

Stubbens, Margaret Ann and Wesley Banks, of Baltimore County, m. 29 Apr 1841 by Rev. John Rice, lic. dated 28 Apr 1841

Sturgess, John, d. after 1847 (death noted in Class List) [*Ed. Note:* Death notice in the *Baltimore Sun* stated that John Sturgess d. 5 Dec 1848.]

Suick, John and Jane Clendinen m. 9 Sep 1850 by Rev. Isaac P. Cook

Suit, Mary E. and John B. Williamson m. 18 Feb 1846 by Rev. Samuel Keppler (date of lic. not recorded)

Sullivan, James W. and Amanda M. Vaughan m. 1 Nov 1849 by Rev. William Hirst, lic. dated 31 Oct 1849

Sullivan, John, see "Matilda Sullivan," q.v.

Sullivan, John C. and Mary Ann Callender m. 29 Nov 1840 by Rev. Samuel Keppler, lic. dated 28 Nov 1840

Sullivan, Martha and Wilsey Fowler, both of Virginia, m. 14 Apr 1845 by Rev. William Hamilton

Sullivan, Matilda, d. circa 1845 (exact date not given in Record of Members) [*Ed. Note:* Death notice in the *Baltimore Sun* stated that Matilda Sullivan, wife of John Sullivan, d. 5 Jul 1845.]

Sullivan, William, see "Ann Disney," q.v.

Summers, George D., d. 1844 (death noted in Class List)

Summers, Joseph G. and Martha Green, both of Baltimore County, m. 19 Jun 1845 by Rev. William Hamilton, lic. dated 18 Jun 1845

Sumwalt, Ann, d. "3 years ago" (death noted in 1847 Record of Members) [*Ed. Note:* Death notice in the *Baltimore Sun* stated that Ann B. Sumwalt, wife of Joshua B. Sumwalt, d. 21 Sep 1844.]

Sumwalt, David S. and Elizabeth Davis m. 10 Mar 1847 by Rev. Wesley Stevenson

Sumwalt, Joshua B. and Annie E. Wood m. 2 Nov 1847 at the house of her father in Baltimore by Rev. Beverly Waugh, lic. dated 1 Nov 1847. See "Ann Sumwalt," q.v.

Sumwalt, Mary J. (S.?) and Barzella Jones m. 1 Jun 1847 by Rev. Wesley Stevenson

Sumwalt, Sarah and Christopher Fifer m. 7 Dec 1846 by Rev. Wesley Stevenson

Sutherland, William and Mary Ann Hilditch m. 3 May 1847 by Rev. Stephen A. Roszel, lic. dated same day

Sutro, Michael, d. circa 1842 (death noted in Probationers Book)

Sutton, Cyrus and Barthy A. Forbush m. 11 Apr 1845 by Rev. Dr. George C. M. Roberts

Sutton, James and Mary Kendall m. 29 Oct 1843 by Rev. Isaac P. Cook

Sutton, Mildred C. and Franklin Blackburn m. 1 Sep 1843 by Rev. Samuel Brison

Swan, Emeline and William James Pennington m. 6 Sep 1848 by Rev. Stephen A. Roszel, lic. dated same day

Swan, Isaac and Maria Blaney m. 6 Jan 1845 by Rev. Isaac P. Cook

Swann, James and Catherine Wroten m. 22 Jun 1846 by Rev. Dr. George C. M. Roberts

Sweetzer, Susan B. and David E. Thomas m. 17 May 1842 by Rev. Dr. George C. M. Roberts

Swift, Ann, d. circa 1845 (death noted in Class List)

Swift, Keziah, d. circa 1845 (death noted in Class List)

Swift, William A. Jr. and Ann Carty m. 20 Jul 1847 by Rev. Stephen A. Roszel, lic. dated same day

Switzer, Caroline and Milton N. Taylor m. 7 May 1848 by Rev. Dr. George C. M. Roberts

Sword, Alexander and Mary E. Bean m. 21 Apr 1840 by Rev. Samuel Keppler, lic. dated 20 Apr 1840

Sword, Margaret Ann Roszel, dau. of Solomon and Louisa Sword, b. 19 Apr 1847, Baltimore, bapt. 25 Jul 1847 by Rev. William M. D. Ryan

Sybrant, Christian and Julia Ann Mulligan m. 24 Jul 1843 by Rev. Dr. George C. M. Roberts

Symington, Charles, son of Thomas and Angeline A. Symington, b. 17 Oct 1848, bapt. 2 Feb 1852 by Rev. Dr. George C. M. Roberts

Symington, John Fife, son of Thomas and Angeline A. Symington, b. 3 Nov 1844, bapt. 2 Feb 1852 by Rev. Dr. George C. M. Roberts

Talbert, Lewis Bissell, son of Abel and Eliza Talbert, b. 16 Nov 1841, bapt. 26 Jun 1842 by Rev. Henry Slicer

Talbott, Charles A. and Emily J. Hutchinson m. 10 Apr 1849 by Rev. Isaac P. Cook

Talbott, Hannah and James W. Orem m. 13 May 1850 by Rev. Joseph Shane

Talbott, Luther Williams, son of Joseph C. and Sarah Ann Talbott, b. 15 Sep 1844, bapt. 18 May 1845 by Rev. Dr. George C. M. Roberts

Talbott, Mary Ann, d. circa 1847 (exact date not given in Record of Members) [Ed. Note: Death notice in the Baltimore Sun stated that Mary A. Talbott d. 18 Nov 1847.]

Talbott, Richard and Rachel Ann Disney m. -- Sep 1843 by Rev. Joseph Shane

Talbott, Sarah Ann, see "Luther W. Talbott," q.v.

Tall, Joseph L. and Sarah J. Willey m. 27 May 1849 by Rev. Dr. George C. M. Roberts

Tapman, Euphemia E. and John Mowbray m. 11 Dec 1849 by Rev. William Hirst, lic. dated 10 Dec 1849

Tarr, Frances, d. circa 1847-1850 (exact date not given in Record of Members)

Taylor, Alverda and Andrew J. Lyons m. 7 May 1850 by Rev. Henry Slicer, lic. dated 6 May 1850

Taylor, Ann and James S. Chandley m. 21 Dec 1840 by Rev. Joseph Shane

Taylor, Benjamin and Mary A. Foard m. 26 Sep 1843 by Rev. Henry Slicer, lic. dated same day

Taylor, Christiana and William E. Stansbury m. 16 Apr 1844 at the house of her father Isaac Taylor in Baltimore County by Rev. Beverly Waugh, lic. dated 15 Apr 1844

Taylor, Christopher and Eliza A. Molestead m. 22 Jun 1844 by Rev. James Sewell, lic. dated 14 Jun 1844

Taylor, Elizabeth A. and John W. Nash m. 25 Oct 1846 by Rev. Dr. George C. M. Roberts

Taylor, Elizabeth J., see "Samuel R. S. Taylor," q.v.

Taylor, Ellen and Philip March m. 10 Nov 1845 by Rev. Joseph Shane

Taylor, Emily A., d. 12 Aug 1847 (death noted in Record of Members) [Ed. Note: Death notice in the Baltimore Sun stated that Emily A. Taylor, wife of Samuel T. Taylor, d. 13 Aug 1847.]

Taylor, Esther Jane and George Hall m. 13 Sep 1849 by Rev. John S. Martin, lic. dated same day

Taylor, Harriot, d. circa 1840 (exact date not given in Class Record)

Taylor, Isaac, see "William E. Stansbury," q.v.

Taylor, Isaiah, see "Major Taylor" and "Mary E. Taylor," q.v.

Taylor, James and Ann Maria Brown m. 30 Apr 1848 by Rev. Dr. George C. M. Roberts

Taylor, James and Martha Ann Wilson m. 22 Mar 1848 by Rev. Stephen A. Roszel, lic. dated same day

Taylor, James and Sarah Jane Black m. 2 Jun 1841 by Rev. Gerard Morgan, lic. dated 1 Jun 1841

Taylor, Jenifer Somerset Smith and Mary Taylor m. 22 Dec 1840 by Rev. Samuel Keppler, lic. dated same day. See "Virginia P. Taylor," q.v.

Taylor, Julia and William Jackson m. 5 Apr 1848 by Rev. Stephen A. Roszel, lic. dated 3 Apr 1848

Taylor, Levi and Rebecca Ebaugh m. 7 Jun 1849 by Rev. Dr. George C. M. Roberts

Taylor, Major, son of Isaiah and Polly Taylor, b. 10 Oct 1835, bapt. 21 Jun 1840 by Rev. John Bear

Taylor, Margaret A. and John Mortimer m. 30 May 1847 by Rev. Isaac P. Cook

Taylor, Mary, d. circa 1844-1847 (exact date not given in Record of Members)

Taylor, Mary and Jenifer Somerset Smith Taylor m. 22 Dec 1840 by Rev. Samuel Keppler, lic. dated same day. See "Virginia P. Taylor," q.v.

Taylor, Mary Ellen, dau. of Isaiah and Polly Taylor, b. 14 Dec 1837, bapt. 21 Jun 1840 by Rev. John Bear

Taylor, Mary Jane and Daniel Hartman, both of Baltimore County, m. 27 Mar 1841 by Rev. John Rice

Taylor, Milton N. and Caroline Switzer m. 7 May 1848 by Rev. Dr. George C. M. Roberts

Taylor, Permelia Jane and Richard Henry Shedrick m. 14 Nov 1847 by Rev. Stephen A. Roszel, lic. dated 8 Nov 1847

Taylor, Polly, see "Major Taylor" and "Mary E. Taylor," q.v.

Taylor, Samuel Robert Sewell, son of Thomas George and Elizabeth J. Taylor, b. 15 Mar 1847, bapt. 7 Aug 1847 by Rev. Dr. George C. M. Roberts

Taylor, Samuel T., see "Emily A. Taylor," q.v.

Taylor, Thomas G., see "Samuel R. S. Taylor," q.v.

Taylor, Virginia Parsons, dau. of Jenifer Somerset S. and Mary Taylor, b. 7 Nov 1842, bapt. 14 Nov 1841 [sic] by Rev. Dr. George C. M. Roberts

Teal, Lorinda and James W. Berry m. 25 Nov 1844 by Rev. Dr. George C. M. Roberts

Tear, Benjamin F., see "Jacob Reese," q.v.

Tear, Joseph Rees, son of Benjamin and Sarah E. Tear, b. 18 Dec 1838, bapt. 30 Jan 1842 by Rev. Gerard Morgan

Terry, Mary Martha, dau. of Isaiah and Martha Ann Terry, b. 27 May 1840, bapt. 4 Mar 1842 by Rev. Robert Emory

Tharle, George W. and Louisa Chaney m. 28 Sep 1847 by Rev. Joseph Shane

Thireon, Maria and Ambrose Lebrun m. 30 Apr 1844 by Rev. Dr. George C. M. Roberts

Tholen, Claas and Elizabeth Ogden m. 19 Dec 1849 by Rev. Aquila A. Reese, lic. dated 18 Dec 1849

Thomas, Benjamin Probart, son of Benjamin and Rebecca Thomas, b. 16 Apr 1842, bapt. 30 Oct 1842 by Rev. Henry Slicer

Thomas, David E. and Susan B. Sweetzer m. 17 May 1842 by Rev. Dr. George C. M. Roberts. See "Florence S. Thomas" and "Mary R. Thomas," q.v.

Thomas, Elizabeth, d. circa 1840 (exact date not given in Class Record)

Thomas, Elizabeth (colored) and Daniel Boston (colored) m. 17 Sep 1846 by Rev. Samuel Keppler

Thomas, Elizabeth Ann and Richard Price m. 21 Jul 1840 at Light Street Church in Baltimore by Rev. Beverly Waugh, lic. dated 18 Jul 1840

Thomas, Florence Sweetzer, dau. of David E. and Susan B. Thomas, b. 3 Nov 1844, bapt. 10 Sep 1845 by Rev. Dr. George C. M. Roberts

Thomas, George C. M. Roberts, son of Capt. Samuel and Millicent C. Thomas, b. 26 Jan 1847, bapt. 31 Jan 1847 by Rev. Dr. George C. M. Roberts

Thomas, George M. and Rachel M. Wade m. 15 Jul 1849 by Rev. Joseph Shane

Thomas, George W. and Henrietta Thomas m. 12 Jan 1841 by Rev. Samuel Keppler, lic. dated same day

Thomas, Henrietta, see "George W. Thomas," q.v.

Thomas, Joseph and Ann Weaver m. 26 Jul 1842 by Rev. Job Guest, lic. dated 25 Jul 1842

Thomas, Margaret, see "Virginia Thomas," q.v.

Thomas, Margaret Elizabeth, dau. of Capt. Samuel and Melicent C. Thomas, b. 1 Apr 1841, bapt. 5 May 1844 by Rev. Dr. George C. M. Roberts

Thomas, Mary and Marshall H. Ferguson m. 8 Aug 1847 by Rev. Isaac P. Cook

Thomas, Mary Rogers, dau. of David E. and Susan B. Thomas, b. 31 Dec 1845, bapt. 19 Nov 1847 by Rev. Dr. George C. M. Roberts

Thomas, Melicent (Millicent), see "Margaret E. Thomas" and ""Richard E. Thomas," q.v.

Thomas, Parker C. and Mary Cacey m. 15 Nov 1849 by Rev. Dr. George C. M. Roberts

Thomas, Rebecca, see "Benjamin B. Thomas," q.v.

Thomas, Richard Evalt, son of Capt. Samuel and Melicent C. Thomas, b. 27 Feb 1844, bapt. 5 May 1844 by Rev. Dr. George C. M. Roberts

Thomas, Samuel, see "Margaret E. Thomas" and ""Richard E. Thomas," q.v.

Thomas, Sarah E. and Tobias Stansbury m. 16 Sep 1842 by Rev. Henry Slicer, lic. dated same day

Thomas, Susan B., see "Florence S. Thomas" and "Mary R. Thomas," q.v.

Thomas, Thomas and Catherine R. Frazier m. 18 May 1845 by Rev. Dr. George C. M. Roberts

Thomas, Virginia, dau. of William and Margaret Thomas, b. 7 Nov 1843, bapt. same day by Rev. Dr. George C. M. Roberts

Thomas, Virginia E. and Paul E. Dorsey, both of Baltimore County, m. 21 Apr 1841 by Rev. Thomas Myers, lic. dated same day

Thomas, William, see "Virginia Thomas," q.v.

Thompson, Absolem C. C. and Sarah A. Hadaway m. 30 May 1844 by Rev. James Sewell, lic. dated same day

Thompson, Amelia and George Bunting, both of Baltimore County, m. 1 Apr 1841 by Rev. John Rice

Thompson, Carey Ann and Elisha Jackson m. 13 Jun 1848 by Rev. Isaac P. Cook

Thompson, Caroline and Edward Clavell m. 1 Feb 1848 by Rev. Stephen A. Roszel, lic. dated 30 Jan 1848 [Ed. Note: His last name looked more like "Claivell" in the church register, but the marriage notice in the Baltimore Sun gave their names as Edward Clavell and Caroline D. Thompson.]

Thompson, Charles H. and Catharine Williams m. 18 Jun 1849 by Rev. John S. Martin, lic. dated same day

Thompson, Deborah, d. 1849 (death noted in Class List) [Ed. Note: Death notice in the Baltimore Sun stated that Deborah D. Thompson, widow of John H. Thompson, d. 1 Aug 1849.]

Thompson, Elizabeth and Washington Gill m. 30 Apr 1843 by Rev. Dr. George C. M. Roberts

Thompson, Elizabeth and William D. Stanley, both of Baltimore County, m. ---- [date not given] by Rev. George D. Chenoweth, lic. dated 13 Mar 1842 [Ed. Note: Their marriage notice in the Baltimore Sun stated that William D. Stanley m. Elizabeth A. Thomson on 31 Mar 1850.]

Thompson, Francis and Abraham Stewart m. 1 Sep 1847 by Rev. James H. Brown, lic. dated 14 Aug 1847

Thompson, John H., see "Deborah Thompson," q.v.

Thompson, Jphar(?) A. and Margaret E. Farling m. 12 Nov 1847 by Rev. Stephen A. Roszel, lic. dated same day [Ed. Note: His first name is unusual as it is written in the church register. Their marriage notice in the Baltimore Sun gave his name only as J. A. Thompson.]

Thompson, Julian and Andrew Peyton m. 18 Feb 1841 by Rev. John Bear

Thompson, Margaret and William G. Delcher m. 28 May 1843 by Rev. Dr. George C. M. Roberts

Thompson, Marion A. and Van Courtland Secord m. 6 Jun 1849 by Rev. Dr. George C. M. Roberts

Thompson, Mary E. G. and Abraham G. Mott m. 4 May 1843 by Rev. Henry Slicer, lic. dated same day

Thompson, Mary Ellen and Nathan Webster Massey, both of Baltimore County, m. 20 Feb 1841 by Rev. John Rice

Thompson, Nancy Jane, dau. of William and Sarah Thompson, b. 28 Mar 1840, bapt. 27 Aug 1840 by Rev. Dr. George C. M. Roberts

Thompson, Oliver and Margaret Farlan m. 9 Mar 1847 by Rev. Joseph Shane

Thompson, Rachel, d. circa 1847-1850 (exact date not given in Record of Members)

Thompson, Rachel M. and Benjamin E. Gittings m. 2 Jul 1850 by Rev. Henry Slicer, lic. dated same day

Thompson, Sarah, see "Nancy J. Thompson," q.v.

Thompson, Sarah A. and Jesse W. Grimes m. 12 Nov 1849 by Rev. Aquila A. Reese, lic. dated 11 Nov 1849

Thompson, Sophia, d. -- Dec 1846 (death noted in Record of Members)

Thompson, Susannah and John W. Collins m. 29 Jan 1845 by Rev. James Sewell, lic. dated 22 Jan 1845

Thompson, William and Martha Debrow m. 4 May 1845 by Rev. Isaac P. Cook

Thompson, William, see "Nancy J. Thompson," q.v.

Thorn, Ann Maria and John Keys m. 5 Aug 1847 by Rev. Dr. George C. M. Roberts

Thornes, James and Ann Gray m. 17 Sep 1843 by Rev. Samuel Brison

Thorrington, William W. and Mary J. Lednum m. 25 May 1843 by Rev. Isaac P. Cook

Thorton, Sarah and John Willett m. 12 Nov 1847 by Rev. Benjamin F. Brooke

Thumlert, James Edwin, son of James E. and Jane Thumlert, b. 2 Jun 1842, bapt. 3 Feb 1850 by Rev. Dr. George C. M. Roberts

Thumlert, Peter Hepburn, son of James E. and Jane Thumlert, b. 17 Jul 1849, bapt. 3 Feb 1850 by Rev. Dr. George C. M. Roberts

Thumlert, William Henry, son of William Henry and Mary Jane Thumlert, b. 30 Nov 1848, bapt. 9 Jan 1849 by Rev. Dr. George C. M. Roberts

Tibbitt, Franklin J. D., son of Walter and Sarah Ann Tibbitt, b. 31 Aug 1839, bapt. 29 May 1842 by Rev. Henry Slicer

Tidings, Susan and Thomas Ford m. 14 May 1843 by Rev. Henry Slicer, lic. dated 13 May 1843

Tier, James and Amanda Marshall m. ---- [blank] by Rev. John S. Martin, lic. dated 17 Sep 1850 [Ed. Note: Their marriage notice in the Baltimore Sun stated James C. Tier m. Mary A. Marshall on 17 Sep 1850.]

Tier, Sarah Ann and William S. Espey m. 28 Nov 1843 by Rev. Henry Slicer, lic. dated same day

Tierny(?), Thomas A. Taylor, son of Elisha and Ann Maria Tierny(?), aged 14 years [b. 1826], b. Baltimore City, bapt. 1840 (exact date not given) by Rev. Gerard Morgan

Tierny(?), John E. Taylor, son of Elisha and Ann Maria Tierny(?), aged 10 months [b. c1839?], b. Baltimore City, bapt. 1840 (exact date not given) by Rev. Gerard Morgan

Tierny(?), John Henry Harrison, son of Elisha and Ann Maria Tierny (?), aged 3 months [b. 1840], b. Baltimore City, bapt. 1840 (exact date not given) by Rev. Gerard Morgan

Tilghman, Josephine and Joel Greenfield m. 5 Sep 1844 by Rev. Isaac P. Cook

Tilghman, Sarah E. and John W. Lambdin m. 29 Nov 1849 by Rev. Dr. George C. M. Roberts [*Ed. Note:* Her last name was misspelled "Tilgman" in the marriage register.]

Tilton, Ann and William B. Rimby m. 17 Sep 1844 by Rev. Isaac P. Cook

Tilyard, James, d. 1843 (death noted in Probationers Book)

Timanus, Amanda and Leonard R. Woolen, both of Baltimore County, m. 15 Sep 1840 by Rev. Bernard H. Nadal

Timanus, George and Margery, see "Sarah Hurley," q.v.

Timanus, Harriet Ann and James Sanks m. 27 Feb 1850 by Rev. Aquila A. Reese, lic. dated 26 Feb 1850

Timmerman, John and Rebecca J. Hebum(?) m. 18 Mar 1844 by Rev. Isaac P. Cook

Tindell, Ann Maria and John H. T. Morton m. 7 Jan 1844 by Rev. Dr. George C. M. Roberts

Tindle, Eliza Jane, dau. of Robert W. and Mary Elizabeth Tindle, b. 6 Aug 1839, bapt. 12 Jun 1840 by Rev. Dr. George C. M. Roberts

Tippett, Edwin Boswell, son of Rev. C. B. and Margaret Tippett, b. 2 Jul 1842, bapt. 25 Mar 1843 by Rev. Dr. George C. M. Roberts

Tippett, George Roberts, son of Rev. Charles B. and Margaret S. Tippett, b. 11 Jan 1847, bapt. 24 Jul 1848 by Rev. Dr. George C. M. Roberts

Tippett, James Henry, son of Rev. C. B. and Margaret Tippett, b. 14 Oct 1840, bapt. 16 Sep 1841 by Rev. Dr. George C. M. Roberts

Tipton, John and Rebecca Baxter m. 30 Apr 1848 by Rev. Isaac P. Cook

Tipton, Susan and Francis Ray m. 16 Mar 1841 by Rev. Joseph Shane

Tisdale, Lucius A. R. and Mahala Burnham m. 28 May 1843 by Rev. Henry Slicer, lic. dated 27 May 1843

Tiser, Thomas and Margaret Hill m. 5 Sep 1847 by Rev. Stephen A. Roszel, lic. dated 26 Aug 1847

Todd, Elizabeth and George W. Disney m. 16 Apr 1844 by Rev. Joseph Shane

Tolbart, Hannah E., see "Hannah Talbott," q.v.

Tolman, William and Sarah J. Mitchell m. 2 Jun 1844 by Rev. Dr. George C. M. Roberts

Tomblinson, Jane D. and Isaac W. Lansdale m. 14 Nov 1848 by Rev. Wesley Stevenson

Tomlinson, Martha Zela, dau. of William and Elizabeth Tomlinson, b. 8 Jul 1839, bapt. 10 Feb 1840 by Rev. Dr. George C. M. Roberts

Tongue, John W. (Rev.), of the Baltimore Annual Conference, and Miss Sophia Grauff(?) Price, of Baltimore County, m. 13 May 1846 by Rev. George Hildt, lic. dated 12 May 1846

Torrence, Ann Jane and James Gardner m. ---- [blank] by Rev. John S. Martin, lic. dated 15 Jan 1850 [*Ed. Note:* Their marriage notice in the *Baltimore Sun* stated James Gardiner m. Ann J. Torrance, dau. of William Torrance, on 23 Jan 1850.]

Tottle, Ann, d. 1845 (exact date not given in Record of Members)

Towes, Mary and James Lloyd m. 3 May 1842 by Rev. Henry Slicer, lic. dated 2 May 1842

Townsend, Martha Ann and John B. Jordan m. 1 Jan 1840 by Rev. John Bear

Townsend, Thomas, son of Thomas and Margaret Townsend, b. 25 Apr 1839, bapt. 17 Jan 1843 by Rev. Elisha D. Owen

Townshend, Susan and Peter Shaw m. 12 May 1847 by Rev. Stephen A. Roszel, lic. dated same day

Towson, James Franklin and Louisa Barker, both of Baltimore, MD, m. 6 Apr 1842 by Rev. John A. Hening

Towson, Mary E. and Lewis W. Essender m. 26 Nov 1850 by Rev. Henry Slicer, lic. dated 20 Nov 1850

Towson, Rebecca, d. circa 1847-1850 (exact date not given in Record of Members)

Towson, Sarah, d. circa 1840 (exact date not given in Class Record)

Tracy, Barbary A. and William M. Jury m. 29 May 1844 by Rev. James Sewell, lic. dated same day

Tracy, Benjamin and Elizabeth Morgan m. 31 Oct 1846 by Rev. Wesley Stevenson

Travers, Eliza Jane and Lewis D. Travers m. 3 Dec 1849 by Rev. Aquila A. Reese, lic. dated 1 Dec 1849

Travers, Elizabeth, d. circa 1849-1850 (exact date not given in Record of Members) [Ed. Note: Death notice in the Baltimore Sun stated that Elizabeth Travers, wife of John Travers, d. 21 Aug 1849.]

Travers, John, see "Elizabeth Travers," q.v.

Travers, Lewis D. and Eliza Jane Travers m. 3 Dec 1849 by Rev. Aquila A. Reese, lic. dated 1 Dec 1849

Travers, Priscilla S. and James B. Perry m. 21 Oct 1847 by Rev. Littleton F. Morgan, lic. dated same day

Travers, Priscilla and John R. Perkins m. 19 Dec 1848 by Rev. Dr. George C. M. Roberts

Travers, Samuel H. and Elizabeth Addison m. 11 Jan 1848 by Rev. Littleton F. Morgan, lic. dated same day

Traverse, Mary and Richard H. Hyatt m. 12 Nov 1849 by Rev. William Hirst, lic. dated same day

Travillo, Ann E. Williamson and Young Owens m. 17 Dec 1850 by Rev. Henry Slicer, lic. dated 16 Dec 1850

Treadway, Eliphalet L. and Susanna Wyman m. 14 Nov 1847 by Rev. Stephen A. Roszel, lic. dated 1 Nov 1847

Treakle, Joseph J. and Ann E. Starr m. 24 Dec 1850 by Rev. Henry Slicer, lic. dated 23 Dec 1850

Tredway, Nicholas and Mary A. Jemison m. 16 Feb 1843 by Rev. Isaac P. Cook

Tregg, Harriett and William Stansberry m. 22 Aug 1841 by Rev. Job Guest, lic. dated 21 Aug 1841

Trego, Elizabeth and Henry Hubbard m. 2 Apr 1843 by Rev. Henry Slicer, lic. dated 1 Mar 1843

Trenton, John R. and Rosetta Jarvis m. 20 Apr 1843 by Rev. Joseph Shane

Trepp, Thomas and Sarah Ann Howard m. 2 Nov 1843 by Rev. Joseph Shane

Tribbett, Hester, d. circa 1847 (death noted in Class List) [Ed. Note: Death notice in the Baltimore Sun stated that Hester Tribut d. 20 Feb 1848.]

Triger, Eliza and Robert Myers m. 24 Dec 1840 by Rev. John Bear

Trimble, Edward Norwood and Elizabeth A. Gott m. 19 Mar 1850 by Rev. Joseph Shane

Trippe, Rachel Elizabeth, dau. of Capt. Joseph and Sarah P. Trippe, b. 19 Jul 1843, bapt. 14 Aug 1843 by Rev. Dr. George C. M. Roberts

Troton, Ferdinand, son of Thomas and Eliza Troton, b. 29 Oct 1839, Fells Point, Baltimore City, bapt. 20 Feb 1840 by Rev. Samuel Keppler

Trott, Elizabeth and George Preston m. 30 Dec 1841 by Rev. Joseph Shane

Trott, Robert W. and V. Mary Dean, both of Baltimore County, m. 4 Oct 1843 by Rev. S. S. Roszel, lic. dated same day

Troxall, Ann Maria and Jacob Patterson m. 28 Jun 1849 by Rev. Aquila A. Reese, lic. dated 27 Jun 1849

Trumbo, Charles H. and Charlotte J. Holebrook, both of Baltimore County, m. ---- [date not given] by Rev. George Hildt, lic. dated 20 May 1845 [*Ed. Note:* Their marriage notice in the *Baltimore Sun* initially stated Charles H. Trumbo m. Charlotta I. Holbrook on 21 May 1845, but her name was later corrected to Charlotte J. Holbrook.]

Tucker, Ann, d. circa 1840 (exact date not given in Class Record)

Tucker, Benjamin and Elizabeth McKenny m. 17 Oct 1841 by Rev. Dr. George C. M. Roberts

Tucker, Eliza A. and Williams Richards, Jr. m. 16 Nov 1848 by Rev. Joseph Shane

Tucker, Evelinia, d. circa 1847-1850 (exact date not given in Record of Members)

Tucker, Frances E., dau. of Henry and Harriot Tucker, b. 13 Mar 1842, bapt. 4 Nov 1842 by Rev. Elisha D. Owen

Tucker, Greenbury and Hannah, see "Wesley J. Tucker," q.v.

Tucker, Harriet Ann, dau. of Greenbury and Hannah Tucker, b. 10 May 1834, bapt. 17 Oct 1841 by Rev. Dr. George C. M. Roberts

Tucker, Harriot and Henry, see "Frances E. Tucker," q.v.

Tucker, James F. and Alverta Peck, both of Baltimore County, m. 7 May 1846 by Rev. George Hildt, lic. dated 18 Apr 1846

Tucker, Mary J. and John B. Perkins m. 2 Jun 1845 by Rev. James Sewell, lic. dated same day

Tucker, Prudence, d. circa 1840-1847 (exact date not given in Record of Members)

Tucker, Wesley Jackson, son of Greenbury and Hannah Tucker, b. 9 Oct 1841, bapt. 17 Oct 1841 by Rev. Dr. George C. M. Roberts

Tudor, Edward Washington, son of John and Sarah Tudor, b. 10 Sep 1849, bapt. 17 Feb 1850 by Rev. Dr. George C. M. Roberts

Tudor, Louisa, dau. of John and Sarah Tudor, b. 2 Oct 1845, bapt. 7 Nov 1845 by Rev. Dr. George C. M. Roberts

Tudsworth, David Howard, son of David H. and Catherine Tudsworth, b. 31 Jul 1841, bapt. 13 Mar 1842 by Rev. Dr. George C. M. Roberts

Tull, Harriett H. and William H. Waters m. 24 Jan 1844 by Rev. Joseph Shane

Turfle, Susan and John Robison, both of Baltimore County, m. 17 Jan 1843 by Rev. Nelson Head

Turner, Charles and Eliza Jane Price, both of Baltimore County, m. ---- [date not given] by Rev. George D. Chenoweth, lic. dated 17 Feb 1842 [*Ed. Note:* Their marriage notice in the *Baltimore Sun* stated they were married on 17 Feb 1842.]

Turner, Dorritee, see "George W. Turner," q.v.

Turner, Edmond and Ann Miller m. 17 Jun 1844 by Rev. James Sewell, lic. dated 10 Jun 1844

Turner, Elizabeth A., see "Harry F. Turner," q.v.

Turner, Elizabeth Ann and Samuel Jeffry m. ---- [blank] by Rev. John S. Martin, lic. dated 15 Apr 1850

Turner, George and Betsey Bannen m. 20 Nov 1843 by Rev. Dr. George C. M.
Roberts

Turner, George J. and Mary S. Watkins m. 25 Nov 1849 by Rev. William Hirst, lic.
dated 17 Nov 1849

Turner, George Warner, son of Isaac W. and Dorritee Turner, b. 1 Mar 1840, bapt.
25 Jul 1841 by Rev. Isaac P. Cook

Turner, Harry Fowler, son of Robert and Elizabeth A. Turner, b. 2 Jan 1844, bapt.
6 Jan 1844 by Rev. Dr. George C. M. Roberts

Turner, John W. and Rachel McCauley m. 24 Dec 1846 by Rev. Dr. George C. M.
Roberts

Turner, Maria and George Gardner m. 20 Oct 1842 by Rev. Dr. George C. M.
Roberts

Turner, Mary Ann and William Simpson m. 13 May 1845 by Rev. Samuel Keppler
(date of lic. not recorded)

Turner, Matthew and Mahala, see "Susan B. Turner" and "William M. D. Turner,"
q.v.

Turner, Robert, see "Harry F. Turner," q.v.

Turner, Sarah Ann and Rev. Joseph S. Morris, both of Baltimore County, m. 1 Oct
1840 by Rev. Thomas Myers, lic. dated 29 Sep 1840

Turner, Susan Amanda and Samuel Maccubbin m. 14 Mar 1849 by Rev. Isaac P.
Cook

Turner, Susan Bankard, dau. of Matthew W. and Mahala Turner, b. 14 Jun 1847,
bapt. 9 Sep 1847 by Rev. Dr. George C. M. Roberts

Turner, William H. H. and Hester Ann Rusk m. 15 Nov 1843 by Rev. Henry Slicer,
lic. dated 13 Nov 1843

Turner, William Morris Duely, son of Matthew and Mahala Turner, b. 19 Feb 1841,
bapt. 22 Aug 1841 by Rev. Dr. George C. M. Roberts

Turner, Zacharia and Ann Elisabeth Cook m. 15 Nov 1841 by Rev. Gerard Morgan,
lic. dated 13 Nov 1841

Turpin, Caroline Keturah, dau. of Joshua and Ann Turpin, b. 24 Mar 1838, bapt.
30 Aug 1840 by Rev. Thomas Myers

Turrington, Margaret and Alexander Wallace m. 9 Nov 1840 by Rev. Samuel
Keppler, lic. dated same day

Tutchton, Nathan and Ann S. Schultz m. 9 Mar 1843 by Rev. Henry Slicer, lic.
dated 8 Mar 1843

Tutsel, Richard J. and Elizabeth Fardwell m. 25 Jul 1842 by Rev. Samuel Brison

Tuttle, Columbus and Anna P. Ginnevan m. 7 Jan 1845 by Rev. Dr. George C. M.
Roberts

Tweedall, John and Mary Gaunt m. 19 Aug 1849 by Rev. William Hirst, lic. dated
18 Aug 1849

Tweedy, Jacob and Caroline Peregoy m. 17 Jan 1850 by Rev. Joseph Shane

Twiford, Virginia A. and Sewell F. Lane m. 24 Mar 1843 by Rev. Isaac P. Cook

Twigg, Mary and Charles Poultner m. 27 Mar 1845 by Rev. Joseph Shane

Tydings, E. V. and Samuel Davis m. 6 Apr 1848 by Rev. William Hirst

Tyler, Euphen Elmira, dau. of George and Elizabeth Taylor, b. -- Apr 1845, bapt.
20 Sep 1846 by Rev. Samuel Keppler

Tyler, George M. Dallas, son of Joseph and Rosanna Tyler, b. 7 Jan 1845, bapt. 15
Sep 1845 by Rev. Dr. George C. M. Roberts

Tyson, Laura E. and Robert A. Greer m. 21 Jul 1847 by Rev. Dr. George C. M. Roberts

Tyson, Thomas and Albensinda(?) Cline m. 13 Jan 1845 by Rev. James Sewell, lic. dated same day

"U.... L.... and M.... O. J...., G. H....offd." m. 4 Oct 1848, lic. dated 25 Oct *[sic]* 1848 [*Ed. Note:* This was written, as shown here with the incomplete names, among the marriages performed by Rev. Stephen A. Roszel.]

Uhler, Eliza P. and Rev. Matthew G. Hamilton m. 9 Jan 1843 at the house of Dr. Davis in Baltimore by Rev. Beverly Waugh, lic. dated 7 Jan 1843

Underwood, Noah, son of Albert and Elizabeth Underwood, b. 28 Apr 1842, bapt. 3 Oct 1842 by Rev. William Prettyman

Ungerer, William F. and Elenora Sadtler m. ---- [blank] by Rev. John S. Martin, lic. dated 20 Apr 1849 [*Ed. Note:* Their marriage notice in the *Baltimore Sun* stated that William T. Ungerer m. Eleanora Sadler on 20 Apr 1849.]

Uppercoe, Sarah Ann and Thomas Kirkley m. 20 Aug 1846 by Rev. Littleton F. Morgan, lic. dated same day

Upton, John Teackle, son of Benjamin and Elizabeth Upton, b. 27 Feb 1846, bapt. 15 Sep 1846 by Rev. Dr. George C. M. Roberts

Valiant, Arianna and William Slate m. 24 Jan 1840 by Rev. Joseph Shane

Valiant, Rebecca S. and William A. Rippey m. ---- [blank] by Rev. John S. Martin, lic. dated 28 Jan 1850 [*Ed. Note:* Their marriage notice in the *Baltimore Sun* stated that William A. Rippey m. Rebecca S. Valiant, dau. of John Valiant, on 28 Jan 1850.]

Valient, John F. and Sarah Jane Walker m. 6 Oct 1846 by Rev. Littleton F. Morgan, lic. dated 5 Oct 1846

Van Fossen, David and Catherine Kerlinger m. 27 Mar 1849 by Rev. Aquila A. Reese, lic. dated 26 Mar 1849

Van Trump, John and Margaret Ann Despeaux m. 20 Oct 1850 by Rev. John S. Martin, lic. dated 17 Oct 1850

Vanderford, Margaret Ann and Lovern M. Personett m. 6 Jul 1840 by Rev. Joseph Shane

Vanderford, Mary and Edward Hamilton m. 19 Feb 1846 by Rev. Dr. George C. M. Roberts

Vanderlille, Marthaetta, dau. of Stephen and Julia Vanderlille, b. 14 Jan 1840, bapt. 4 Aug 1840 by Rev. Dr. George C. M. Roberts

Vansant, Susan, see "Susan Varsans," q.v.

Vanwagner, John Washington, son of John and Julian Vanwagner, b. 10 Feb 1840, bapt. 22 Apr 1840 by Rev. Joseph Shane

Varina, Edward C. and Mary E. Disney m. 15 May 1842 by Rev. Dr. George C. M. Roberts

Varina, Thomas H. and Sarah Ann Wilkerson m. 8 May 1843 by Rev. Samuel Brison

Varsans, Susan and James B. Alderson, both of Baltimore County, m. ---- [date not given] by Rev. George Hildt, lic. dated 13 Jan 1846 [*Ed. Note:* Their marriage notice in the *Baltimore Sun* gave her name as Susan Vansant and the marriage date as 14 Jan 1846.]

Vaughan, Amanda M. and James W. Sullivan m. 1 Nov 1849 by Rev. William Hirst, lic. dated 31 Oct 1849

Vaughn, Daniel D. and Maria Allen m. 27 Oct 1841 by Rev. Gerard Morgan, lic. dated same day

Venables, Benjamin and Tabitha Ewell, both of Baltimore County, m. 29 Oct 1844 by Rev. William Hamilton

Vernon, Roseana and George W. C. McCabe m. 11 Feb 1842 by Rev. Joseph Shane

Vetry, Frances E. and Henry Buckmaster m. ---- [blank] by Rev. John S. Martin, lic. dated 21 Mar 1850

Vickers, Ann L. and Thomas W. Kendall m. 2 May 1849 by Rev. Joseph Shane

Vickers, Ann and William Snook m. 27 Dec 1843 by Rev. Dr. George C. M. Roberts

Vickers, Margaret M. and William T. Harris m. 8 Nov 1848 by Rev. Dr. George C. M. Roberts

Vickers, Margaret S. H. and Michael Cole m. ---- [blank] by Rev. John S. Martin, lic. dated 13 Mar 1850 [*Ed. Note:* Their marriage notice in the *Baltimore Sun* stated they married on 31 Mar 1850.]

Vickers, Mary Ann and William Brady m. 29 Nov 1840 by Rev. Samuel Keppler, lic. dated 23 Nov 1840

Vickory, Charles B. and Emilie A. Gregory m. 5 Dec 1847 by Rev. Stephen A. Roszel, lic. dated 4 Dec 1847

Vincent, Mary Louisa, dau. of John and Mary Vincent, b. 15 May 1840, bapt. 3 Dec 1840 by Rev. Dr. George C. M. Roberts

Viney, Mary and James H. Plummer m. 12 Aug 1849 by Rev. Dr. George C. M. Roberts

Vinsen, Susan and William T. Spies m. 6 Jan 1850 by Rev. William Hirst, lic. dated 4 Jan 1850

Vinton, Olivia Elenor, dau. of Rev. Robert S. and Juliet M. Vinton, b. 23 Oct 1845, bapt. 14 Nov 1845 by Rev. Dr. George C. M. Roberts

Visher, John and Louisa Cunoal m. 27 Mar 1845 by Rev. Isaac P. Cook

Voice, Julia Ann and Thomas A. Lennox m. 4 May 1843 by Rev. Dr. George C. M. Roberts

Von Hollan, John and Sarah Ellen Ward m. 1 Oct 1848 by Rev. Dr. George C. M. Roberts

Wade, Ann O. and John Bryden (Buyden?) m. 16 Dec 1841 by Rev. Joseph Shane

Wade, Joseph G. and Mary Larimer m. 17 Dec 1843 by Rev. Phillip B. Reese (date of lic. not recorded)

Wade, Rachel M. and George M. Thomas m. 15 Jul 1849 by Rev. Joseph Shane

Wadlow, Frances and William Lyons m. 18 Apr 1848 by Rev. Stephen A. Roszel, lic. dated same day

Wadman, Lucretia and Richard Cole m. 16 Jan 1843 by Rev. Joseph Shane

Waggner, Isaiah, b. 8 Oct 1819, bapt. 27 Sep 1846 by Rev. Samuel Keppler

Waggner, John H. and Margaret A. Peal m. 10 Nov 1844 by Rev. James Sewell, lic. dated 9 Nov 1844

Waggner, Josiah and Ann E. Horney m. 9 Nov 1845 by Rev. James Sewell, lic. dated 7 Nov 1845

Waggnier, Lemuel and Ann C. Berry m. 26 Dec 1844 by Rev. James Sewell, lic. dated same day

Wagner, Elizabeth and Richard Wise m. 21 Jan 1846 by Rev. James Sewell, lic. dated same day

Waite, Ann Augusta, dau. of Richard C. and Jane Waite, b. 2 Sep 1840, bapt. 27 Oct 1840 by Rev. Charles B. Tippett

Waite, Mary Clarissa, dau. of Richard B. and Elizabeth Waite, b. 3 Oct 1845, bapt. 1 May 1850 by Rev. Dr. George C. M. Roberts

Waite, Samuel Ringold, son of William W. and Louisa M. Waite, b. 15 Aug 1846, bapt. 19 Aug 1847 by Rev. Dr. George C. M. Roberts

Waits, Jane, d. circa 1844-1847 (exact date not given in Record of Members)

Wales, Elizabeth Jane, dau. of Joseph and Mary Wales, b. 11 Nov 1830, Fells Point, Baltimore City, bapt. 13 Apr 1840 by Rev. Samuel Keppler

Walker, Ann and Robert Keith m. 26 Dec 1844 by Rev. James Sewell, lic. dated 13 Dec 1844

Walker, Elizabeth, d. circa 1840 (exact date not given in Class Record)

Walker, Elizabeth and Samuel Peacock m. 12 Jan 1843 by Rev. Job Guest, lic. dated same day

Walker, James and Mary North m. 6 Sep 1843 by Rev. Henry Slicer, lic. dated same day

Walker, Jesse and Victorine Graham m. 5 Aug 1845 by Rev. Isaac P. Cook

Walker, John and Elizabeth Mitchell m. 16 Dec 1841 by Rev. Dr. George C. M. Roberts

Walker, Joseph S. and Margaret Duhaey m. 6 Jul 1845 by Rev. Isaac P. Cook

Walker, Luther C. and Mary Jane Wardell m. 1 Aug 1848 by Rev. Dr. George C. M. Roberts

Walker, Margaret and Arthar [sic] Onell m. ---- [no date given] by Rev. John Miller, lic. dated 19 Jun 1850

Walker, Mary, d. circa 1847 (death noted in Class List)

Walker, Sarah Jane and John F. Valient m. 6 Oct 1846 by Rev. Littleton F. Morgan, lic. dated 5 Oct 1846

Walker, Thomas and Mary Kirby m. 11 Jun 1849 by Rev. Dr. George C. M. Roberts

Walkins (Watkins?), Robert Emory, son of Thon (Thos.?) and Elizabeth Walkins (Watkins?), b. 17 Jan 1842, bapt. -- Feb 1842 by Rev. Robert Emory

Wall, Ann and James B. Andrews, both of Baltimore County, m. 10 Mar 1845 by Rev. William Hamilton

Wall, John F. and Hester Ann Grim m. 2 Jul 1850 by Rev. Henry Slicer, lic. dated same day

Wall, John Melchor, son of John Melchor and Ann Reb [sic] Wall, b. 16 Jul 1840, bapt. -- Oct 1840 by Rev. Charles B. Tippett

Wallace, Alexander and Margaret Turrington m. 9 Nov 1840 by Rev. Samuel Keppler, lic. dated same day

Wallace, Elizabeth Gatt, dau. of William and Sarah Wallace, b. 3 Mar 1838, Baltimore City, bapt. 30 May 1841 by Rev. Gerard Morgan

Wallace, James Alexander, son of Alexander and Margaret Wallace, b. 28 Apr 1842, bapt. 12 Jun 1842 by Rev. Henry Slicer

Wallace, John, son of John and Emily Wallace, b. 29 Oct 1839, bapt. 19 May 1840 by Rev. John Bear

Wallace, Joseph, see "Laura V. Wallace," q.v.

Wallace, Laura Virginia, dau. of Dr. Joseph and Elizabeth Wallace, b. 21 Feb 1838, bapt. 9 Oct 1846 by Rev. Dr. George C. M. Roberts

Wallace, Margaret and Edward Riggs m. 13 Dec 1848 by Rev. Stephen A. Roszel, lic. dated same day

Wallace, Ruth Ann and Samuel G. Coleman m. 23 Mar 1847 by Rev. Isaac P. Cook

Wallace, William, see "Elizabeth G. Wallace," q.v.

Waller, Elizabeth and William H. Mitchell m. 31 Oct 1849 by Rev. William Hirst, lic. dated same day

Wallis, John and Eliza Ann Eaisbouns(?) m. 19 Mar 1846 by Rev. Joseph Shane

Walls, George W. d. circa 1844-1847 (exact date not given in Record of Members)

Walls, Mary, d. circa 1845-1847 (exact date not given in Record of Members) [Ed. Note: Death notice in the Baltimore Sun stated that a Mary Wall d. 15 Mar 1846.]

Walmsley, Catharine and George Washington Shiningham m. 25 Jul 1848 by Rev. Stephen A. Roszel, lic. dated 24 Jul 1848

Walmsley, Isaac, d. circa 1841-1842 (exact date not given in Record of Members) [Ed. Note: Death notice in the Baltimore Sun stated that Isaac Walmsley d. 1 Jul 1842.]

Walmsley, James T. and Mary E. Ellis m. 30 May 1850 by Rev. Henry Slicer, lic. dated same day [Ed. Note: His last name was spelled "Wamsley" in the church register.]

Walmsley, Robert M. and Harriet McCauley m. 28 Oct 1841 by Rev. Dr. George C. M. Roberts

Walsh, John A. and Cornelia Legoe m. 18 Jul 1843 by Rev. Henry Slicer, lic. dated same day

Walter, Cornelia Landstreet, dau. of George K. and Albina L. Walter, b. 29 Oct 1847, bapt. same day by Rev. Dr. George C. M. Roberts

Walter, John and Maria, see "Maria Walters," q.v.

Walter, Louisa and Rufus Bennett m. 11 Oct 1849 by Rev. Aquila A. Reese, lic. dated 10 Oct 1849

Walter, Margaretta, dau. of George K. and Albina L. Walter, b. 3 Jan 1846, bapt. 29 May 1847 by Rev. Dr. George C. M. Roberts

Walters, Maria, d. circa 1847-1848 (exact date not given in Record of Members) [Ed. Note: Death notice in the Baltimore Sun stated that Maria Walter, wife of John Walter and dau. of Hiram Cochran, d. 28 Feb 1847.]

Walters, Mary Anna, dau. of William C. and Margaret M. Walters, b. 7 Jan 1847, bapt. 24 Jul 1848 by Rev. Dr. George C. M. Roberts

Walters, Rebecca and Joseph Weaver m. 13 Apr 1847 by Rev. Joseph Shane

Walton, Ann, d. 1841 (death noted in Class List) [Ed. Note: Death notice in the Baltimore Sun stated that Ann Walton, wife of Edward Walton and dau. of Samuel and Elizabeth Kretch, d. 23 Feb 1841.]

Walton, Edward, see "Ann Walton," q.v.

Walton, John and Diana Gladding m. 17 Nov 1847 by Rev. Dr. George C. M. Roberts

Walton, Mary Ann, dau. of Elijah and Elizabeth Walton (residence on Lombard St. near the corner of Hanover St.), b. 14 Oct 1842, bapt. 11 Jul 1857 by Rev. William B. Edwards

Walton, Robert James, son of Elijah and Elizabeth Walton (residence on Lombard St. near the corner of Hanover St.), b. 23 Dec 1847, bapt. 11 Jul 1857 by Rev. William B. Edwards

Walton, Sarah Elizabeth, dau. of Elijah and Elizabeth Walton (residence on Lombard St. near the corner of Hanover St.), b. 19 Mar 1844, bapt. 11 Jul 1857 by Rev. William B. Edwards

Walts, Sarah and Francis Hart m. 16 May 1847 by Rev. Joseph Shane

Walworthy, John and Sarah Green m. 6 Jan 1846 by Rev. Dr. George C. M. Roberts

Wane, Elizabeth, d. circa 1840 (exact date not given in Class Record)

Wanel, Samuel and Rachel Morris m. 24 Jul 1843 by Rev. Dr. George C. M. Roberts

Ward, Arietta Jedavie, dau. of William J. and Harriet Ward, b. 24 Jan 1836, bapt. 13 Sep 1841 by Rev. Dr. George C. M. Roberts

Ward, E. A. and B. F. Bennett m. 23 Aug 1848 by Rev. William Hirst [*Ed. Note:* Their marriage notice in the *Baltimore Sun* states Benjamin F. Bennett and E. A. Ward m. 24 Aug 1848.]

Ward, Edward J., see "Sarah Elizabeth Ward," q.v.

Ward, Elizabeth W. and John J. Marselas m. 4 Sep 1843 by Rev. Henry Slicer, lic. dated same day

Ward, John W. and Charlotte M. Jones m. 30 Jul 1844 by Rev. James Sewell, lic. dated same day

Ward, Mary Jane and William Casey m. 6 Nov 1842 by Rev. Job Guest, lic. dated 5 Nov 1842

Ward, Sarah Elizabeth, dau. of Edward J. and Mary E. Ward, b. 9 Dec 1848, bapt. 13 May 1849 by Rev. Dr. George C. M. Roberts

Ward, Sarah Ellen and John Von Hollan m. 1 Oct 1848 by Rev. Dr. George C. M. Roberts

Ward, Sarah J. and James G. McCutchen m. 29 Feb 1844 by Rev. Joseph Shane

Ward, William, see "Arrietta J. Ward," q.v.

Wardell, Mary Jane and Luther C. Walker m. 1 Aug 1848 by Rev. Dr. George C. M. Roberts

Warfield, Oliver Charles, son of William and Sarah Jane Warfield, b. 20 May 1841, bapt. 19 Jun 1841 by Rev. Robert Emory

Warfield, Rufus and Sarah Ann Wells m. 1 Oct 1846 by Rev. Wesley Stevenson

Warfield, Sarah E. and James L. Chapline m. 9 May 1844 by Rev. Joseph Shane

Waring, Basil and Elizabeth, see "Mary Jane Keppler," q.v.

Warner, Elizabeth, d. 1844 (exact date not given in Record of Members) [*Ed. Note:* Death notice in the *Baltimore Sun* stated that Elizabeth Warner, wife of Richard Warner, d. 11 Aug 1844.]

Warner, Richard and Elizabeth Ann Holtstein, both of Baltimore County, m. 21 Sep 1842 by Rev. Nelson Head

Warns, Mary F. and John W. Davis m. 21 Dec 1848 by Rev. Wesley Stevenson

Warren, Charles and Mary Jane Cudlipp m. 14 Oct 1848 by Rev. Isaac P. Cook

Warrington, Charles Francis James, son of John E. W. and Susan Ann James Warrington, b. 8 Oct 1849, bapt. 7 Nov 1856 by Rev. Dr. George C. M. Roberts

Warrington, Elizabeth M. and Frances E. Quarley m. 19 Feb 1844 by Rev. Samuel Brison

Warrington, John E. and Susan A. James m. 18 Nov 1846 by Rev. Dr. George C. M. Roberts

Wasmus, Frederick Henry and Elizabeth Corsey m. 2 Jun 1845 by Rev. Dr. George C. M. Roberts

Watchman, Esther and Emanuel Corbitt m. 9 Oct 1849 by Rev. Dr. George C. M. Roberts

Watchman, Margaret and Robert McClean m. 16 Apr 1850 by Rev. Dr. George C. M. Roberts

Waters, Elizabeth and John W. Clark m. 28 Aug 1845 by Rev. Dr. George C. M. Roberts

Waters, Elizabeth, d. circa 1845 (exact date not given in Record of Members) [Ed. Note: Death notice in the Baltimore Sun stated that Elizabeth Waters, widow of Richard Waters and mother of Zebulon Waters, d. 17 Sep 1845.]

Waters, James B., see "Joshua T. Waters," q.v.

Waters, James Nicholas, son of John Henry and Elizabeth Waters, aged 10 months [sic], bapt. 1 Nov 1840 by Rev. Charles B. Tippett. See "John Henry Waters," q.v.

Waters, John Henry, son of John Henry and Elizabeth Waters, aged 11 months [sic], bapt. 1 Nov 1840 by Rev. Charles B. Tippett. See "James Nicholas Waters," q.v.

Waters, Joshua Trimer, son of James B. and Emily Jane Waters, b. 20 Nov 1843, bapt. 24 Nov 1843 by Rev. Dr. George C. M. Roberts

Waters, Letitia A. and George W. Woodrow m. 14 Oct 1847 by Rev. Dr. George C. M. Roberts

Waters, Mary E. and Jacob Lehmen m. 30 Apr 1846 by Rev. Littleton F. Morgan, lic. dated 27 Apr 1846

Waters, Richard, see "Elizabeth Waters," q.v.

Waters, William H. and Harriett H. Tull m. 24 Jan 1844 by Rev. Joseph Shane

Waters, Zebulon, see "Elizabeth Waters," q.v.

Watkins (Walkins?), Robert Emory, son of Thon (Thos.?) and Elizabeth Watkins (Walkins?), b. 17 Jan 1842, bapt. -- Feb 1842 by Rev. Robert Emory

Watkins, Elizabeth, dau. of Nicholas E. and Mary W. Watkins, b. 6 Mar 1842, bapt. 13 Oct 1851 by Rev. Dr. George C. M. Roberts

Watkins, Francis Dungan, son of Thomas C. and Elizabeth A. Watkins, b. 25 Mar 1847, bapt. 6 Apr 1848 by Rev. Dr. George C. M. Roberts

Watkins, Gassaway, d. circa 1840 (exact date not given in Record of Members) [Ed. Note: Death notice in the Baltimore Sun stated that Gassaway Watkins d. 8 Sep 1840.]

Watkins, James and Mary Kane m. 17 Jun 1845 by Rev. James Sewell, lic. dated 16 Jun 1845

Watkins, John H., see "Mary F. H. Watkins," q.v.

Watkins, Louis J. and Ann Hardy m. 20 Apr 1843 by Rev. Dr. George C. M. Roberts

Watkins, Margaret Fanny, dau. of Nicholas E. and Mary W. Watkins, b. 13 May 1847, bapt. 13 Oct 1851 by Rev. Dr. George C. M. Roberts

Watkins, Mary Frances Hendly, dau. of John H. and Maria Ann Watkins, b. 21 May 1841, bapt. 3 Jan 1842 by Rev. Dr. George C. M. Roberts

Watkins, Mary S. and George J. Turner m. 25 Nov 1849 by Rev. William Hirst, lic. dated 17 Nov 1849

Watkins, Mary Wyan, dau. of Nicholas E. and Mary W. Watkins, b. 11 Feb 1838, bapt. 13 Oct 1851 by Rev. Dr. George C. M. Roberts

Watkins, Nicholas E., see "Elizabeth Watkins" and "Margaret F. Watkins" and "Mary W. Watkins" and "Rebecca W. Watkins" and "Thomas M. Watkins" and "William E. Watkins," q.v.

Watkins, Noble G. and Adeline Logan m. 10 Dec 1848 by Rev. Joseph Shane

Watkins, Rebecca Watters, dau. of Nicholas E. and Mary W. Watkins, b. 11 Dec 1839, bapt. 13 Oct 1851 by Rev. Dr. George C. M. Roberts

Watkins, Thomas Montgomery, son of Nicholas E. and Mary W. Watkins, b. 5 Mar 1845, bapt. 13 Oct 1851 by Rev. Dr. George C. M. Roberts

Watkins, Thomas B. and Ann E. Bowen m. 7 Apr 1846 by Rev. Dr. George C. M. Roberts

Watkins, Thomas C., see "Francis D. Watkins," q.v.

Watkins, William C., see "William F. Watkins," q.v.

Watkins, William J. and Margaret Ann Jubb m. 28 Jun 1846 by Rev. Joseph Shane

Watkins, William Edwin, son of Nicholas E. and Mary W. Watkins, b. 6 Sep 1849, bapt. 13 Oct 1851 by Rev. Dr. George C. M. Roberts

Watkins, William Francis, son of William C. and Margaret W. Watkins, b. 15 Jan 1850, bapt. 24 Aug 1851 by Rev. Dr. George C. M. Roberts

Watson, Cassandra, d. circa 1847-1850 (exact date not given in Record of Members)

Watson, Emily and Daniel West m. 20 Apr 1847 by Rev. Isaac P. Cook

Watson, Henry H. and Susannah Dungan m. 15 Jun 1847 by Rev. Dr. George C. M. Roberts

Watson, James Edward and Sally Kent m. 29 Jun 1841 by Rev. Job Guest, lic. dated same day

Watson, John, see "William G. F. Watson," q.v.

Watson, Mahala and Charles F. Burnham m. 9 Sep 1840 by Rev. Samuel Keppler, lic. dated same day

Watson, Margaret, d. circa 1840-1847 (exact date not given in Record of Members)

Watson, William George Francis, son of John and Susannah Watson, b. 24 Oct 1841, bapt. 28 Nov 1841 by Rev. William Prettyman

Watters, Elizabeth and Denis [sic] Wesley m. 18 Apr 1844 by Rev. Joseph Merriken

Watters, James A. G. and Charlotte J. Spencer, both of Baltimore County, m. 23 Feb 1843 by Rev. Nelson Head

Watts, John, son of John and Ann Watts, b. 14 Mar 1840, Fells Point, Baltimore City, bapt. 13 Apr 1840 by Rev. John Alday

Watts, Joseph and Mary Ellen Wright m. 13 Nov 1844 by Rev. Joseph Shane

Watts, Mary Elizabeth (adult), b. ---- [blank], Fells Point, Baltimore City, bapt. 13 Apr 1840 by Rev. John Alday

Waugh, B., see "William Mason" and "George W. Zeigler," q.v.

Waugh, Henrietta and James B. Dodson m. 28 Sep 1840 at her father's house in Washington, D.C. by Rev. Beverly Waugh, lic. dated same day

Waugh, Henrietta M., d. circa 1845 (exact date not given in Record of Members) [Ed. Note: Death notice in the Baltimore Sun stated that Henrietta Waugh, niece of Jonathan Roberts, d. 17 Jun 1845.]

Weathers, Joseph S. and Araminta Graff m. 4 Oct 1842 by Rev. Job Guest, lic. dated -- Oct 1842

Weathers, Sarah Elizabeth, dau. of Joseph and Araminta Weathers, b. 2 Nov ---- [blank], bapt. 30 May 1844 by Rev. James Sewell

Weaver, Ann and Joseph Thomas m. 26 Jul 1842 by Rev. Job Guest, lic. dated 25 Jul 1842

Weaver, Catharine and James Earpe m. 10 Apr 1849 by Rev. Isaac P. Cook

Weaver, Elizabeth, see "Ursilla Weaver," q.v.

Weaver, Joseph and Rebecca Walters m. 13 Apr 1847 by Rev. Joseph Shane

Weaver, Mary Ellen, dau. of William and Mary Weaver, b. 4 Jul 1840, bapt. 12 Sep 1842 by Rev. Elisha D. Owen

Weaver, Ursilla, dau. of Elizabeth Weaver, b. 18 Dec 1847, bapt. 31 Dec 1847 by Rev. Dr. George C. M. Roberts

Weaver, William, see "Mary E. Weaver," q.v.

Webb, Charles Jr. and Hester Cox, both of Baltimore County, m. 7 Oct 1844 by Rev. William Hamilton

Webb, Jacob H. and Eliza Ann Hacket m. 23 Mar 1844 by Rev. Isaac P. Cook

Webb, Rebecca and James Hudson, both of Baltimore County, m. 10 Feb 1846 by Rev. George Hildt, lic. dated same day

Webb, Timon [sic] Watson, child of ---- [blank], b. -- Jul 1848, bapt. 1849 (exact date not given) by Rev. John S. Martin

Webb, William J. and Sarah J. Elder m. 3 Oct 1850 by Rev. Joseph Shane

Weeden (Weedon), Ann R. and Robert B. Hampton m. 12 Dec 1845 by Rev. Dr. George C. M. Roberts

Weeden, Mary Ellen, dau. of Thomas and Mary Weeden, b. 8 Aug 1840 (twin of Thomas James Weeden) Baltimore City, bapt. 29 Jan 1841 by Rev. Samuel Keppler

Weeden, Thomas James, son of Thomas and Mary Weeden, b. 8 Aug 1840 (twin of Mary Ellen Weeden), Baltimore City, bapt. 29 Jan 1841 by Rev. Samuel Keppler

Weeks, John S. and Margaret Kirkland m. 16 Oct 1850 at the house of her father in Baltimore by Rev. Beverly Waugh, lic. dated 14 Oct 1850

Weems, Georgianna, dau. of Capt. Mason L. and Matilda Weems, b. 27 May 1845, bapt. 8 Jul 1848 by Rev. Dr. George C. M. Roberts

Weems, Mason Locke, son of Capt. Mason L. and Matilda Weems, b. 9 Jun 1850, bapt. 16 Jul 1850 by Rev. Dr. George C. M. Roberts

Weems, Matilda Sparrows, dau. of Capt. Mason L. and Matilda Weems, b. 8 Jun 1848, bapt. 8 Jul 1848 by Rev. Dr. George C. M. Roberts

Weems, Sutton J. and Cassandra S. Dare m. 10 Dec 1845 by Rev. Dr. George C. M. Roberts

Weivelle, Charlotte and John Ireland m. 27 Jul 1843 by Rev. Dr. George C. M. Roberts

Welch, John, see "Sarah Ann Corner," q.v.

Welch, Sarah Ann and Baptist Mezick Corner m. 14 Jan 1841 by Rev. Samuel Keppler, lic. dated 12 Jan 1841

Welch, Sarah Rebecca, dau. of John and Mary P. Welch, b. 5 Dec 1846, Baltimore, bapt. 11 May 1847 by Rev. Stephen A. Roszel

Welch, William A. and Ann Emma Shaffer m. 10 Jun 1845 by Rev. Samuel Keppler (date of lic. not recorded)

Weldon, Sarah, d. 19 Jun 1847 (death noted in Record of Members) [Ed. Note: Death notice in the Baltimore Sun verified that Sarah Weldon d. 19 Jun 1847.]

Wellen, Mary Amanda and James Harris m. 6 Sep 1846 by Rev. Dr. George C. M. Roberts

Wellender, Maria J., dau. of Thomas W. and Mary E. Wellender, b. 30 Apr 1847, bapt. 23 Sep 1849 by Rev. John S. Martin

Wellender, Mary E., dau. of Thomas W. and Mary E. Wellender, b. 18 Mar 1849, bapt. 23 Sep 1849 by Rev. John S. Martin

Welling, Sarah Ann and George W. Johnson m. 19 Jul 1849 by Rev. Dr. George C. M. Roberts

Wells, Andrew, see "Emma E. Wells," q.v.

Wells, Benjamin, d. 1841 (death noted in Class List) [Ed. Note: Death notice in the Baltimore Sun stated that a Benjamin T. Wells, son of Peter and Eliza Wells, d. 22 Sep 1841.]

Wells, Emila Willing, dau. of John W. and Georgiana Wells, b. 27 Jan 1844, bapt. 1 May 1844 by Rev. James Sewell

Wells, Emma Eliot, dau. of Andrew and Elizabeth Wells, b. 8 Apr 1843, bapt. 1 May 1844 by Rev. James Sewell

Wells, John W., see "Emila W. Wells," q.v.

Wells, Margarett and Rezin Shipley m. 28 Apr 1844 by Rev. Joseph Shane

Wells, Nathaniel B. and Ann L. Louderman m. 23 Apr 1850 by Rev. Henry Slicer, lic. dated same day

Wells, Peter, d. circa 1849-1850 (death noted in Class List) [Ed. Note: Death notice in the Baltimore Sun stated that Peter Wells d. 15 Oct 1850.] See "Benjamin Wells," q.v.

Wells, Rachel and Frederick Caples m. 28 Jan 1841 by Rev. Joseph Shane

Wells, Sarah Ann and Rufus Warfield m. 1 Oct 1846 by Rev. Wesley Stevenson

Wells, Susan and Frederick Byers m. 27 Jun 1844 by Rev. Isaac P. Cook

Wells, William and Deborah Fort m. 11 Feb 1844 by Rev. Joseph Shane

Welsh, Alonzo and Susan Morgan m. 28 Feb 1849 by Rev. Joseph Shane

Welsh, Lewis E., son of William and Sarah Welsh, aged 3 weeks, bapt. 7 Jan 1840 by Rev. Gerard Morgan

Welsh, Lucretia A. and Joseph F. Skillman m. 24 Sep 1849 by Rev. William Hirst, lic. dated same day

Welsh, Thomas Edward, son of Edward and Martha Welsh, b. -- Mar 1840, bapt. 20 Sep 1840 by Rev. Thomas Myers

Welsh, William, see "Lewis E. Welsh," q.v.

Welsh, William Charles and Mary Jane Siscoe m. 28 Sep 1845 by Rev. Isaac P. Cook

Wempsat, Mary Ann and Isaiah Holland m. 15 Apr 1844 by Rev. Joseph Merriken

Wentworth, Abigail Catherine, dau. of Thomas and Ann Wentworth, b. 16 Jun 1843, bapt. 16 Jul 1843 by Rev. Dr. George C. M. Roberts

Wentworth, Alonzo Snow, son of Thomas and Ann Wentworth, b. 12 Mar 1840, bapt. 6 Jun 1840 by Rev. Dr. George C. M. Roberts

Wentworth, Catherine, dau. of Thomas J. and Aunt [sic] Wentworth, b. 11 May 1846, bapt. 7 Jun 1846 by Rev. Dr. George C. M. Roberts

Wesley, Denis [sic] and Elizabeth Watters m. 18 Apr 1844 by Rev. Joseph Merriken

Wesley, Eliza Ann and Albin P. Davis m. 8 Jan 1850 by Rev. Aquila A. Reese, lic. dated 7 Jan 1850

West, Ann A. and William H. Carpenter m. 20 Nov 1848 by Rev. William Hirst

West, Daniel and Emily Watson m. 20 Apr 1847 by Rev. Isaac P. Cook

West, Emily J. and James Karny m. 26 Dec 1845 by Rev. Dr. George C. M. Roberts

West, George H. and Mary E. Smith m. 15 Jan 1845 by Rev. James Sewell, lic. dated 13 Jan 1845

West, James C., son of James and Barbara West, b. 11 Jun 1839, bapt. 15 Feb 1842 by Rev. Isaac P. Cook

West, John and Harriet Jane Evans m. 3 Sep 1844 by Rev. Dr. George C. M. Roberts

Westerman, Eliza Ann, dau. of Nathan and Sarah Westerman, aged 5 months [b. 1841], bapt. 11 Jul 1841 by Rev. Wesley Stevenson

Wetherill, Jeremiah, son of James H. and Susan Wetherill, b. 12 Mar 1839, Harford County, MD, bapt. 21 Sep 1840, Baltimore City, by Rev. John Alday

Wever, John and Elizabeth Pamer m. 2 Sep 1847 by Rev. Stephen A. Roszel, lic. dated same day

Whapping, Frances and Nathan Adams m. 3 Dec 1846 by Rev. Wesley Stevenson

Wheeler, A. C., see "Ann M. Wheeler" and "Laura V. Wheeler," q.v.

Wheeler, Ann Eliza and William H. Douglas m. 11 Aug 1845 by Rev. Samuel Keppler (date of lic. not recorded)

Wheeler, Ann Matilda, dau. of A. C. and Ann Wheeler, b. 12 Apr 1840, bapt. 23 Dec 1840 by Rev. Charles B. Tippett

Wheeler, Barrack, see "Henry C. Wheeler," q.v.

Wheeler, Charles Henry, son of Samuel James and Susanna Wheeler, b. 12 Feb 1843, bapt. 27 Jul 1843 by Rev. Dr. George C. M. Roberts

Wheeler, Elizabeth C. and John A. Durkee m. 4 Feb 1841 by Rev. Samuel Keppler, lic. dated 1 Feb 1841

Wheeler, Emeline and Christian Steiver m. 31 Dec 1848 by Rev. Joseph Shane

Wheeler, George Edward, son of Henry A. and Sarah Wheeler, b. 1 Aug 1841, bapt. 12 Aug 1841 by Rev. Dr. George C. M. Roberts

Wheeler, George and Hannah, see "Mary E. B. Wheeler," q.v.

Wheeler, Henry [sic] and Thomas McCauley m. 28 Dec 1847 by Rev. Joseph Shane

Wheeler, Henry A., see "George E. Wheeler," q.v.

Wheeler, Henry Clay, son of Capt. Barrack and Sarah G. Wheeler, aged 8 months [b. 1839], bapt. 30 Jan 1840 by Rev. Thomas Myers

Wheeler, Jacob Zigler, son of Capt. Samuel J. and Susanna Wheeler, b. 28 Nov 1847, bapt. 1 Jul 1850 by Rev. Dr. George C. M. Roberts

Wheeler, Laura Virginia, dau. of A. C. and Ann Wheeler, b. 23 Dec 1837, bapt. 23 Dec 1840 by Rev. Charles B. Tippett

Wheeler, Mary Eliza Berry, dau. of George and Hannah Wheeler, b. -- Sep 1841, bapt. 19 Sep 1841 by Rev. Dr. George C. M. Roberts

Wheeler, Oliver W. and Elizabeth A. Holland m. 20 Dec 1849 by Rev. Aquila A. Reese, lic. dated 19 Dec 1849

Wheeler, Rebecca Conine, dau. of Capt. Samuel J. and Susanna Wheeler, b. 8 May 1850, bapt. 1 Jul 1850 by Rev. Dr. George C. M. Roberts

Wheeler, Samuel James, son of Samuel J. and Susanna Wheeler, b. 11 May 1841, bapt. 25 May 1840 [sic] by Rev. Dr. George C. M. Roberts. See "Charles H. Wheeler" and "Jacob Z. Wheeler," q.v.

Whitaker, Joshua and Avarilla Brison(?) m. 21 Apr 1842 by Rev. Job Guest, lic. dated same day

White, Andrew D. and Jane H. Jones m. 3 May 1849 by Rev. Joseph Shane

White, Charles B. and Rebecca B. Smith m. 4 Nov 1841 by Rev. Dr. George C. M. Roberts. See "Gideon White" and "Mary S. White," q.v.

White, David, see "Nathaniel S. White," q.v.

White, Gideon, son of Charles B. and Rebecca White, b. 27 Nov 1842, bapt. 10 Apr 1843 by Rev. Dr. George C. M. Roberts

White, Hannah, dau. of John and Hannah White, aged 10 days, bapt. 1 Feb 1843 by Rev. Wesley Stevenson

White, Hannah, d. after 1844 (exact date not given in Record of Members) [*Ed. Note:* Death notice in the *Baltimore Sun* stated that Hannah White d. 19 Nov 1847.]

White, Henry, see "Mary Elizabeth White," q.v.

White, Howard, see "Rose Ann White," q.v.

White, James E. and Elenor Brown m. 4 Apr 1841 by Rev. Gerard Morgan, lic. dated 3 Apr 1841

White, John T. and Elizabeth Phillips m. 28 Mar 1848 by Rev. Stephen A. Roszel, lic. dated 24 Mar 1848. See "Sarah L. White," q.v.

White, Joseph K. T. and Mary Ann Perry m. 25 Jan 1842 by Rev. Isaac P. Cook

White, Martin and Catherine Libbart m. 2 Nov 1845 by Rev. James Sewell, lic. dated 1 Nov 1845

White, Mary E. and William Bell m. 8 Mar 1842 by Rev. Gerard Morgan, lic. dated 7 Mar 1842

White, Mary Elizabeth, dau. of Henry and Margaret White, b. 15 Mar 1838, bapt. 23 Sep 1840 by Rev. Charles B. Tippett

White, Mary Elizabeth and John W. Maurace (Manrace?) m. 2 Dec 1847 by Rev. Dr. George C. M. Roberts

White, Mary Smith, dau. of Charles B. and Rebecca B. White, b. 2 Oct 1847, bapt. 18 Jun 1848 by Rev. Dr. George C. M. Roberts

White, Nathaniel Spicer, son of David and Jane White, b. ---- "not given" [*sic*], bapt. 29 Oct 1843 by Rev. Isaac P. Cook

White, Rose Ann, dau. of Howard and Sarah White, b. 1838, Baltimore, bapt. 27 Jun 1847 by Rev. Stephen A. Roszel

White, Sarah Louisa, dau. of John T. and Elizabeth White, b. 12 Aug 1842, bapt. 3 Oct 1842 by Rev. Henry Slicer

White, Sarah A. and Henry S. Hainesworth m. 20 Sep 1847 by Rev. Dr. George C. M. Roberts

White, Sarah A. and George E. Shaffer m. 9 Dec 1845 by Rev. James Sewell, lic. dated 8 Dec 1845

Whiteford, Elizabeth and William Corns m. 12 Apr 1849 by Rev. Isaac P. Cook

Whiteford, John J. and Mary Frances Bosworth, both of Baltimore County, m. 29 Jan 1843 by Rev. Nelson Head

Whiteford, Mary Jane and Charles E. Magness m. 15 Oct 1848 by Rev. Stephen A. Roszel, lic. dated 14 Oct 1848

Whiteman, George and Caroline Rusk, both of Baltimore County, m. 6 Jan 1845 by Rev. William Hamilton

Whitson, Sarah and David C. Ronsaville, both of Baltimore City, m. 15 Apr 1841 by Rev. Robert Emory

Whittaker, George W. and Mary H. Wood m. 21 Apr 1849 by Rev. William Hirst

Whitten, William R. and Debora Dawson m. 22 Oct 1844 by Rev. James Sewell, lic. dated same day

Whittier, Joseph Hathaway and Pauline Barnard Way m. 28 Nov 1849 by Rev. John S. Martin, lic. dated 27 Nov 1849

Whittington, Drusilla, d. after 1847 (exact date not given in Record of Members) [*Ed. Note:* Death notice in the *Baltimore Sun* stated that Drucilla C. Whittington, wife of John Whittington, d. 18 Nov 1850.]

Whittington, John and Drucilla Long, both of Baltimore County, m. 18 Mar 1845 by Rev. William Hamilton

Whittington, Matilda, d. circa 1843-1844 (exact date not given in Record of Members) [*Ed. Note:* Death notice in the *Baltimore Sun* stated that Matilda Whittington, wife of John Whittington, d. 8 May 1843.]

Whittington, Matilda Emily, dau. of John and Matilda Emily Whittington, b. 5 Feb 1843, bapt. 16 Apr 1843 by Rev. Dr. George C. M. Roberts

Whittington, William Colburn, son of John and Matilda Whittington, b. 14 Nov 1840, bapt. 19 Jul 1840 by Rev. Dr. George C. M. Roberts

Whittle, Benjamin and Rosina Kinzendolff m. 9 Jul 1844 by Rev. Joseph Shane

Whittle, David and Lucretia Hobbs m. 2 Apr 1843 by Rev. Isaac P. Cook

Whittle, Thomas and Sarah Flayhart m. 20 Oct 1842 by Rev. Isaac P. Cook

Wideman, Samuel and Ellenora Hissey m. 15 Jun 1842 by Rev. Joseph Shane

Wields, John L. and Ann Eliza Noblet m. 1 Apr 1849 by Rev. John S. Martin, lic. dated 31 Mar 1849

Wilcox, Esheldia Ann, dau. of Thomas S. and Elizabeth Wilcox, b. 10 Oct 1843, bapt. 27 Dec 1843 by Rev. Dr. George C. M. Roberts

Wilcox, Mary Ann and Isaiah Brown m. 2 Jul 1850 by Rev. Isaac P. Cook

Wilcox, Thomas Sewell, son of Thomas S. and Elizabeth Wilcox, b. 8 Sep 1848, bapt. 28 Feb 1850 by Rev. Dr. George C. M. Roberts

Wilds, John and Elizabeth Forice m. 24 Aug 1849 by Rev. Joseph Shane

Wiley, David N. and Jane Lloyd m. 6 Jun 1840 by Rev. John Bear

Wiley, Kenedy, d. circa 1840-1847 (exact date not given in Class Record)

Wilkerson, Margaret W. and Thomas Floyd m. 21 Oct 1841 by Rev. Gerard Morgan, lic. dated 19 Oct 1841

Wilkerson, Sarah Ann and Thomas H. Varina m. 8 May 1843 by Rev. Samuel Brison

Wilkes, Jabez and Catharine R. Ferrel m. 16 May 1849 by Rev. John S. Martin, lic. dated same day

Wilkins Bartus, see "Charles H. Wilkins" and "Edward Wilkins" and "Mary C. Wilkins," q.v.

Wilkins, Charles Henry, son of Bartus and Frances Wilkins, b. 4 Jan 1840, bapt. 28 Dec 1841 by Rev. Dr. George C. M. Roberts

Wilkins, Edward, son of Bartus and Frances Wilkins, b. 1 Feb 1836, bapt. 28 Dec 1841 by Rev. Dr. George C. M. Roberts

Wilkins, Henrietta Morgan, dau. of William N. and Elizabeth A. Wilkins, b. 22 Feb 1842, bapt. 4 May 1842 by Rev. Henry Slicer

Wilkins, John, d. circa 1840-1842 (exact date not given in Record of Members) [*Ed. Note:* Death notice in the *Baltimore Sun* stated that John Wilkins d. 24 Jul 1842.]

Wilkins, Mary Caroline, dau. of Bartus and Frances Wilkins, b. 4 May 1838, bapt. 28 Dec 1841 by Rev. Dr. George C. M. Roberts

Wilkins, William Albert, dau. of Bartus and Frances Wilkins, b. 16 Nov 1841, bapt. 28 Dec 1841 by Rev. Dr. George C. M. Roberts

Wilkins, William N., see "Henrietta M. Wilkins," q.v.

Wilkinson, Edward H. and Susanna H. Baker m. 15 Dec 1840 by Rev. Samuel Keppler, lic. dated 5 Dec 1840

Wilkinson, Elizabeth and Thomas Pool m. 14 Mar 1850 by Rev. Isaac P. Cook

Wilkinson, Jabez S. and Sarah Smith m. 24 Sep 1843 by Rev. Dr. George C. M. Roberts

Wilkinson, Jane and Henry W. McIntire m. 1 Jun 1841 by Rev. Dr. George C. M. Roberts

Wilkinson, Jesse Carter, son of Joseph and Mary Ann Wilkinson, b. 4 Jun 1842, bapt. 15 Nov 1843 by Rev. Dr. George C. M. Roberts

Wilkinson, Joseph and Mary, see "Jesse C. Wilkinson" and "William U. Wilkinson," q.v.

Wilkinson, Mary Elizabeth, dau. of Edward and Susanna Wilkinson, b. 6 Jul 1842, bapt. 12 Oct 1842 by Rev. Elisha D. Owen

Wilkinson, Sarah C. and Henry Pruett m. 7 Mar 1850 by Rev. Isaac P. Cook

Wilkinson, William Uriah, son of Joseph and Mary Wilkinson, b. 30 Jan 1840, bapt. 31 Jan 1841 by Rev. Dr. George C. M. Roberts

Willard, Sarah, d. circa 1841 (death noted in Class List) [Ed. Note: Death notice in the Baltimore Sun stated that Sarah Willard d. 28 Dec 1842.]

Willett, John and Sarah Thorton m. 12 Nov 1847 by Rev. Benjamin F. Brooke

Willett, Mary Ann and Edward L. Bowen m. 21 Feb 1850 by Rev. Aquila A. Reese, lic. dated 20 Feb 1850

Willey, Sarah J. and Joseph L. Tall m. 27 May 1849 by Rev. Dr. George C. M. Roberts

Williams, Alexander and Eleanora Longly m. 11 Mar 1849 by Rev. Joseph Shane. See "John A. Williams," q.v.

Williams, Catharine and Charles H. Thompson m. 18 Jun 1849 by Rev. John S. Martin, lic. dated same day

Williams, Charles, see "George D. D. Williams," q.v.

Williams, Charles G. and Georgianna C. Ames m. 21 Jan 1845 by Rev. Dr. George C. M. Roberts

Williams, Eleanor and Henry T. Houck m. 9 Jun 1840 by Rev. John Bear

Williams, Elijah D. and Mary G. Baxley m. 28 Sep 1847 by Rev. James H. Brown, lic. dated same day

Williams, Eliza, d. circa 1840 (exact date not given in Class Record)

Williams, Francis A. and Juliet S. Hall m. ---- [no date given] by Rev. John Miller, lic. dated 16 May 1850

Williams, George Dorsey Dyer, son of Charles and Catherine Williams, b. 3 Jun 1840, bapt. 6 Jun 1840 by Rev. Dr. George C. M. Roberts

Williams, Giles, d. circa 1841 (death noted in Class List) [Ed. Note: Death notice in the Baltimore Sun stated that Giles Williams d. 16 Feb 1842.]

Williams, Henry and Elizabeth Darby m. 8 Apr 1850 by Rev. Dr. George C. M. Roberts

Williams, Jacob, see "James M. Williams" and "Mary L. Williams," q.v.

Williams, Jacob, son of Maurice and Joanna Williams, b. 24 Feb 1818, bapt. 3 Jul 1842 by Rev. Henry Slicer

Williams, James, see "Louisa A. Williams," q.v.

Williams, James D., see "Laura Williams," q.v.

Williams, James Morris, son of Jacob and Mary Ann Williams, b. 4 Feb 1843, bapt. 22 Mar 1842 by Rev. Dr. George C. M. Roberts

Williams, John and Agnes Cox m. 14 Jan 1847 by Rev. Joseph Shane

Williams, John Alexander, son of Alexander and Eleanor Elizabeth Williams, b. 10 Feb 1850, bapt. 21 Jul 1850 by Rev. Dr. George C. M. Roberts

Williams, Joseph (colored) and Ann Reece (colored) m. 9 Sep 1841 by Rev. Gerard Morgan, lic. dated same day

Williams, Laura, dau. of James Dunlop and Louisa Ann Williams, b. 11 Jul 1848, bapt. 2 Sep 1848 by Rev. Dr. George C. M. Roberts

Williams, Louisa Ann, dau. of James and Mary M. Williams, b. 13 Nov 1823, bapt. 2 Sep 1848 by Rev. Dr. George C. M. Roberts

Williams, Mary, d. 1849 (death noted in Class List)

Williams, Mary Ann and Austen Clifford m. 9 Feb 1843 by Rev. Dr. George C. M. Roberts

Williams, Mary E. and Ralph P. Etchberger m. 10 May 1840 by Rev. Samuel Keppler, lic. dated 8 May 1840

Williams, Maurice, see "Jacob Williams," q.v.

Williams, Mary Louisa, dau. of Jacob and Mary Ann Williams, b. 3 Jan 1840, bapt. 22 Mar 1842 by Rev. Dr. George C. M. Roberts

Williams, Peter and Catharine Hitch m. 18 Oct 1847 by Rev. Stephen A. Roszel, lic. dated same day

Williams, Robert, son of Samuel and Mary Williams, b. 26 Jun 1840, bapt. 4 Jul 1840 by Rev. Isaac P. Cook

Williams, Samuel, see "Robert Williams," q.v.

Williams, Sarah Ann and John Thomas Legg m. 5 Jul 1849 by Rev. John S. Martin, lic. dated same day

Williams, Solomon and Rachel E. Sewell m. 27 Dec 1848 by Rev. Stephen A. Roszel, lic. dated 23 Dec 1848

Williams, William and Elizabeth Simms m. 6 May 1844 by Rev. Joseph Shane

Williams, William and Victoria Fitzgerald m. 25 Jan 1848 by Rev. Dr. George C. M. Roberts

Williams, William (colored) and Arley Ann Johnson (colored) m. 3 Mar 1842 by Rev,. Gerard Morgan (date of lic. not recorded)

Williamson, Ann E., see "Young Owens," q.v.

Williamson, John B. and Mary E. Suit m. 18 Feb 1846 by Rev. Samuel Keppler (date of lic. not recorded)

Williamson, William, d. 1840 (death noted in Class List) [Ed. Note: Death notice in the Baltimore Sun stated that William Williamson d. 11 Jun 1840.]

Williar, Henry Dugal, son of George P. and Catherine Williar, b. 4 May 1847, bapt. 27 Dec 1847 by Rev. Dr. George C. M. Roberts

Willis, Ann, d. circa 1840-1842 (exact date not given in Record of Members) [Ed. Note: Death notice in the Baltimore Sun stated that Ann Willis, widow of Henry Willis, d. 16 Feb 1842.]

Willis, Henry, see "Ann Willis," q.v.

Willis, John and Mary Elizabeth Hooker m. 18 Jun 1840 by Rev. Samuel Keppler, lic. dated 2 Jun 1840

Willis, Mary Ann and Judson Gillman m. 7 Jun 1845 by Rev. Dr. George C. M. Roberts

Willis, Thomas and Josephine E. Davis m. 18 Dec 1849 by Rev. Aquila A. Reese, lic. dated 17 Dec 1849

Wills, Mary C., d. circa 1847-1850 (exact date not given in Record of Members)

Wilson, Allen L. and Margaret A. Hackett m. 18 Mar 1849 by Rev. Aquila A. Reese, lic. dated 17 Mar 1849

Wilson, Allen Nelson, son of George and Rachel Wilson, b. 20 Jul 1839, bapt. 28 Oct 1844 by Rev. Isaac P. Cook

Wilson, Andrew F. and Mary A. Burkholder m. 2 Dec 1843 by Rev. Isaac P. Cook

Wilson, Andrew Gregg, son of William and Elizabeth Wilson, b. 21 Jan 1850, bapt. 12 Jun 1851 by Rev. Dr. George C. M. Roberts

Wilson, Catherine and William Carman m. 8 Oct 1843 by Rev. Joseph Shane

Wilson, Catherine and John Combes m. 5 Jan 1846 by Rev. Joseph Shane

Wilson, Delia, d. circa 1847 (exact date not given in Record of Members) [Ed. Note: Death notice in the Baltimore Sun stated that Delilah Wilson d. 10 Nov 1847.]

Wilson, Drucilla and William Mitchell m. 16 May 1844 by Rev. Dr. George C. M. Roberts

Wilson, Edward M. (colored) and Sarah Dillen (colored) m. 3 Jul 1844 by Rev. James Sewell

Wilson, Eliza and Charles Brown m. 8 Jun 1842 by Rev. Dr. George C. M. Roberts

Wilson, Elizabeth, d. circa 1849-1850 (exact date not given in Record of Members) [Ed. Note: Death notice in the Baltimore Sun stated that Elizabeth Wilson d. 10 Dec 1849.]

Wilson, Frances W., see "William B. Wilson," q.v.

Wilson, George, see "Allen N. Wilson" and "Jesse L. Wilson," q.v.

Wilson, George and Teresa J. Corrie m. 28 Jun 1844 by Rev. Dr. George C. M. Roberts

Wilson, George, d. 1840 (death noted in Class List) [Ed. Note: Death notice in the Baltimore Sun stated that George Wilson d. 14 Apr 1840.]

Wilson, Harriet and Joseph Miller m. 1 Jun 1843 by Rev. Joseph Shane

Wilson, Henrietta and Wesley Hamilton m. 1 Oct 1843 by Rev. Joseph Shane

Wilson, Jane, d. circa 1840-1842 (exact date not given in Record of Members) [Ed. Note: Death notice in the Baltimore Sun stated that Jane Wilson, widow of William Wilson, d. 8 Nov 1842.]

Wilson, Jesse Lee, son of George and Rachel Wilson, aged 4 (14?) months [b. 1843 or 1844], bapt. 28 Oct 1844 by Rev. Isaac P. Cook

Wilson, John and Mary Moores m. 27 Feb 1844 by Rev. Samuel Brison

Wilson, John and Caroline M. Andrews m. 14 Oct 1849 by Rev. John S. Martin, lic. dated 13 Oct 1849

Wilson, Lydia and Vachel R. Pumphrey m. 24 Dec 1843 by Rev. Isaac P. Cook

Wilson, Margaret Elizabeth and Charles J. Kruse m. 8 Sep 1850 by Rev. Isaac P. Cook

Wilson, Martha Ann and James Taylor m. 22 Mar 1848 by Rev. Stephen A. Roszel, lic. dated same day

Wilson, Mary, d. circa 1845 (death noted in Class List)

Wilson, Mary and Philip O. Dawson, both of Baltimore County, m. 31 Oct 1844 by Rev. William Hamilton

Wilson, Mary Jane and John Henry Osborne m. 8 Dec 1846 by Rev. Isaac P. Cook

Wilson, Olivia and Silas Driver m. 23 Apr 1846 by Rev. Joseph Shane

Wilson, Peter and Virginia Hennace m. 28 Jul 1845 by Rev. Samuel Keppler (date of lic. not recorded)

Wilson, Samuel B. and Sarah J. Hance m. 5 Dec 1847 by Rev. Littleton F. Morgan, lic. dated 4 Dec 1847

Wilson, Thomas M. and Eleanor Birth m. 20 Oct 1842 by Rev. Samuel Brison

Wilson, William, see "Andrew J. Wilson" and "Jane Wilson," q.v.

Wilson, William Buckler, son of Capt. Francis W. and Elizabeth A. Wilson, b. 17 Feb 1846, bapt. 15 Mar 1846 by Rev. Dr. George C. M. Roberts

Wilson, William C. and Maria L. Myers m. 16 Jul 1843 by Rev. Henry Slicer, lic. dated 15 Jul 1843

Wimesly, Martha Cornelia, dau. of Benjamin and Martha Wimsely, b. 11 Aug 1846, bapt. 25 Aug 1846 by Rev. Samuel Keppler

Winchester, Catherine Sophronia, dau. of Samuel and Ruth E. Winchester, b. 4 Aug 1841, bapt. 19 Dec 1841 by Rev. Dr. George C. M. Roberts

Winchester, George Hubbard, son of Samuel and Ruth E. Winchester, b. 22 Feb 1839, bapt. 19 Dec 1841 by Rev. Dr. George C. M. Roberts

Winchester, Hannah and Charles Butcher m. 26 Nov 1848 by Rev. Dr. George C. M. Roberts

Winchester, Mary Virginia, dau. of Samuel C. and Celia Ann Winchester, b. 10 Jun 1848, bapt. 18 Jun 1848 by Rev. Dr. George C. M. Roberts

Winchester, Oliver Augustus, son of Samuel and Ruth E. Winchester, b. 2 Jan 1837, bapt. 19 Dec 1841 by Rev. Dr. George C. M. Roberts

Winchester, Ruth E., d. circa 1845-1847 (exact date not given in Record of Members) [Ed. Note: Death notice in the Baltimore Sun stated that Ruth E. Winchester, wife of Samuel C. Winchester, d. 26 Jun 1846.]

Winchester, Ruth Isabella, dau. of Samuel C. and Ruth E. Winchester, b. 27 Jun 1846, bapt. 28 Jun 1846 by Rev. Dr. George C. M. Roberts

Winchester, Samuel, see "Catherine S. Winchester" and "George H. Winchester" and "Mary V. Winchester" and "Oliver A. Winchester" and "Ruth E. Winchester" and "Ruth I. Winchester" and "Samuel G. Winchester," q.v.

Winchester, Samuel Gridley, son of Samuel and Ruth E. Winchester, b. 1834, bapt. 19 Dec 1841 by Rev. Dr. George C. M. Roberts

Winchester, Sophia and William A. Hitchkiss m. 19 Oct 1848 by Rev. William Hirst

Windslow, Letitia, d. 1847 (death noted in Class List) [Ed. Note: Death notice in the Baltimore Sun stated that Letitia Winslow d. 19 Mar 1847.]

Windsor, Elizabeth R. G., dau. of Jessee and Matilda Windsor, b. 17 Aug 1841, bapt. 29 Jun 1842 by Rev. William Prettyman

Wingate, Major C. R. and Mary R. Wooten m. 17 Jun 1845 by Rev. James Sewell, lic. dated same day

Wingert, Rose A. and James W. Jones m. 27 May 1849 by Rev. John S. Martin, lic. dated 26 May 1849

Winks, John W. and Mary A. Morse m. 21 Oct 1847 by Rev. Stephen A. Roszel, lic. dated 19 Oct 1847

Winks, Robert C. and Sarah Ann Marshall m. ---- [blank] by Rev. John S. Martin, lic. dated 19 Sep 1850 [Ed. Note: Their marriage notice in the Baltimore Sun stated they married on 19 Sep 1850.]

Winnafield, Elizabeth, d. circa 1847-1850 (exact date not given in Record of Members)

Winslow, Letitia, see "Letitia Windslow," q.v.

Wirt, James and Elizabeth Arnold m. 31 Dec 1850 by Rev. Joseph Shane

Wirts, Benjamin Franklin, son of John and Ellen Wirts, aged 13 months [b. 1840], bapt. 9 Sep 1841 by Rev. John A. Hening

Wise, Anna Pedan, dau. of Tully and Celinda Wise, b. -- Nov 1838, bapt. 5 Jan 1841 by Rev. Charles B. Tippett

Wise, Elizabeth Wells, dau. of Tully and Celinda Wise, b. -- Nov 1833 (twin), bapt. 5 Jan 1841 by Rev. Charles B. Tippett

Wise, Richard and Elizabeth Wagner m. 21 Jan 1846 by Rev. James Sewell, lic. dated same day

Wise, William McKeel, son of Tully and Celinda Wise, b. -- Nov 1833 (twin), bapt. 5 Jan 1841 by Rev. Charles B. Tippett

Wiseman, James R. and Amelia Bassett m. 27 May 1845 by Rev. James Sewell, lic. dated same day

Wisner, Sarah and Philip Johnson m. 14 Nov 1850 by Rev. Henry Slicer, lic. dated 22 Oct 1850

Wisner, Susan A. and William Dubard m. 4 May 1845 by Rev. Joseph Shane

Woelper, Rebecca J. and Alexander R. Barker m. 8 Oct 1850 by Rev. John S. Martin, lic. dated 7 Oct 1850

Wolf, Ann Maria and Isaac Clare Poteet m. 7 Dec 1846 by Rev. Joseph Shane

Wolf, Charlotte and Henry Shillingberger m. 1 Nov 1847 by Rev. Joseph Shane

Wolf, Peter and Elizabeth Short m. 8 Dec 1844 by Rev. Joseph Shane

Wolf, Sophia and Edward A. McKeldin m. 13 Nov 1845 by Rev. Joseph Shane

Wolfe, George and Caroline Mace m. 11 Jun 1846 by Rev. Joseph Shane

Wolford, Joseph B. and Susan E. Junnock m. 6 Jan 1848 by Rev. Dr. George C. M. Roberts

Womble, Pembrook M. (Dr.) and Amanda J. Chappell m. 20 Dec 1849 by Rev. William Hirst, lic. dated 18 Dec 1849

Wondersford, Maria and James Mewshaw m. 25 Mar 1845 by Rev. Joseph Shane

Wood, Ann, see "Sarah E. Wood," q.v.

Wood, Annie E. and Joshua B. Sumwalt m. 2 Nov 1847 at the house of her father in Baltimore by Rev. Beverly Waugh, lic. dated 1 Nov 1847

Wood, Charles, see "George R. Wood," q.v.

Wood, George Roberts, son of Charles and Mary Wood, b. 6 Nov 1842, bapt. 14 May 1843 by Rev. Dr. George C. M. Roberts

Wood, Harriet C. and Frederick Bloomer m. 19 Jan 1840 by Rev. Samuel Keppler, lic. dated 27 Jan 1840

Wood, Isaac and Sarah German m. 16 Feb 1843 by Rev. Henry Slicer, lic. dated 15 Feb 1843

Wood, James H. and Lavenia Russell m. 3 Jun 1846 by Rev. Dr. George C. M. Roberts

Wood, John and Hesther Lankford m. ---- [blank] by Rev. John S. Martin, lic. dated 5 Oct 1850 [Ed. Note: Their marriage notice in the Baltimore Sun stated that John Woods m. Hester Lankford on 6 Oct 1850.]

Wood, Maria Louisa and George W. Duvall m. 19 Nov 1845 at the house of her father in Baltimore by Rev. Beverly Waugh, lic. dated 18 Nov 1845

Wood, Mary Ann, d. circa 1847-1850 (exact date not given in Record of Members)

Wood, Mary H. and George W. Whittaker m. 21 Apr 1849 by Rev. William Hirst

Wood, Richard and Elizabeth Doughlas m. 30 Mar 1844 by Rev. Joseph Shane

Wood, Samuel and Catherine Kauffman m. 9 Oct 1842 by Rev. Joseph Shane

Wood, Samuel and Margery Lowman m. 12 Sep 1848 by Rev. Joseph Shane

Wood, Sarah Elizabeth, dau. of William and Ann Wood, b. 28 Sep 1838, bapt. 25 Sep 1840 by Rev. Thomas Myers

Wood, William and Sarah J. Coulter m. 11 Feb 1841 by Rev. Joseph Shane

Woodcock, Almira F. and George Rawlings m. 20 Jan 1847 by Rev. Dr. George C. M. Roberts

Woodcock, Amelia B., d. circa 1849-1850 (exact date not given in Record of Members) [Ed. Note: Death notice in the Baltimore Sun stated that Amelia B. Woodcock, wife of William Woodcock, d. 28 Jun 1849.]

Woodrow, George W. and Letitia A. Waters m. 14 Oct 1847 by Rev. Dr. George C. M. Roberts

Woods, Charles L. and Mary E. Fitzpatrick m. 9 Dec 1841 by Rev. Dr. George C. M. Roberts

Woods, Dorothy Ann and Charles Adams m. 14 May 1843 by Rev. Dr. George C. M. Roberts

Woods, Elizabeth Ann and John R. Faulkner m. 15 Sep 1846 by Rev. Dr. George C. M. Roberts

Woods, Ellen and Wesley Jones m. 12 Aug 1841 by Rev. Dr. George C. M. Roberts

Woods, John, see "John Wood," q.v.

Woods, Margaret A. and Augustus W. Cassnill m. 5 May 1849 by Rev. John S. Martin, lic. dated same day

Woods, Sarah Ann and James Ballard m. 13 Jun 1843 by Rev. Wesley Stevenson

Woodward, Abraham and Margaret E. Littig m. 30 Apr 1844 by Rev. James Sewell, lic. dated 29 Apr 1844

Woodward, Ruth Ann and John Gregg m. 22 May 1845 by Rev. Dr. George C. M. Roberts

Woodward, Sarah Margaret, dau. of William W. and Dorothea Woodward, b. 27 Nov 1846, bapt. 5 Aug 1847 by Rev. Dr. George C. M. Roberts

Woodward, William W. and Dorothy Spencer m. 25 Sep 1845 by Rev. Dr. George C. M. Roberts

Woolcott, Hannah E. and Francis A. Rose m. 15 May 1845 by Rev. Dr. George C. M. Roberts

Woolen, Leonard R. and Amanda Timanus, both of Baltimore County, m. 15 Sep 1840 by Rev. Bernard H. Nadal

Woolen, Mary Ann, d. circa 1844-1847 (exact date not given in Record of Members)

Woolford, Sarah A. and Joshua W. Myers m. 12 Jul 1841 by Rev. Gerard Morgan, lic. dated same day

Woolford, Stephen and Ann Dorsey m. 24 Jan 1850 by Rev. Joseph Shane

Woolford, Stephen and Sarah A. Burke m. 22 Mar 1842 by Rev. Dr. George C. M. Roberts

Wooten, Mary R. and Major C. R. Wingate m. 17 Jun 1845 by Rev. James Sewell, lic. dated same day

Working, Mary, d. circa 1840-1847 (exact date not given in Record of Members)

Worrell, Sarah and Peter Newell m. 17 Jan 1841 by Rev. John Bear

Worthington, Ann E. and Theodore Owings m. 31 Jul 1849 by Rev. Aquila A. Reese, lic. dated 30 Jul 1849

Wotten, George W. and Emeline Frazier m. 25 Apr 1845 by Rev. Dr. George C. M. Roberts

Wright, Amanda M. and James Carr m. 15 Nov 1849 by Rev. Aquila A. Reese, lic. dated 14 Nov 1859

Wright, Ann Maria and John Rutter m. 30 Sep 1847 by Rev. Stephen A. Roszel, lic. dated 27 Sep 1847

Wright, Caroline and Edwin Phillips m. 14 Aug 1846 by Rev. Joseph Shane

Wright, Charles Roberts, son of Jeremiah C. and Margaret R. Wright, b. 14 Aug 1847, bapt. 6 Apr 1848 by Rev. Dr. George C. M. Roberts

Wright, Emily L. and William Hemmack m. 21 Feb 1850 by Rev. Aquila A. Reese, lic. dated 20 Feb 1850

Wright, George W. and Julia A. C. Dunn m. 27 Jun 1843 by Rev. Henry Slicer, lic. dated same day

Wright, Jeremiah C., see "Charles R. Wright," q.v.

Wright, John W. and Margaret A. Disney m. 8 Jun 1848 at the house of her father in Baltimore by Rev. Beverly Waugh, lic. dated 7 Jun 1848

Wright, Mary Ann and David N. Auld m. 5 Aug 1848 by Rev. James H. Brown, lic. dated 2 Aug 1848

Wright, Mary Ellen and Joseph Watts m. 13 Nov 1844 by Rev. Joseph Shane

Wright, Matilda A. and William Sloan m. ---- [blank] by Rev. John S. Martin, lic. dated 1 Mar 1850 [Ed. Note: Their marriage notice in the Baltimore Sun stated they married on 2 Mar 1850.]

Wright, Valeria, d. 1844 (death noted in Class List) [Ed. Note: Death notice in the Baltimore Sun stated that Valeria Wright d. 29 Jan 1844.]

Wrightson, Samuel Clay, son of John and Mary Wrightson, b. 21 Jul 1846, Baltimore, bapt. 7 Mar 1847 by Rev. Samuel Keppler

Wrightson, Thomas H. and Ann Eliza R. Dawson m. 28 Jun 1849 by Rev. John S. Martin, lic. dated 21 Jun 1849

Wrightson, William L. and Mary Elizabeth Germain m. 4 Oct 1849 by Rev. John S. Martin, lic. dated 3 Oct 1849

Wroten, Catherine and James Swann m. 22 Jun 1846 by Rev. Dr. George C. M. Roberts

Wyant, Nicholas and Clorinda Hammond m. 19 Nov 1843 by Rev. Dr. George C. M. Roberts

Wyatt, Daniel and Amanda Longe m. 21 May 1849 by Rev. Joseph Shane

Wylie, Sarah and William Brundage m. 4 Dec 1849 by Rev. Aquila A. Reese, lic. dated 3 Dec 1849 [Ed. Note: Their marriage notice in the Baltimore Sun gave their names as William Brundige and Sarah Wiley.]

Wyman, Isaac and Mary Jane Simms m. 28 Sep 1848 by Rev. Stephen A. Roszel, lic. dated 7 Sep 1848 by Rev. Stephen A. Roszel, lic. dated

Wyman, Jackson and Mary Nace m. 6 May 1846 by Rev. Isaac P. Cook

Wyman, Susanna and Eliphalet L. Treadway m. 14 Nov 1847 by Rev. Stephen A. Roszel, lic. dated 1 Nov 1847

Yager, Charles and Mary Shaffer m. 31 Dec 1844 by Rev. Wesley Stevenson

Yeager, Ann, dau. of John and Catherine Yeager, b. 26 Feb 1841, bapt. 24 Mar 1841 by Rev. Dr. George C. M. Roberts

Yeager, James and Rachel Constantine m. 31 Jan 1843 by Rev. Wesley Stevenson

Yearley, Alexander, son of Thomas C. and Elizabeth Ann Yearley, b. 19 Jun 1843, bapt. 10 Oct 1847 by Rev. Dr. George C. M. Roberts

Yearley, Anna Jane, dau. of Thomas C. and Elizabeth Ann Yearley, b. 14 Jul 1845, bapt. 10 Oct 1847 by Rev. Dr. George C. M. Roberts

Yearley, Elizabeth Ann Israel, dau. of Thomas C. and Elizabeth Ann Yearley, b. 14 Sep 1847, bapt. 10 Oct 1847 by Rev. Dr. George C. M. Roberts

Yearly, Sarah E. and John W. Slagel m. 25 Jun 1846 by Rev. Dr. George C. M. Roberts

Yeates, George W., see "Elizabeth Cordrey," q.v.

Yehrman, William and Mary Ann Comeges m. 10 Jul 1844 by Rev. Joseph Shane

Yeo, Alexander and Permelia S. Dull m. ---- [blank] by Rev. John S. Martin, lic. dated 7 Feb 1850 [*Ed. Note:* Their marriage notice in the *Baltimore Sun* stated Alexander Yeo m. Permelia J. Dull, dau. of James and Jane R. Dull, on 7 Feb 1850.]

Yost, Margaret and Edward Flayhart m. 22 Jan 1843 by Rev. Isaac P. Cook

Young, Eliza Ann and Jeremiah Johnson m. 28 Sep 1845 by Rev. Dr. George C. M. Roberts

Young, Eliza Jane and William Airey m. 30 Oct 1844 by Rev. Joseph Shane

Young, Elizabeth, d. circa 1840 (exact date not given in Record of Members) [*Ed. Note:* Death notice in the *Baltimore Sun* stated that Elizabeth Young, widow of Robert Young, d. 1 Mar 1840.]

Young, George W. and Sarah Lawson, both of Baltimore County, m. 18 May 1843 by Rev. S. S. Roszel, lic. dated same day

Young, Harriet E. and William Pulley m. 16 Nov 1845 by Rev. Dr. George C. M. Roberts

Young, Laura Jane, dau. of James and Margaret Young, b. ---- [blank], bapt. 8 Mar 1840 by Rev. Thomas Myers

Young, Mary, dau. of Walter and Ann Young, aged 14 months [b. 1840, Baltimore City], bapt. 1841 (exact date not given) by Rev. Gerard Morgan

Young, Mary and James Butler m. 8 Aug 1846 by Rev. Isaac P. Cook

Young, Mary Ann and James Arnold m. 2 Aug 1846 by Rev. Joseph Shane

Young, Narcissa and Edwin Creswell Frazier m. 13 Jan 1848 at the house of her father in Shrewsbury, PA by Rev. Beverly Waugh, no lic. required

Young, Walter, see "Mary Young," q.v.

Young, William, see "Elizabeth Young," q.v.

Young, William H. Harrison, son of William and Jane Young, aged 11 days, b. Baltimore City, bapt. 1840 (exact date not given) by Rev. Gerard Morgan

Younger, Ann Jane and William Henry Riley m. 23 Oct 1841 by Rev. Wesley Stevenson

Youngman, Emily and Alexander D. Howe m. 14 Apr 1842 by Rev. Job Guest, lic. dated 8 Feb 1842

Zeigler, George W. and Mary E. Johnson m. 4 Mar 1845 at the house of B. Waugh in Baltimore by Rev. Beverly Waugh, lic. dated 3 Mar 1845

Zeigler, Margaret and William C. Emerson m. 7 Apr 1850 by Rev. Dr. George C. M. Roberts

Zeigler, Mary and John Keiffer m. 29 Sep 1846 by Rev. Dr. George C. M. Roberts

Zepp, Reubin and Mary Howard m. 18 Aug 1844 by Rev. Joseph Shane

Zigler, Louisa and Thomas Harrington m. 26 Aug 1841 by Rev. Dr. George C. M. Roberts

Zimmerman, David C. and Ann Burns m. 4 Oct 1849 by Rev. Aquila A. Reese, lic. dated 3 Oct 1849

Zimmerman, John W., b. 23 Apr 1817, bapt. 25 Dec 1842 by Rev. Henry Slicer
Zimmerman, John W. and Harriet Graves m. 27 Jan 1841 by Rev. Samuel Keppler,
  lic. dated same day. See "Roberta V. G. Zimmerman," q.v.
Zimmerman, Mary, d. 1844 (exact date not given in Record of Members)
Zimmerman, Roberta V. G., dau. of J. W. and Harriot Zimmerman, b. 2 Jun 1842,
  bapt. 25 Dec 1842 by Rev. Henry Slicer
Zimmerman, Sarah and Peter Hoover m. 19 Jul 1846 by Rev. Littleton F. Morgan,
  lic. dated 16 Jul 1846
Zimmers, Michael, d. 4 Oct 1847 (death noted in Record of Members)